Java® and Flex®
Integration Bible

D1027764

Java® and Flex® Integration Bible

**Matthew Keefe and
Charles A. Christiansen Jr.**

WILEY
Wiley Publishing, Inc.

Java® and Flex® Integration Bible

Published by
Wiley Publishing, Inc.
10475 Crosspoint Boulevard
Indianapolis, IN 46256
www.wiley.com

Copyright © 2009 by Wiley Publishing, Inc., Indianapolis, Indiana

Published by Wiley Publishing, Inc., Indianapolis, Indiana

Published simultaneously in Canada

ISBN: 978-0-470-40074-6

Manufactured in the United States of America

10 9 8 7 6 5 4 3 2 1

In memory of my best friend, Andrew Lenihan.

To Eileen, for all your love and support;
and to my mom, who always wanted to see my name in print.

About the Authors

Charles A. Christiansen Jr. is a full-time Java application developer. Over the past 11 years, he has worked on teams that have developed a wide variety of e-learning and classroom management applications. Charles has written applications by using the gamut of Java application technologies, from the heavy client Java application using RMI over dialup connections to fast, lightweight Web applications using Spring and Hibernate. He holds a Master of Science degree in Internet Engineering from the Graduate Center of Marlboro College.

Charles lives in the metro Boston area with his wife Eileen and their irascible cat Tigger. In his spare time, he enjoys cooking, especially barbecue, and photography.

Matthew Keefe is a new-media designer, developer, author, and trainer with a strong background in application development for the Web and offline platforms. Originally a full-time graphic artist, he found that much of the programming associated with his design work was being outsourced. Matthew quickly learned programming for the Web and uncovered a valuable but little-known skill set in this industry: the ability to build a site and to also powerfully design it.

Matthew recently authored the *Flash and PHP Bible*, has contributed to various Flex and Flash magazines, and runs `http://scriptplayground.com` for other programmers to learn from. You can find more information on his personal site at `http://mkeefe.com`.

Matthew has worked with several companies and studios, including Inverted Creative, Delphi, PhotoshopCAFE, Kineticz Interactive, Organi Studios, Bent 360, and ORCA Media, Inc. He lives in Carver, Massachusetts.

Credits

Acquisitions Editor
Courtney Allen

Project Editor
Christopher Stolle

Technical Editor
Darron Schall and Gerry Power

Copy Editor
Marylouise Wiack

Editorial Manager
Robyn Siesky

Business Manager
Amy Knies

Senior Marketing Manager
Sandy Smith

Vice President and Executive Group Publisher
Richard Swadley

Vice President and Executive Publisher
Barry Pruett

Project Coordinator
Lynsey Stanford

Graphics and Production Specialists
Ana Carrillo
Jennifer Mayberry
Sarah Philippart

Quality Control Technicians
Laura Albert
Amanda Graham

Proofreading
Kathy Simpson

Indexing
Sharon Shock

Contents at a Glance

Acknowledgments xvii
Introduction xix

Part I: Installation and Getting Started .1
Chapter 1: Setting Up the Java Development Environment 3
Chapter 2: Configuring Flex for Java Development 37
Chapter 3: Similarities between Java and Flex 61
Chapter 4: Understanding the Flex Application Development Process 85

Part II: Connecting Java and Flex 111
Chapter 5: Sending Data from Flex 113
Chapter 6: Writing Java Web Applications 123
Chapter 7: Using JUnit and FlexUnit to Test Your Applications 167
Chapter 8: Relational Databases 203
Chapter 9: Java and Databases 233
Chapter 10: Building a Basic Database-Powered Flex Application 265
Chapter 11: Developing a Stock Ticker with BlazeDS 285

Part III: Building Advanced Applications 305
Chapter 12: Developing a Storefront Server Application with Java 307
Chapter 13: Developing a Storefront Server Application with Flex 371
Chapter 14: Building a Real-Time Messaging System 399
Chapter 15: Extending Java and Flex Development 435
Chapter 16: Advanced Development 477

Appendix: Installing Adobe Flex and Adobe Flex Builder 499
Glossary 509

Index 513

Contents

Acknowledgments xvii

Introduction xix

Part I: Installation and Getting Started   1

Chapter 1: Setting Up the Java Development Environment 3

The Java Programming Language 3
    Object-oriented programming 4
    Key Java concepts 4
    Java syntax 5
The Java SE Development Kit 7
    Installing the JDK 8
    Configuring the JDK 11
The JBoss Application Server 14
    Installing JBoss 14
    Configuring JBoss 14
Apache Ant 17
    Installing Apache Ant 18
    Configuring Apache Ant 18
The Eclipse Integrated Development Environment 20
    Installing the Eclipse IDE 21
    Configuring the Eclipse IDE 22
Summary 36

Chapter 2: Configuring Flex for Java Development 37

Configuring Flex 37
    The Java and Flex project type 38
    The Flex Library project type 46
Testing the Configuration 48
    Testing online 48
    Reading debug messages 54
Summary 60

Chapter 3: Similarities between Java and Flex 61

What Makes Java and Flex Similar? 61
    Code structure 62
    Libraries 67
    Development tools 73

Contents

How These Similarities Help with Integration 83

    Team building...83

    Multiapplication integration 83

Summary 84

Chapter 4: Understanding the Flex Application Development Process ... 85

Working with Packages and Classes..85

    Packages..85

    Classes 86

    Extending classes 90

MXML and ActionScript 91

Understanding Events in Flex 93

Data Providers 94

Working with Item Renderers..96

    Setting up an item renderer 96

    Creating an MXML component file...98

    Overriding a value..100

Building a Sample Flex Application..104

Summary 110

Part II: Connecting Java and Flex   111

Chapter 5: Sending Data from Flex. 113

Understanding the Sending Process 113

    ActionScript approach..114

    Using HTTPService 114

    Handling the response of the HTTPService call 115

Writing the Sample Test..116

    Building the Flex application...116

    Adding the components 116

    Aligning the components 117

    Adding the ActionScript...118

Summary 122

Chapter 6: Writing Java Web Applications 123

The Model-View-Controller Pattern 123

The Spring Framework 124

Writing a Simple Web Application...126

    The project directory structure 126

    Creating an Eclipse project 128

    Configuring the Eclipse project 130

    Writing the Web application...141

    Writing the Ant build script 156

    Enhancing the Web application 164

Summary 166

Chapter 7: Using JUnit and FlexUnit to Test Your Applications **167**

Working with JUnit 167
   Importing the testing library 168
   Building the testing suite 177
Working with FlexUnit 188
   Using unit testing 188
   Configuring FlexUnit 189
   Developing the unit test 190
   Working with the FlexUnit Runner 197
Summary 201

Chapter 8: Relational Databases **203**

Relational Database Concepts 203
   Tables 203
   SQL queries 206
   Stored procedures 209
The MySQL Database Server 209
   Installing and configuring MySQL 209
   Creating a simple database in MySQL 218
Summary 231

Chapter 9: Java and Databases **233**

Java Database Connectivity 233
   Overview of JDBC 233
   Using JDBC with MySQL 234
The Hibernate Framework 244
   Overview of Hibernate 245
   Using Hibernate with MySQL 245
Summary 264

Chapter 10: Building a Basic Database-Powered Flex Application **265**

Understanding the Database Application 265
   Defining the application 265
   File outline 266
Building the Database Application 266
   Designing the application 266
   Creating the product editor popup 269
   Creating the product grid ItemRenderer 272
Developing the Database Communication with Java 273
   Building a custom data class 274
   Adding the class methods 275
   Handling the response from the server 276
Connecting the Database Application 278
   Main application code 278
   Adding the methods 279
Summary 284

Contents

Chapter 11: Developing a Stock Ticker with BlazeDS 285

Installing BlazeDS 286
Understanding Messaging in Flex...286
    Producer and Consumer messaging components...286
    Managing the destination service..289
Developing a Stock Ticker Application...290
    Setting up the messaging config file..290
    Developing the Java back end..291
    Building the Flex user interface 295
    Setting the J2EE Server options 295
    Building the user interface...296
    Developing the ActionScript...297
    Bindable variables 297
    Using the labelFunction 299
Summary 303

Part III: Building Advanced Applications   305

Chapter 12: Developing a Storefront Server Application with Java 307

Application Best Practices 307
    Code modularity 308
    Separation of interface and implementation 308
Developing the Java 309
    The MySQL database...310
    The Eclipse project 319
    The model layer 329
    The data access layer 348
    The service layer...355
    The Ant build file 365
Deploying and Testing the Web Application 367
Summary 370

Chapter 13: Developing a Storefront Server Application with Flex 371

Designing and Developing the Flex Front End 371
    Communicating with the Java back end 372
    Developing the product viewer 382
    Developing the payment solution 395
Summary 397

Chapter 14: Building a Real-Time Messaging System 399

Understanding the Application Process..399
Writing the Java Code...400
    Setting up the Eclipse project 400
    The chat server..403

Writing the Flex Code..408
Connecting the Java and Flex Pieces 420
    The Web application configuration 420
    The BlazeDS configuration 421
    Configuring Ant and Eclipse to build the application 422
    Connecting to the chat server...430
    Testing the chat application..431
Summary 433

Chapter 15: Extending Java and Flex Development 435

Building Mashups 435
    Libraries for mashups...436
    Advanced example 436
Overview of Developing Custom Flex Interfaces 463
    Custom interfaces using CSS 463
    Custom interfaces using ActionScript 464
    Creating the Flex mashup UI 465
    Skinning the Flex mashup UI 473
Summary 476

Chapter 16: Advanced Development 477

Advanced Java Concepts 477
    Enterprise-level Java development...477
    More library components 485
Advanced Flex Concepts 492
    Requirements for charting components.................................492
    Configuring the charting component in Flex 493
Summary 498

Appendix: Installing Adobe Flex and Adobe Flex Builder 499

Glossary 509

Index 513

Acknowledgments

Charles A. Christiansen Jr.: I would like to thank Matthew Keefe for asking me to do this book with him, my lovely wife Eileen for encouraging me through this whole process, Courtney Allen and Christopher Stolle for being so great to work with, Kevin Polk for bringing me into the world of Java development so many years ago, and my parents for teaching me the value of hard work and encouraging me to fully pursue my interests.

Matthew Keefe: I would like to thank all the folks at Wiley for making this book a reality. A special thanks to acquisitions editor Courtney Allen and project editor Christopher Stolle. I would also like to thank my friends and family — Philip, Daz, Colin, Teisha, John, Brooke, Frank, and my mom — for their support. And lastly, I would like to thank my dad for getting me started in technology when I was younger and making it possible to do what I love.

Introduction

For years, Java has been used to develop Web applications that allow users to access server-side data through user interfaces presented in a Web browser. Generally, the user interfaces for these applications have been presented to the user as HTML by using technologies such as Java Server Pages (JSP) to insert server-side data into the user interface to create dynamic, data-driven applications.

Flex offers another possibility for Web application user interfaces — the highly visual, fluid, and rich experience provided by Adobe Flash Player and Flash movies. Flex puts the richness and power of Flash into the hands of application developers by providing a software development kit and user interface components that allow developers to create Flash applications by using familiar software development tools and methodologies.

When you integrate Java and Flex in a Web application, you get the best of both worlds. You get the power and stability that Java provides on the server side and the rich, dynamic user interfaces that Flex and Adobe Flash Player make possible. In this book, you learn to marry the two to create applications with the data your customers need and the visually compelling user experience they want.

There are many applications on the Web — some you probably use without even knowing it. When you want these online applications to offer a richer experience to the end user, you need to use the right tools.

Flex is one of these tools, but that only accounts for half the requirements. For an application to be truly useful, it needs a dynamic back end to process the user's information and add the overall usefulness for the end user.

Java can help you write the back end that provides data to your Flex applications and makes them more dynamic and useful. Java has a number of frameworks, development tools, and libraries that can make developing powerful, data-driven Web applications faster and less complicated than other platforms.

In this book, you learn how to connect Flex — by using the stand-alone IDE and Eclipse plug-in — to a Java back end. Once the basics of installing and configuring Java and Flex are completed, you learn how to build real-world applications, such as a chat client, a storefront, and a back-end administration tool for the same store.

This book is for beginning to advanced developers interested in developing rich Internet applications that go beyond the standard HTML-based development model. While this book assumes that you have at least some programming knowledge, previous experience with Java and Flex isn't assumed. The basic concepts of the Java and Flex languages are explained in detail in part one of the book, so those with programming experience should be able to come up to speed quickly.

Using the Icons

This book includes several icons that should help you with your understanding of the topics:

 **From time to time, you may find that you want to review some Java and Flex concepts explained in another chapter. These icons point you to that information.**

NOTE **These icons note interesting tidbits. For example, a Note might alert you to upcoming releases of development tools that you need to be aware of.**

TIP **These icons indicate a power-user secret that might help you develop successful projects, such as handy shortcuts to use within the development tools.**

How This Book Is Organized

This book is divided into three parts. In the first part of the book, you learn to install and/or configure Java, Flex, and various development tools for each. You also learn some basic concepts involved in Java and Flex programming, including more about the syntax and constructs of each language. Once you've finished part one, you have the basic foundation you need to start diving into development.

The second part builds upon this foundation and introduces you to specific Java and Flex development topics. You learn how to work with relational databases, develop Java Web applications, and send data from a Flex application. You also learn about unit testing in both Java and Flex, allowing you to ensure that your code is functioning as you expect. After completing this part, you understand how to develop applications by using Java and Flex and then how to test those applications.

In the final part, you apply what you've learned in the first two parts to the development of specific, real-world applications. You develop a functioning chat application, a Web store, and a mashup application that uses data from multiple services on the Web and then combines that data in a new way. You end the book by learning about a number of other libraries available for both Java and Flex to aid in the development of reliable, scalable enterprise applications.

The book also includes an appendix that details the installation and configuration of the Flex Builder integrated development environment (IDE) and Flex software development kit (SDK). There's also a glossary that defines some terms related to Java and Flex development that you may not be familiar with.

Once you've finished reading this book, you should have the necessary knowledge to build your own rich Internet applications that users will find useful and that you'll enjoy developing.

So, what are you waiting for? Chapter 1 is only a few short pages away!

Part I

Installation and Getting Started

IN THIS PART

Chapter 1
Setting Up the Java Development Environment

Chapter 2
Configuring Flex for Java Development

Chapter 3
Similarities between Java and Flex

Chapter 4
Understanding the Flex Application Development Process

Chapter 1

Setting Up the Java Development Environment

efore you start working with Java, you need to set up a Java development environment. This includes installing the Java Standard Edition (SE) Development Kit and the JBoss application server and then configuring the server to use the Java Development Kit (JDK) you just installed. After that, you must install Apache Ant and the Eclipse integrated development environment (IDE), which you also configure to use the same JDK and to control your JBoss server.

Because Java is multiplatform, and JBoss, Ant, and Eclipse are themselves written in Java, it's possible to use this Java development environment setup wherever Java runs. This chapter, though, covers only setup in Windows.

IN THIS CHAPTER

The Java programming language

The Java SE Development Kit

The JBoss application server

Apache Ant

The Eclipse integrated development environment

The Java Programming Language

The Java programming language is one of the most popular choices for Web application development for a number of reasons. First, Web applications written in Java are portable. That means that the same Java application you write for a Windows machine can also be run on Mac OS, Linux, or Solaris without the need for changes to your code.

In addition to portability, Java is well-supported by a number of development tools that make developing and deploying Java Web applications much easier. The Eclipse IDE, when configured to work together with other development tools, can help you write code, compile it, package and deploy the application to a server, and even run and debug the application — all from within the IDE. In fact, Eclipse, Ant, and JBoss are all written in Java themselves — a testament to the versatility of the language.

Object-oriented programming

Java is said to be an *object-oriented* programming language. In the world of object-oriented programming, *programs* are simply collections of interacting objects. *Objects* are programmatic representations of things in the real world. They are collections of *properties* (things the object has) and *behaviors* (things the object does).

The basic building block in object-oriented programming is called a *class*. A class describes the properties and behaviors of an object. For example, a Car class might contain properties such as color, bodyStyle, currentSpeed, and mileage. It might also have behaviors such as accelerate, stop, and start.

An object is a specific *instance* of a class. Whereas a class merely describes the properties and behaviors of an object, an instance contains specific values and implementations of those properties and behaviors. For example, an instance of the Car class might have a color of "blue", a bodyStyle of "sedan", and a currentSpeed of "55". The accelerate behavior might increase the value of currentSpeed by one each time it's invoked. Each instance of a class shares the properties and behaviors of the class with all other instances of that class, but the values and implementations of those properties and behaviors can differ.

Classes may also *inherit* properties and behaviors from other classes. A Convertible class might inherit all the properties and behaviors of the Car class while adding a topColor property and raiseTop and lowerTop behaviors. The properties of the Car class, known as the *superclass* of Convertible, are also accessible by Convertible, which is considered a *subclass* of Car. Any code that requires a Car object may also use a Convertible (or any other subclass of Car) and then use it just like any other Car. This is known as *polymorphism* — the ability of an object to act or be treated like another object.

These concepts are the basic building blocks of all object-oriented programming languages, including Java. Understanding these concepts helps you comprehend the way object-oriented programming in Java works.

Key Java concepts

As an object-oriented language, Java makes use of all the concepts just discussed. Java also has a few key concepts that separate it from other programming languages. Among these concepts are the following:

- **Write once, run anywhere.** Applications written in Java don't run natively in the operating system. Instead, Java provides a virtual machine that runs natively in the operating system. In turn, Java programs run inside this virtual machine, which acts as a translator between the compiled Java application and the operating system, converting the Java program instructions into operating system instructions. Virtual machines are available for most major operating systems, including multiple versions of Windows, Mac OS X, and Linux.

- **Built-in libraries.** Java comes with a number of useful libraries right out of the box. These include libraries for networking, working with databases, and creating graphical user interfaces.

■ **Automatic memory management.** In many other programming languages, the programmer is responsible for making sure that any memory used up by objects created by the program is freed when it's no longer needed. This is problematic for a couple of reasons. The first reason is that it requires that memory management code be mixed in with application logic, which makes the application logic harder to maintain. The second is that if the programmer forgets to add memory management code everywhere it's needed, the application could end up with what's known as a *memory leak*. An application with a memory leak continues to use more and more memory until it runs out altogether, causing the application to crash.

Java has an automatic memory manager, known as the *garbage collector*, that monitors all the objects created in the virtual machine and disposes of the ones that are no longer in use by any part of the application, thus freeing up the memory used by those objects. In this way, the Java virtual machine removes the burden of memory management from the program, leaving the programmer to concentrate on the logic of the application, not memory management.

Java syntax

This code listing shows how the previously discussed Car class might be written in Java:

```java
package com.wiley.jfib.ch01;

public class Car
{
    public String color;
    public String bodyType;
    public boolean isStarted;
    public int currentSpeed;

    public Car()
    {
        currentSpeed = 0;
    }

    public void accelerate()
    {
        currentSpeed += 1;
    }

    public void start()
    {
        isStarted = true;
    }

    public void stop()
    {
        isStarted = false;
    }
}
```

The first line of this class is known as the *package declaration*. A package in Java is a means of grouping related classes together.

The next line of this class is known as the *class declaration*. The keyword `public` indicates that the class is able to be *instantiated* — that is, new instances of this class can be created by other code.

The next four lines of this class define the properties of the class and their data types. `Color` and `bodyType` are both *strings*, which contain character data. The `isStarted` property is a *boolean*, which is a value that can be set to `true` or `false`. The `currentSpeed` property is an *int*, which contains integer values.

The block of code starting with `public Car()` and including the code within the curly braces is known as the *constructor*. The constructor is used by other code to *instantiate* (construct an instance of) a class by using the new operator. For example, if some code requires an instance of the `Car` class, it can include this line to create one:

```
Car carInstance = new Car();
```

The next three blocks of code, which define the `accelerate`, `start`, and `stop` behaviors, are known as *methods*. A method in a Java class provides an interface for invoking a behavior. The `public` keyword indicates that each of these methods is available for any other code to invoke. Other method access keywords are `private`, which means that only the class itself can invoke the method, and `protected`, which means that subclasses and any classes in the same package as the class can invoke the method. The `void` keyword indicates that these methods return no value when they've finished executing. Methods can return no value; simple types of values, such as `int` or `boolean`; or any object.

Here's the code listing for the `Convertible` class:

```
package com.wiley.jfib.ch01;

public class Convertible extends Car
{
    public String topColor;
    public boolean isTopUp;

    public Convertible()
    {
        super();
        isTopUp = true;
    }

    public void raiseTop()
    {
        isTopUp = true;
    }
```

```
public void lowerTop()
{
        isTopUp = false;
}
}
```

The syntax for the Convertible class is the same as for the Car class, with a few differences. First, in the class declaration, notice that Convertible extends Car. This indicates that the Convertible class inherits the properties and behaviors of the Car class. Second, in the constructor, there's a call to super(). This call tells the constructor of the Convertible class to invoke the constructor of the Car class, the superclass of Convertible.

This final code listing shows an example of a method in another class that uses the Car class:

```
public void driveToWork()
{
    Car companyCar = new Car();
    companyCar.color = "black";
    companyCar.bodyType = "sedan";
    companyCar.start();
    while(companyCar.currentSpeed < 55)
    {
            companyCar.accelerate();
    }

    // some logic to determine when the
    // car arrives at work would go here

    companyCar.stop();
}
```

This method instantiates a new Car object by using the Car class's constructor, sets its color and bodyType properties, invokes its start() method, and invokes accelerate() until the value of the currentSpeed property reaches 55. Finally, the Car object's stop() method is invoked.

The Java SE Development Kit

The first thing you need to get started with Java development is Java itself. The Java SE Development Kit, or JDK, contains both the Java runtime needed to run Java applications and the Java compiler needed to compile Java source code into Java applications. Much like Flex, where your MXML and ActionScript files are compiled into one or more SWF files, Java source code files are compiled into binary Java class files that can be run inside the Java virtual machine.

Installing the JDK

The most recent version of the JDK for all platforms is always available from Sun at `http://java.sun.com/javase/downloads/index.jsp`. As of this writing, JDK 6 Update 10 is the current version.

 **Updates to the JDK are likely, so use the current version available.**

The JDK for Windows is packaged as a standard Windows installer. Once the installer has finished installing the JDK, some additional configuration steps are required.

To download the installer from the Java Web site, follow these steps:

1. **Click the Download button for the current version of the JDK on the download page, as shown in Figure 1.1.** You're automatically redirected to the next page.

2. **On the next page, as shown in Figure 1.2, choose the Windows operating system and Multi-language options from the dropdown lists, click the check box to indicate your acceptance of the license agreement, and then click Continue to go to the next page.**

FIGURE 1.1

On the Java 6 download page, click the Download button for the current version of the JDK.

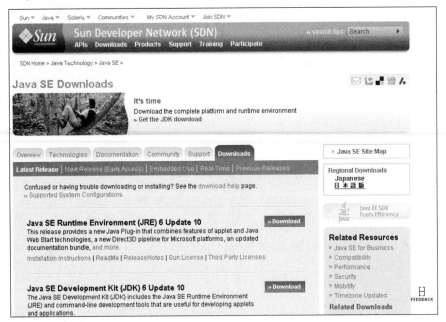

3. **On the final page, as shown in Figure 1.3, click the** `jdk-6u10-windows-i586-p.exe` **link for the Windows Offline Installation.** The offline installation option is a larger download but doesn't require a network connection to install once downloaded.

4. **Choose Save rather than Run to save the file to your computer.** Pick a location that you can remember.

FIGURE 1.2

On the next page of the Java download Web site, select the Windows operating system and Multi-language options from the dropdown lists and click the check box to accept the license agreement.

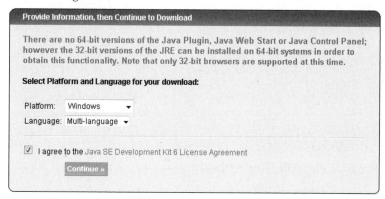

FIGURE 1.3

On the final page of the Java download Web site, click the Windows Offline Installation to download the installer.

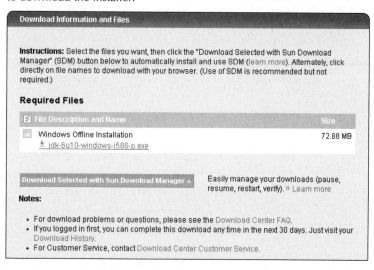

To run the installer from the saved location, follow these steps:

1. **Double-click the installer executable.**

2. **Read the Sun Binary Code License Agreement for the JDK and then click the Accept button to continue.**

3. **On the second screen, as shown in Figure 1.4, choose the location where you want to install the JDK and which features to include and then click Next to continue.** The default values are suitable for most users. If you need to change the install location, click Change and then choose a new location. In either case, be sure to note the location. The JDK installer displays a progress bar that shows the progress of the JDK installation before going to the next step.

 By default, the installer installs all features, including demos and sample code. The sample code is worth a look if you're new to Java development.

4. **Once the JDK has finished installing, choose the installation location for the stand-alone Java Runtime Environment (JRE) and Java browser plug-in, as shown in Figure 1.5.** These components allow Java applications installed on your computer as well as Java applets hosted on Web sites to run. The default values are suitable for most users. If you need to change the install location, click the Change button and then choose a new location. The JDK installer displays a progress bar that shows the progress of the JRE installation before going to the next step.

5. **Click Finish to exit the installer.** Installation of the JDK and JRE is now complete.

FIGURE 1.4

The default installation location and settings. These are acceptable for most installations.

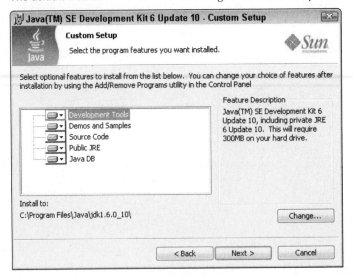

FIGURE 1.5

The Java Runtime Environment and Java browser plug-in are installed separately from the JDK. Again, the default values are acceptable for most installations.

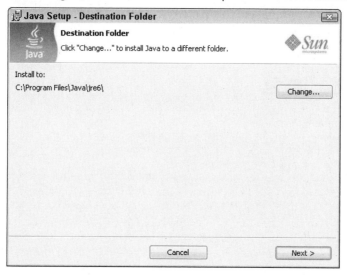

Configuring the JDK

Although it's possible to run the tools in the JDK without any configuration, taking the time now to perform a few simple configuration steps makes it easier to configure other Java development tools later. Most Java development tools and servers expect (or at least prefer) that a couple of system environment variables have been set. These environment variables make it easier for other applications to locate your installed JDK and to execute the Java compiler and runtime without needing to configure the full path to the Java installation in each development tool you install.

To modify the environment variables, follow these steps:

1. **Open the System Properties dialog box, as shown in Figure 1.6:**

   - **In Windows Vista:** Choose Start ⇨ Control Panel ⇨ System and Maintenance ⇨ System ⇨ Advanced System Settings.

   - **In Windows XP using the Control Panel's Classic View:** Choose Start ⇨ Control Panel ⇨ System and then click the Advanced tab.

   - **In Windows XP using the Control Panel's Category View:** Choose Start ⇨ Control Panel ⇨ Performance and Maintenance ⇨ System and then click the Advanced tab.

2. **Click the Environment Variables button.** The Environment Variables dialog box opens. As shown in Figure 1.7, the dialog box is divided into two sections:

   - **User variables.** These are specific to the environment of the user currently logged into the Windows system.

   - **System variables.** These are globally available to any application run by any user on the system.

FIGURE 1.6

The Advanced tab in the System Properties dialog box is where you set necessary environment variables.

NOTE   Typically, you only add or modify environment variables in the User variables section. However, if your Java development machine is shared among multiple developers with different logins, it may make sense to set environment variables in the System variables section. Setting System variables may require a Windows user account with Administrator privileges.

3. **Click the New button in the User variables section.** The New User Variable dialog box opens.

4. **Type** JAVA_HOME **in the Variable name text field, type the full path to your JDK installation in the Variable value text field, as shown in Figure 1.8, and then click OK.** The JAVA_HOME variable lets other applications know where your JDK is installed. Both the JBoss application server and the Eclipse IDE use this environment variable.

FIGURE 1.7

The Environment Variables dialog box. User variables are available only to the
logged-in user, while System variables are globally available.

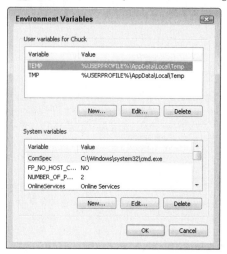

5. **Click the New button in the User variables section.** The New User Variable dialog box
   opens.

6. **Type** PATH **in the Variable name text field, type** %JAVA_HOME%\bin **in the Variable
   value text field, and then click OK.** The PATH environment variable tells the system the
   specific locations to look for executable programs. By adding the JAVA_HOME\bin entry
   to the PATH environment variable, the system can find the Java compiler and runtime
   executables when they're called.

7. **Click OK to exit the Environment Variables dialog box and then click OK to save
   your settings.** Now that you've installed and configured the JDK, you can install other
   development tools that use it.

FIGURE 1.8

In the New User Variable dialog box, type JAVA_HOME in the Variable name text field
and the full path to your JDK (C:\Program Files\Java\jdk1.6.0_10, for example)
in the Variable value text field.

 If you're adding environment variables to the System variables section, the PATH variable likely already exists. If so, select the PATH variable from the variables list and then click the Edit button rather than the New button. Type the full path to the bin directory inside the JDK installation folder (for example, C:\Program Files\Java\jdk1.6.0_10\bin) at the end of the path, preceded by a semicolon to separate it from the rest of the values.

The JBoss Application Server

Java Web applications consist of a combination of compiled Java code; standard Web assets, such as HTML files and images; and Java Server Pages (JSPs), which allow dynamic content to be retrieved from the server and displayed in a browser. Java Web applications are typically packaged in a Web Application Archive (WAR) file and then deployed to an application server, which is responsible for providing the runtime resource management that the Web application needs.

The application server used to run the applications in this book is JBoss. JBoss is an open-source application server for Java Web applications. JBoss is popular for Java development because it's free to download and use, closely follows Java standards, and is easy to configure. As mentioned previously, JBoss is written in Java. You use the JDK you previously installed to run JBoss.

Installing JBoss

The JBoss application server can be downloaded from the JBoss Web site at www.jboss.org/jbossas/downloads. As of this writing, the latest stable version of JBoss is 4.2.3GA.

 JBoss version 5.0.0 is in its release candidate phase and may be available by the time you read this. Installation and configuration may be slightly different for this version.

Clicking the Download link for the latest stable version takes you to the file-listing page for that release. For JDK 6 for Windows, click the download link labeled jboss-<version number>-jdk6.zip (for example, jboss-4.2.3.GA-jdk6.zip). Save the archive to your machine and then extract it to a directory of your choice. JBoss is packaged in and runs from a self-contained folder. No installation is required.

Configuring JBoss

Initial configuration of JBoss involves setting an environment variable and optionally editing JBoss's run.bat startup batch file. Once you're ready to deploy your Web application to JBoss, more detailed configuration may be necessary. The configuration steps listed here allow you to run JBoss with its default settings, which are appropriate for the Web applications in this book.

To run JBoss with its default settings, follow these steps:

1. **Open the System Properties dialog box:**

   ■ **In Windows Vista:** Choose Start ➪ Control Panel ➪ System and Maintenance ➪ System ➪ Advanced System Settings.

- **In Windows XP using the Control Panel's Classic View:** Choose Start ⇨ Control Panel ⇨ System and then click the Advanced tab.

- **In Windows XP using the Control Panel's Category View:** Choose Start ⇨ Control Panel ⇨ Performance and Maintenance ⇨ System and then click the Advanced tab.

2. **Click the Environment Variables button.** The Environment Variables dialog box opens.

3. **Click the New button in the User variables section.** The New User Variable dialog box opens.

4. **Type** JBOSS_HOME **in the Variable name text field, type the full path to your JBoss installation in the Variable value text field, and then click OK.** The JBOSS_HOME variable lets other applications know where JBoss is installed on your system. This helps you use automated tools to handle deploying your compiled Java applications to the JBoss server without needing to remember or type the full installation path each time.

5. **Click OK to exit the Environment Variables dialog box and then click OK to save your settings.**

The batch file run.bat, as shown in Figure 1.9, is located in the bin subfolder of your JBoss install directory. This file is used to start the JBoss server for Windows and contains a number of parameters that are passed to the Java virtual machine (JVM) when starting up the JBoss server. Most of the default parameters are fine for development purposes. However, one parameter almost certainly needs to be changed.

Using Notepad, open the run.bat file by choosing File ⇨ Open from the menu and then navigating to the bin subfolder of your JBoss install to select it. When you have opened the file, look for the following line:

```
JAVA_OPTS=%JAVA_OPTS% -Xms128m -Xmx512m
```

This line configures two parameters: -Xms128m and -Xmx512m refer to the minimum and maximum Java heap size, respectively. The *heap size* is the amount of physical memory Java uses to store its objects. These are the parameters you most likely need to adjust. When dealing with large Java applications, these default values may not be enough to meet the server's memory requirements. If you're using a development machine with a healthy amount of RAM, consider increasing the minimum and maximum heap sizes. By increasing the minimum heap size, you decrease the likelihood that the JVM needs to take the time to allocate more memory to the heap. By increasing the maximum heap size, you decrease the likelihood that the JVM runs out of memory, thus causing your application to stop responding altogether. In production environments, it's typical to set the minimum and maximum heap sizes to the same value. For development environments, the minimum heap size is less important. If you eventually find that JBoss runs out of memory with the specified maximum heap size, increase that value as needed by replacing the -Xmx512m value with a higher number.

> **NOTE**   Although it's not strictly necessary to do so, using increments of 128MB is standard practice for adjusting the heap size value.

 Don't set the maximum heap size higher than the amount of memory your system has. The system may become unstable if the JVM tries to use all the memory your system has.

To test your JBoss installation, double-click run.bat. You see a Windows command prompt window open and some startup information scroll by. When the scrolling has stopped, the bottom line in the window indicates that the server has started. You can verify this by opening a browser and then typing the following in the address bar:

```
http://localhost:8080
```

You should see the JBoss welcome page shown in Figure 1.10. The JBoss welcome page includes links to the JBoss site, including documentation and discussion forums. These are great resources for becoming familiar with JBoss.

FIGURE 1.9

The run.bat file, which starts the JBoss server in Windows and contains arguments for the JVM that runs JBoss

```
run.bat - Notepad
File  Edit  Format  View  Help

:ADD_TOOLS

set JAVA=%JAVA_HOME%\bin\java

rem A full JDK with toos.jar is not required anymore since jboss web packages
rem the eclipse jdt compiler and javassist has its own internal compiler.
if not exist "%JAVA_HOME%\lib\tools.jar" goto SKIP_TOOLS

rem If exists, point to the JDK javac compiler in case the user wants to
rem later override the eclipse jdt compiler for compiling JSP pages.
set JAVAC_JAR=%JAVA_HOME%\lib\tools.jar

:SKIP_TOOLS

rem If JBOSS_CLASSPATH or JAVAC_JAR is empty, don't include it, as this will
rem result in including the local directory in the classpath, which makes
rem error tracking harder.
if not "%JAVAC_JAR%" == "" set RUNJAR=%JAVAC_JAR%;%RUNJAR%
if "%JBOSS_CLASSPATH%" == "" set RUN_CLASSPATH=%RUNJAR%
if "%RUN_CLASSPATH%" == "" set RUN_CLASSPATH=%JBOSS_CLASSPATH%;%RUNJAR%

set JBOSS_CLASSPATH=%RUN_CLASSPATH%

rem Setup JBoss specific properties
set JAVA_OPTS=%JAVA_OPTS% -Dprogram.name=%PROGNAME%

rem Add -server to the JVM options, if supported
"%JAVA%" -server -version 2>&1 | findstr /I hotspot > nul
if not errorlevel == 1 (set JAVA_OPTS=%JAVA_OPTS% -server)

rem JVM memory allocation pool parameters. Modify as appropriate.
set JAVA_OPTS=%JAVA_OPTS% -Xms128m -Xmx512m

rem With Sun JVMs reduce the RMI GCs to once per hour
set JAVA_OPTS=%JAVA_OPTS% -Dsun.rmi.dgc.client.gcInterval=3600000 -Dsun.rmi.dgc.server.gcInterval=3600000

rem JPDA options. Uncomment and modify as appropriate to enable remote debugging.
rem set JAVA_OPTS=-Xdebug -Xrunjdwp:transport=dt_socket,address=8787,server=y,suspend=y %JAVA_OPTS%

rem Setup the java endorsed dirs
set JBOSS_ENDORSED_DIRS=%JBOSS_HOME%\lib\endorsed

echo ===============================================================================
echo.
echo  JBoss Bootstrap Environment
echo.
echo  JBOSS_HOME: %JBOSS_HOME%
echo.
echo  JAVA: %JAVA%
echo.
echo  JAVA_OPTS: %JAVA_OPTS%
echo.
```

FIGURE 1.10

The JBoss welcome page provides verification of a correctly installed and configured JBoss server. It also provides links to documentation on the JBoss Web site.

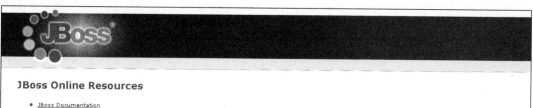

JBoss Online Resources

- JBoss Documentation
- JBoss Wiki
- JBoss JIRA
- JBoss Forums

JBoss Management

- Tomcat status (full) (XML)
- JMX Console
- JBoss Web Console

Apache Ant

It's possible to do all the compilation of your Java applications simply by using the compiler included with the JDK. In reality, that process doesn't scale up well for larger projects. For example, consider a large enterprise application consisting of multiple Web applications and libraries. To build such an application by using only JDK tools would involve invoking the Java compiler with a lengthy classpath argument to compile the code, invoking separate commands to package up each Web application into its own Web application archive (WAR) file, invoking yet another command to package the WAR files and any libraries needed by the applications into an enterprise application archive (EAR) file, and finally manually copying the EAR file to the application server's deployment directory. With this many manual steps, the chance of problems arising increases.

Large software projects typically use automated build processes that not only handle the compilation of source code but also take care of other tasks, such as the packaging and deployment of the compiled application and even running unit tests to ensure that the compiled application works as expected before it's deployed to a production environment. In order to effectively automate the build process, it's necessary to use build tools that run easily and consistently every time.

The most widely used build tool in Java development is Apache Ant. Ant is a command-line tool written in Java that uses XML build files to build your Java projects. Ant's build files divide builds into discrete sets of tasks called *targets*. Ant allows you to chain together targets in such a way that a single command can compile your code, package up your application, and deploy it to the application server.

CROSS-REF For a detailed example of writing an Ant build file and using it to deploy your application to the JBoss server, see Chapter 6.

Installing Apache Ant

Apache Ant can be downloaded from the Apache Ant project's Web site at `http://ant.apache.org/bindownload.cgi`. As of this writing, the latest stable version of Apache Ant is 1.7.1.

Apache Ant comes packaged as a ZIP archive file. Click the download link labeled `apache-ant-<version>-bin.zip` (for example, `apache-ant-1.7.1-bin.zip`). Save the archive to your machine and then extract it to the directory of your choice. Apache Ant is self-contained and doesn't require installation.

Configuring Apache Ant

As with the JDK, you need to set a few environment variables in order to make it easy for other applications to find and work with Ant.

To modify the environment variables, follow these steps:

1. **Open the System Properties dialog box:**

   - **In Windows Vista:** Choose Start ⇨ Control Panel ⇨ System and Maintenance ⇨ System ⇨ Advanced System Settings.

   - **In Windows XP using the Control Panel's Classic View:** Choose Start ⇨ Control Panel ⇨ System and then click the Advanced tab.

   - **In Windows XP using the Control Panel's Category View:** Choose Start ⇨ Control Panel ⇨ Performance and Maintenance ⇨ System and then click the Advanced tab.

2. **Click the Environment Variables button.** The Environment Variables dialog box opens.

3. **Click the New button in the User variables section.** The New User Variable dialog box opens.

4. **Type ANT_HOME in the Variable name text field, type the full path to your Apache Ant installation (`c:\apache-ant-1.7.1`, for example) in the Variable value text field, and then click OK.** The `ANT_HOME` variable lets other applications know where Ant is installed on your system.

5. **Click the New button in the User variables section again.** The New User Variable dialog box opens.

6. **Type ANT_OPTS in the Variable name text field, type the maximum heap size for Ant to use in the Variable value text field, and then click OK.** Because Ant is written in Java, it uses a Java heap to manage the objects it uses, much like JBoss does. Some tasks in Ant require more memory than others, and building projects with large amounts of source code or many resources to package could cause Ant to run out of memory if the heap size is too small. Setting the `ANT_OPTS` environment variable allows you to specify enough of a maximum heap size to ensure that Ant has enough memory and to easily adjust the amount of memory as your project grows. Set the value of the `ANT_OPTS` variable to the same maximum heap size as your JBoss installation by using the same `-Xmx` notation you saw in the JBoss run.bat configuration file, as shown in Figure 1.11.

FIGURE 1.11

Set the value of the ANT_OPTS environment variable to the same maximum heap size you set in JBoss's run.bat file (-Xmx512m, for example).

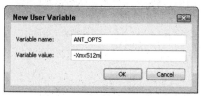

7. **Click the PATH environment variable in the User variables section and then click the Edit button.** The Edit User Variable dialog box opens, and the Variable name and Variable value text fields are populated with the current values for the PATH variable.

8. **Add %ANT_HOME%\bin to the Variable value by using a semicolon to separate it from the %JAVA_HOME%\bin entry and then click OK.** See Figure 1.12. Apache Ant's executables are now available to other applications.

9. **Click OK to exit the Environment Variables dialog box and then click OK to save your settings.**

FIGURE 1.12

Add **%ANT_HOME%\bin** to the PATH environment variable. Separate it from the existing values by using a semicolon.

NOTE   If you're adding environment variables to the System variables section, the PATH variable likely already exists. If so, select the PATH variable from the variable list and then click the Edit button rather than the New button. Type the full path to the bin directory inside the Ant installation (for example, C:\apache-ant-1.7.1\bin) at the end of the path, preceded by a semicolon to separate it from the rest of the values.

To test your Apache Ant installation, follow these steps:

1. **Open a command prompt:**

   ■ **In Windows Vista:** Choose Start, type **cmd** in the Start Search box, and then choose cmd.exe from the Programs list to open the command prompt.

■ **In Windows XP:** Choose Start ⇨ Run, type **cmd** in the Run dialog box that opens, and then click OK to open the command prompt.

2. **Type** ant -version **in the command prompt window and then press Enter.** You should see a message, as shown in Figure 1.13, indicating the version of Apache Ant you installed. If you see a message stating that ant isn't recognized as a command, double-check that your PATH environment variable entry is accurate.

FIGURE 1.13

If Apache Ant is installed and configured correctly, running the ant command with the -version option should print a message similar to this.

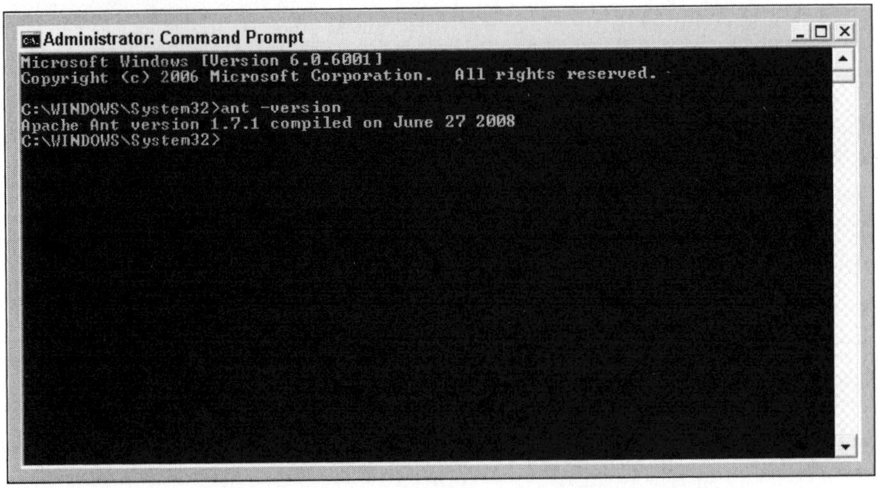

The Eclipse Integrated Development Environment

Eclipse is an open-source integrated development environment (IDE) for Java and other languages. Eclipse is the most popular IDE for Java development because it's not only packed with features such as code completion and templates, but it also integrates with other standard Java tools, such as Ant and JBoss, and is extensible with a wide variety of plug-ins. Eclipse itself is written in Java, and you use the JDK you installed previously to run Eclipse as well as compile the Java code you write by using Eclipse.

Installing the Eclipse IDE

The Eclipse IDE can be downloaded from the Eclipse project's Web site at `www.eclipse.org/downloads/packages`. There are a number of packages available on this page. You should download the Eclipse IDE for Java EE Developers package. This package contains a number of tools, such as database views and XML editors, that are useful for your Java development work. As of this writing, the latest stable version of Eclipse is code-named Ganymede.

To download the Eclipse archive file, follow these steps:

1. **Click the Eclipse IDE for Java EE Developers link on the download page.** The next page opens with a list of mirror sites from which Eclipse can be downloaded, as shown in Figure 1.14. The mirror sites in this list are clones of the main Eclipse download site. Their purpose is to take some of the load off the main Eclipse download site by offering other locations from which you can download Eclipse.

2. **Click the link for the mirror site closest to you.** Choosing a mirror site that's geographically closer to you usually results in a faster download time.

3. **Click Save to download the archive to a location of your choice.**

FIGURE 1.14

The list of mirror sites where Eclipse can be downloaded. Choose the one closest to you geographically.

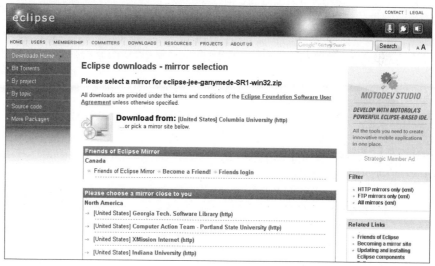

4. **Extract the archive to a location of your choice.** Eclipse is self-contained and doesn't require installation.

5. **Start Eclipse by double-clicking** eclipse.exe **in the Eclipse directory you just extracted.** The Workspace Launcher dialog box, as shown in Figure 1.15, opens.

FIGURE 1.15

The Workspace Launcher dialog box allows you to choose a location for your Eclipse workspace and set that workspace as the default. The workspace contains Eclipse settings and properties. The default value is appropriate for most installations.

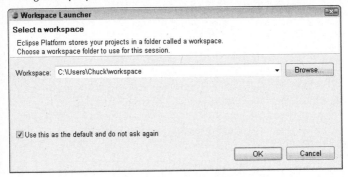

6. **Leave the default value for Workspace, click the Use this as the default and don't ask again check box, and then click OK.** Eclipse launches.

The workspace in Eclipse is a folder in which project configuration, global preferences, and project resources (such as source code) are stored. The default location is a folder named `workspace` under your user files directory. It's possible to have more than one workspace in Eclipse and switch between them at will. This allows you to maintain logical groupings of related projects and keep separate preferences and window layouts for each workspace. For the projects in this book, you need only one workspace.

When Eclipse opens for the first time, the Welcome view is displayed. The Welcome view, as shown in Figure 1.16, provides icons that link to an overview of the Eclipse IDE, descriptions of new features in this version of Eclipse, samples, and tutorials. If you're new to Eclipse or Java development in general, it's worth spending some time with these materials.

Configuring the Eclipse IDE

Eclipse is almost infinitely configurable, and the list of configuration options can be daunting. For the Java and Flex development you do in this book, only a couple of configuration options are necessary.

FIGURE 1.16

The Welcome view in Eclipse contains links to documentation, tutorials, and other valuable information for both new and experienced developers.

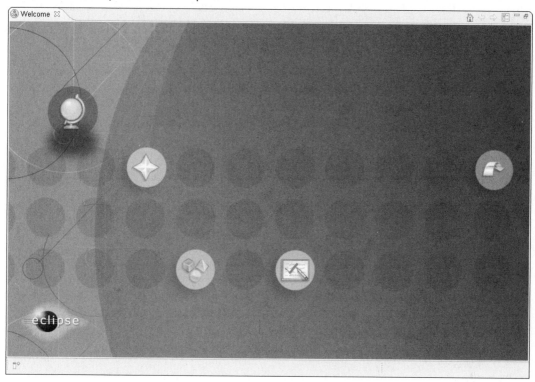

Follow these steps to configure Eclipse:

1. **Choose Window ⇨ Preferences.** The Preferences dialog box opens.

2. **In the left pane, click the arrow next to Java.** The Java submenu is expanded.

3. **Choose Installed JREs from the Java submenu.** The Installed JREs list appears in the right pane, as shown in Figure 1.17. Because you set the JAVA_HOME environment variable when you installed the JDK, you see it listed here and selected as the default option. If the JDK you installed doesn't appear here, follow these steps to add it by using the Add JRE wizard:

FIGURE 1.17

The expanded Java submenu with the Installed JREs item selected in the Preferences dialog box

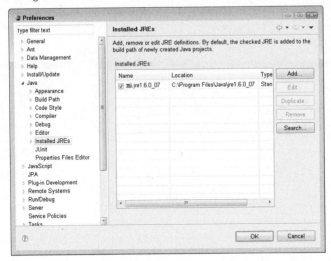

1. **Click the Add button next to the Installed JREs list.** The Add JRE wizard opens.

2. **Choose Standard VM from the dropdown list and then click Next.** See Figure 1.18.

3. **Click Directory, navigate to your JDK installation directory, and then click OK.** The wizard populates the JRE name and JRE system libraries text fields for you, as shown in Figure 1.19.

4. **Click Finish.** The Add JRE wizard closes. Your JDK now appears in the Installed JREs list.

4. **In the left pane of the Preferences dialog box, click the arrow next to Ant.** The Ant submenu is expanded. Eclipse has its own built-in version of Apache Ant, but it's best for the sake of consistency to use the same Ant installation both inside and outside the Eclipse environment.

5. **Choose Runtime from the Ant submenu.** The Runtime properties appear in the right pane, with the Classpath tab selected, as shown in Figure 1.20.

6. **Click the Ant Home button on the Classpath tab.** The Browse for Folder dialog box opens.

7. **Choose your Apache Ant install directory and then click OK.** The Ant Home Entries item now shows the path to your Apache Ant installation. Expand that item to see the set of Java archive (JAR) files corresponding to your Apache Ant installation, as shown in Figure 1.21.

8. **In the left pane, click the arrow next to Server.** The Server submenu is expanded.

FIGURE 1.18

The first screen of the Add JRE wizard. Choose Standard VM from the dropdown list.

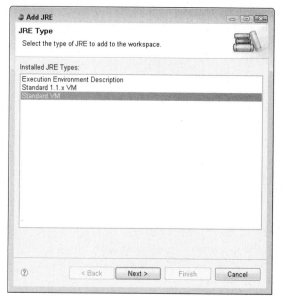

FIGURE 1.19

After you select your JDK installation directory in the second screen of the Add JRE wizard, the wizard automatically fills in the JRE name and JRE system libraries text fields for you.

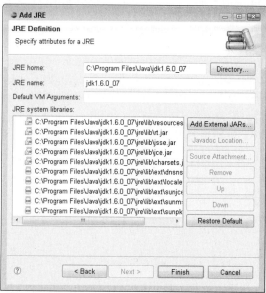

FIGURE 1.20

The expanded Ant submenu with the Runtime item selected in the Preferences dialog box. The Classpath tab is selected by default.

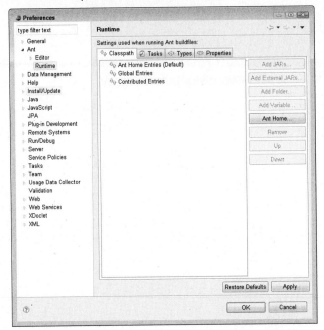

9. **Choose Runtime Environments from the Server submenu.** The Server Runtime Environments list appears in the right pane, as shown in Figure 1.22. Here, you add your JBoss installation to your Eclipse configuration. This allows you to take advantage of Eclipse's debugging features. You're able to step through your code running on your JBoss server, start and stop the server, and more — all from within Eclipse.

10. **Click the Add button next to the Server runtime environments list.** The New Server Runtime Environment wizard opens.

11. **Click the arrow next to JBoss, choose JBoss v4.2 from the expanded list, click the Create a new local server check box, and then click Next.** See Figure 1.23.

FIGURE 1.21

Once you've chosen your Ant installation directory in the Browse for Folder dialog box, Eclipse fills in the Ant Home Entries with the Ant installation's runtime JAR files.

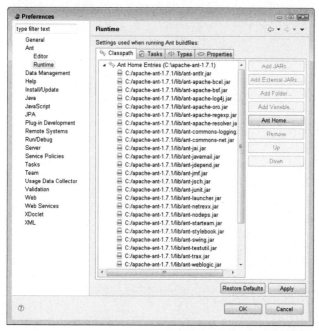

12. **Click the Browse button next to the Application Server Directory text box.** The Browse for Folder dialog box opens.

13. **Choose your JBoss installation folder, click OK, and then click Next.** See Figure 1.24.

14. **Click Finish.** The default values for Address, Port, JNDI Port, and Server Configuration, as shown in Figure 1.25, are acceptable. Your JBoss configuration now appears in the Server runtime environments list.

15. **Click OK.** The Preferences dialog box closes.

FIGURE 1.22

The expanded Server submenu in the Preferences dialog box, with the Runtime Environments item selected

FIGURE 1.23

The New Server Runtime Environment wizard, with the JBoss v4.2 item selected

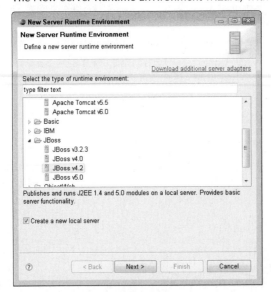

FIGURE 1.24

Choose your JBoss installation folder from the Browse for Folder dialog box.

FIGURE 1.25

The default values for Address, Port, JNDI Port, and Server Configuration in the last screen of the New Server Runtime Environment wizard are fine as they are.

To test your JBoss configuration, close the Welcome tab by clicking the X on the top-right corner of the tab and then follow these steps:

1. **Choose Window ➪ Show View ➪ Servers.** The Servers view, as shown in Figure 1.26, opens. You should see your JBoss configuration listed in the Servers view with the value Stopped in the State column.

FIGURE 1.26

The Servers view showing the stopped JBoss server

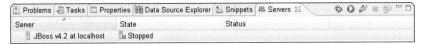

2. **Choose your JBoss server and then either click the Start the Server button (the round green button with the white arrow to the right of the Servers view tab) or press Ctrl+Alt+R.** As JBoss starts up, the Console view opens and displays JBoss startup messages. Once JBoss has started successfully, Eclipse switches back to the Servers view, and the value Started appears in the State column, as shown in Figure 1.27.

3. **Choose your JBoss server and then either click the Stop the Server button (the square red button to the right of the Servers view tab) or press Ctrl+Alt+S.** As JBoss shuts down, the Console view opens and displays JBoss shutdown messages. Once JBoss has stopped successfully, Eclipse switches back to the Servers view, and the value Stopped appears in the State column.

FIGURE 1.27

The Servers view showing the started JBoss server

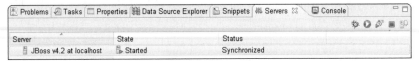

As mentioned previously, one of the things that makes Eclipse a popular choice among Java developers is the ability to extend its functionality through a plug-in system. The last part of configuring Eclipse for the Web applications in this book is installing one such plug-in: the Spring IDE plug-in. The Spring IDE plug-in provides a number of useful tools for developing applications by using the popular Spring Framework.

CROSS-REF For more on the Spring Framework, see Chapter 6.

Eclipse plug-ins are typically installed by providing Eclipse's software update manager with a URL where the plug-in can be downloaded and then choosing the features you want to install. This process is used to install the Spring IDE plug-in.

To install the Spring IDE plug-in for Eclipse, follow these steps:

1. **Choose Help ⇨ Software Updates.** The Software Updates and Add-ons dialog box opens with the Installed Software tab selected, as shown in Figure 1.28.

FIGURE 1.28

The Software Updates and Add-ons dialog box consists of two tabs. The Installed Software tab, selected by default, shows a list of currently installed features.

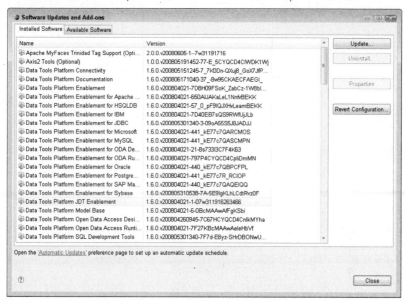

2. **Click the Available Software tab.** The list of currently configured software update sites is displayed, as shown in Figure 1.29. The update sites listed here are those for the features Eclipse provides upon installation. These sites can be used to add features or update existing features.

FIGURE 1.29

The Available Software tab of the Software Updates and Add-ons dialog box lists currently configured software update sites. Software update sites in Eclipse are sites where Eclipse features and plug-ins can be downloaded and installed from within Eclipse.

3. **Click the Add Site button.** The Add Site dialog box opens.

4. **Type** http://dist.springframework.org/release/IDE **in the Location text field, as shown in Figure 1.30, and then click OK.** The Add Site dialog box closes, and the Spring IDE Update Site is added to the list of update sites and is expanded to display the features available for installation, as shown in Figure 1.31. There are a number of features available with Spring IDE. Aside from the Core, which provides the basic Spring IDE installation and is required, only a few of the other options are necessary here:

   ■ **The Spring IDE AOP Extension and Spring IDE AOP Developer Resources provide tools that help with aspect-oriented programming.** Among other things, aspect-oriented programming helps developers deal with modularizing *cross-cutting concerns* — functionality such as logging and error handling that affects multiple modules in an application.

   ■ **The Spring IDE Security Extension and Spring IDE Security Developer Resources provide tools that help with implementing Spring Security in Web applications.** Spring Security provides functionality for handling authentication, resource protection, and other features to make sure only users with proper credentials have access to application resources.

FIGURE 1.30

Type the URL for the Spring IDE update site in the Location text field of the Add Site dialog box.

FIGURE 1.31

Once you provide Eclipse with the URL for the Spring IDE update site, it appears in the list of configured software update sites and expands to display the features available for installation.

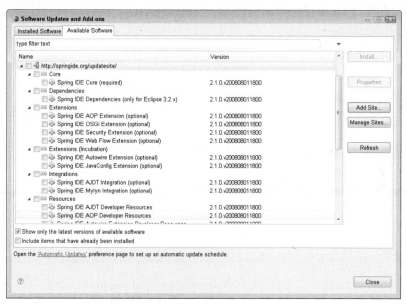

5. **Click the check boxes next to Spring IDE Core, Spring IDE AOP Extension, Spring IDE Security Extension, Spring IDE AOP Developer Resources, and Spring IDE Security Extension Developer Resources and then click the Install button.** Eclipse resolves any dependencies to make sure any selected features don't require other features that aren't present. Upon successful dependency resolution, the Install wizard, as shown in Figure 1.32, opens.

6. **Click the Next button.** The Review Licenses screen, as shown in Figure 1.33, opens. Review the license for each feature you're installing.

7. **Click the radio button to accept the license agreement for each feature and then click the Finish button.** The Install dialog box opens, showing the progress of the feature download and installation, as shown in Figure 1.34. Once all features have been installed, the Install dialog box closes, and the Software Updates dialog box opens, recommending that Eclipse be restarted.

8. **Click the Yes button to restart Eclipse.** Eclipse closes and then reopens.

9. **Once Eclipse has reopened, choose Window ⇨ Show View ⇨ Other.** You should see a Spring folder in the list of views.

Once you install an Eclipse plug-in and restart Eclipse, the new plug-in is available in Eclipse. Each Eclipse plug-in adds different features, views, and menu items to Eclipse. Eclipse may or may not notify you about new features available when a plug-in is installed, so it's best to read the documentation for any Eclipse plug-ins you install to understand what features the plug-ins add. The Spring IDE plug-in adds some Spring views and project types to Eclipse.

FIGURE 1.32

Once Eclipse has made sure that all required dependencies for the features you're installing are present, the Install wizard opens, displaying a list of the chosen features.

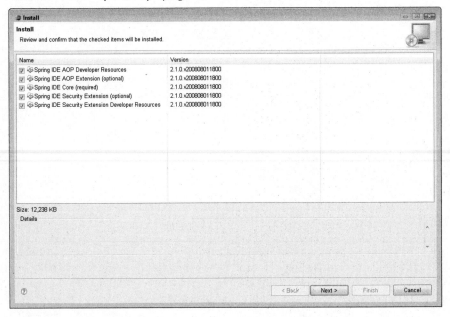

FIGURE 1.33

The Review Licenses screen displays the license agreements for the features you're installing. You can click each feature on the left side of the screen to display the license that applies to that feature.

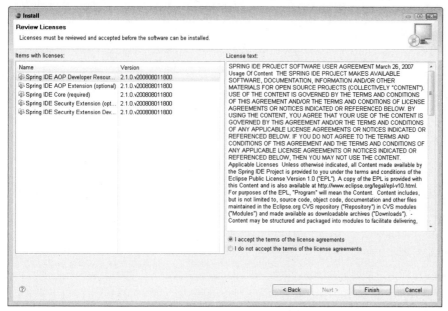

FIGURE 1.34

After you accept the license agreements, Eclipse displays the progress of the feature installation. After all features have been installed, you need to restart Eclipse to ensure that all features are available.

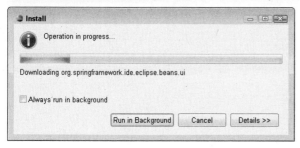

Summary

In this chapter, I discussed the installation and configuration of the tools you use to develop, compile, and run your Java applications. These include the Java SE Development Kit, which contains the compiler and runtime code for Java applications; the JBoss application server, the server environment in which Java Web applications are run; the Apache Ant build tools, which make the process of building, packaging, and deploying applications easier to manage and automate; and the Eclipse IDE, the development environment in which you write, compile, and debug the code for your Java Web applications.

Chapter 2

Configuring Flex
for Java Development

There are a number of different ways to configure your Flex development projects, depending on the amount of code involved, the intended usage of your Flex code, and other factors. In this chapter, you learn several ways to configure your Flex projects for these various scenarios as well as explore a few useful libraries to include in your projects that make working with Java on the server side easier.

IN THIS CHAPTER

Configuring Flex

Testing the configuration

> **NOTE** This chapter assumes that you've already installed the Flex SDK and the Flex Builder IDE. For more information on installing these tools, see Appendix A.

Configuring Flex

There are a number of options available to you when writing a Flex project by using Flex Builder. Among the project types available in Flex Builder are:

- **Flex project.** This type of project involves creating a main application MXML file along with any other resources, such as ActionScript classes, images, and CSS files. The code you write is compiled by the Flex compiler into an SWF file. An HTML wrapper file for the SWF file can also be optionally generated to run your compiled SWF file in a Web browser. Flex projects allow you to develop by using a visual editor that lets you add components directly to your application via drag and drop as well as visually resize and lay out components. Flex projects also make use of a property editor that lets you modify the properties of your components, such as text labels and styles. You can also directly edit the MXML source code.

- **ActionScript project.** This type of project involves creating a set of ActionScript classes by using the Adobe Flash API. This type of project doesn't use the Flex framework and, as such, doesn't include a visual editor or Design view in Flex Builder. Rather than creating application UI classes by using MXML files and visual components, an ActionScript project typically consists of both visual and nonvisual components written in ActionScript code exclusively. You compile these projects into stand-alone SWF files just like a Flex application and then run them in the stand-alone Flash Player. ActionScript code can be used in Flex applications, Flash applications, and Adobe AIR applications.

- **Flex Library project.** This type of project involves creating MXML files, ActionScript classes, and other resources that are compiled and packaged into an SWC file. An SWC file in a Flex application is much like a JAR file in a Java application. It acts as a library whose resources are made available to a Flash or Flex application at runtime. A library can be used in a couple of different ways. First, the resources of the library can be included in the SWF file of an application when that application is compiled. In this case, only the specific resources needed by the application are included in the compiled SWF file. Second, the library can be deployed with the application and the resources in the library accessed at runtime by the application. This is most similar to the Java way of doing things.

Let's take a look at these Flex and Flex Library project types and how to configure them. In general, each of the different project types has the same structure. A source folder holds all the ActionScript and MXML resources, which are compiled to some output folder. Any external libraries needed by the application are included in the project's build path, along with any necessary Flex framework code, such as JavaScript files that help determine the user's version of Flash Player and work with the browser's history for accessibility purposes.

NOTE Because you won't use the ActionScript project type in this book, it's not discussed in detail here. The Flex Builder documentation can provide you with more information about ActionScript projects should you choose to explore them on your own.

The Java and Flex project type

To create a Flex project with Java code in Flex Builder, follow these steps:

1. **Choose Window ⇨ Open Perspective ⇨ Other.** The Open Perspective dialog box, as shown in Figure 2.1, opens.

2. **Choose Flex Development from the list and then click OK.** The Flex Development perspective, as shown in Figure 2.2, opens. The Flex Development perspective is used to create all three types of Flex projects in Flex Builder: Flex projects, ActionScript projects, and Flex Library projects. The tab in the top-left corner of the Flex Builder window is the Flex Navigator view. This view is where your Flex projects appear when created.

FIGURE 2.1

The Open Perspective dialog box allows you to choose a perspective for development. A perspective in Flex Builder and Eclipse is a context in which a certain kind of development (Java or Flex, for example) takes place.

FIGURE 2.2

The Flex Development perspective is the development context used to create Flex projects, ActionScript projects, and Flex Library projects. The Flex Navigator view in the top-left corner is where your Flex projects appear.

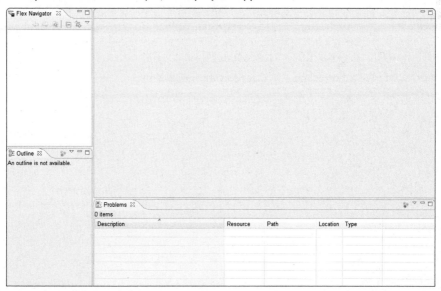

3. **Right-click in the Flex Navigator view and then choose New⇨Flex Project from the popup menu.** The New Flex Project wizard, as shown in Figure 2.3, opens.

The New Flex Project wizard allows you to supply the settings for your new Flex project.

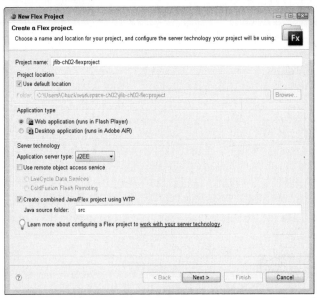

4. **Type** jfib-ch02-flexproject **in the Project name text field, choose J2EE from the Application server type dropdown list, deselect the Use remote object access service check box, and then click Next.** The Configure J2EE Server screen of the New Flex Project wizard, as shown in Figure 2.4, opens.

5. **Choose your J2EE server configuration:**

   ■ If your JBoss configuration appears in the Target runtime dropdown list, choose it from the list.

   ■ If your JBoss configuration doesn't appear in the Target runtime dropdown list, follow these steps to add it:

1. **Click the New button next to the Target runtime dropdown list.** The New Server dialog box, as shown in Figure 2.5, opens.

The Configure J2EE Server screen of the New Flex Project wizard allows you to type the settings for your JBoss server configuration and the project structure of your combined Java and Flex project.

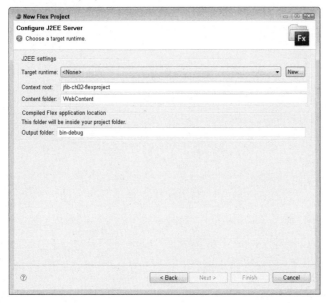

2. **Click the arrow next to JBoss to expand it and then choose JBoss v4.2 from the list.** The default values are appropriate.

3. **Click Next.** The first screen of the New JBoss v4.2 Runtime wizard, as shown in Figure 2.6, opens.

FIGURE 2.5

The New Server dialog box allows you to choose and configure a server setup for your projects.

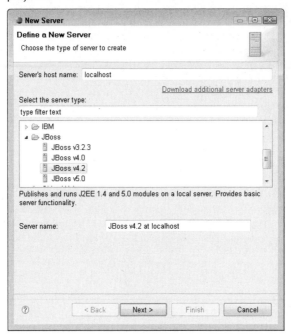

4. **Click the Browse button next to the Application Server Directory text field.** The Browse for Folder dialog box opens.

5. **Choose the root of your JBoss installation from the Browse for Folder dialog box** (c:\jboss-4.2.3.GA, **for example) and then click OK.** The Browse for Folder dialog box closes, and the path to your JBoss installation appears in the Application Server Directory text field on the New JBoss v4.2 Runtime wizard screen.

FIGURE 2.6

The New JBoss v4.2 Runtime screen lets you choose the root folder of your JBoss installation to make that server available to your applications.

6. **Click Next.** The next screen of the New JBoss v4.2 Runtime wizard, as shown in Figure 2.7, opens. The default values are appropriate.

7. **Click Finish.** The New JBoss v4.2 Runtime wizard closes.

8. **Choose JBoss v4.2 from the Target runtime dropdown list.**

FIGURE 2.7

The second screen of the New JBoss v4.2 Runtime wizard contains settings for the address and port of your JBoss server.

6. **Click Next.** The Create a Flex project screen of the New Flex Project wizard, as shown in Figure 2.8, opens. The default values are appropriate.

7. **Click Finish.** The New Flex Project wizard closes. The newly created Flex project appears in the Flex Navigator view, and the `Main.mxml` application file opens in the editor, as shown in Figure 2.9.

A Java and Flex project contains the following folder structure:

- `bin-debug`. This folder contains the compiled SWF files and HTML wrapper files for your project, along with any necessary Flex libraries and JavaScript utility files.

- `flex_libs` and `flex_src`. These two folders contain any Flex libraries needed to compile the application and the source MXML and ActionScript files for the application, respectively.

- `html-template`. This folder also contains the utility JavaScript files as well as an HTML template used to generate the HTML wrapper file for the application SWF at run-time. The HTML template contains parameters passed into the SWF when the HTML page is loaded into a browser and JavaScript code that checks to see whether the Flash Player is installed in the browser and that it's the version of the Flash Player that the SWF needs to run. These values are determined by the compile options in the Flex Builder project.

- `src`. This folder contains the Java source files for your project.

- `WebContent`. This folder contains all the deployment configuration files for the Web application, such as the `web.xml` file.

 **For more on the various Flex user interface components and classes, see Chapter 4.**

FIGURE 2.8

The Create a Flex project screen of the New Flex Project wizard contains a couple of tabs that let you add more source folders and libraries to your project if necessary.

FIGURE 2.9

Once the New Flex Project wizard is finished, the newly created Flex project appears in the Flex Navigator view, and the `Main.mxml` application file is opened in the editor.

The Flex Library project type

Ensure that the Flex Development perspective is still open. Then, to create a Flex Library project, follow these steps:

1. **Right-click in the Flex Navigator view and then choose New ⇨ Flex Library Project from the popup menu.** The New Flex Library Project wizard, as shown in Figure 2.10, opens.

FIGURE 2.10

The New Flex Library Project wizard contains the settings and configuration for creating a new Flex Library project.

2. **Type** jfib_ch02_libraryproject **as the project name.** Note the use of underscores here rather than dashes. The default values for the other settings are appropriate.

3. **Click Next.** The second screen of the New Flex Library Project wizard, as shown in Figure 2.11, opens.

4. **On the Classes tab, click the check box next to the** src **folder.**

5. **Click the Assets tab and then click the check box next to the** src **folder.**

6. **Click Finish.** The New Flex Library Project wizard closes, and the newly created project appears in the Flex Navigator view.

FIGURE 2.11

On the second screen of the New Flex Library Project wizard, you can choose the ActionScript class folders as well as the folders containing nonembedded assets that are added to your library.

This project contains only two folders: an src folder that contains the source code for ActionScript and MXML files to be included in the library and a bin folder to hold the compiled SWC file created from the source code. Remember that an SWC file isn't something that runs on its own but instead contains code that's referenced by other MXML or ActionScript code that's compiled into an SWF application.

When you create this project, Flex Builder places a red X next to the project in the Flex Navigator view. If you click the Problems tab at the bottom of the workspace, you see that the red X indicates that there are no source code files included in the library. This makes sense because a library that includes nothing isn't much of a library! Once you add some ActionScript and MXML files to the `src` folder for this library project, you can add them to the classes included in the library by right-clicking the file and then choosing Include Class in Library from the popup menu.

It's useful to create a library when you have a set of ActionScript or MXML code that can be reused in several Flex applications. For example, you might create an ActionScript class that contains mathematical or string manipulation functions that you can use in multiple applications.

Testing the Configuration

Because you've configured Flex Builder to output to your configured JBoss application server, you can quickly test your Flex Builder project configurations to make sure that your applications deploy and run properly on the server. First, you learn to deploy your application to the JBoss server and then run it online. After that, you learn how to add debug information to the compiler and then trace information to your Flex code to help you debug your Flex applications from within the Flex Builder IDE.

Testing online

You can build, deploy, and test your Java and Flex projects all from within Flex Builder with a single command. There's a simple configuration change that's needed in order to set things up properly to allow this to work correctly.

In a Java Web application, a configuration file called `web.xml` contains information about the Web application, including definitions for any Java servlets, servlet *filters* (Java classes that are run before the servlets when a request is made to the server for a particular servlet), and other identifying information about the Web application.

CROSS-REF For more on Java Web applications, see Chapter 6.

One of the other things defined in `web.xml` is a set of welcome files. These files are the ones used if no specific file is given in a URL. Typically, `index.html` is the default welcome file. If you visit a URL such as `www.somewebserver.com`, the Web server uses the default welcome file to fulfill the request, so that the page you're actually visiting is `www.somewebserver.com/index.html`. In a Java Web application, you can specify multiple welcome files in the `web.xml` configuration file. The application server checks for each one of them in the order specified and then uses the first one it finds to fulfill the request.

When Flex Builder creates the Flex project for a Java and Flex application, it adds a default set of welcome files to the `web.xml` configuration file. However, none of these files actually exist in the project. The only HTML file that's created by Flex Builder when you create your Java and Flex project is a wrapper HTML file with the same name as your MXML application file. By default, Flex Builder names the MXML application file `Main.mxml` and the corresponding HTML file `main.html`. In order to deploy and run your project from inside Flex Builder, you must do one of two things:

- **Add an HTML file or JSP page to your project that uses one of the names listed in the `web.xml` configuration file.** This option is most likely to be used in a production environment, where you may want the user to log in or choose between a Flash and non-Flash site before entering your main application area.

- **Add the `main.html` file to the welcome file list in the `web.xml` configuration file.** This is a quick configuration change that can get your application up and running in Flex Builder quickly so that you can experiment and test things as you develop.

Because this project is currently just a shell with no real application logic yet, adding the `main.html` file to the list of welcome files in the `web.xml` configuration file is the quickest way to get started with this project. To modify the `web.xml` configuration file and build, deploy, and run the project within Flex Builder, follow these steps:

1. **Click the arrow next to the `jfib-ch02-flexproject` project in the Flex Navigator view to expand it.**

2. **Click the arrow next to the `WebContent` folder to expand it and then click the arrow next to the `WEB-INF` folder to expand it.**

3. **Double-click `web.xml` to open it in the editor.** The code listing is shown in Figure 2.12.

FIGURE 2.12

The code listing for the `web.xml` configuration file

```
main.mxml      jfib_ch02_actionscriptproject.as      web.xml

<?xml version="1.0" encoding="UTF-8"?>
<web-app id="WebApp_ID" version="2.4" xmlns="http://java.sun.com/xml/ns/j2ee" xmlns:xsi="http:
    <display-name>jfib-ch02-flexproject</display-name>
    <welcome-file-list>
        <welcome-file>main.html</welcome-file>
        <welcome-file>index.html</welcome-file>
        <welcome-file>index.htm</welcome-file>
        <welcome-file>index.jsp</welcome-file>
        <welcome-file>default.html</welcome-file>
        <welcome-file>default.htm</welcome-file>
        <welcome-file>default.jsp</welcome-file>
    </welcome-file-list>
</web-app>
```

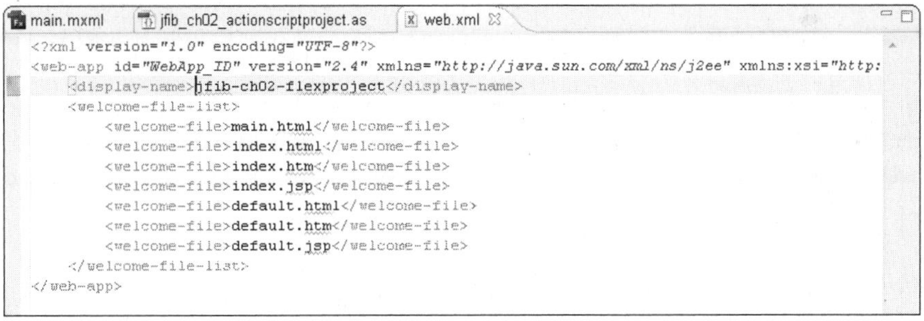

4. **Add the `main.html` file to the top of the list of welcome files.** Be sure to put it between opening and closing `<welcome-file>` tags like the rest of the welcome files in the list.

5. **Click the Save button or choose File ⇨ Save from the menu to save the `web.xml` configuration file.**

6. **Right-click the** `jfib-ch02-flexproject` **project in the Flex Navigator view and then choose Run As⇨ Run On Server from the popup menu.** Alternatively, you can choose Run ⇨ Run As ⇨ Run On Server from the Flex Builder menu. The Run On Server dialog box, as shown in Figure 2.13, opens.

7. **Click the** `JBoss v4.2 at localhost` **item in the server selection box and then click Finish.** The Run On Server dialog box closes.

When you click the Finish button to close the Run On Server dialog box, a few things happen:

- An Ant build script is run, which packages all the files in the application into a Java Web application archive (WAR) file and then deploys that WAR file to the JBoss application server.

- The JBoss server is started.

- Once the JBoss server is started, the Web browser built into Flex Builder is launched with the URL of your project. Java Web applications are given a *context*, which is a way of deploying several applications to the same application server while keeping them separate from one another by providing a specific URL pattern in which they run. A Web application can specify a context, but if no context is specified, the default context name is the name of the WAR file without the `.war` extension. In this case, the application was built and deployed as `jfib-ch02-flexproject.war`, so the URL is `http://localhost:8080/jfib-ch02-flexproject/`. The address of the application server is `localhost`. It runs on port `8080` — the port must be specified if the application isn't running on the default HTTP port of 80. Finally, the application runs in the context `jfib-ch02-flexproject`.

CROSS-REF For more on installing Apache Ant, see Chapter 1. For more on Apache Ant build scripts, see Chapter 6.

You can see what the application running inside the Flex Builder Web browser looks like in Figure 2.14. It opens in its own tab in the editor view, alongside any source code files you have open in the editor.

The MXML file created by the New Flex Project wizard contains only empty opening and closing `<mx:Application>` MXML tags, so the resulting compiled SWF isn't very interesting. Close the Flex Builder Web browser by clicking the X on the right side of the tab.

FIGURE 2.13

The Run On Server dialog box lets you choose a server configuration to deploy and run your application on. The JBoss configuration you created previously appears here for you to use.

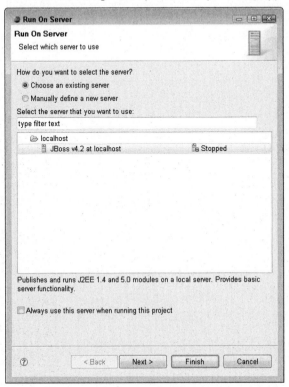

FIGURE 2.14

Using the Run On Server dialog box causes the application to be built and packaged into a WAR file, deployed to the JBoss application server, and launched in Flex Builder's built-in Web browser.

```
Problems   Servers   Console

JBoss v4.2 at localhost [Generic Server] C:\Program Files\Java\jre1.6.0_07\bin\javaw.exe (Oct 26, 2008 1:31:35 PM)
13:31:51,912 INFO  [securedTopic] Bound to JNDI name: topic/securedTopic
13:31:51,927 INFO  [testDurableTopic] Bound to JNDI name: topic/testDurableTopic
13:31:51,927 INFO  [testQueue] Bound to JNDI name: queue/testQueue
13:31:51,974 INFO  [UILServerILService] JBossMQ UIL service available at : /127.0.0.1:8093
13:31:52,021 INFO  [DLQ] Bound to JNDI name: queue/DLQ
13:31:52,177 INFO  [ConnectionFactoryBindingService] Bound ConnectionManager 'jboss.jca:service=Co
13:31:52,349 INFO  [TomcatDeployer] deploy, ctxPath=/jfib-ch02-flexproject, warUrl=.../tmp/deploy/
13:31:52,458 INFO  [TomcatDeployer] deploy, ctxPath=/jmx-console, warUrl=.../deploy/jmx-console.wa
```

To give you a sneak preview of Flex development and show how Flex Builder makes it easy to redeploy your applications as you develop to see how they're progressing, add a few components to the MXML file by following these steps:

1. Click the arrow next to the `jfib-ch02-flexproject` project in the Flex Navigator view to expand it.

2. Click the arrow next to the `flex_src` folder to expand it and then double-click `Main.mxml`. The `Main.mxml` file opens in the editor in Source view.

3. Click the Design button below the `Main.mxml` tab in the editor. The `Main.mxml` file editor switches to Design view, and the Flex Properties, States, and Components views, as shown in Figure 2.15, open.

4. Click the arrow next to Controls in the Components view to expand it and then click `TextInput` and drag it onto the `Main.mxml` application in the editor. A `TextInput` control appears inside the `Main.mxml` application.

5. Click `Button` in the Components view and then drag it onto the `Main.mxml` application in the editor below the `TextInput` control. A `Button` control appears inside the `Main.mxml` application. The application should look like Figure 2.16.

FIGURE 2.15

When you switch the `Main.mxml` editor from Source view to Design view, a number of other Flex views also open. The States view opens in the top-right corner, the Flex Properties view opens in the bottom-right corner, and the Components view opens in the bottom-left corner.

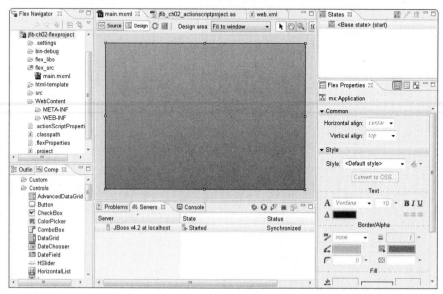

FIGURE 2.16

After adding `TextInput` and `Button` controls, the `Main.mxml` application should look like this.

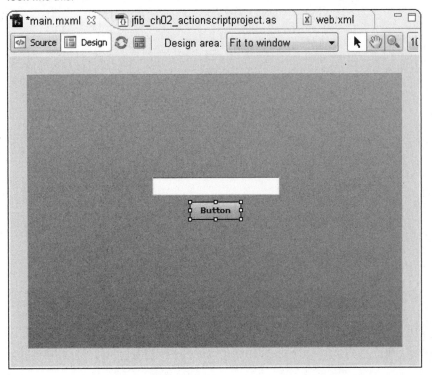

6. **Click the `TextInput` control in the `Main.mxml` application.** The Flex Properties view on the right changes to show the properties of the `TextInput` control.

7. **Type theMessage in the ID text field of the Flex Properties view.**

8. **Click the `Button` control in the `Main.mxml` application.** The Flex Properties view on the right changes to show the properties of the `Button` control.

9. **Type theButton in the ID text field of the Flex Properties view.**

10. **Type Get A Message! in the Label text field of the Flex Properties view.**

11. **Type theMessage.text = "Hello, World!" in the On click text field of the Flex Properties view.**

12. **Click the Save button to save the `Main.mxml` application.** The file is saved, and the Ant build script is run to rebuild the application.

Redeploy and run the application by using the previous steps. This time, when the Web browser opens the application, you see the Button and TextInput controls you added to the application. Click the Button control, and you see the message you added to the Button control's on-click event appear in the TextInput control, as shown in Figure 2.17.

After adding some controls to the application, you can rebuild, deploy, and run it on the JBoss application server the same way you did before to see the updated version. Being able to update and run the application while developing helps you see how your application functions as you add more features and lets you correct problems as you go.

Reading debug messages

During Flex development, it's sometimes helpful to be able to see messages and inspect the code during runtime to diagnose any problems that arise. This is especially true in large applications, where many MXML and ActionScript files make up a single application and the application flows through code in many different files. Two means of examining what's going on in your code are adding trace messages and setting debugging breakpoints.

The trace() function in Flex allows you to print out messages to the console while running in Flex Builder so that you can see what's happening in an application at any given point. This is useful if, for example, your application code uses many different functions for a given feature and you want to print out a message in each one to be sure they're all being called — and in the proper order.

You typically don't leave trace messages in your final application — they're useful only during development, where you can see them being output in the Flex Builder console. In production applications, they only add unnecessary overhead.

To view trace messages in Flex Builder, your application must be running in Debug mode within Flex Builder. Debug mode allows you to inspect the output of any trace messages as well as set breakpoints in your application. A breakpoint pauses execution of the application at the selected location. You can use Flex Builder's Flex Debugging perspective to inspect the values of variables while the application is paused or to step through the application one line at a time to see what the code is doing. To debug with Flex Builder, your application must be compiled with debug information added. This increases the size of the final SWF file, so it's not recommended that this information be included in the final release version of your application. Flex Builder automatically compiles your Flex applications with debug information included for use in development. For production releases, you can create an optimized SWF file by choosing Project ⇨ Export Release Build from the Flex Builder menu.

To demonstrate using trace messages and debugging the application, you can change the click action of the `Button` control to call an ActionScript function that performs a few functions. Then, you can add a trace message to the ActionScript function and set a breakpoint to see how the debugger operates.

Click the Source button below the `Main.mxml` editor tab to switch the editor back to Source view. The MXML code for the `Button` and `TextInput` controls has been added to the source code. Add the following MXML block to the `Main.mxml` application just above the `<mx:TextInput>` tag:

```
<mx:Script>
    <![CDATA[
        private function setMessage(e:MouseEvent):void
        {
            trace("entering setMessage function");
            var buttonLabel:String = (e.target as Button).label;
            var dateTime:Date = new Date();
            var dateString:String = dateTime.
toLocaleDateString();
            var timeString:String = dateTime.
toLocaleTimeString();
            theMessage.text = "Clicked " + buttonLabel + " on "
+ dateString + " at " + timeString;
            trace("exiting setMessage function");
        }
    ]]>
</mx:Script>
```

CROSS-REF **For more on Flex and ActionScript code and concepts, see Chapter 4.**

This code constructs a `String` based on the label of the button that was clicked as well as the date and time and then sets the text property of the `TextInput` control to that `String`. At the beginning and end of the function, Flex trace messages are output to the console. To tie this function to the clicking of the `Button` control, change the `click` attribute of the `<mx:Button>` tag to the following:

```
click="setMessage(event)"
```

To set a breakpoint in the code in Flex Builder, you simple double-click the left margin next to the line of code at which you want the application execution to pause. Double-click the left margin next to the second line of the `setMessage()` function where the value of the `buttonLabel` variable is set. You see a blue dot icon appear in the left margin, as shown in Figure 2.18.

NOTE   When you debug your application, Flex Builder may launch it in your default system Web browser rather than the internal Flex Builder Web browser. You must have the debug version of Flash Player installed, which is included by default when you install Flex Builder.

FIGURE 2.18

When you set a breakpoint in Flex Builder, a blue dot icon appears in the margin to the left of the line containing the breakpoint. The highlighted line has this icon before it.

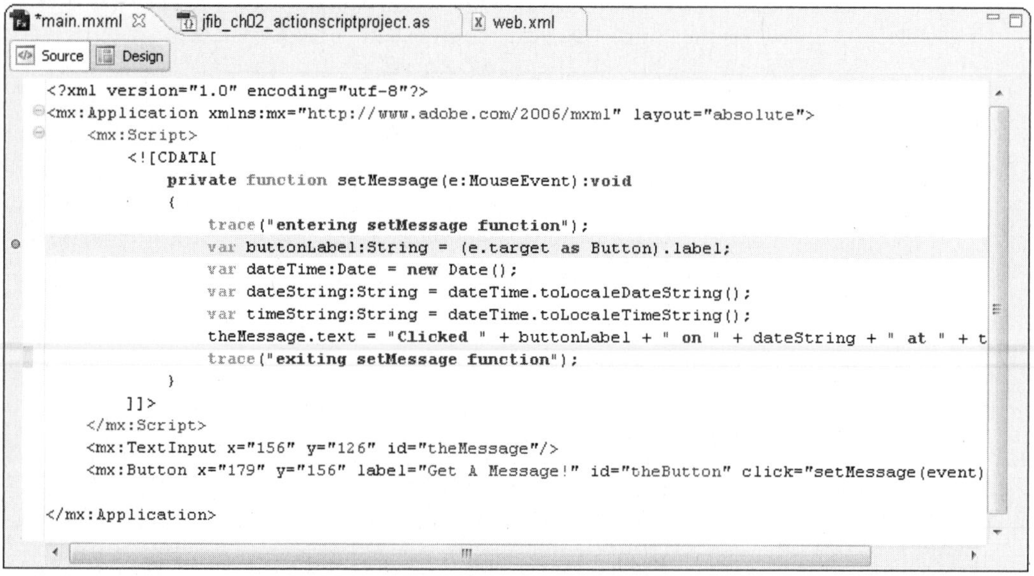

```
<?xml version="1.0" encoding="utf-8"?>
<mx:Application xmlns:mx="http://www.adobe.com/2006/mxml" layout="absolute">
    <mx:Script>
        <![CDATA[
            private function setMessage(e:MouseEvent):void
            {
                trace("entering setMessage function");
                var buttonLabel:String = (e.target as Button).label;
                var dateTime:Date = new Date();
                var dateString:String = dateTime.toLocaleDateString();
                var timeString:String = dateTime.toLocaleTimeString();
                theMessage.text = "Clicked " + buttonLabel + " on " + dateString + " at " + t
                trace("exiting setMessage function");
            }
        ]]>
    </mx:Script>
    <mx:TextInput x="156" y="126" id="theMessage"/>
    <mx:Button x="179" y="156" label="Get A Message!" id="theButton" click="setMessage(event)

</mx:Application>
```

To run your application, follow the steps you previously used to build, deploy, and run the application on the JBoss server. Once the application is started, close the internal Flex Builder Web browser by clicking the X on the right side of the tab and then start up the debugger by following these steps:

1. **Right-click the** `jfib-ch02-flexproject` **project in the Flex Navigator view and then choose Debug As ➪ Flex Application from the popup menu.** A Web browser launches with the application running.

2. **Click the** `Get A Message!` **button in the application.** The Flex Builder window returns to the front, and a dialog box opens, asking you to switch to the Flex Debugging perspective, as shown in Figure 2.19.

FIGURE 2.19
_____

When a breakpoint is hit in your application, the Flex Debugging perspective is opened. If you've not previously debugged in Flex Builder, a dialog box opens, asking you to switch to this perspective.

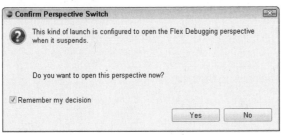

3. **Click the Remember my decision check box and then click Yes.** The Flex Debugging perspective, as shown in Figure 2.20, opens.

Take a moment to explore the Flex Debugging perspective. In the top-right corner is a set of views that includes the Variables, Breakpoints, and Expressions views. The Variables view lets you see the current value of variables in your application at the point where the application has paused. The Breakpoints view lets you see and toggle your breakpoints on and off. The Expressions view lets you type expressions whose value you want to evaluate. In the Console view at the bottom of the screen, the trace message you set at the beginning of the `setMessage()` function has been output to the console.

The Flex Debugging perspective contains a number of views that let you inspect variable values, see and toggle breakpoints, and step through the code one line at a time.

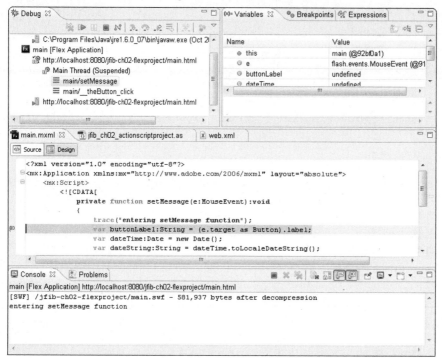

To step to the next line of the application, press F6. As you step line by line through the application code, the Variables view updates the values of the variables as they're set. The first time you press F6, for example, the value of the buttonLabel variable changes from undefined to Get A Message! Step through the code line by line, and watch all the variable values change in the Variables view. When you reach the end of the function, the final trace message is printed out to the Console view. If you keep pressing F6, the debugger actually steps into the internals of the Flex framework. To continue running your application, press the green Run arrow button in the Debug view to the left of the Variables view.

Now switch to the Breakpoints view and then click the check box next to the breakpoint to toggle it off. Switch back to your Web browser and then click the Get A Message! button again. This time, the application doesn't stop, but going back into Flex Builder reveals that the trace messages still print out to the Console view. The ability to turn breakpoints on and off as needed comes in handy when stepping through a large body of code to try to pinpoint the location of a problem. You can have the application stop at some breakpoints and skip others while still keeping the locations of all breakpoints intact.

Using trace() is most appropriate during development by using the debug version of the Flash Player. However, you probably want to be able to also log errors and other information in your deployed applications. Flex includes a logging framework that allows you to write such information out to log files. Flex logging consists of two main components:

- The *target* tells the logging framework where to output log messages. Flex includes a target implementation, TraceTarget, that outputs log messages by using the same internal mechanism as the trace() function. You can also implement a custom Flex logging target by extending the Flex AbstractTarget class and providing an implementation of the abstract logEvent() function.

- The *logger* is the component that actually sends the log messages to the target. The logger provides details about the code sending the message, the level of the message (info, debug, error, etc.), and the text of the message itself. The logger also contains the set of targets that receive the messages. Multiple targets can be added to a logger, and each of these targets can be configured to receive a subset of the logged messages based on which code is logging them and the level of the message.

Changing the Main.mxml application to use the Flex logging framework requires only a few changes to the code. First, add the following code to the Main.mxml file just above the setMessage() function:

```
import mx.logging.*;
import mx.logging.targets.TraceTarget;

private function setupLogger():void
{
    var target:TraceTarget = new TraceTarget();

    // possible values: ALL, DEBUG, INFO, WARN, ERROR, FATAL
    target.level = LogEventLevel.ALL;
    target.includeCategory = true;

    // log the level
    target.includeLevel = true;

    // log the date and time
    target.includeDate = true;
    target.includeTime = true;

    Log.addTarget(target);
}
```

First, the Flex logging classes are imported into the Main.mxml application. This code uses the built-in TraceTarget. The setupLogger() function configures the target and adds it to the logger. This target logs messages at all levels (LogEventLevel.ALL), but you could specify a less verbose level of logging by choosing a specific value. Each level includes messages at that level or higher.

For example, specifying `LogEventLevel.WARN` logs messages at the `WARN`, `ERROR`, and `FATAL` levels. The target is then configured to include category, level, date and time information along with the message being logged. Finally, the target is added to the logger.

To ensure that the `setupLogger()` function is executed when the application begins, add a `creationComplete` attribute to the `<mx:Application>` tag so that it matches the following code:

```
<mx:Application xmlns:mx="http://www.adobe.com/2006/mxml"
    creationComplete="setupLogger();" layout="absolute">
```

The `creationComplete` attribute specifies a function to be run once the application has been fully instantiated. Here, the `setupLogger()` function runs, and the logging framework is configured and ready to use.

Now change the two `trace()` statements in the `setMessage()` function to use the logger instead. The first statement changes from this:

```
trace("entering setMessage function");
```

to this:

```
Log.getLogger("main").debug("entering setMessage function");
```

This statement retrieves the logger for the category `"main"`, referring to the `Main.mxml` application, and sends a debug level message. This message is sent to the `TraceTarget` added to the logger, which in turn outputs this message — along with the category, level, date, and time information — by using the trace mechanism.

Although this example uses the `TraceTarget` class, you could also implement a custom logging target that extends `AbstractTarget` and sends the output to a server (by using a Web service or other remote call, for example) or splits the output among multiple log files on the client machine. Using the logging framework rather than simply using `trace()` provides more flexibility for getting debug and error information from your deployed applications.

Summary

In this chapter, you learned how to set up your Flex Builder configuration for integration with Java applications and deployment to the JBoss application server.

First, you learned about the different Flex project types available to you in the Flex Builder IDE. Next, you looked at each project type individually and explored their similarities and differences. After that, you learned how to test your configuration and then deploy it to the JBoss server in the Flex Builder IDE.

Finally, you learned how to add trace information, logging configuration, and breakpoints to your Flex applications so they can be run in the Flex debugger to provide valuable information to you while you develop your Flex code.

Chapter 3

Similarities between Java and Flex

IN THIS CHAPTER

What makes Java and Flex similar?

How these similarities help with integration

O ne difficulty that often crops up when writing Web applications is that the tools and languages used to develop the server-side code and the client-side code are quite different. For example, a Web developer who specializes in HTML, CSS, and JavaScript development may face a steep learning curve if the need arises for him or her to learn Perl CGI scripting. Similarly, not every server-side developer finds the task of combining HTML, graphics, CSS, and JavaScript into a functional user interface to be easy to do.

Developing Web applications by using Java and Flex takes away some of this difficulty because there are many similarities between Java and Flex. In this chapter, you learn about the similarities between the two technologies and how these similarities can make it easier to develop Web applications by using Java and Flex together.

What Makes Java and Flex Similar?

There are a number of things that make Java and Flex similar. These can be broken down into a few categories:

- **Code structure and language constructs.** ActionScript, the primary programming language for Flex applications (and specifically ActionScript 3, the version covered in this book), shares a number of style conventions, construct names, and programming concepts with the Java programming language.

- **Libraries.** Java and Flex each have libraries available that provide similar functionality. Furthermore, libraries exist that help connect Java and Flex code.
- **Development tools.** A number of development tools exist that allow you to develop your Java and Flex applications in a similar way.

Let's go over each of these items in detail.

Code structure

Most of the coding you do in Flex is in the form of MXML files. These files contain tags that define, among other things, the user interface elements and layout that make up the application and ActionScript files that provide programmatic functionality for manipulating the data that populates the user interface elements as well as the user interface elements themselves.

Earlier versions of ActionScript were based on ECMAScript, the standardized scripting language most notably found in Web programming in the form of JavaScript. ActionScript 3 implements some features based on a draft specification of ECMAScript 4. However, the ECMAScript 4 specification has since evolved to remove some of the features implemented in ActionScript 3. Therefore, ActionScript 3 development will continue on its own, implementing many features of ECMAScript while also implementing features outside the scope of the ECMAScript specification. Beginning with ActionScript 2 and continuing with the current version, ActionScript 3, the syntax of the language took on more object-oriented characteristics and constructs to the point where ActionScript now more closely resembles other modern object-oriented languages.

Java has been an object-oriented language since its beginnings. A great deal of Java's syntax is derived from another object-oriented language: C++. However, one of the design goals of Java was to eliminate some of the complexity and low-level programming requirements of C++, such as memory management. Java was also designed such that programs could be written once and run on any operating system by using a virtual machine to run code and translate between compiled Java classes, called *bytecode,* and instructions that could be understood by the host operating system. This is similar to how a compiled Flex SWF application file is run inside a browser plug-in, which allows the same compiled Flex application to run in multiple browsers on multiple operating systems without changing.

To further understand the similarities between the ActionScript code used to develop Flex applications and Java application code, take a look at the following code listings. Both are classes that represent a car. The first is a code listing for `Car.java`:

```
package com.wiley.jfib.ch03;

public class Car
{
    private String make;
    private String model;
    private int year;
```

```
private int numDoors;

public Car()
{
}

/**
 * @return the make
 */
public String getMake()
{
      return make;
}
/**
 * @param make the make to set
 */
public void setMake(String make)
{
      this.make = make;
}
/**
 * @return the model
 */
public String getModel()
{
      return model;
}
/**
 * @param model the model to set
 */
public void setModel(String model)
{
      this.model = model;
}
/**
 * @return the year
 */
public int getYear()
{
      return year;
}
/**
 * @param year the year to set
 */
public void setYear(int year)
{
      this.year = year;
}
```

```
/**
 * @return the numDoors
 */
public int getNumDoors()
{
        return numDoors;
}
/**
 * @param numDoors the numDoors to set
 */
public void setNumDoors(int numDoors)
{
        this.numDoors = numDoors;
}
}
```

Now compare the Java version with this ActionScript code representing the same Car object:

```
package com.wiley.jfib.ch03
{

    public class Car
    {
            private var _make:String;
            private var _model:String;
            private var _year:int;
            private int _numDoors:int;

            public function Car ():void
            {
            }

            /**
             * return the make
             */
            public function get make():String
            {
                    return _make;
            }

            public function set make(val:String):void
            {
                    this._make = val;
            }

            public function get model():String
            {
                    return _model;
            }
```

```
public function set model(val:String):void
{
        this._model = val;
}

public function get year():int
{
        return _year;
}

public function set year(val:int):void
{
        this._year = val;
}

public function get numDoors():int
{
        return _numDoors;
}

public function set numDoors(val:int):void
{
        this._numDoors = val;
}

        }
}
```

There are a number of similarities that you should immediately notice. First, both the Java version and the ActionScript version of this class contain a *package declaration* as the first statement. Recall that in Java, *a package declaration* is a logical grouping of classes into a single unit. The same is true for packages in ActionScript. One difference to note in the syntax is that the Java package declaration is a single statement ending in a semicolon, whereas the ActionScript package declaration opens a code block that encloses the remainder of the ActionScript class.

CROSS-REF For more on packages in Java, see Chapter 1.

After the package declaration is the declaration of the class itself. Here, though, the syntax between the Java class and the ActionScript class is identical. ActionScript also uses the same syntax as Java for declaring interfaces and for declaring classes that extend other classes or implement an interface. For example, the following declarations are valid for both ActionScript and Java:

```
public interface StreetLegal
public class Convertible extends Car implements StreetLegal
```

Both the Java and ActionScript class declarations for the Car class use the keyword public to indicate their access level. The public keyword is known as the *access modifier*, and it tells the application what other code has access to this code. Java and Flex share the following access modifiers:

- public. This access modifier means that the class, function, or property marked public is accessible by any other code.

- private. This access modifier means that the class, function, or property marked private is accessible only by any enclosing code. For example, only the Car class is able to access any of its private properties directly. If some other piece of ActionScript or Java code tried to access them, it would not compile.

Java and Flex also have another access modifier in common. The protected access modifier exists in both Java and Flex but means different things in each language. In ActionScript, the protected access modifier means that the class, function, or property is available only to a class or any of its subclasses. In Java, protected means that the class, function, or property is available to a class, any of its subclasses, or any class in the same package. ActionScript's equivalent of the protected access modifier in Java is the internal access modifier. If you don't specify an access modifier in ActionScript, the access level defaults to internal. When no access modifier is specified in Java, a fourth modifier type called default is used. The default access modifier in Java is the equivalent of ActionScript's protected modifier — only classes in the same package have access to the class, function, or property. Subclasses in other packages do not.

Both versions of the Car class contain a constructor used by other application code to create an instance of the object. In Java, the constructor is written as a method, with the name of the class serving as both the function name and return type. In ActionScript, the constructor uses the same function keyword as all other functions in the class and declares a return type of void, which means that no value is returned.

CROSS-REF   For more on classes, instances, and other object-oriented programming concepts, see Chapter 1.

To provide access to the private properties of the Car object, both the Java and ActionScript versions provide methods called *getters* and *setters*. In Java, the methods are by convention named getFoo() and setFoo() for a property named foo. A Java class that contains private properties and getter and setter methods following these conventions is known as a *Java bean*. Many Java development tools understand this naming convention for Java classes and are able to use it to display property editors and other code visualization tools to help with development. As a result, this convention is quite common.

NOTE   The naming convention for getters of boolean (true/false) properties in a Java class is slightly different. For the boolean property named foo, the getter function would be named isFoo() rather than getFoo().

In the ActionScript class, the getter and setter functions are somewhat different. The get and set keywords aren't part of the actual function names but instead declare what type of functions they are. The way these functions are called also differs between the Java and ActionScript versions. In Java, to get the `make` property of a `Car` object, you would call `car.getMake()`. In ActionScript, to get the `_make` property, you would call `car.make`, with no parentheses.

The location of the function return type declaration is also different between Java and ActionScript. In Java, the return type is declared immediately following the access modifier. In ActionScript, the return type is given following a colon after the closing parenthesis at the end of the function declaration.

Despite a few differences, you can see that the syntax and constructs of classes, functions, and properties are very similar between ActionScript and Java. Even with these syntactical differences, it's clear that the two languages have a great deal of similarity. Developers familiar with one language should be able to read and understand code written in the other and experience a minimal learning curve if they need to debug or write code in the language they're less familiar with.

Libraries

In addition to similarities in the language constructs, Java and Flex each have a number of third-party libraries available for use in your applications. In some cases, libraries exist for each development environment to provide the same functionality. Two such areas of functionality are implementations of the Model-View-Controller design pattern and unit testing libraries.

Model-View-Controller implementations

Model-View-Controller (MVC) is a popular design pattern that separates the user interface pieces of an application from the data and business logic pieces. As the name implies, the MVC pattern consists of three main layers:

- **The model** represents the data and *business logic* (data manipulation functionality) of the application.
- **The view** represents the user interface elements of the application.
- **The controller** is responsible for communicating user input from the view to the business logic code in the model.

 For more on the MVC design pattern, see Chapter 6.

The MVC design pattern is popular because the separation of the interface code from the business logic code makes it easier to reuse the business logic code with a different user interface and to fix or enhance one or more of the layers without having to worry about code in the other layers. Third-party libraries exist for both Java and Flex, providing implementations of the MVC design pattern.

For Java, there's the Spring Framework's Spring Web MVC module. The Spring Framework is a Java application framework that contains a number of separate modules that can be used on their own or in conjunction with one another. In addition to the MVC module, there are modules for working with databases, managing transactions within an application, and much more.

CROSS-REF   For more on the Spring Framework, see Chapter 6.

The Spring Web MVC module provides a set of Java classes and interfaces that map to the different layers of the MVC design pattern. The `Controller` interface, for example, maps to the controller layer of the MVC design pattern. Classes that implement the `Controller` interface implement a `handleRequest()` method that receives requests from the user interface (the view layer), passes the parameters of those requests off to the business logic (the model layer) to retrieve the requested data, and then returns the results of the request to the view for display to the user. The data and a reference to the view to be displayed are packaged up together in a Spring `ModelAndView` object, which is the type returned from the `handleRequest()` method.

Here's a code listing for a simple class that implements the Spring Framework's `Controller` interface:

```
/**
 *
 */
package com.wiley.jfib.ch03;

import javax.servlet.http.HttpServletRequest;
import javax.servlet.http.HttpServletResponse;
import org.springframework.web.servlet.ModelAndView;
import org.springframework.web.servlet.mvc.Controller;

/**
 * @author Chuck
 *
 */
public class SimpleExampleController implements Controller {

    private MyModel myModel;

    @Override
    public ModelAndView handleRequest(HttpServletRequest req,
                HttpServletResponse resp) throws Exception {
        String param = req.getParameter("param");
        String dataResult = getMyModel().getRequestedData(param);
        return new ModelAndView("WEB-INF/jsp/myview.jsp",
        "data",dataResult);
    }
```

```
public MyModel getMyModel() {
    return myModel;
}

public void setMyModel(MyModel myModel) {
    this.myModel = myModel;
}
}
```

CROSS-REF For more on Spring Web MVC, see Chapter 6.

For Flex development, one of the most widely used MVC libraries is PureMVC. PureMVC has been ported to many languages aside from ActionScript, including Java. However, its most widespread use remains in the ActionScript realm. In addition to ActionScript in Flex, PureMVC can be used in Adobe AIR and Flash.

The overarching piece of a PureMVC-based application is a class known as the Façade. The Façade is responsible for controlling all the communication between the other components of the PureMVC application. Flex applications developed using PureMVC use an event- and notification-driven asynchronous means of communication. *Asynchronous* communication means that messages are sent without the sender's being concerned with receiving a response or the timing of the message delivery. Typically, an interaction with the user interface results in a notification being fired off with or without some data attached. The notification is listened for by other code, which performs whatever task it's meant to perform in response to the event. Once that code is finished performing its task, it sends another notification, again optionally attaching some data to the body of the note it sends. Finally, code receives the notification and makes use of the attached data, if any.

The basic concepts of the model, view, and controller layers are present in PureMVC, but they go by different names:

- **The model layer** in PureMVC is represented by the Proxy class and IProxy interface. The Proxy class contains functions for setting and retrieving data as well as functions that are called when the proxy is registered and unregistered with the view layer. Proxy classes are responsible for retrieving data to be presented to the view layer, the same as model classes in Spring Web MVC. The proxy can retrieve data from a variety of sources: value objects in the application, Web services or other remote services, or files in the file system. This layer is somewhat different from the model layer in Spring Web MVC in that a specific class and interface are used when implementing PureMVC proxies, whereas the model layer in a Spring Web MVC application doesn't need to extend a specific class or implement a specific interface.

- **The view layer** in PureMVC is represented by the Mediator class and IMediator interface. The Mediator class is responsible for managing all interaction with the user interface components of the Flex application, for populating the UI components with data received from the proxies, and for passing requests for new data to the proxies.

■ **The controller layer** in PureMVC is represented by the `SimpleCommand` class and `ICommand` interface. The `SimpleCommand` class and `ICommand` interface are analogous to the `Controller` interface in Spring Web MVC. The `SimpleCommand` class implements a single method, `execute()`, which receives a notification in response to some user interaction with the user interface and executes a command in response to the notification; this is much like the Spring `Controller` interface's `handleRequest()` method, which executes code in response to a request from the user interface. `SimpleCommand` subclasses are registered with the `Façade`, which maps commands to notification names, much like a Spring controller is mapped to a URL string in the Spring configuration file. When the notification is received, the `SimpleCommand` subclass's `execute()` method is called with the notification as a parameter.

Compare the following code listing for a PureMVC controller layer `SimpleCommand` with the Spring Web MVC controller's Java code:

```
package com.wiley.jfib.ch03.controller
{
    import com.wiley.jfib.ch03.model.MyProxy;

    import org.puremvc.as3.interfaces.*;
    import org.puremvc.as3.patterns.command.*;
    import org.puremvc.as3.patterns.observer.*;

    public class SimpleExampleCommand extends SimpleCommand implements ICommand
    {

        /**
         * Initialize the SimpleExampleCommand.
         */
        override public function execute( note:INotification ) : void
        {
            var param:String = note.getBody() as String;
            var myProxy:MyProxy = facade.retrieveProxy(MyProxy.NAME) as MyProxy;
            myProxy.getRequestedData(param);
        }
    }
}
```

The PureMVC `SimpleExampleCommand`'s `execute()` method is very similar to the Java `SimpleExampleController`'s `handleRequest()` method. The parameter is retrieved from the body of the note sent along with the notification. The proxy is retrieved from the `Façade` rather than being a property of the `SimpleExampleCommand`, as the model is a property of the Java controller. Finally, the proxy's `getRequestedData()` method is invoked to retrieve the data.

There's no variable here that's assigned the value returned from the proxy. In most cases, the proxy retrieves the data and then sends a notification with the data attached. This notification is received by the mediator that's managing the relevant view component. The mediator uses the data to populate the appropriate portions of the interface.

Unit testing libraries

Unit testing is a development methodology that involves testing your code a single unit at a time. Most of the time in Java and Flex development, a *unit* means a single function or method in a Java or ActionScript class. These tests should test the functionality of the unit in isolation, without relying on the functionality of other units of code. For example, if a method in a Java class calls into a method of a second Java class, a unit test that tests the method in the first class provides some well-known value to the method rather than having it rely on the second method's functioning properly.

CROSS-REF For more on unit testing in Java and Flex, see Chapter 7.

Java and Flex have very similar unit testing libraries available to them. Java unit testing is done with the JUnit library, whereas Flex ActionScript unit testing makes use of the FlexUnit library. JUnit and FlexUnit share a number of concepts:

- **Unit tests are grouped into a test case.** A *test case* typically contains all the unit tests that fully cover a single class (that is, they test all the methods in the class).

- **Test cases are grouped together into a test suite.** A *test suite* typically contains all the unit tests pertaining to a package, a functional area, or an entire application.

- **Test cases and test suites are run by using a test runner.** The *test runner* runs all the unit tests in each test case or test suite and then outputs information about whether the test passed and the reason for failure if it fails. A test runner may have a graphical user interface to make the results of the testing easier to understand.

Unit testing makes it easier to keep track of your development as you go and reduces the number of errors in your code when you deliver your application. Constantly writing and running unit tests as you develop your application allows you to catch a lot of coding errors along the way because the unit tests fail if any piece of functionality changes in such a way that it no longer operates as expected.

The syntax of JUnit and FlexUnit is nearly identical. To illustrate this, consider a simple math object called `Divider` with a single function called `divide()` that accepts two integer values as parameters and then returns the rounded quotient of the two values.

In Java, this method looks like this:

```
public static int divide(int numerator, int denominator) throws
    ArithmeticException
{
    return denominator / denominator;
}
```

In Flex, the function looks like this:

```
public static function divide(numerator:int, denominator:int):int
{
    if(denominator == 0)
    {
        throw new Error ("Division by Zero!");
    }
    return denominator / denominator;
}
```

Both the Java method and the ActionScript function have an error — namely, that they're dividing the denominator by itself. Any application that calls this code either receives an error or the value 1, depending on whether the denominator is equal to 0.

Unit testing would catch this error fairly quickly. First, look at this JUnit test case for the Java class:

```
package com.wiley.jfib.ch03.test;

import static org.junit.Assert.*;

import org.junit.After;
import org.junit.Before;
import org.junit.Test;

public class DividerTest {
    @Before
    public void setUp() throws Exception {
    }

    @After
    public void tearDown() throws Exception {
    }

    @Test
    public void testDivide() {
        try
        {
            int num = 12;
            int den = 3;
            int result = Divider.divide(num,den);
            assertEquals(4,result);
        }
        catch(Exception e)
        {
            fail("Unexpected Exception encountered");
        }
    }

    @Test(expected = ArithmeticException.class)
```

```
        public void testDivideByZero() throws Exception
        {
                int num = 12;
                int den = 0;
                int result = Divider.divide(num,den);
        }


}
```

Now compare it with the FlexUnit test for the Flex version:

```
    package com.wiley.jfib.ch03.test {

    import flexunit.framework.TestCase;

    public class DividerTest extends TestCase {
        public function testDivide():void {
            var num:int = 12;
            var den:int = 3;
            var result:int = Divider.divide(num,den);
            assertEquals(4,result);
        }
        public function testDivideByZero():void {
            listenForEvent(Divider, ErrorEvent.ERROR,
    EVENT_EXPECTED);
                var num:int = 12;
                var den:int = 0;
                var result:int = Divider.divide(num,den);
        assertEvents("Received expected division by zero");
        }
    }
    }
```

Each test case here contains two tests. The first one tests for a correct result from valid division, and the second one tests that if an invalid division-by-zero operation is attempted, the expected exception or error is thrown by the code. You can see that these two classes are very similar. Both follow the unit testing naming convention of starting the names of functions that perform the tests with the lowercase word `test`. The Flex test case extends a `TestCase` base class. In Java, JUnit 4 no longer requires a test case to extend a `TestCase` class, but in JUnit 3, which is still widely used, test cases also extend a `TestCase` class. Finally, both sets of unit tests use very similar `assert` statements to determine whether the results of the test are as expected.

Development tools

Another area where Java and Flex share some common ground is the availability of development tools that work well with both development environments. In particular, Flex has excellent compatibility with two development tools most commonly used in the Java programming world: the Eclipse integrated development environment and the Apache Ant build tools.

The Eclipse IDE is written in Java and used primarily to develop Java code. It includes a number of wizards and code templates that make creating Java applications much faster and easier. It's also designed to be highly flexible and extensible by allowing functionality to be added through the use of plug-ins. Eclipse plug-ins exist for a wide variety of languages and can also provide tools such as database browsers that help with other areas of application development.

CROSS-REF   For more on Eclipse, see Chapter 1.

Adobe has developed an Eclipse plug-in for Flex development called Flex Builder. Flex Builder installs in Eclipse like any other Eclipse plug-in and provides a number of wizards and project templates for creating Flex projects in Eclipse.

Flex Builder isn't free, but Adobe does offer a free trial on its Web site. The Flex Builder trial can be downloaded at `www.adobe.com/go/flex_trial`. As of this writing, the latest version of Flex Builder is 3.0.1.

NOTE   Only Flex Builder version 3.0.1 (and later) is compatible with the latest release of Eclipse (version 3.4, code-named Ganymede). Make sure that you're using the latest version of Flex Builder if you're using this version of Eclipse. Updates to Flex Builder are likely, so use the current version available.

Downloading the Flex Builder plug-in trial for Eclipse requires you to have an account on the Adobe Web site. Registering for an account is free. This installation guide assumes that you have an Adobe account and are able to log in with it. It also assumes that you have Eclipse installed.

NOTE   The Flex development in this book is done by using the stand-alone Flex Builder development environment, whose installation is covered in Appendix A.

Installing the Flex Builder plug-in trial for Eclipse here is optional, but it does provide a good look at how a Java developer coming into Flex for the first time might go about getting started.

To download and install Flex Builder, follow these steps:

1. **Open your Web browser, type** www.adobe.com/go/flex_trial **in the address bar, and then press Enter.** The Flex Builder 3 download page opens, as shown in Figure 3.1.

2. **Scroll to the bottom of the page and click the Download button to download the trial Flex Builder Eclipse plug-in for your operating system.** The Adobe sign-in screen, as shown in Figure 3.2, opens. If you need to create an account with Adobe, you must do so here. Once you have created the account, you're automatically directed to the download choice screen.

3. **Type your Adobe username and password and then click Sign in.** The Flex Builder plug-in download page, as shown in Figure 3.3, opens.

FIGURE 3.1

The Flex Builder 3 download page

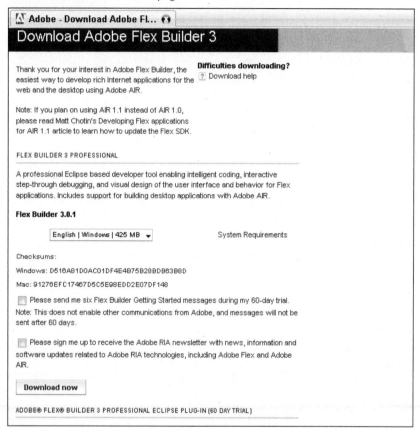

4. **Choose the version of the plug-in that's appropriate for your language (for example, English|Windows) and then click Download.** The Save File dialog box opens, asking you to save the file `FB3_WWEJ_Plugin.exe`.

5. **Click Save to save the file to your computer in a location where it's easy to find, such as the desktop.** The file is then downloaded.

6. **Double-click the `FB3_WWEJ_Plugin.exe` file.** The installer starts and prepares the installation wizard. Once the installer preparation is complete, the first screen of the installation wizard, as shown in Figure 3.4, opens.

FIGURE 3.2

The Adobe sign-in screen. This tutorial assumes that you already have an Adobe account. You must create an account to continue with the download process.

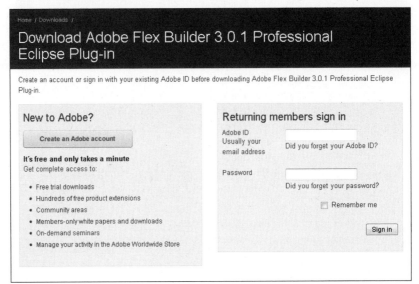

FIGURE 3.3

The Flex Builder plug-in download page

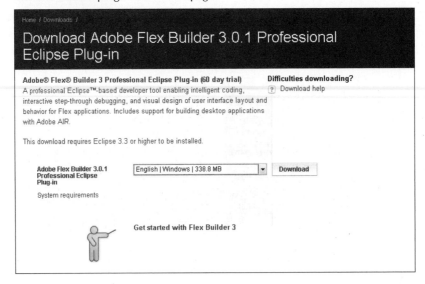

7. **Choose your language from the dropdown list and then click OK.** The next wizard screen opens.

8. **Close all programs as it recommends and then click Next.** The license agreement screen opens.

9. **Click the radio button indicating your acceptance of the license agreement and then click Next.** The installation location screen, as shown in Figure 3.5, opens.

10. **Leave the default installation location selected and then click Next.** The Choose Eclipse Folder to be Extended screen, as shown in Figure 3.6, opens.

11. **Type the location of your Eclipse installation (for example, c:\eclipse) in the text field and then click Next.** The wizard asks you to wait while the Flex Builder plug-in is being configured for your system. When finished, the Additional Installations screen, as shown in Figure 3.7, opens. The items of interest on this screen are the installation options for the debug version of Flash Player. This Flash Player version allows you to connect Flash Player to your debugger, allowing you to debug your Flex applications in Eclipse the same way you debug Java applications. You should install the debug version of Flash Player in at least one browser.

12. **Click Next.** The Pre-Installation Summary screen, as shown in Figure 3.8, opens. This screen shows you all the installation options you chose.

13. **Review the installation information to make sure the installation path and Flash Player options are what you wanted and then click Install.** The installer installs Flex Builder to the directory you chose, showing a progress bar. When finished, the installer confirms that the installation succeeded.

14. **Click Done.** The installer closes.

FIGURE 3.4

The first screen of the Flex Builder plug-in installation wizard

FIGURE 3.5

The installation location screen allows you to choose the location to which Flex Builder is installed. The default location is suitable for most installations, but you can change it if needed.

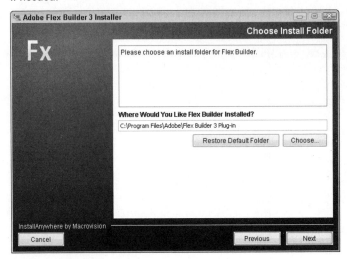

FIGURE 3.6

The Choose Eclipse Folder to be Extended screen

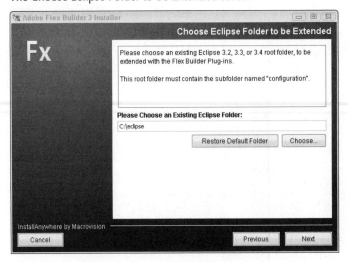

FIGURE 3.7

The Additional Installations screen allows you to install the debug version of Flash Player into one or more browsers. This allows you to debug your Flex applications within Eclipse the same way you debug Java applications.

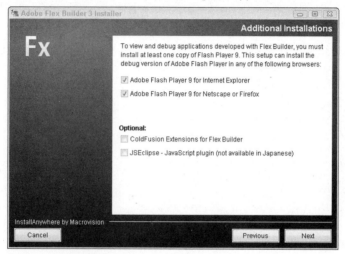

FIGURE 3.8

The Pre-Installation Summary screen shows information about the installation. Before continuing, ensure that the options shown here match what you chose.

To see what Flex Builder has added to Eclipse, follow these steps:

1. **Navigate to your Eclipse install directory and double-click** `eclipse.exe`. Eclipse launches.

2. **Choose Window ⇨ Open Perspective.** The Open Perspective dialog box, as shown in Figure 3.9, opens. Notice the three Flex perspectives that have been added as options in Eclipse.

3. **Choose Flex Development from the list of perspectives and then click OK.** The Flex Development perspective opens, displaying the Flex Navigator view in the top-left corner, as shown in Figure 3.10.

4. **Right-click in the Flex Navigator view and then choose New from the popup menu.** A menu opens, as shown in Figure 3.11, with a selection of Flex and ActionScript types that can be created by using wizards and dialog boxes.

Because the Flex development in this book uses the stand-alone Flex Builder development environment, this chapter doesn't go into detail about working with Flex projects and code. The point is that Java developers likely already have Eclipse installed on their development machines. For those who want or need to develop front-end code for their Java Web application in Flex, the Flex Builder plug-in for Eclipse allows them to use Flex from within the familiar development setup of Eclipse.

FIGURE 3.9

After installing the Flex Builder plug-in for Eclipse, three new Flex perspectives are added to the Open Perspective dialog box in Eclipse.

FIGURE 3.10

The Flex Development perspective's main view is the Flex Navigator in the top-left corner. Much like the Project Explorer in Java views, the Flex Navigator view is used to display the structure of your Flex projects.

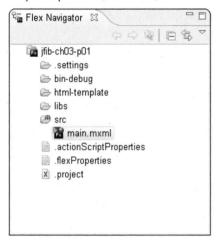

FIGURE 3.11

In the Flex Development perspective, a number of Flex and ActionScript types are available for you to create by using wizards and dialog boxes.

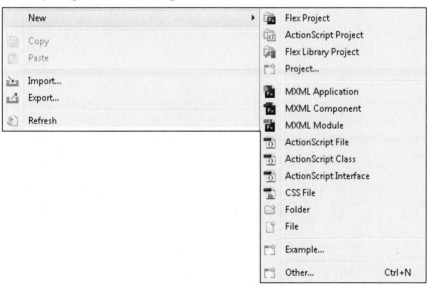

When the time comes to build and deploy a Flex application, Java developers have another familiar tool at their disposal: the Apache Ant build tool. Ant is a build utility written in Java that uses XML build scripts to divide the building of a project into compilation and deployment tasks that can be chained together so that a single command can compile code, package it up into an application archive file, and then deploy that file to the application server to be run.

Ant build files are divided into targets and tasks. A *target* is the command that's run to perform one or more tasks. Adobe provides a set of Ant *tasks* for compiling Flex applications with the Flex SDK download. These tasks are defined in the `flexTasks.tasks` file in the Ant directory within the Flex SDK distribution. They can be included in the same build script as other Ant tasks that deal with Java code and are invoked the same way.

Look at this example of an Ant target that includes tasks for compiling both Java and Flex code:

```
<target name="build" description="Compile main source tree java
files">
    <mkdir dir="${build.dir}"/>
    <javac destdir="${build.dir}" source="1.5" target="1.5"
debug="true"
        deprecation="false" optimize="false"
failonerror="true">
        <src path="${src.dir}"/>
        <classpath refid="cp"/>
    </javac>
    <mxmlc file="${APP_ROOT}/Chat.mxml"
    keep-generated-actionscript="false">

<load-config filename="${FLEX_HOME}/frameworks/flex-config.xml"/>
        <source-path path-element="${FLEX_HOME}/frameworks"/>
            <services>web/WEB-INF/services-config.xml</services>
        </mxmlc>
    </target>
```

CROSS-REF For more on the structure of Ant build files, see Chapter 6. For more on importing the `<mxmlc>` task and then using it in an Ant build file, see Chapter 14.

In this target, the `<javac>` task invokes the `javac` command from the JDK to compile the Java code into class files, and the `<mxmlc>` task invokes the `mxmlc` command from the Flex SDK to compile the MXML files and ActionScript code into SWF files.

Because Ant is familiar to Java developers, it can be used to compile Java and Flex projects even by Java engineers who don't know Flex and don't develop in it.

How These Similarities Help with Integration

Now that you understand a few of the similarities between Java and Flex and the tools and libraries they use, you can start to see how using Java and Flex to develop the client and server pieces of your application might help the application development process go more smoothly.

Team building

In large development houses, there's often a level of specialization that occurs on development teams. Graphic designers and artists work on the user interface portions of an application, including creating graphics, CSS, and HTML files. Software engineers develop the back-end components. Database administrators create databases, maintain SQL code, and fine-tune performance of the database servers. There may even be engineers responsible for creating, maintaining, and running build scripts and the source code control system.

In smaller development groups, however, engineers are often required to be multitaskers, doing front-to-back application development, including all these pieces. Using technologies that are similar stylistically and syntactically with the ability to use the same development tools across the entire application scope helps developers get up to speed more quickly and feel more comfortable working in all these technologies. When switching between Java and Flex development doesn't require leaving a single development environment with a well-known project methodology, developers spend less time figuring out how to do things and more time actually doing them. Developers new to a project can spend more time digging into the specifics of what the code does rather than spending a lot of time learning the syntax of a language or the ins and outs of a new development environment.

Multiapplication integration

Any application integration effort — especially between a Flex front end that can be written to stand alone by using static data and a Java Web application that might potentially be returning data to a variety of front-end clients (such as desktop browsers running HTML or Flex front ends or mobile browsers with more compact data needs) — must be concerned with a couple of questions. First, can the server reliably know that the client will accept data in the format it's sending (and, conversely, can the client reliably know that the server will send data in the expected format)? Second, can the integrated applications be successfully packaged and deployed together on the server to run as expected?

Once again, the commonality between the tools available to Java and Flex helps answer these two questions. First, developers can write and run similar parallel unit tests for the client and server pieces that test the expected input and output to and from the server and client. Because FlexUnit and JUnit are so similar, Java and Flex developers can each look at the tests written for both the client and server and understand whether they're accurately testing the correct things. With the unit tests approved and agreed upon by both the client-side and server-side application developers, both sides can be confident that if all the unit tests for both the client and server pass, then the pieces of the application work as expected. When integration testing begins, developers dealing with any problems that are discovered can focus on the small amount of code that actually communicates between the two applications rather than the codebase at large, which has already satisfactorily passed unit testing.

Furthermore, unit testing can be automated as part of the build process. Ant has tasks that can build the Java code, build the Flex code (by using targets provided by the Flex SDK), and run the unit tests for each piece once the code is built. Ant can also be used to package and deploy the code to the application server, whether on a developer's machine or a quality-assurance testing server. Automated continuous integration systems can use Ant to build code and run unit tests whenever a change is made to the codebase, ensuring that the integrated pieces of Java and Flex code continue to work as expected at all times. And again, if something does happen to go wrong with a build or a unit test fails, the code and unit testing libraries are similar enough that a Java development engineer could help debug and fix the Flex code — and vice versa.

Summary

Although they're substantially different technologies, there are many ways in which Java and Flex are similar. They share a number of syntactical conventions, architectural elements, and naming conventions. They each have a variety of third-party libraries available that provide similar functionality, such as MVC frameworks and unit testing libraries, across the two platforms. The leading Java development environment, Eclipse, can be used with the Flex Builder plug-in to develop Java and Flex applications together in the same environment, and Apache's Ant build tool can be used to script the compilation and packaging of your Java and Flex applications.

The similarities between Java and Flex can help your development team get up to speed quickly on both front- and back-end development for your applications. The ability to use common development, build, and deployment tools makes it easier to automate your application build process, saving time and developer resources. These similarities also facilitate communication and a common understanding of code between front- and back-end development teams. Combined, these factors can help you rapidly develop quality applications and bring them to market more quickly.

Chapter 4

Understanding the Flex Application Development Process

I n this chapter, you learn how to develop Flex applications by using Flex Builder. You learn how to set up and use classes and packages while also learning how to use a mixture of MXML and ActionScript.

The last part of the chapter takes you through the process of building a basic application to make sure that you understand the fundamentals before moving on to other chapters that involve the Flex development process.

Working with Packages and Classes

Unless this is your first time using Flex, you've probably worked with ActionScript classes at some point. However, you may not have built your own custom classes; this is explained in the following section.

Packages

A *package* is a bundle of classes that function in one easy-to-use container. Packages are common in class-based development because they add another level of separation for your code. Packages allow you to share pieces of classes without also exposing that content to foreign code.

The most common way to determine a path for a package definition is to use reverse domain format. Let's say you have a class `Person` located in your project. The reverse domain format takes your Web domain, and starting with the `com`, you define the package path, as in the following example:

```
com.example.people.Person
```

IN THIS CHAPTER

Working with packages and classes

MXML and ActionScript

Understanding events in Flex

Data providers

Working with item renderers

Building a sample Flex application

In this example path, `Person` is the class name, and `com.example.com` is the domain name. This is used to ensure that packages and classes don't collide with other libraries because it's likely that you would name your classes, but another developer may not.

CAUTION Make sure you check your package paths to ensure that they don't collide. This can cause many long nights of debugging.

Now that you have the package path, let's take a look at a sample package declaration:

```
package com.example.people
{
    class Person
    {
        .
        .
        .
    }
}
```

The package path that you see in this example is also in the directory structure. For this example, it means that the `Person` class would be located in the following directory structure:

```
com/example/people/People.as
```

Classes

A *class* is built up of methods and properties. Classes can be placed inside a package, which is essentially a folder of classes that most likely have some similarities.

Here's an example of a very basic class:

```
class HelloWorld
{
    public function HelloWorld()
    {

    }
}
```

This `HelloWorld` class isn't all that useful; it doesn't even actually have a use other than to explain the concept. Let's add a *method*, which is a function inside a class:

```
class HelloWorld
{
    public function HelloWorld()
    {

    }
```

```
public function sayIt():void
{
        trace("Hello World!");
}
}
```

You can start to see the class coming to life, but for a useful class, you would probably need to assign a property. A *property* is a variable within a class. Properties can be defined as public, private, internal, or protected. Public and private are the most common properties and are used extensively in this book. A private property means that it exists only within the class. This is useful when you want to store sensitive information or data that you don't want to expose to the public.

An internal property is accessible to other classes within the same package. This is also the default attribute of classes in ActionScript 3. A protected property is accessible to the class it's created in and classes that are subclasses.

Now that you know about the different property types in a class, let's look at a few examples that warrant a protected or private property.

One example of a class that should contain private properties is a users class that's subclassed for each specific user.

By contrast, defining a property as public means that anyone can read it or write to it, as shown in the following sample of code. The sayIt() method accesses the public property myString and outputs it to the Output panel:

```
class HelloWorld
{

    public var myString:String = "Hello, World!";

    public function HelloWorld()
    {

    }

    public function sayIt():void
    {
            trace(myString);
    }
}
```

Getters/setters

One of the ways to write a class is to make all the properties private, using getter and setter methods to modify them. This allows you to limit access to and modification of a variable. Let's say you have the following Person class:

```
class Person
{
    public var personName:String;

    function Person()
    {

    }
}
```

Malicious coding could directly access that variable and change it to anything, such as in the following example:

```
var person:Person = new Person();
person.personName = "9999";
```

Obviously, this isn't a good thing. One of the ways around this potential issue is to make the property private and use a getter/setter to access and modify the value. The getter and setter functions make it so that the variable can't be directly accessed.

The Accessor, or *getter*, is a simple method like any other:

```
public function get personName():String
{
    return _personName;
}
```

Conversely, the Mutator, or *setter*, would have some level of security to ensure that the proper value is sent:

```
public function set personName(s:String):void
{
    if(s.length > 0 checkID(s))
    {
        _personName = s;
    }
}
```

The method first checks to ensure that the length of the string is greater than 0 (nonempty) and then ensures that the value is a proper string. If you typed your value properly as a string (`:String`), you probably wouldn't need the second check, but it's a best practice when dealing with security.

NOTE   The typing in ActionScript is called *post-colon syntax* and is part of the ECMAScript standard.

The completed `Person` class with the proper methods and properties is shown below. This should give you a good understanding of how your classes should be built.

```
class Person
{
    private var _personName:String;

    function Person()
    {

    }

    public function get personName():String
    {
        return _personName;
    }

    public function set personName(s:String):void
    {
        if(s.length > 0 && typeof(s) == String)
        {
            _personName = s;
        }
    }
}
```

Multiple classes in the same file

ActionScript does allow you to create multiple classes in the same file. However, only one of the classes can be marked as public. All the other classes must be marked as internal and placed outside the class declaration. Here's a quick example:

```
package
{

    public class Person()
    {

    }

    internal class Role()
    {

    }

    internal class WorkHistory()
```

```
        {

        }

        .
        .
        .

    }
```

> **CAUTION**   You can't overload methods or constructors in ActionScript, but you can set default
> values for method parameters.

> **NOTE**   Any classes with required arguments can't be instantiated in MXML tags.

At this point, you should have a basic understanding of classes. For a more in-depth look, you can pick up the *ActionScript 3.0 Bible* or a similar title.

Extending classes

A more advanced topic of classes is *extending*, which is also referred to as *inheritance*. Inheritance is useful when you want to use properties and methods of another class but don't want to manage two classes.

Let's look at a simple example to better understand extending classes. The first class is `Person`, and the second class is `Runner`:

```
    class Person
    {

        public var name:String;
        public var age:uint;

        function Person()
        {

        }
    }

    class Runner
    {

        function Runner()
        {

        }

    }
```

It's safe to assume that a `Runner` is a person; thus, the name and age of the runner don't need to be duplicated in the `Runner` class. A better option is to extend the `Person` class. This makes it so that the `Runner` class has access to the contents of the `Person` class:

```
class Runner extends Person
{

    function Runner()
    {

    }

}
```

Here's an example that shows the relationship of the classes:

```
var runner:Runner = new Runner();
runner.name = "Jamie";
runner.age = 24;

trace(runner.name) // outputs: Jamie
```

As you can see, the `name` variable can be set because the `Person` class is being extended. Extending a class isn't limited to variables. You can borrow methods, constants, or properties. Extending classes offers a greater level of customization and allows you to manage the code without breaking something else. However, be aware that private variables won't be inherited.

Extending classes allows you to write less but more manageable code.

MXML and ActionScript

MXML is an XML-based set of tags used to instruct the compiler how to build an application. In fact, almost anything you can do with MXML, you can also achieve by using standard ActionScript.

The MXML code is typed in the Flex Builder IDE in the editor portion of the Flex Development perspective. You can type it directly in Source view or add components by using the visual Design view. Start off by creating a new Flex project and then jump into Source view to start writing MXML code.

The simplest code you could write would have to be a button:

```
<mx:Button label="Click Me" />
```

The components in Flex that are standard normally start with `mx`, which is the namespace. A *namespace* is a container created to hold a group of unique identifiers. In this case, that would be the default components. As you get into custom component development, you define your own namespace — just like you did with the package creation earlier in this chapter — which is covered later in this chapter.

You can define actions directly in MXML tags, such as by adding a click event handler to a button. Actions are not the only element you can define in MXML. Remember the `label=""` in the previous component example? This property, along with overall style, can also be defined by using standard MXML attributes:

```
<mx:Button label="Click Me" click="trace('I am a button')" />
```

However, for a more complete application, you would create ActionScript code in external files or directly in the MXML component. If you choose to code directly in the MXML file, all ActionScript code is placed between script tags:

```
<mx:Script>
<![CDATA[

]]>
</mx:Script>
```

If you've developed in JavaScript in the past, that code may look familiar to you. The structure of the `Script` block is very similar to the code block found in JavaScript, as defined by the `<script>` tags. Building on the simple button example from before, let's add a bit more ActionScript to the example:

```
<mx:Script>
<![CDATA[

    private function buttonClick():void
    {
        trace("Button Clicked!");
    }

]]>
</mx:Script>

<mx:Button label="Click Me" click="buttonClick()" />
```

This approach is much cleaner and allows greater modification without having to work entirely in the MXML tags. You can also create this example entirely in ActionScript, which is covered later in this chapter.

If you move over to Design view, you see your `Button` component on the canvas, which you created with MXML. However, for more complex applications, you may want to drag and drop the components and then code the remainder. In this case, Flex also has you covered. Simply toggle to Design view and then locate the Components panel to the left of the screen. Drag out any of those components to the stage and then switch back to Source view. You see that Flex Builder automatically created the necessary MXML code.

Flex Builder only adds the required properties into a component tag unless you set others in the Properties view. As a result, if you resize the component on the canvas and then return to the code, you see Flex Builder has now added the width and height properties because you modified the size of the component.

Understanding Events in Flex

In the button example, you added a click event but never defined the event handler function. To do that, you start by importing the necessary class. For example, you import the `MouseEvent` class for a button click:

```
<mx:Script>
<![CDATA[

    import flash.events.MouseEvent;

    private function buttonClick(e:MouseEvent):void
    {
            trace(e.currentTarget.label);
    }

]]>
</mx:Script>

<mx:Button label="Click Me" click="buttonClick(event)" />
```

Notice that the MXML `Button` tag has the word `event` as the argument. This is a special object in MXML that refers to the tag's events. In this case, that would be the mouse click.

The `buttonClick` method now has an argument, which is typed as a `MouseEvent`. In order to send a proper event, you must place the variable `event` in the method call located within the `click()` event in the `Button` component.

You should now have a basic grasp of MXML and how to mix it with ActionScript to make your applications more useable. This is only the beginning of MXML usage in Flex; throughout this book, you're introduced to various topics surrounding the MXML tags and overall usage.

Now that you've seen how to create this simple `Button` component example by using MXML, let's look at how to create exactly the same application by using only ActionScript. Well, almost exclusively using ActionScript; you still need an MXML script block and an event to kick off the entire process:

```
<mx:Application ... initialize="init()">

    <mx:Script>
    <![CDATA[

        import flash.events.MouseEvent;

        private var button:Button;

        private function init():void
        {
                button = new Button();
                button.label = "Click Me!";
```

```
                button.x = 20;
                button.y = 20;

                button.addEventListener(MouseEvent.CLICK,
                        buttonClick);

                addChild(button);
        }

        private function buttonClick(e:MouseEvent):void
        {
                trace(e.currentTarget.label);
        }

    ]]>
    </mx:Script>

</mx:Application>
```

The contents of the `init()` method are where the `Button` component is created, moved, and added to the display list. The `addEventListener()` method of the `Button` is used to define the click event, which is similar to its MXML sibling.

The `addChild()` method is where the `Button` is sent to the display list and is visible on the canvas. In a more complete application, you may have various levels of display to ensure that the data was properly loaded and initialized.

The ActionScript code is fairly similar to the MXML version. The neat thing about Flex is the ability to choose whichever option works best for your application or coding style. Some developers like to work entirely in ActionScript files, whereas others prefer MXML. You may prefer a mixture of both and find it very useful to know about both ways. MXML does offer the ability to work with other technologies, such as Thermo (its code name), an upcoming graphics product from Adobe.

Data Providers

A more advanced topic of Flex development is data providers. You will probably use them in almost every application you develop.

Let's assume that you have a simple chat application. That application would be responsible for packaging and sending messages and for receiving messages from others. Data providers give you a way to achieve an almost automatic way of updating data. Rather than setting up complex event listeners or timers to watch variables, Flex gives you the ability to subscribe to a variable's changes and then automatically display them.

Going back to the chat application concept, you would have some process polling a server for changes, and when they existed, you would need to update a list box or some other similar component. As an example, let's take a look at some pseudo-code that better explains how to use a data provider.

You start off by assigning the metadata tag [Bindable] to the variable definition. What this does is tell all the items that are assigned to that variable of any changes that occur:

```
[Bindable]
private var messages:ArrayCollection;
```

Once the variable is set as Bindable, you can assign a component to that variable. For example, bind the messages property to a List component dataProvider.

```
<mx:List dataProvider="{messages}" />
```

Now whenever new entries are added to the messages property, the List component automatically shows them. This is, of course, a very simple example of Bindable variables, but it gets you started, and you can continue to explore binding on your own.

Let's look at a sample chat application in pseudo-code that takes advantage of this Bindable variable ability:

```
<mx:Application ... initialize="init()">

    <mx:Script>
    <![CDATA[

        [Bindable]
        private var messages:ArrayCollection;

        function init():void
        {
            messages = new ArrayCollection();

            // enable server loading process
        }

        function getNewMessages(e:ResultEvent):void
        {
            messages = ArrayCollection(e.result);
        }

    ]]>
    </mx:Script>

    <mx:List dataProvider="{messages}" />

</mx:Application>
```

Working with Item Renderers

Flex offers many components to build your applications with. Some of these are purely for display (such as `Canvas`, `HBox`, and `VBox`); the others are for data management and interaction. Each of these data components is built up of rows and columns called *items*. In fact, they all share the `ListBase` subclass. These components all start with a default and similar view. Applications often call for a little customization to these components.

Flex offers the item renderer to let you achieve this level of customization without having to build your own component. The item renderer gives developers the ability to custom-design each of the columns in a data component. An item renderer can also be used to modify data.

For example, you could have a data grid with a row that displays pricing information and, based on an amount, changes the background color of the column for that one entry. This is certainly not a feature of the standard data grid, so you could develop your own component or use an item renderer.

Setting up an item renderer

The definition of an item renderer is placed in the `DataGridColumn`. There's no limit to how many columns can have an item renderer, and each column could use the same one, although that isn't likely.

Start by opening a new Flex project. Once the new project is opened, jump into Design view and drag out a `DataGrid` component to the canvas, as shown in Figure 4.1. Once the `DataGrid` is on the canvas, jump back to Source view to see the code Flex created.

Here's the default `DataGrid` code:

```
<mx:DataGrid x="128" y="108">
    <mx:columns>
        <mx:DataGridColumn headerText="Column 1" dataField="col1"/>
        <mx:DataGridColumn headerText="Column 2" dataField="col2"/>
        <mx:DataGridColumn headerText="Column 3" dataField="col3"/>
    </mx:columns>
</mx:DataGrid>
```

Each column in the `DataGrid` is assigned by a `DataGridColumn` node. In order to ensure that the item renderer is placed in the correct row, it's added to the `DataGridColumn` node.

For this example, the `itemRenderer` has been named `PricingView`. This name corresponds with an MXML component file, which is built in just a moment:

FIGURE 4.1

The `DataGrid` on the canvas in Design view

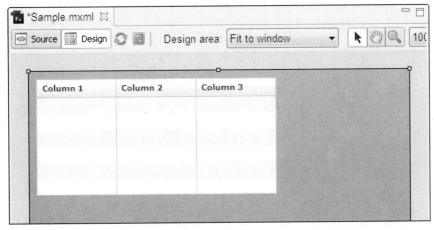

```xml
<mx:DataGrid x="128" y="108">
    <mx:columns>
        <mx:DataGridColumn headerText="Column 1" dataField="col1"/>
        <mx:DataGridColumn headerText="Column 2" dataField="col2"/>
        <mx:DataGridColumn headerText="Column 3" dataField="col3"
    itemRenderer="PricingView"/>
    </mx:columns>
</mx:DataGrid>
```

If you were to run this code, you would likely receive an error because that item renderer doesn't exist, and Flex would have no way to render that column properly.

Before creating the item renderer, it's a good idea to fill the data grid with some fake data, at least for testing purposes, unless you're already loading real data, in which case you can simply use that.

You can use MXML or ActionScript to create fake data. The contents of a `DataGrid` are in an array/object type.

Following is a sample `ArrayCollection` that's prefilled with product data for testing. This `ArrayCollection` is technically identical to one created entirely in ActionScript. In order to add it to the `DataGrid`, you need to place it within the `<DataGrid>` node to mimic the `dataProvider` property:

```
<mx:DataGrid x="128" y="108">

    <mx:ArrayCollection>
        <mx:Object col1="Product 1" col2="35.00" />
        <mx:Object col1="Product 2" col2="20.00" />
        <mx:Object col1="Product 2" col2="50.00" />
    </mx:ArrayCollection>

    <mx:columns>
        <mx:DataGridColumn headerText="Column 1" dataField="col1"/>
        <mx:DataGridColumn headerText="Column 2" dataField="col2"/>
        <mx:DataGridColumn headerText="Column 3" dataField="col3"
itemRenderer="PricingView"/>
    </mx:columns>
</mx:DataGrid>
```

Now that you've filled the `DataGrid` with sample data, you can continue with the development of the custom item renderer.

Creating an MXML component file

An MXML component file is used to build custom components or subapplications that are used in the main application. Follow these steps:

1. **Choose File ⇨ New ⇨ MXML Component.** The New MXML Component dialog box, as shown in Figure 4.2, opens. The dialog box shows the tree structure of your application. Make sure that the `src` directory is selected to ensure that the file is saved in the correct location.

2. **In the Filename text field, type** PricingView.mxml. You can leave the Based on: option with its default.

3. **Set both the Width and Height to 100 (percent) so that the component fills the entire column.**

4. **Click OK to create the component.**

You should see a skeleton of the `Canvas` component in the component file that has just been created. The width and height that were set in the configuration screen appear toward the end of the `Canvas` node:

```
<?xml version="1.0" encoding="utf-8"?>
<mx:Canvas xmlns:mx="http://www.adobe.com/2006/mxml"
    width="100%"
    height="100%">

</mx:Canvas>
```

FIGURE 4.2

The New MXML Component dialog box

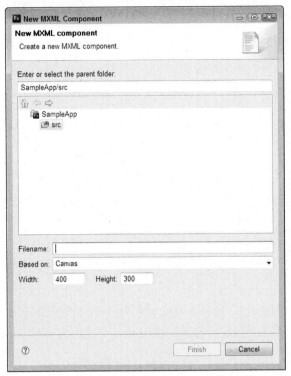

If you ran the sample application now, you would notice that the text for the custom column has disappeared. That's because the item renderer takes the place of the default view. In order to add the text back, you need to create some form of a text view for the DataGrid to display. You can use a Label or Text component; it really doesn't matter which one you decide to use.

Here's the Canvas code with a Label component added. The Label component is given a unique id of "lbl", which is required when the data needs to be displayed:

```
<?xml version="1.0" encoding="utf-8"?>
<mx:Canvas xmlns:mx="http://www.adobe.com/2006/mxml"
    width="100%"
    height="100%">

    <mx:Label id="lbl" />

</mx:Canvas>
```

Using the id property isn't the only way you can add the content. You can also use data binding, which you learned about earlier in this chapter. The item renderer has a globally defined data object, which currently holds the contents of this row's data. To quickly set the Label value, you can add this code:

```
<mx:Label text="{data.col2}" />
```

This code takes the data object and extracts the col2 property, which in this example is holding the price. The { } is telling Flex that the value being requested is a bindable property and can be updated automatically.

However, this doesn't allow you to modify or update this value but simply to display it. In order to modify the value, you must use a process called overriding.

Overriding a value

Overriding is creating a method to take the place of a default process. In a way, an item renderer is like an override but for display.

In this case, you want to override the data property, so you need to set up a custom setter function. The data property holds the values for the components. You find that almost all the components have the data property, which can be set in MXML and ActionScript code. In MXML coding, you would set the dataProvider attribute:

```
<mx:Script>
    <![CDATA[

        override public function set data(value:Object):void
        {

        }

    ]]>
</mx:Script>
```

That method sits before the data is sent to this component and allows you to modify it. However, you still need to allow the original process to run, as you never really know what Flex is doing behind the scenes.

> **NOTE** You can Ctrl+click a method or property and then see the origination of it. This is a common way to learn the abilities of a class.

The super() method is used to call the original process:

```
<mx:Script>
    <![CDATA[
```

```
override public function set data(value:Object):void
{
        super.data = value;
}

]]>
</mx:Script>
```

Once you've made a call to the original process, you can begin modifying the data. Let's set the code to look for a price value and then set the background color of the canvas based on the amount. If the price is above $25, make the background red; otherwise, make it green:

```
<mx:Script>
    <![CDATA[

        [Bindable] private var bgColor:uint;

        override public function set data(value:Object):void
        {
                if(value != null)
                {
                        super.data = value;
                        if(value.col2 > 25)
                        {
                                bgColor = 0xFF0000;
                        }
                        else
                        {
                                bgColor = 0x00FF00;
                        }
                }
        }

    ]]>
</mx:Script>
```

This code is setting a property of bgColor to the specified color, but you may have noticed that the color is never sent to the canvas. This isn't a problem, as the bgColor property is marked as Bindable, so you can easily add it to the Canvas node, as follows:

```
<mx:Canvas xmlns:mx="http://www.adobe.com/2006/mxml"
    backgroundColor="{bgColor}" ...>
```

Figure 4.3 shows the result of adding this code to the previous code example.

FIGURE 4.3

An example of `DataGrid` coloring

The background of the canvas is now changing properly, but the label isn't being filled. Using the label `id` you assigned earlier, you can set the `text` property:

```
<mx:Script>
<![CDATA[

    [Bindable] private var bgColor:uint;

    override public function set data(value:Object):void
    {
        if(value != null)
        {
            super.data = value;
            if(value.col2 > 25)
            {
                bgColor = 0xFF0000;
            }
            else
            {
                bgColor = 0x00FF00;
            }

            lbl.text = String(value.col2);
        }
    }

]]>
</mx:Script>
```

Now that the function is changing the background color properly and updating the label, the last step is to alert other components that the data has changed. This is done by using the `dispatch Event()` method. This code creates a new `FlexEvent` and sets up a broadcast to any objects or items that are watching for the DATA_CHANGE event.

```
dispatchEvent(new FlexEvent(FlexEvent.DATA_CHANGE));
```

You must also add an import at the top of your ActionScript for the `FlexEvent` class. If you didn't load this class, Flex is unable to generate the event and throws an error:

```
import mx.events.FlexEvent;
```

At this point, you have completed the custom item renderer. Feel free to add to this concept or adapt it to your other work.

Here's the completed item renderer:

```xml
<?xml version="1.0" encoding="utf-8"?>
<mx:Canvas xmlns:mx="http://www.adobe.com/2006/mxml"
    backgroundColor="{bgColor}" alpha="0.4" width="100%"
    height="100%">

    <mx:Script>
    <![CDATA[

        import mx.events.FlexEvent;

        [Bindable] private var bgColor:uint;
        [Bindable] private var myLabel:String;

        override public function set data(value:Object):void
        {
            if(value != null)
            {
                super.data = value;

                if(value.col2 > 25)
                {
                    bgColor = 0xFF0000;
                }
                else
                {
                    bgColor = 0x00FF00;
                }

                lbl.text = String(value.col2);
            }
```

```
                    // Dispatch the dataChange event.
                    dispatchEvent(new FlexEvent(FlexEvent.DATA_CHANGE));
            }


        ]]>
        </mx:Script>

        <mx:Label id="lbl" />

    </mx:Canvas>
```

Building a Sample Flex Application

Now that you've been introduced to the various aspects of Flex application development, let's take that information and build a sample application. Most Web sites have some form of RSS feed, so let's build a simple reader application.

Start by creating a new Flex project. Keep all the default options and then click Finish to wrap up the project-building process. Open the MXML file that's displayed to the left in the Flex Navigator. Switch to Source view to start building the application.

This RSS feed displays the entries in a DataGrid, and when the user clicks a row, the contents of that entry are displayed in a TextArea component. A Button component is used to start the XML loading, but you could easily modify the code to load the feed once the application starts:

```
<?xml version="1.0" encoding="utf-8"?>
<mx:Application xmlns:mx="http://www.adobe.com/2006/mxml"
    layout="absolute">

    <mx:Button x="308" y="12" label="Get RSS Feed"/>
    <mx:TextArea id="desc" x="10" y="178" width="400" height="150"/>
    <mx:DataGrid x="10" y="40" width="400" height="125">
        <mx:columns>
        <mx:DataGridColumn headerText="Title" dataField="title"/>
        <mx:DataGridColumn headerText="Date" dataField="date"/>
        </mx:columns>
    </mx:DataGrid>

</mx:Application>
```

Once the overall application is designed, you can start adding the events and bindable variables to the DataGrid and Button components:

```
    .
    .
    .
```

```
<mx:Button x="308" y="12" label="Get RSS Feed" click="getFeed()"/>
<mx:DataGrid ...
   dataProvider="{feed}"
   itemClick="storySelected(event)">

   .
   .
   .
```

The next step is to begin writing the code for this application. Start by importing the necessary packages and then defining the variables. In this application, two bindable variables and one standard variable direct the code to the XML file:

```
<mx:Script>
<![CDATA[

    import mx.collections.ArrayCollection;

    [Bindable]
    private var feed:ArrayCollection;

    [Bindable]
    private var feedTitle:String;

    private var feedURL:String = "http://mkeefedesign.com/blog/feed";

]]>
</mx:Script>
```

When the user clicks the Get Feed button, an event is dispatched that calls the getFeed() method. This method creates a URL request to the server and attempts to load the XML data. A URLLoader instance is also created to set up a response function that handles the XML being returned.

The last part of the getFeed() method makes the actual call to the server-side file, passing the URL request object as an argument:

```
<mx:Script>
<![CDATA[


    .
    .
    .


    private function getFeed():void
    {
        var urlRequest:URLRequest = new URLRequest(feedURL);
        var urlLoader:URLLoader = new URLLoader();
```

```
                urlLoader.addEventListener(Event.COMPLETE, feedLoaded);
                urlLoader.load(urlRequest);
        }


]]>
</mx:Script>
```

Once the XML data has been loaded, you need to build a handler to take that XML data and display it in the `DataGrid` component. This is painlessly achieved by using E4X in ActionScript 3. E4X is a way to traverse XML data. In previous versions of ActionScript, you had to use `childNodes[]` and actually drill down into the XML object in order to find the information you were searching for.

Now in ActionScript 3, you can simply say `xml..itemToBeFound`, and it automatically finds that correct item. If there were multiple items, you would build a loop to go through them. This is exactly what's needed for this example.

You start off by retrieving the XML data, building a new XML instance, and then using a `for..each` loop to traverse the block of data:

```
<mx:Script>
<![CDATA[


        .
        .
        .


    private function feedLoaded(e:Event):void
    {
            var urlLoader:URLLoader = URLLoader(e.target);
            var xml:XML = XML(urlLoader.data);

            feedTitle = String(xml..title[0]);

            feed = new ArrayCollection();

            for each(var item:* in xml..item)
            {
                    feed.addItem({
                            title:item..title,
                            date:item..pubDate,
                            body:item..description
                    });
            }
    }

]]>
</mx:Script>
```

That `for..each` loop goes through the XML object and pulls out all the `item` nodes, sticks them in the `item` variable, and then continues on the loop. For each item in the XML object, you need to create a row in the `DataGrid`.

The `feed` property is bindable, so any changes to it are automatically displayed in the `DataGrid`. If you could slow down this loading process, you would see that each row is added to the `feed` variable and then placed in the `DataGrid`.

The `addItem()` method is part of the `ArrayCollection` class and is how you push new data in to the array. The type of data it accepts is an object, so one is created automatically for each row in the XML:

```
feed.addItem({title:item..title, ...});
```

Now that the `DataGrid` is being filled properly, the last part of the code is an event handler for whenever the user clicks a row. This action displays the body of the message in the `TextArea` component you added earlier:

```
<mx:Script>
<![CDATA[

    .
    .
    .


    private function storySelected(e:Event):void
    {
        desc.htmlText = DataGrid(e.target).selectedItem.body;
    }

]]>
</mx:Script>
```

In order to display the proper entry, you need to reference the correct row in the `DataGrid`. One of the properties of the `DataGrid` is `selectedItem`. This property holds the data for that current row. The `e.target` makes a reference to the object that called this event, which in this example would be the `DataGrid`.

The property that you're looking for is `body`. This property is stored in the `selectedItem` object, so a simple bit of code, such as the following, does the trick:

```
DataGrid(e.target).selectedItem.body
```

The `DataGrid()` portion of the code is ensuring that the value is typed as a `DataGrid` instance. This is done to ensure that your data is pure. This is especially important if this code handled something of a more secure nature, such as a login or access-specific action.

Whenever a user clicks that DataGrid row, the correct story is loaded into the TextArea. Now that the application is complete, you can test it and expand it to your liking. You may have noticed that this application was loading a remote XML file.

If you happen to be working offline, below is the XML structure; simply create a new XML file and then load this file locally. You can also replace the feedURL with another feed that's online. The structure that's expected is the one found in any WordPress RSS feed:

```xml
<?xml version="1.0" encoding="UTF-8"?>
<rss version="2.0"
    xmlns:content="http://purl.org/rss/1.0/modules/content/"
    xmlns:wfw="http://wellformedweb.org/CommentAPI/"
    xmlns:dc="http://purl.org/dc/elements/1.1/"
    xmlns:atom="http://www.w3.org/2005/Atom"
    >

<channel>
    <title>Sample Feed</title>
    <description>Sample feed for flex app</description>
    <pubDate>Tue, 19 Jul 2008 16:04:28 +0000</pubDate>

    <item>
        <title>Sample Story</title>
        <pubDate>Tue, 08 Jul 2008 15:57:45 +0000</pubDate>
        <dc:creator>mkeefe</dc:creator>
        <description><![CDATA[Contents of the story here.]]>
        </description>
    </item>
    <item>
        <title>Sample Story 2</title>
        <pubDate>Tue, 01 Jul 2008 15:57:45 +0000</pubDate>
        <dc:creator>mkeefe</dc:creator>
        <description><![CDATA[Contents of the story here.]]>
        </description>
    </item>
    <item>
        <title>Sample Story 3</title>
        <pubDate>Tue, 20 June 2008 15:57:45 +0000</pubDate>
        <dc:creator>mkeefe</dc:creator>
        <description><![CDATA[Contents of the story here.]]>
        </description>
    </item>

</channel>
</rss>
```

You have now completed a sample application that should give you a firm understanding of Flex application development. At this point, you can start building your own applications, and with the knowledge you obtain in the rest of this book, those applications will be very well-developed.

Here's the sample application in its entirety:

```
<?xml version="1.0" encoding="utf-8"?>
<mx:Application xmlns:mx="http://www.adobe.com/2006/mxml"
    layout="absolute">

<mx:Script>
<![CDATA[

    import mx.collections.ArrayCollection;

    [Bindable]
    private var feed:ArrayCollection;

    [Bindable]
    private var feedTitle:String;

    private var feedURL:String = "http://mkeefedesign.com/blog/feed/";

    private function getFeed():void
    {
            var urlRequest:URLRequest = new URLRequest(feedURL);
            var urlLoader:URLLoader = new URLLoader();
            urlLoader.addEventListener(Event.COMPLETE, feedLoaded);
            urlLoader.load(urlRequest);
    }

    private function feedLoaded(e:Event):void
    {
            var urlLoader:URLLoader = URLLoader(e.target);
            var xml:XML = XML(urlLoader.data);

            feedTitle = String(xml..title[0]);

            feed = new ArrayCollection();

            for each(var item:* in xml..item)
            {
                    feed.addItem({
                            title:item..title,
                            date:item..pubDate,
                            body:item..description
                    });
            }
    }

    private function storySelected(e:Event):void
    {
```

```
                desc.htmlText = DataGrid(e.target).selectedItem.body;
      }

]]>
</mx:Script>

<mx:Button x="308" y="12" label="Get RSS Feed" click="getFeed()"/>
<mx:TextArea id="desc" x="10" y="178" width="400" height="150"/>

<mx:DataGrid x="10" y="40" width="400" height="125"
   dataProvider="{feed}"
   itemClick="storySelected(event)">
   <mx:columns>
         <mx:DataGridColumn headerText="Title" dataField="title"/>
         <mx:DataGridColumn headerText="Date" dataField="date"/>
   </mx:columns>
</mx:DataGrid>
<mx:Label x="10" y="10" text="{feedTitle}" fontSize="14"/>

</mx:Application>
```

Summary

In this chapter, you learned how to develop Flex applications. You first learned how classes and packages are built and then how you can benefit from using them. You also learned that the majority of standard Flex coding is built up of packages and classes, even when it comes to the MXML format.

You were also introduced to events and how they can be used to create more responsive and more solid applications. The event section also gave you a firm understanding of how events are used in MXML development.

Later in the chapter, you learned about data providers and how binding is used to create more interactive applications. You also learned that data binding allows you to keep track of variables without a lot of extra coding.

Being introduced to this information as well as the item renderers should put you well on your way to developing very interesting and useful applications. Now that you understand the basics, it's time to move on to connecting Flex with Java data services.

Part II

Connecting Java and Flex

IN THIS PART

Chapter 5
Sending Data from Flex

Chapter 6
Writing Java Web Applications

Chapter 7
Using JUnit and FlexUnit to Test Your Applications

Chapter 8
Relational Databases

Chapter 9
Java and Databases

Chapter 10
Building a Basic Database-Powered Flex Application

Chapter 11
Developing a Stock Ticker with BlazeDS

Chapter 5

Sending Data from Flex

I n this chapter, you learn how to send data from Flex. The concepts you learn aren't specific to Java because no matter what back-end language you decide to work with, you still need to send and load some form of data.

The actual process of sending data consists of packages and classes that ship with Flex, paired with a custom response handler that the developer would create and which you will now learn to create.

IN THIS CHAPTER

Understanding the sending process

Writing the sample test

Understanding the Sending Process

The process of sending data in Flex requires an object to send the data and another to handle the response that's captured once the requested server returns a result. This is because Flex uses an *asynchronous* sending process, which means that the response calls are assigned to an response handler because it's not known when the response will be available. In a *synchronous* (blocking) process, the application waits until the response is available.

The object for the asynchronous call is also used to hold any variables that need to be passed to the server.

When creating a service to send data, first you need to determine the purpose and functionality of the service. For example, if you want to load a user's information from a server-based database, you would make a request with a user ID and expect a *slug* (fragment) of XML or a formatted string that contains the response.

ActionScript approach

The above scenario may look something like this when developed by using ActionScript:

```
private function sendData():void
  {
var url:String = "http://localhost/app/getUser";

var variables:URLVariables = new URLVariables();
variables.userID = 2;

var urlRequest:URLRequest = new URLRequest(url);
urlRequest.data = variables;

var loader:URLLoader = new URLLoader();
loader.addEventListener(Event.COMPLETE, handleServerResponse);
loader.load(urlRequest);
  }

 private function handleServerResponse(e:Event):void
 {
       // handle server response here
 }
```

This code is a simplified example of creating a service to contact the server. You start off by creating an instance of the URLVariables object, which contains the parameters that are passed to the server. Next is the URLRequest instance, which is stored in the urlRequest variable.

Then you create a new URLLoader instance, passing in the previous URLRequest, and add an event listener that's called once the response has been loaded.

All that probably looks pretty straightforward and familiar to you if you've worked with Flex before. Now let's look at a simpler approach using HTTPService.

Using HTTPService

Building the service by using ActionScript is only one option. When using Flex, most of the ActionScript you develop can be re-created by using only MXML, depending on how you construct your application.

The HTTPService tags simplify the process of building a request service and require only a few bits of code to re-create what the previous ActionScript approach contained.

Start by adding the HTTPService tag to your document. The placement within the MXML file doesn't matter because it's purely for runtime use; you won't see anything on the stage or in your completed application as a result of simply adding the HTTPService tag:

```
<mx:HTTPService
    id="httpService"
    url="http://example.com"
    method="POST"
/>
```

The `HTTPService` tag is given an `id`, which would be referred to within your script block. The `url` parameter is the fully qualified path to the back-end server processor, similar to the one you would connect to in the previous section.

The last parameter, `method`, is used to define the method that sends the data. Valid options would be `GET` and `POST`, exactly the same as you would find in an HTML-based application.

 **You can find other methods, such as PUT and DELETE, in third-party libraries.**

The `HTTPService` code can be assigned to a binding response. This allows your application to be updated automatically, minimizing the amount of code that's required to handle the response.

Here's an example of a bindable response based on the previous `HTTPService` tag:

```
<mx:Label
    text="Response: { httpService.lastResult.id }"
/>
```

 **The `lastResult` variable is cleared after each call. It's a good idea to store this response in case you want to use it later.**

Handling the response of the HTTPService call

You don't have to assign the service call to a bindable string. You can manually handle the response from the server. Start by adding a function to the `result` property, which is called once the response is complete:

```
<mx:HTTPService
    id="httpService"
    result="xmlResponse"
```

Then, once the tag has been updated, the next step is to create the function, which in this example is `xmlDecodeResponse`:

```
public function xmlResponse(xml:*):void
{
    trace("User ID: " + xml.firstChild.attributes.userID);
}
```

Writing the Sample Test

Now that you know how to send data from Flex, let's take a moment to develop a sample test, which you can refer to in case you run into problems.

Building the Flex application

Before you write the sending process, start off by creating a new Flex application and adding the components.

To create a new Flex project, follow these steps:

1. **Choose File ⇨ New ⇨ Flex Project.** The Flex Project dialog box opens.
2. **Type SendingData in the Project name text field.**
3. **Click OK to create the project.**

Adding the components

Switch to the Design view and then drag out three Button components and a TextArea component, as shown in Figure 5.1. The buttons are used to call functions, which are created when you start to define the code for this example.

FIGURE 5.1

The Button and TextArea components are dragged from the Components panel to the application display list.

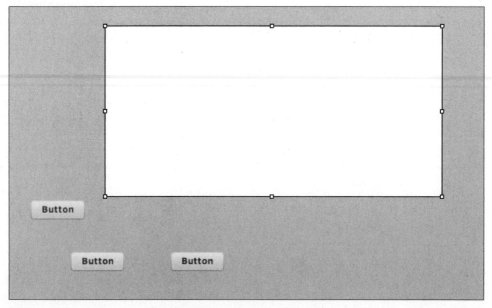

Aligning the components

The next step is to align the components by dragging them together until the snap line appears, as shown in Figure 5.2, for graphics purposes. You can then assign unique ids to each component by using the Flex Properties panel.

 You can modify most of the component parameters in the Flex Properties panel or in the Code editor; they both create the same result.

The components are properly aligned on the application display list.

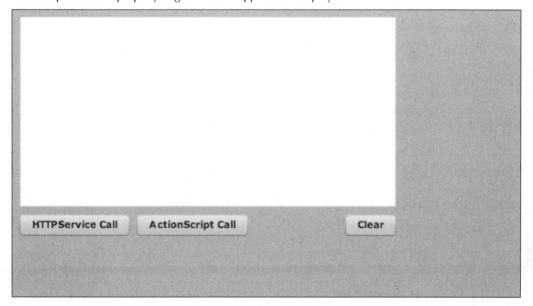

You should now have the components and ids defined. The exact alignment of the elements isn't important for this example. The code in the Source view should look similar to the following block of text:

```
<?xml version="1.0" encoding="utf-8"?>

<mx:Application
    xmlns:mx="http://www.adobe.com/2006/mxml"
    layout="absolute"
>

    <mx:TextArea
        id="debugTxt"
        x="10"
        y="10"
```

```
            width="406"
            height="199"
        />


        <mx:Button x="10" y="217" label="HTTPService Call" id="httpBtn"/>
        <mx:Button x="137" y="217" label="ActionScript Call" id="asCall"/>
        <mx:Button x="361" y="217" label="Clear" id="clearBtn"/>

    </mx:Application>
```

The next step is to add the HTTPService call, which — as you learned before — is achieved by adding a line (formatted as more than one here) of MXML code:

```
<mx:Application
    xmlns:mx="http://www.adobe.com/2006/mxml"
    layout="absolute"
>

    <mx:HTTPService
        id="httpService"
        url="http://localhost/app/getUser"
        method="POST"
        result="xmlResponse"
    />

    ...

    </mx:Application>
```

Adding the ActionScript

Now that the basic MXML code has been created, the next step is to begin adding the ActionScript, which is called whenever one of the Button components is clicked. Start by adding the Script tags, which contain the ActionScript:

```
<mx:Script>
    <![CDATA[

    ]]>
</mx:Script>
```

The first method, asCallHandler(), handles the ActionScripted version of the sending process. Start by creating a URLVariables instance and then attach that variable object to a new URLRequest instance.

A URLLoader is then set up to control the actual calling of the server. A more complete application uses a Java back end. But in this example, the server is nothing more than a simple HTML file:

```
private function asCallHandler():void
{
    var url:String = "http://localhost/app/getUser";

    var variables:URLVariables = new URLVariables();
    variables.userID = 2;

    var urlRequest:URLRequest = new URLRequest(url);
    urlRequest.data = variables;

    var loader:URLLoader = new URLLoader();
    loader.addEventListener(Event.COMPLETE, handleServerResponse);
    loader.load(urlRequest);
}
```

The second method, handleServerResponse(), is called when the data in the previous method is loaded.

For this example, the response is captured and displayed in the TextField component that's located within the application:

```
private function handleServerResponse(e:Event):void
{
    trace("User data is loaded");
    debugTxt.text = e.currentTarget.response;
}
```

The third method, httpBtnHandler(), handles the call to the HTTPService request. A call to the send() method starts the process. This is to ensure that the calls aren't made when the application loads:

```
private function httpBtnHandler():void
{
    httpService.send({userID:2});
}
```

The last method, xmlResponse(), is called when the HTTPService returns a response. In this example, the response data is passed into the TextArea component. The response is XML:

```
public function xmlResponse(xml:*):void
{
    debugTxt.text = xml.firstChild.attributes.response;
}
```

At this point, you've completed the example. You can now load the application in your browser, which should look similar to Figure 5.3.

FIGURE 5.3

The completed application as seen when loaded in a browser

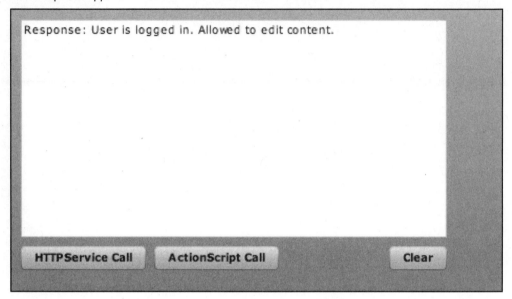

Here's the code for the completed application:

```
<?xml version="1.0" encoding="utf-8"?>
<mx:Application
    xmlns:mx="http://www.adobe.com/2006/mxml"
    layout="absolute"
>

    <mx:Script>
        <![CDATA[

        private function asCallHandler():void
        {
            var url:String = "http://localhost/app/getUser";

            var variables:URLVariables = new URLVariables();
            variables.userID = 2;

            var urlRequest:URLRequest = new URLRequest(url);
            urlRequest.data = variables;

            var loader:URLLoader = new URLLoader();
            loader.addEventListener(Event.COMPLETE,
```

```
                    handleServerResponse);

          loader.load(urlRequest);
     }
     private function handleServerResponse(e:Event):void
     {
          trace("User data is loaded");

          debugTxt.text = e.currentTarget.response;
     }

     private function httpBtnHandler():void
     {
          httpService.send({userID:2});
     }

     public function xmlDecodeResponse(xml:*):void
     {
          debugTxt.text = xml.firstChild.attributes.response;
     }

     ]]>
</mx:Script>

<mx:HTTPService
     id="httpService"
     url="http://localhost/app/getUser"
     method="POST"
     xmlDecode="xmlDecodeResponse"
/>

<mx:TextArea
     x="10"
     y="10"
     width="406"
     height="199"
     id="debugTxt"
/>

<mx:Button
     click="httpBtnHandler()"
     x="10"
     y="217"
     label="HTTPService Call"
     id="httpBtn"
/>
<mx:Button
     click="asCallHandler()"
     x="137"
```

```
        y="217"
        label="ActionScript Call"
        id="asCall"
    />
    <mx:Button
        x="361"
        y="217"
        label="Clear"
        id="clearBtn"
    />

</mx:Application>
```

Summary

In this chapter, you learned how to send data to Flex by using two different processes. The first process was an MXML version that used `HTTPService` tags. The second process used `URLLoader` and constructed a complete server handler made entirely of code.

You also created a complete sample application, allowing you to clearly see the differences between the two processes. You should now have a good understanding of how to send data with Flex, which you can use in your future Java development.

Chapter 6

Writing Java Web Applications

Even the most dynamic Flex user interface needs live data to make it more valuable than just a static page. Web applications typically get their data from an application server that handles requests from the user interface and then returns the requested data for the user interface to display. Java is well-suited to meet this need. Java application servers and Web application frameworks have been around for a number of years now and provide a stable back-end base upon which to build your dynamic Web applications.

In this chapter, you build a simple Web application to receive the request from the Flex client. The Web applications you build throughout this book use a popular open-source Java application framework called Spring. This chapter starts with a look at the Model-View-Controller pattern, followed by an introduction to the Spring Framework. After that, you write a simple Web application using Spring and then compile and deploy it to a server by using an Ant build script.

IN THIS CHAPTER

The Model-View-Controller pattern

The Spring Framework

Writing a simple Web application

The Model-View-Controller Pattern

In software development, an *architectural pattern* refers to a proven, repeatable way to describe the structure of an application. Java Web applications are typically written by using the Model-View-Controller (MVC) architectural pattern. The objective of using the MVC pattern is to separate the user interface from the data and business logic so that changes to one don't require changes to the other. For example, if a Web application is written with a JSP/HTML user interface, and the requirements for the next version include changing the user interface to Flex, using the MVC pattern would allow the user interface portion of the application to be replaced without touching the business logic.

The MVC pattern divides application code into three parts:

- **The model** consists of the objects representing the application's data and the business logic code that handles and manipulates those objects.
- **The view** consists of the code and user interface elements that together make up the user interface for the application.
- **The controller** consists of the code that handles communication to the model about actions taken on the user interface elements in the view (for example, a request to the model for data when a user interface button is clicked).

Typically, some event in the user interface sends a request to a controller. The controller retrieves the parameters for the request and then passes them on to the business logic in the model. The model retrieves or manipulates data based on the parameters passed on by the controller and then returns the requested data to the controller. Finally, the controller places the data into the view and then returns that view to the user.

The Spring Framework

The *Spring Framework* is a lightweight Java framework whose purpose is to make developing complex Java applications easier and to allow a programmer to create loosely coupled, highly reusable code. *Loosely coupled* means that code modules are as independent of one another as possible. This makes it easier to alter one part of an application without touching other parts. This is invaluable in large software projects but also desirable in smaller projects where modules that interact with one another are subject to frequent changes. Without loosely coupled code, changes to one module would likely require changes to one or more other modules. This can lead to maintenance problems, as it becomes harder and harder to keep up with all the required changes.

Spring's most widely used feature is known as dependency injection. *Dependency injection* allows the Spring Framework to provide an object with the other objects it needs to work instead of the object needing to create or locate those objects itself. When an object that's managed by the Spring Framework (known in Spring terminology as a *Spring bean*) needs some other object to do its work, the Spring container provides the needed object. The Spring container is said to inject the object with its dependencies so that they're available to the object when needed.

The Spring Framework consists of a number of modules, and going into detail about them would require a book of its own. But because Spring is modular, you can pick and choose the pieces you want to use and ignore the others or you can use different pieces of the framework as they become appropriate. For the first application, you use a handful of Spring modules. As the applications grow in size and complexity, more pieces of the Spring Framework enter the picture.

For the first Web application, the following Spring modules are used:

- **Application context.** The Spring application context module builds upon Spring's core. It provides the basic Spring functionality, such as dependency injection, as well as support for more advanced functionality, such as remote services.

- **Spring MVC.** This is the Spring Framework's implementation of the Model-View-Controller pattern. It includes a number of classes and interfaces that help create applications that follow the MVC paradigm.

- **Spring Web.** Spring's Web module contains support for using MVC code within Spring's application context. It also contains functionality that allows form fields and other request parameters in a Web application to be bound directly to server-side Java objects and provides integration with various view technologies.

The Spring Framework can be downloaded from the Spring Framework Web site at `http://springframework.org/download`. As of this writing, the latest stable version of Spring is 2.5.5. Click the Download link for the latest release to go to the download file listing page, as shown in Figure 6.1. Click the link labeled `spring-framework-<version>-with-dependencies.zip` (for example, `spring-framework-2.5.5-with-dependencies.zip`). Save the archive to your machine and then extract it to a directory of your choice.

 Updates to the Spring Framework are likely, so use the current version available.

Each of the Spring Framework modules is packaged in its own JAR file. The core Spring modules, such as the application context module, are located in the `spring.jar` file in the `dist` directory of the Spring Framework distribution. Other Spring modules, such as Spring Web MVC, are located in their own JAR files in the `dist\modules` directory. The Spring Framework distribution also comes packaged with other libraries that can be used for such things as application logging and using JSP tag libraries in Web applications.

Documentation for the Spring Framework can be found in the `docs` folder of the Spring Framework distribution. Plenty of valuable examples and reference materials are found there. It's worth spending some time going through these materials to get a feel for what the Spring Framework provides.

The file listing page on the Spring Framework download Web site contains a few different options for download. Download the `-with-dependencies` version, which contains everything needed to run and build the Spring Framework.

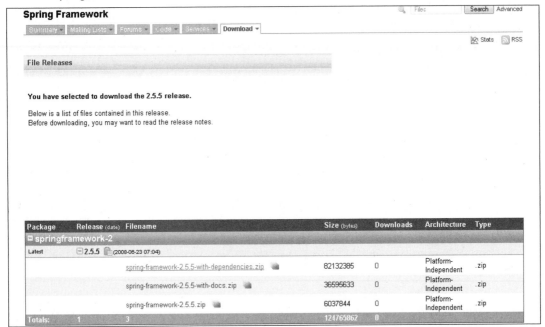

Writing a Simple Web Application

Now that you know a little more about Spring Framework and what it provides, it's time to write a simple Web application using Spring — a Spring Web application version of the classic "Hello, World!" application. First, you create a new project inside your Eclipse workspace. Next, you configure the project properties. Finally, you write the code and configuration files for the application.

The project directory structure

A Java Web application project typically consists of Java source files, XML configuration files, JSP files, and Web assets, such as HTML and image files. Using a consistent directory structure for all your Java Web application projects helps speed development by separating these various pieces into well-known areas. It also helps you reuse Ant build files by allowing you to put common, generic paths into your build files and separating out project-specific settings into a properties file that the build file can import.

The Web application projects in this book all use a consistent directory structure. Some projects may have pieces that others don't, but they all share a few basic pieces. Figure 6.2 shows the project directory structure for the simple Web application you write in this chapter. This structure is created for you by Eclipse when you start developing your Web application.

Typically, the top-level directory has the same name as your application. Below this directory, there are three other directories:

- **The** bin **directory** contains the compiled Java class files.
- **The** src **directory** contains Java source code files.
- **The** web **directory** contains non-Java files for the application, including XML configuration files, JSP pages, and images. Below this web folder is a WEB-INF folder, which contains configuration files for the Web application and any other resources needed by the Web application that shouldn't be directly accessible through the Web browser (for example, JSP views that should be served up only by calls to services on the server). Below the WEB-INF folder is a lib folder, which contains library JAR files needed by the Web application.

FIGURE 6.2
_____

A typical Java Web application directory structure contains folders for Java source code, Web application code, and compiled Java class files. Using a standardized directory structure is a best practice when developing a Java Web application.

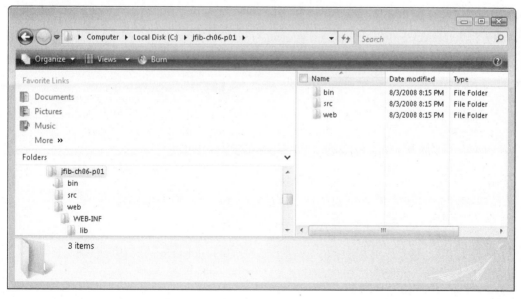

> **NOTE** When you're using JBoss, library JAR files must be placed directly in the `WEB-INF\lib` folder. They can't be placed in subfolders beneath the `WEB-INF\lib` folder. Other application servers, such as IBM's Websphere, do allow subfolders for library JAR files.

Now that you've seen what the directory structure for a Java Web application project looks like, you can set up a project in Eclipse.

Creating an Eclipse project

Although you can create this directory structure on your own, because you're using the Eclipse IDE, you can let Eclipse set up this directory structure for you by creating a new project in Eclipse. Eclipse creates much of the necessary directory structure by using a wizard. Once the project has been created, you can add any other needed folders and files as necessary within the Eclipse environment.

To create a new project in Eclipse, follow these steps:

1. **Open Windows Explorer by choosing Start ⇨ All Programs ⇨ Accessories ⇨ Windows Explorer.**

2. **Navigate to the Eclipse install directory and then double-click `eclipse.exe`.** Eclipse launches. If you didn't click the Use this as the default and don't ask again check box the first time you ran Eclipse, Eclipse again asks you to choose a workspace directory.

3. **Leave the default value in place and then click OK.**

4. **Create a new project by choosing File ⇨ New ⇨ Project or right-clicking within the Project Explorer view and choosing New ⇨ Project from the popup menu.** The New Project dialog box, as shown in Figure 6.3, opens.

5. **Click the arrow next to Spring to expand it, choose Spring Project, and then click Next.** The New Spring Project dialog box, as shown in Figure 6.4, opens.

6. **Type a name for the project and then click Finish.** The dialog box closes, and the newly created project appears in the Project Explorer view.

In the New Spring Project dialog box, the default values in the Source Folder Name and Output Folder Name text fields are `src` and `bin`, respectively. These names match the names discussed in the previous section. Eclipse creates these directories for you when you create a new project, and Eclipse can also automatically compile the Java code in the `src` directory and then output the compiled Java class files to the `bin` directory as you work.

FIGURE 6.3

The New Project dialog box in Eclipse is the first step in creating a new project. Eclipse supports many different types of projects out of the box, and you can add more types by using plug-ins.

Take a few minutes to explore the newly created project. Click the arrow to the left of the project name in the Project Explorer view to expand the project, as shown in Figure 6.5.

When you create a new Spring project in Eclipse, it adds a few elements to the project automatically:

- **The Spring Elements item** lets you visualize the relationships among your Spring beans.
- **The JRE System Library item** includes all the standard Java libraries from your installed JDK. These libraries are what Eclipse uses to compile your Java code.
- **The src folder** is the place where you add your Java source code.

Even though the New Spring Project dialog box contains an item for an output folder named bin, this item doesn't appear in the expanded project. This is because Java class files are binary and won't ever be edited.

FIGURE 6.4

The New Spring Project dialog box contains settings for creating a new Spring project. The default values conform to standard Spring project development practices and shouldn't be changed for most applications.

FIGURE 6.5

Eclipse automatically adds a few necessary elements to newly created projects.

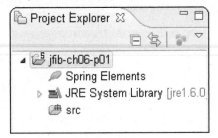

Configuring the Eclipse project

Before diving into coding, you have some project configuration steps to do. Once the project has been configured, you can write, compile, deploy, and test your first application.

To configure the Eclipse project, follow these steps in Eclipse:

1. **Right-click your project in the Project Explorer view and then choose New ⇨ Folder from the popup menu.** The New Folder dialog box, as shown in Figure 6.6, opens.

FIGURE 6.6

The New Folder dialog box allows you to add new folders to your project. You can type nested folder paths here (for example, web\WEB-INF\lib) and then Eclipse creates the entire structure for you.

2. **Type web\WEB-INF\lib in the Folder name text field and then click Finish.** The New Folder dialog box closes, and the newly created folder structure is added to the project, as shown in Figure 6.7.

3. **Right-click the lib folder and then choose Import from the popup menu.** The Import dialog box, as shown in Figure 6.8, opens.

4. **Click the arrow next to the General item to expand it, choose File System from the list, and then click Next.** The Import dialog box, as shown in Figure 6.9, opens.

5. **Click the Browse button next to the From directory text field.** The Import from directory dialog box, as shown in Figure 6.10, opens.

FIGURE 6.7

Folders are displayed in the project in a nested structure much like Windows Explorer.

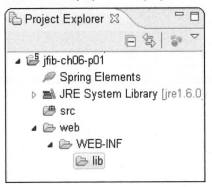

FIGURE 6.8

The Import dialog box allows you to import resources for your project from a variety of sources.

6. **Navigate to your extracted Spring Framework directory, select it, and then click OK.** The directory appears in the left pane of the Import dialog box, as shown in Figure 6.11. Clicking the Spring Framework directory displays its contents in the right pane of the dialog box. Clicking the arrow next to the directory name on the left expands it to display its subfolders.

7. **Click the arrow next to the Spring Framework directory in the left pane to expand it, click the `dist` folder in the left pane, and then click the check box next to `spring.jar`, which is in the right pane.**

8. **Click the arrow next to the `dist` folder in the left pane to expand it, click the `modules` folder in the left pane and then click the check box next to `spring-webmvc.jar`, which is in the right pane, as shown in Figure 6.12.**

9. **Click the arrow next to the `lib` folder under the expanded Spring Framework folder in the left pane to expand it, click the `j2ee` folder in the left pane, and then click the check box next to `jstl.jar`, which is in the right pane, as shown in Figure 6.13.**

FIGURE 6.9

The Import dialog box lets you bring resources from your computer's file system into your project. Resources are copied from their original locations into your project's directory structure.

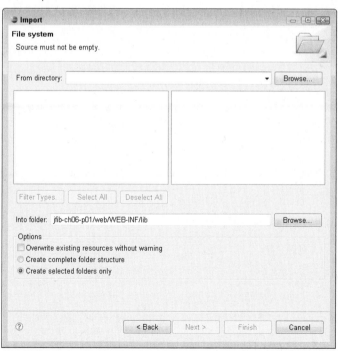

FIGURE 6.10

The Import from directory dialog box allows you to choose directories and resources to import into your project.

FIGURE 6.11

Once you've chosen your extracted Spring Framework directory, it appears in the left pane of the Import dialog box, and its contents appear in the right pane. Clicking the arrow next to the directory in the left pane expands it to display its subfolders.

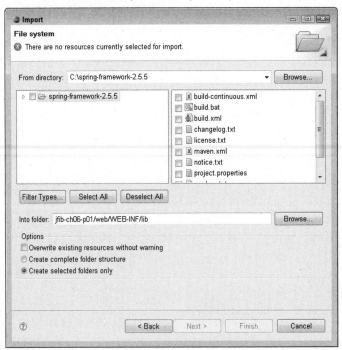

10. **Click the** `jakarta-taglibs` **folder under the expanded** `lib` **folder in the left pane and then click the check box next to** `standard.jar`, **which is in the right pane, as shown in Figure 6.14.** The `spring.jar`, `spring-webmvc.jar`, `jstl.jar`, and `standard.jar` libraries contain all the pieces of the Spring Framework that you need for this application. As you move on to more complex projects where more pieces of Spring are needed, you can use this same import process to easily bring them into your projects.

11. **Click Finish.** The Spring Framework libraries you just added appear beneath the `web\WEB-INF\lib` folder in subfolders, as they were in the Spring Framework directory.

12. **Drag the JAR files from their subfolders directly into the web\WEB-INF\lib folder, right-click each of the empty folders, and then choose Delete from the popup menu.** When you finish, the Project Explorer view should look like the one in Figure 6.15, with all the JAR files appearing directly within the `lib` folder and the empty subfolders gone. Dragging the JAR files directly into the `web\WEB-INF\lib` folder is required because library JAR files for a Web application must be placed directly in the `lib` directory under `WEB-INF` in order to be found by JBoss.

FIGURE 6.12

Click the `spring.jar` and `spring-webmvc.jar` libraries to be imported from the `dist` and `dist\modules` folders, respectively, under the extracted Spring Framework folder.

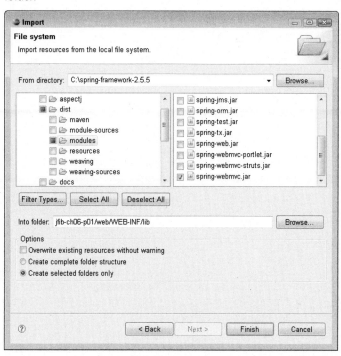

Although you added the Spring libraries to your project, Eclipse doesn't use them to compile your Java code unless you explicitly configure it to do so. Eclipse uses a setting called the Java Build Path to tell it where Java source code is kept, where Java class files should be output, and where libraries needed to compile the Java source code into Java class files can be found. The Java Build Path in Eclipse is essentially the same as the classpath that needs to be set when compiling Java classes manually by using the JDK's Java compiler. You need to configure this setting next.

FIGURE 6.13

Choose the `jstl.jar` library to be imported from the `lib\j2ee` folder under the extracted Spring Framework folder.

FIGURE 6.14

Choose the `standard.jar` library to be imported from the `lib\jakarta-taglibs` folder under the extracted Spring Framework folder.

FIGURE 6.15

After you drag the library JAR files from their subfolders into the `web\WEB-INF\lib` folder and then delete the emptied subfolders, the Project Explorer view should look like this.

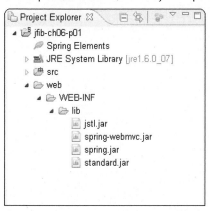

To configure the Java Build Path for your project, follow these steps:

1. **Right-click your project in the Project Explorer view and then choose Properties from the popup menu.** The Properties dialog box opens.

2. **Click Java Build Path in the left navigation pane of the Properties dialog box.** The Java Build Path tabbed section opens in the right pane, as shown in Figure 6.16.

Choosing Java Build Path in the left pane of the Properties dialog box opens the Java Build Path tabbed section in the right pane.

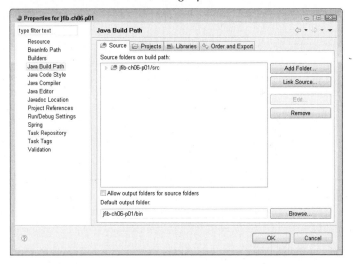

3. **Click the Libraries tab.** A list of library JAR files and class folders appears. As shown in Figure 6.17, the JRE System Library from the installed JDK is already included in this list.

4. **Click the Add JARs button.** The JAR Selection dialog box opens.

5. **Click** `jstl.jar`, `spring-webmvc.jar`, `spring.jar`, **and** `standard.jar`, **as shown in Figure 6.18, and then click OK.** The files are added to the library list, as shown in Figure 6.19.

6. **Click the Add External JARs button.** The JAR Selection dialog box opens.

7. **Navigate to the client folder within your JBoss installation, choose the** `servlet-api.jar` **file, and then click OK.** The `servlet-api.jar` library is added to the library list, as shown in Figure 6.20.

NOTE If you have JAR files that need to be deployed with your application, you import them into your project first and then add them to the build path using the Add JARs button. For JAR files that don't need to be deployed with your application, simply add them to the build path for your project by using the Add External JARs button. This allows Eclipse to use the JAR library to compile your Java code, but it doesn't copy it into your project. In this case, you need to package and deploy the Spring Framework JAR files with the application, but the `servlet-api.jar` file is already part of the JBoss server, so you don't need to deploy it with your application.

8. **Click OK.** The Properties dialog box closes.

FIGURE 6.17

The JRE System Library from your installed JDK is automatically added to the JAR files and class folders list in the Library tab.

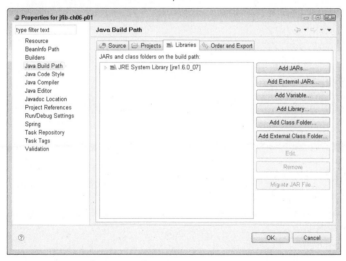

FIGURE 6.18

Click the `jstl.jar`, `spring-webmvc.jar`, `spring.jar`, and `standard.jar` files
in the JAR Selection dialog box to add them to the build library path for your project.

FIGURE 6.19

The JAR files now appear in the build library path.

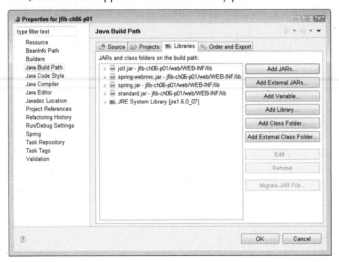

FIGURE 6.20

The `servlet-api.jar` is added to the build library path. The entry shows the full path to the JAR on your computer. This indicates that the JAR file hasn't been copied into the project but instead is referenced externally.

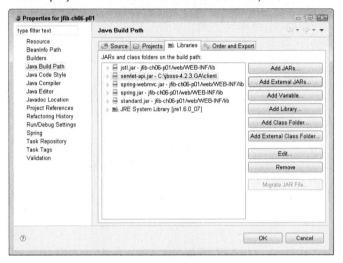

Writing the Web application

Now that the Eclipse project has been configured, it's time to start writing the application. Using the Spring Framework Web MVC module, this application follows the Model-View-Controller (MVC) pattern. Here's how the pieces of the application fit into the pattern:

- **The model represents the data and business logic for the application.** In this case, there isn't any real business logic, just data: the "Hello, World!" message.

- **The controller receives requests from the user interface, passes the parameters from the request off to the business logic and receives the requested data, and then passes that data back to the user interface view.** A Java class implementing Spring Web MVC's `Controller` interface handles that task.

- **The view is the user interface for the application, and the view contains the data from the model.** The view for this application is a JSP that receives the "Hello, World!" message and displays it.

The Model and Controller

Spring's `Controller` interface contains a single method, `handleRequest`, that receives requests from the user interface and responds with the requested data. Eclipse can create the stub of a controller for you by using a wizard.

In Java development, classes are divided into smaller groups of related functionality called *packages*. Packages for Web applications are typically named following a pattern that describes the company or organization the code is being written for, the specific project the code is part of, and what functionality the code provides. For example, the application in this chapter uses the package `com.wiley.jfib.ch06.helloworld.service` for the controller. Controllers are often referred to as *services*, as they service the requests of clients.

CROSS-REF For more on packages and other Java concepts, see Chapter 1.

To create the controller class, follow these steps:

1. **Right-click the `src` folder of your project in the Project Explorer view and then choose New ⇨ Package from the popup menu.** The New Java Package dialog box opens.

2. **Type com.wiley.jfib.ch06.helloworld.service in the Name text field, as shown in Figure 6.21, and then click Finish.** The new package appears under the project's `src` folder in the Project Explorer, as shown in Figure 6.22.

3. **Right-click the newly created package and then choose New ⇨ Class from the popup menu.** The New Java Class dialog box, as shown in Figure 6.23, opens. The Source folder and Package text fields are already filled in for you with the correct values.

4. **Type HelloWorldService in the Name text field.**

FIGURE 6.21

Type the package name in the Name text field of the New Java Package dialog box.

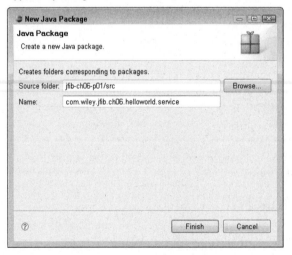

FIGURE 6.22

The newly created package appears under the `src` folder of your project in the Project
Explorer view.

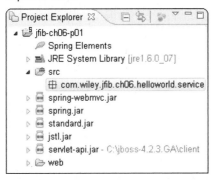

FIGURE 6.23

The New Java Class dialog box, with the Source folder and Package text fields already
filled in with the correct values

5. **Click the Add button next to the Interfaces list box.** The Implemented Interfaces Selection dialog box opens.

6. **Type** Controller **in the Choose interfaces text field.** As you type, the Matching items list box fills in potential matches, as shown in Figure 6.24.

7. **Choose** `Controller - org.springframework.web.servlet.mvc` **from the list box and then click OK.** The Implemented Interfaces Selection dialog box closes, and the Controller interface is added to the Interfaces list box in the New Java Class dialog box, as shown in Figure 6.25.

8. **Click the Generate comments check box and then click Finish.** The New Java Class dialog box closes, and the newly created `HelloWorldService` class opens in the editor, as shown in Figure 6.26.

FIGURE 6.24

As you type in the Choose interfaces text field of the Implemented Interfaces Selection dialog box, the Matching items list begins to fill in with interfaces that match what you type.

It's worth taking a look at the various pieces of this Java class before moving on. It may help you to display the line numbers for the file to make it easier to follow along. To show the line numbers, right-click the left margin of the editor and then choose Show Line Numbers from the popup menu. The line numbers appear in the left margin of the editor.

Eclipse also has a feature called *folding*, which allows you to expand or collapse sections of the file, such as import statements, comment blocks, and code blocks. This feature makes working with large Java files easier. When you're interested in only one particular piece of code, you can use folding to collapse the rest. Folded blocks of code have a small + button next to them, which can be clicked to expand them. Expanded blocks can be folded again by clicking the small − button next to them. In this case, being able to see all the code in this small file is more useful for walking through the various pieces. You can quickly expand all folded sections in a Java file by right-clicking the left margin of the editor again and then choosing Folding ⇨ Expand All from the popup menu.

FIGURE 6.25

After you select an interface in the Implemented Interfaces Selection dialog box, it appears in the Interfaces list box in the New Java Class dialog box. A Java class can have multiple interfaces.

FIGURE 6.26

Once you've finished with the New Java Class dialog box, the newly created Java class stub is opened in the editor.

```java
/**
package com.wiley.jfib.ch06.helloworld.service;

import javax.servlet.http.HttpServletRequest;

/**
 * @author Chuck
 *
 */
public class HelloWorldService implements Controller {

    /* (non-Javadoc)
     * @see org.springframework.web.servlet.mvc.Controller#ha
     */
    @Override
    public ModelAndView handleRequest(HttpServletRequest arg0
            HttpServletResponse arg1) throws Exception {
        // TODO Auto-generated method stub
        return null;
    }

}
```

Line 4 of the `HelloWorldService` Java class is the *package statement*, which lets Java know what package the class is in. Lines 6 through 10 are import statements. *Import statements* are used to inform this class of the locations of other classes it needs. On its own, a class has access only to other classes in the same package and any classes in the standard `java.lang` package that's part of the JDK. For `HelloWorldService`, four other classes are also needed:

- `javax.servlet.HttpServletRequest`. This class represents the request coming from an HTTP client, such as a Web browser, to the server. It contains information about the client's locale, any cookies relevant to the application, authentication information, and other information the server may need to know about the client. An instance of this class is passed as a parameter to `HelloWorldService`'s `handleRequest` method.

- `javax.servlet.HttpServletResponse`. This class represents the response going from the server to the HTTP client. This typically includes things that a Web browser might need to know, such as server status codes and HTTP headers. An instance of this class is passed as a parameter to `HelloWorldService`'s `handleRequest` method.

- `org.springframework.web.servlet.ModelAndView`. This class is a convenient container for both the model data packaged up for use by the view and a reference to the view itself. An instance of this class is returned by `HelloWorldService`'s `handleRequest` method.

- `org.springframework.web.servlet.mvc.Controller`. This interface is implemented by `HelloWorldService`.

Line 16 is the *class declaration*. The class declaration contains the name of the class, the name of the class it extends (optional), and the names of any interfaces it implements (optional). Extending a class means adding functionality to or modifying functionality in an existing class. When a Java class extends another class, it has access to all the public member variables and methods in the extended class and can override those public methods with its own implementations. Unless otherwise specified, all Java classes extend the `Object` class in the `java.lang` package. `HelloWorldService` extends `Object`, so there's no `extends` statement in the class declaration. An interface in Java is a set of one or more methods without implementations. When a Java class implements an interface, it's then required to provide an implementation for any methods in the interface. In this example, `HelloWorldService` implements the `Controller` interface from the `org.springframework.web.servlet.mvc` package. The `Controller` interface has one method: `handleRequest`. Because `HelloWorldService` implements `Controller`, it needs to provide an implementation for the `handleRequest` method. Eclipse provides a default implementation of `handleRequest` when it generates the stub class file.

CROSS-REF   For more on Java syntax, see Chapter 1.

You can now change the default implementation of `handleRequest` with code that returns a "Hello, World!" message to the client. To do this, you change the `handleRequest` method so that it looks like this:

```
/* (non-Javadoc)
 * @see org.springframework.web.servlet.mvc.
   Controller#handleRequest(javax.servlet.http.HttpServletRequest,
   javax.servlet.http.HttpServletResponse)
 */
@Override
public ModelAndView handleRequest(HttpServletRequest arg0,
        HttpServletResponse arg1) throws Exception {
    // the message for the client
    return new ModelAndView("WEB-INF/jsp/hello-world.jsp",
            "message","Hello, World!");
}
```

The Spring Web MVC module's `ModelAndView` object holds both the model and the view and allows the controller to return both at once. The constructor used here for the `ModelAndView` object has three parameters. The first parameter is the location of the view. The view for `HelloWorldService` is a JSP page named `hello-world.jsp` located in the `WEB-INF/jsp` folder. The second parameter is the name of the model. The view uses this name to retrieve the model. The model for this request is named `message`. The final parameter is the model itself. The data being returned to the client in this case is the string `"Hello, World!"`

The View

Now that you've got a controller that can handle a request and return data, you need to create the view that displays the data. For this example, you write a simple JSP page to act as the view.

To create the JSP page for the view, follow these steps:

1. **Right-click the** `web/WEB-INF` **folder in the Project Explorer view and then choose New ➪ Folder from the popup menu.** The New Folder dialog box opens.

2. **Type** jsp **in the Folder name text field and then click Finish.** The New Folder dialog box closes, and the newly created folder appears below the `WEB-INF` folder in the Project Explorer view.

3. **Right-click the** `web/WEB-INF/jsp` **folder in the Project Explorer view and then choose New ➪ Other from the popup menu.** The Select a wizard dialog box opens.

4. **Click the arrow next to Web to expand it, click JSP, and then click Next.** The New JavaServer Page wizard, as shown in Figure 6.27, opens.

5. **Type** hello-world.jsp **in the File name text field and then click Next.** The Select JSP Template screen, as shown in Figure 6.28, opens.

FIGURE 6.27

The first screen of the New JavaServer Page wizard is where you give the JSP file a name.

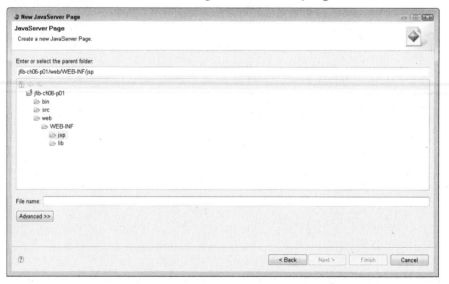

The second screen of the New JavaServer Page wizard allows you to choose a template for your JSP. Templates include many of the required HTML tags and JSP directives, allowing you to concentrate on filling in the details.

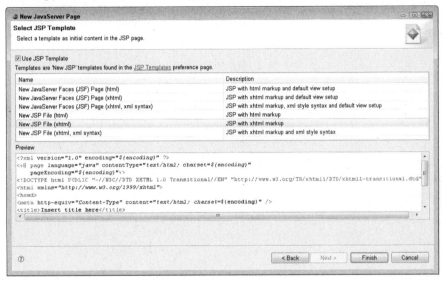

6. **Click New JSP File (xhtml) in the JSP template list and then click Finish.** The New JavaServer Page wizard closes, and the newly created JSP is opened in the editor, as shown in Figure 6.29.

A JSP is basically just a regular HTML or XHTML file with a few special tags that have meaning to the server. When a JSP is requested, the server actually compiles the JSP into a Java class file in much the same way that a regular Java file is compiled. The code in the compiled JSP then outputs HTML or XHTML to a browser to be displayed.

Take a look at lines 2 and 3 of the `hello-world.jsp` file. These lines are referred to as a JSP directive. A *JSP directive* is a special tag that begins with the characters `<%@`. There are many types of JSP directives. This one is called a *page directive*, which tells the server what language the code on the page is written in (`java`, in this case), what the returned content MIME type is (`text/html`), and the character set used by the page (`ISO-8859-1`). Page directives can also be used to import Java classes into the page, much like the import statement in a Java file.

Now that you have a JSP stub, you need to get your model data into it and display it. You do that by adding some more JSP directives to the page to retrieve the data and then another to output it in the page.

FIGURE 6.29

After you complete the New JavaServer Page wizard, the newly created JSP appears in the editor. The template chosen in the last step of the wizard provides the basic HTML tags and JSP directives, allowing you to concentrate on filling in the details.

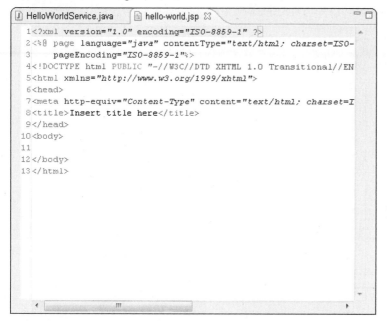

Add the following line of code immediately after the page directive in the JSP file:

```
<%@ taglib prefix="c" uri="http://java.sun.com/jsp/jstl/core" %>
```

This is a tag library (`taglib`) directive. A *tag library* is a set of custom tags that provides extended functionality to JSP pages outside the built-in functionality. This example uses the Java Server Pages Standard Tag Library (JSTL) to add tags that allow you to access and output data in the model more easily. The `prefix` attribute of the `taglib` directive specifies the namespace prefix that the tag libraries' tags use. This is necessary because different tag libraries might include tags with the same name. The prefix ensures that the server knows which tag library a given tag belongs to. This JSP uses the prefix c to identify tags contained in the JSTL tag library. The `uri` attribute tells the server where the description of the tag library can be found. The server uses this description to validate that tags used in the JSP follow the correct syntax. The code for the JSTL tag library itself is contained in the `jstl.jar` file you previously imported into the project. The JAR file needs to be deployed to the server with the application in order for the JSTL tag libraries to be available to the application at runtime.

Change the text in the title tag to something more descriptive than `Insert title here` and then add this line of code to the empty space between the start and end `<body>` tags:

```
<c:out value="${message}"/>
```

The `c` prefix indicates that this is a tag from the JSTL tag library: the `out` tag. The `out` tag simply outputs the contents of its `value` attribute to the JSP. The `value` attribute of this tag is a variable reference to a variable named `message`. A *variable reference* contains the name of some variable surrounded by `${}`. Notice that `message` is also the name you gave your model in the `HelloWorldService` controller. This tag reads the value of `message` from the model and then outputs its value to the JSP view.

Wiring the pieces together

You now have a controller that provides model data to a JSP view. To get everything working together, you need to create and edit some configuration files.

The first configuration file is `web.xml`. This file is the application descriptor file used by all Java Web applications. Among other things, `web.xml` contains entries for any Java servlets in the Web application and the URL patterns that map to those servlets.

In standard Spring Web MVC applications, you generally don't need to write servlets yourself. Spring provides a servlet, the `DispatcherServlet`, that receives incoming requests and passes those along to the appropriate controller. The controllers do the work of gathering the data into the model and then packaging it up for the view.

The Spring `DispatcherServlet` is configured in `web.xml`. The controllers are configured in one or more Spring configuration files. These are additional XML files that provide definitions for the controller classes and URL mappings that tell the `DispatcherServlet` which controller is responsible for which URL.

To create the `web.xml` configuration file, follow these steps:

1. **Right-click the `web/WEB-INF/` folder in the Project Explorer view and then choose New ➪ Other from the popup menu.** The Select a wizard dialog box opens.

2. **Click the arrow next to XML to expand it, click XML in the submenu, and then click Next.** The New XML File wizard, as shown in Figure 6.30, opens.

3. **Type web.xml in the File name text field and then click Next.** The Create XML File From screen, as shown in Figure 6.31, opens.

4. **Click the Create XML file from an XML template radio button and then click Next.** The Select XML Template screen, as shown in Figure 6.32, opens.

5. **Click the xml declaration template in the list and then click Finish.** The New XML File wizard closes, and the newly created `web.xml` file opens in the editor.

The XML schema definition for web.xml can be found online at `http://java.sun.com/xml/ns/j2ee/web-app_2_4.xsd`. There are a number of tags and attributes that can be found in a web.xml file, too numerous to go through in their entirety here. For the HelloWorld application, only the following basic structure is required:

```
<web-app>
    <servlet>
            <servlet-name></servlet-name>
            <servlet-class></servlet-class>
            <load-on-startup></load-on-startup>
    </servlet>
    <servlet-mapping>
            <servlet-name></servlet-name>
            <url-pattern></url-pattern>
    </servlet-mapping>
</web-app>
```

FIGURE 6.30

The first screen of the New XML File wizard is where you give the XML file a name.

FIGURE 6.31

The second screen of the New XML File Wizard allows you to create a new XML file from a template.

The <web-app> tag is the topmost tag of the web.xml file and is required. It has attributes for the Web application version and the XML schema definition location. The <web-app> tag contains two child tags:

- **The** <servlet> **tag** contains child tags that define the servlet name, Java class, and whether the servlet should be loaded when the server starts up.
- **The** <servlet-mapping> **tag** contains child tags that map a servlet name to a URL pattern.

FIGURE 6.32

The Select XML Template screen allows you to choose an XML template.

The entire web.xml file for the HelloWorld application is shown in the listing below. Add this code to the web.xml file in your project and then save the file:

```xml
<?xml version="1.0" encoding="UTF-8"?>
<web-app version="2.4"
 xmlns="http://java.sun.com/xml/ns/j2ee"
 xmlns:xsi="http://www.w3.org/2001/XMLSchema-instance"
 xsi:schemaLocation="http://java.sun.com/xml/ns/j2ee
 http://java.sun.com/xml/ns/j2ee/web-app_2_4.xsd" >
<servlet>
<servlet-name>spring-dispatcher</servlet-name>
<servlet-class>org.springframework.web.servlet.DispatcherServlet
</servlet-class>
<load-on-startup>1</load-on-startup>
</servlet>

<servlet-mapping>
<servlet-name>spring-dispatcher</servlet-name>
<url-pattern>*.htm</url-pattern>
</servlet-mapping>
</web-app>
```

One servlet is being defined in the `<servlet>` tag, and that servlet is being mapped to a single URL pattern in the `<servlet-mapping>` tag. The servlet is named `spring-dispatcher` and is a Spring `DispatcherServlet`. The servlet is mapped to the URL pattern `*.htm`. This pattern matches any incoming server request that ends in `.htm`. Wildcard characters such as `*` are allowed in mappings, and you can make a mapping as general or as specific as necessary for your application. For the `HelloWorld` application, all requests ending in `.htm` go through the `Dispatcher Servlet`. It's possible to simply use `*` for the URL pattern. However, mapping specific suffixes to specific servlets makes adding more servlets easier.

Now that configuration of the `DispatcherServlet` in `web.xml` is complete, you need a Spring beans configuration file to tell the `DispatcherServlet` which requests to map to your controller. Follow the same steps you just used to create `web.xml` to create another XML file in the `web\WEB-INF` directory. Name the file `spring-dispatcher-servlet.xml`. This file derives its name from the value of the `<servlet-name>` tag for the `DispatcherServlet` in `web.xml`, followed by `-servlet.xml`.

The XML schema definition for the Spring beans configuration file can be found at `www.springframework.org/schema/beans/spring-beans-2.5.xsd`. As with `web.xml`, there are too many tags and attributes to fully cover here. For the `HelloWorld` application, only the following basic structure is required:

```
<beans>
    <bean></bean>
</beans>
```

The `<beans>` tag is the topmost tag of the `spring-dispatcher-servlet.xml` file and is required. It has attributes for the XML schema definition location. The `<beans>` tag contains one `<bean>` tag for each controller to be mapped to a URL. The `name` attribute maps to the URL the controller should handle, and the `class` attribute maps to the controller Java class.

The entire `spring-dispatcher-servlet.xml` file for the `HelloWorld` application is shown in the following listing. Add this code to the `spring-dispatcher-servlet.xml` file in your project and then save the file:

```
<?xml version="1.0" encoding="UTF-8"?>
<beans xmlns="http://www.springframework.org/schema/beans"
 xmlns:xsi="http://www.w3.org/2001/XMLSchema-instance"
 xsi:schemaLocation="http://www.springframework.org/schema/beans
 http://www.springframework.org/schema/beans/spring-beans-2.5.xsd">
    <bean name="/hello-world.htm"
    class="com.wiley.jfib.ch06.helloworld.service.HelloWorldService"/>
</beans>
```

In this file, the `HelloWorldService` class is mapped to the URL `/hello-world.htm` by using the `name` attribute. When a request comes into the server for `/hello-world.htm`, it's first passed to the `DispatcherServlet`, as it matches the `*.htm` pattern mapped to that servlet. The `DispatcherServlet` then looks up which controller should handle the specific request by using the information in `spring-dispatcher-servlet.xml`. Because `/hello-world.htm` is mapped to the `HelloWorldService` controller, the request is handed off to that controller, which packages the requested data into the model and then sends it off to be displayed in the view.

All the application code and configuration is now complete. The last step is to create an Ant build script to compile, package, and deploy the application. After that, the application is ready to run under JBoss.

Writing the Ant build script

Although it's possible to compile, package, and deploy your Web application manually by using tools included with the JDK, such an approach doesn't provide an easily adaptable and maintainable build strategy. If more library JAR files are added to your application's build path or the Web application becomes part of a larger Java enterprise application that needs to be deployed to many different application servers, keeping up with long compilation commands, multiple batch files, and deployment paths becomes an error-prone process. Fortunately, thanks to Apache Ant, it's not necessary to manually build your application.

Ant uses an XML build file that contains one or more projects, each of which in turn contains one or more targets. An Ant *target* is a grouping of related *tasks*, which are individual units of work in an Ant target. For example, many Ant build files contain a target named `build`. The `build` target might contain tasks that create output directories and compile Java code.

Projects in an Ant build file are groupings of targets for a particular application. In addition to the targets for building and deploying the application, projects can contain properties that can be substituted into targets and tasks by using variables. Properties can also be defined in a separate properties file that can be included in the build file. This makes it easier to change the value of a property if needed, as you need to change the value in only one place rather than throughout the build file. Projects can also contain path resources that group sets of files under a single ID, which can then be referenced by other parts of the build file.

The Ant build file for the `HelloWorld` application contains a couple of properties, a path resource, and two targets. One of the properties is a reference to an external properties file, which you create now. The properties file simply contains a set of name-value pairs.

To create the `build.properties` file, follow these steps:

1. **Right-click the `jfib-ch06-p01` project in the Project Explorer view and then choose New ⇨ File from the popup menu.** The New File dialog box opens.
2. **Type** helloworld-build.properties **in the File name text field and then click Finish.** The New File dialog box closes, and the `helloworld-build.properties` file opens in the editor.

The code listing for the `helloworld-build.properties` file is as follows:

```
# Ant build properties for helloworld
src.dir=src
web.dir=web
build.dir=${web.dir}/WEB-INF/classes

name=helloworld

appserver.home=${env.JBOSS_HOME}/server/default
appserver.lib=${appserver.home}/lib
deploy.path=${appserver.home}/deploy
```

The first three properties are related to the compiling of the Java code. The `src.dir` property tells the build script where the source code for the application can be found. The `web.dir` property tells the build script where the Web code and configuration files can be found. Finally, the `build.dir` property tells the build scripts where to output the compiled Java classes. This property makes use of the previously defined `web.dir` property by using the `${}` variable substitution notation.

The final four properties are related to packaging and deploying the compiled application to the JBoss server. The `name` property defines the name of the application; the build script packages the application into a WAR file called `${name}.war`. The `appserver.home` property tells the build script where to locate the base of the JBoss installation. There are two things to notice about this property. First, notice the `${env.JBOSS_HOME}` variable substitution used here. It's possible to set a build file property that allows you to access environment variables on your computer. This property accesses the value of the `JBOSS_HOME` environment variable you set when you configured JBoss. Second, notice that you're setting `appserver.home` to the default server instance under the JBoss installation.

It's possible to have multiple server configurations configured under JBoss, and applications need to be deployed to one or more of these specific configurations rather than just deployed to JBoss in general. The `appserver.lib` property uses the `appserver.home` property to tell the build script where the JBoss server libraries are. Remember that the application needs JBoss's `servlet-api.jar` file to build. Finally, the `deploy.path` property tells the build script where to place the built and packaged application. The JBoss server configuration deploys any applications in its deploy directory when it starts up.

Now that the properties file is in place, the Ant build file can be created. By convention, Ant build files are always named `build.xml`.

To create the `build.xml` file, follow these steps:

1. **Right-click the `jfib-ch06-p01` project in the Project Explorer view and then choose New ⇨ Other from the popup menu.** The Select a wizard dialog box opens.

2. **Click the arrow next to XML to expand it, click XML in the submenu, and then click Next.** The New XML File wizard opens.

3. **Type build.xml in the File name text field and then click Next.** The Create XML File From screen opens.

4. **Click the Create XML file from an XML template radio button and then click Next.** The Select XML Template screen opens.

5. **Click the xml declaration template in the list and then click Finish.** The New XML File wizard closes, and the newly created `build.xml` file opens in the editor.

The code listing for the `build.xml` file is as follows:

```xml
<?xml version="1.0" encoding="UTF-8"?>
<project name="helloworld" basedir="." default="usage">
    <property environment="env"/>
    <property file="helloworld-build.properties"/>

    <path id="cp">
        <fileset dir="${web.dir}/WEB-INF/lib">
            <include name="*.jar"/>
        </fileset>
        <fileset dir="${appserver.lib}">
            <include name="servlet-api.jar"/>
        </fileset>
        <pathelement path="${build.dir}"/>
    </path>

    <target name="usage">
        <echo message=""/>
        <echo message="${name} build file"/>
        <echo message="---------------------------------"/>
        <echo message=""/>
        <echo message="Available targets are:"/>
        <echo message=""/>
        <echo message="build --> Build the application"/>
        <echo message="deploy --> Deploy application as a WAR
file"/>
        <echo message=""/>
    </target>

    <target name="build" description="Compile main source tree java
files">
        <mkdir dir="${build.dir}"/>
        <javac destdir="${build.dir}" source="1.5" target="1.5"
        debug="true" deprecation="false" optimize="false"
        failonerror="true">
            <src path="${src.dir}"/>
            <classpath refid="cp"/>
        </javac>
    </target>
```

```
   <target name="deploy" depends="build" description="Deploy
   application as a WAR file">
         <war destfile="${name}.war"
                  webxml="${web.dir}/WEB-INF/web.xml">
              <fileset dir="${web.dir}">
                    <include name="**/*.*"/>
              </fileset>
         </war>
         <copy todir="${deploy.path}" preservelastmodified="true">
              <fileset dir=".">
                    <include name="*.war"/>
              </fileset>
         </copy>
   </target>
</project>
```

This listing looks long, but it's really fairly simple when broken down into its basic parts:

- The first <property> tag sets the system environment to the variable env. This property allows you to use variables, such as ${env.JBOSS_HOME}, used in the helloworld-build.properties file.

- The second <property> tag loads the properties located in the helloworld-build.properties file. It's important that this property is listed after the environment property, as the environment property is used in the helloworld-build.properties file.

- The <path> tag puts together a few sets of files and assigns the list to a variable named cp. You can see from the <fileset> and <pathelement> tags inside the <path> tag that this set includes all the JAR files in the WEB-INF/lib directory, the servlet-api.jar file from the JBoss server, and the compiled class files from the HelloWorld application. This set of files is used as the classpath when compiling the application.

- The first <target> tag defines the usage target. This is the default target, which is run if Ant is executed with no target specified. The usage target simply prints out a list of available targets in this build file to the console.

- The second <target> tag defines the build target. This target contains two tasks. The first, the mkdir task, creates the output directory for the compiled Java classes if it doesn't already exist. The second, the javac task, invokes the Java compiler to compile the source code in the source directory by using libraries in the classpath referenced by the cp variable defined earlier in the <path> tag. The failonerror attribute of the javac task ensures that the build won't continue if there are errors in the source code.

- The final <target> tag defines the deploy target. This target also contains two tasks. The first, the war task, packages up all the files for the Web application into a WAR file by using the name defined in the properties file. The second, the copy task, copies the WAR file into the JBoss deploy directory. The <target> tag has a depends attribute that lists build as a dependency. That means that the deploy target depends on the build target having been run. If the build target hasn't been run and code has changed in the meantime, the deploy target actually runs the build target first to make sure that the compiled code is up to date before packaging and deploying the application.

To run the Ant build script from within Eclipse, you need to add it to the Ant view in your project. To add the build script to the Ant view, follow these steps:

1. **Choose Window ⇨ Show View ⇨ Other.** The Show View dialog box, as shown in Figure 6.33, opens.

FIGURE 6.33

Choose the Ant view in the Show View dialog box.

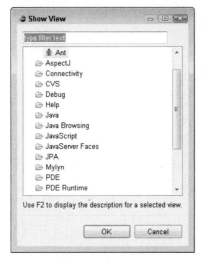

2. **Click the arrow next to Ant to expand it, click Ant in the expanded menu, and then click OK.** The Ant view, as shown in Figure 6.34, opens.

FIGURE 6.34

The Ant view is where the build file for your application appears, allowing you to run build targets from within Eclipse.

3. **Click the Add Buildfiles button in the Ant view.** The Add Buildfiles button is the left-most button in the Ant view, depicting an ant next to a plus sign. The Buildfile Selection dialog box opens.

4. **Click the arrow next to the project name to expand it, click the** `build.xml` **file, as shown in Figure 6.35, and then click OK.** The Buildfile Selection dialog box closes, and the build file is added to the Ant view, as shown in Figure 6.36.

FIGURE 6.35

Choose the `build.xml` file for your project in the Buildfile Selection dialog box to add it to the Ant view.

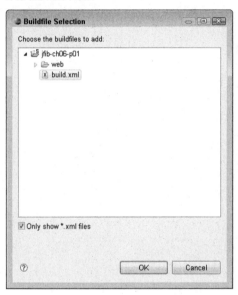

Click the arrow next to the build file entry in the Ant view to expand it and see the available build targets. The three targets you saw in the `build.xml` file appear here. Double-click the `usage` target to run it. Eclipse switches to the Console view, and the messages defined in the `<echo>` tags in the `usage` target print out in the console, as shown in Figure 6.37. Click the Ant tab to switch back to the Ant view.

Now double-click the `deploy` target to run it. Study the output of the console, as shown in Figure 6.38, and notice that because the `build` target has never been run, the `deploy` target launches the `build` target first. The ability to chain dependencies like this in your build files is a very powerful advantage over building manually. Using dependencies like this, you can ensure that you never deploy outdated code to your application server.

FIGURE 6.36

The build file appears in the Ant view with the name of the project as defined in `build.xml`.

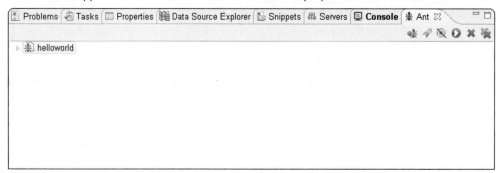

FIGURE 6.37

The console output from running the `usage` target of the Ant build

```
Buildfile: C:\Users\Chuck\workspace\jfib-ch06-p01\build.xml
usage:
     [echo] helloworld build file
     [echo] ----------------------------------------
     [echo] Available targets are:
     [echo] build    --> Build the application
     [echo] deploy   --> Deploy application as a WAR file
BUILD SUCCESSFUL
Total time: 390 milliseconds
```

FIGURE 6.38

The console output from the `deploy` target demonstrates its dependency on the `build` target. Because the `build` target had not yet been run, the `deploy` target launched it before proceeding with its own tasks.

```
Buildfile: C:\Users\Chuck\workspace\jfib-ch06-p01\build.xml
build:
    [javac] Compiling 1 source file to C:\Users\Chuck\workspace\jfib-ch06-p01\web\WEB-INF\cl
deploy:
      [war] Building war: C:\Users\Chuck\workspace\jfib-ch06-p01\helloworld.war
     [copy] Copying 1 file to C:\jboss-4.2.3.GA\server\default\deploy
BUILD SUCCESSFUL
Total time: 2 seconds
```

Once the application has been successfully deployed, you can start up JBoss and see the application in action. To start JBoss and test your application, follow these steps:

1. **Switch to the Servers view by clicking the Servers tab.**

2. **Click the Start the Server button.** Eclipse switches to the Console view while JBoss starts up. Once the server startup has completed, Eclipse switches back to the Servers view and shows the state of the JBoss server as Started, as shown in Figure 6.39.

3. **Open your Web browser, type** http://localhost:8080/helloworld/hello-world.htm **in the address bar, and then press Enter.** You should see the screen shown in Figure 6.40.

FIGURE 6.39

Once the JBoss server has started successfully, the Servers view shows its state as Started.

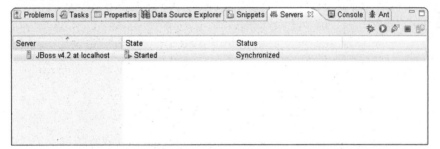

FIGURE 6.40

This screen indicates that the `HelloWorld` application has been successfully deployed to JBoss.

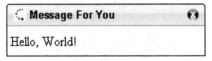

You may be curious about the URL. Web applications are deployed to their own application context on the server. That way, multiple applications can be run on the same server without having conflicting resource names (`index.html`, for example). By default, the application context URL path is the name of the application. In this case, the application is deployed as `helloworld.war`, so the application context name is `helloworld`. Therefore, it can be said that the URL points to the resource `hello-world.htm` within the application context `helloworld` on the `local host` server.

If for some reason you receive an error instead of the screen in Figure 6.40, there are a couple of things you can do to check your work and see what went wrong:

- Be sure you typed the URL correctly in the browser's address bar. Remember to include a colon between `localhost` and `8080` and that the URL ends in `hello-world.htm`, not `hello-world.html`.

- Double-check that there were no compilation errors in your code by looking for red X icons in the left margin of the `HelloWorldService` editor. If you've misspelled any keywords, forgotten parentheses or semicolons, or made other errors, you can correct them in the editor and then rebuild and deploy the application by using Ant as described earlier. You don't need to restart JBoss; it detects that the application WAR file has been updated and redeploys it on the fly.

- Switch to the Console view by clicking the Console tab. If the Console view isn't open, you can open it by choosing Window ⇨ Show View ⇨ Console. The Console view contains output from the JBoss server. If an error has occurred, JBoss may have output it to the console. If you see an error in the Console view, the error output contains information about the line number in your code where the error occurred. Using this information, you can correct the error. After correcting the error, you can rebuild and deploy the application by using Ant as described earlier. Again, you don't need to restart JBoss for your changes to take effect.

Enhancing the Web application

While the `HelloWorld` application builds, deploys, and runs, it's otherwise not very interesting. Adding the ability to accept input from the user interface is the next logical step for this application.

Open the `HelloWorldService` file by double-clicking it in the Project Explorer view. Replace the existing `handleRequest` method with the following:

```
/**
 *
 */
package com.wiley.jfib.ch06.helloworld.service;

import javax.servlet.http.HttpServletRequest;
import javax.servlet.http.HttpServletResponse;

import org.springframework.web.servlet.ModelAndView;
import org.springframework.web.servlet.mvc.Controller;

/**
 * @author Chuck
 *
 */
public class HelloWorldService implements Controller {
```

```
/* (non-Javadoc)
 * @see org.springframework.web.servlet.mvc.
Controller#handleRequest(javax.servlet.http.HttpServletRequest,
javax.servlet.http.HttpServletResponse)
 */
@Override
public ModelAndView handleRequest(HttpServletRequest arg0,
            HttpServletResponse arg1) throws Exception {
    // Receive the language parameter from the client
    String language = arg0.getParameter("lang");
    String message = "";

    // customize the message based on the language
    if(language == null)
        message = "I don't know what language you speak!";
    else if("english".equalsIgnoreCase(language))
        message = "Hello, World!";
    else if("spanish".equalsIgnoreCase(language))
        message = "Hola, mundo!";
    else if("french".equalsIgnoreCase(language))
        message = "Bonjour, monde!";
    else if("german".equalsIgnoreCase(language))
        message = "Hallo, Welt!";
    else if("italian".equalsIgnoreCase(language))
        message = "Ciao, mondo!";
    else
        message = "I'm sorry. I don't speak your language.";

    // return the message for the client
    return new ModelAndView("WEB-INF/jsp/hello-world.jsp",
    "message",message);
    }

}
```

The handleRequest method now attempts to retrieve a parameter named lang from the client's request. The message returned to the client is customized based on the language received, if any.

Save the file and then click the Ant tab below the editors to switch back to the Ant view. Double-click the deploy target to rebuild and redeploy the application.

If you didn't stop the JBoss server, you may notice that the Console view switches back to the JBoss server console after a few moments. JBoss is able to detect applications that have been updated and then reload them on the fly. This means you don't have to stop and restart JBoss to deploy changes to your application. If you had previously stopped JBoss, restart it by switching to the Servers view and then clicking the Start the Server button.

Open your Web browser and then type the same URL you used previously: **http://localhost:8080/ helloworld/hello-world.htm**. Instead of the "Hello, World!" message, you see a message stating, "I don't know what language you speak!" Now change the URL by adding **?lang=spanish** to the end and then press Enter. The part of the URL after the question mark is called the *query string*. The query string is one way of passing parameters to the server. The application now greets you in Spanish, as shown in Figure 6.41.

FIGURE 6.41

The application is now able to display a dynamic message based on the `lang` parameter of the query string.

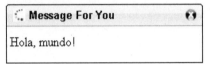

Summary

In this chapter, you wrote, built, deployed, and ran a complete Java Web application by using the Spring Framework's Web MVC module. First, you learned the basics of the Model-View-Controller architectural pattern. The model refers to the data and business logic of the application. The view is the user interface in which the model data is displayed. The controller is the service code that handles requests from the clients, gathers data from the model, and packages it up to be displayed in the view. Next, you learned about the Spring Framework and the various modules and functionality it provides. After that, you set up a Spring project in Eclipse and then configured it for writing a Spring Web MVC application. Finally, you wrote a simple Web application by using Spring Web MVC, built and deployed the application with an Ant build file, and added the ability to accept query string parameters to enhance the application.

Although the application in this chapter is rudimentary, the concepts, code, and configuration files used here are a good starting point for any Web application. Most Web applications include the same basic building blocks that make up this application and add to them or build upon them as needed. With these basics in hand, you can move on to building larger and more complex Web applications.

Chapter 7

Using JUnit and FlexUnit to Test Your Applications

As you begin to develop an application, you need to make sure that everything within the application is working properly before getting in too deep. For a small project, you can trace some commands to the Output panel and then check the results, but that approach simply doesn't work for larger-scale applications.

In this chapter, you look at unit testing tools for Java and Flex. These tools give you the ability to examine elements of a larger application and ensure that your code is well-built.

Primarily, you look at JUnit for Java and FlexUnit for Flex because they're the standard testing kits for their respective programming languages.

Working with JUnit

JUnit is a unit testing library for Java applications and is written in Java itself. It supports the creation of individual test cases and the grouping of those test cases into a test suite that can run all the unit tests together.

The *unit* in unit testing is meant to refer to the smallest possible testable piece of code. In the Java world, this typically means a single method in a class. Some methods, such as those whose only function is to set and retrieve properties of a Java bean class (getter and setter methods), are considered too simple to break and are typically not tested. Any method that does more than that should be tested.

CROSS-REF For more on Java bean classes and getter and setter methods, see Chapter 9.

Importing the testing library

Eclipse has built-in support for creating and running JUnit tests. This makes it easy to write tests and then run them as you develop your applications. Because of this built-in support, there's nothing you need to download or install to run JUnit tests with Eclipse.

CROSS-REF   For more on installing and configuring Eclipse, see Chapter 1.

As an example of a class you would want to test, consider the case of a transfer between two different bank accounts. A bank account has, among other things, an account number and a balance. To transfer funds from one account to the other, the funds must be debited from one account (provided that the amount to be transferred doesn't exceed the balance!) and credited to the other. Testing this functionality is prudent because if something goes wrong, someone might end up with more or less money than he or she should have.

If it's not currently running, launch Eclipse by navigating to your Eclipse install directory and double-clicking `eclipse.exe`. First, you create a project and Java classes to represent a bank account and a system for processing a transfer. After that, you import the JUnit libraries into the project so that you can create some unit tests for the bank account transfer code.

To create the project and the two Java classes, follow these steps:

1. **Right-click inside the Project Explorer view and then choose New ⇨ Project from the popup menu.** The Select a wizard dialog box, as shown in Figure 7.1, opens.

FIGURE 7.1

The Select a wizard dialog box allows you to choose a project type.

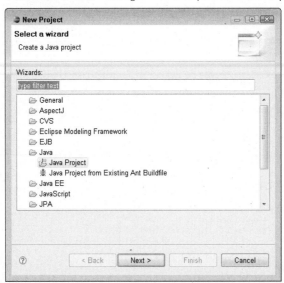

2. **Click the arrow next to Java to expand it, select Java Project, and then click Next.** The Create a Java Project wizard, as shown in Figure 7.2, opens.

3. **Type a name for your project and then click Finish.** The wizard closes, and the new project appears in the Project Explorer view, as shown in Figure 7.3.

4. **Right-click the `src` folder under the new project in the Project Explorer view and then choose New ⇨ Package from the popup menu.** The New Java Package dialog box, as shown in Figure 7.4, opens.

5. **Type com.wiley.jfib.ch07 for the package name and then click Finish.** The default value for the Source folder text field is appropriate. The new package appears in the `src` folder under the project, as shown in Figure 7.5.

FIGURE 7.2

The Create a Java Project wizard

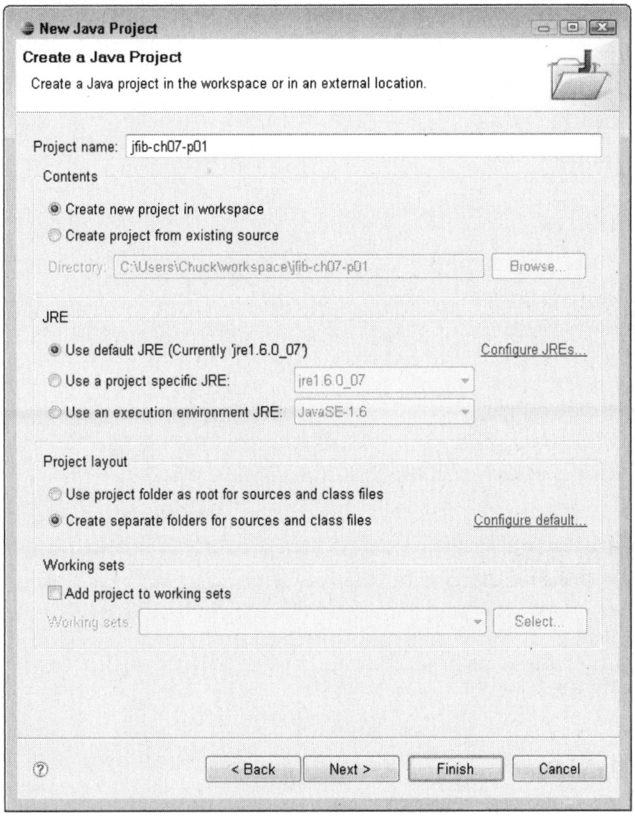

FIGURE 7.3

The newly created project appears in the Project Explorer view once the wizard is complete.

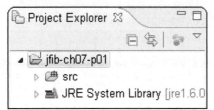

FIGURE 7.4

The New Java Package dialog box

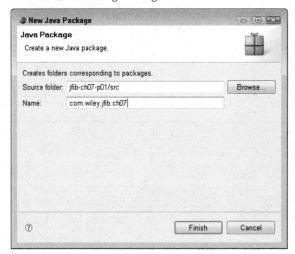

FIGURE 7.5

The newly created package appears in the src folder under the project in the Project Explorer view.

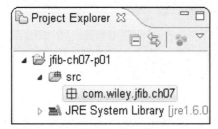

6. **Right-click the** `com.wiley.jfib.ch07` **package in the Project Explorer view and then choose New ⇨ Class from the popup menu.** The New Java Class dialog box, as shown in Figure 7.6, opens.

FIGURE 7.6

The New Java Class dialog box

7. **Type** Account **in the Name text field, click the Generate comments box, and then click Finish.** The new Java class is created and opens in the editor, as shown in Figure 7.7.

8. **Right-click the** `com.wiley.jfib.ch07` **package in the Project Explorer view and then choose New ⇨ Class from the popup menu.** The New Java Class dialog box opens.

9. **Type** AccountManager **in the Name text field, click the Generate comments box, and then click Finish.** The new Java class is created and opens in the editor.

The newly created Java class opens in the editor.

```
Account.java ⊠
  1⊕/**☐
  4 package com.wiley.jfib.ch07;
  5
  6⊖/**
  7  * @author Chuck
  8  *
  9  */
 10 public class Account {
 11
 12 }
 13
```

Edit the `Account` class to match this code listing:

```java
/**
 *
 */
package com.wiley.jfib.ch07;

/**
 * @author Chuck
 * The Account class represents a simple bank account
 */
public class Account
{
    private long accountNumber;
    private double balance;

    /**
     * Constructor
     * @param accountNumber
     * @param balance
     */
    public Account(long accountNumber, double balance)
    {
        this.accountNumber = accountNumber;
        this.balance = balance;
    }

    /**
     * Withdraw an amount from the account
     * @param amount the amount to withdraw
     * @return the balance after the withdrawal
     * @throws Exception if the available balance is less than
```

```
        * the attempted withdrawal.
        */
       public double debit(double amount) throws Exception
       {
          if(amount > balance)
             throw new Exception(
                     "Not enough available funds to withdraw $" + amount
                     + " from account #" + accountNumber
                     + ". Current balance: $" + balance);
          balance -= amount;
          return balance;
       }

       /**
        * Deposit an amount into the account
        * @param amount the amount to deposit
        * @return the balance after the deposit
        */
       public double credit(double amount)
       {
             balance += amount;
             return balance;
       }

       /**
        * Get the account number
        * @return the account number
        */
       public long getAccountNumber()
       {
             return accountNumber;
       }

       /**
        * Get the balance
        * @return the balance
        */
       public double getBalance()
       {
             return this.balance;
       }
   }
```

The `Account` class contains properties for account number and balance, methods to retrieve those properties, and methods to debit and credit the account. The `getAccountNumber()` and `get Balance()` methods do nothing but retrieve variables, which puts them into the too-simple-to-test category. However, the `debit()` and `credit()` methods also perform mathematical operations. Furthermore, the `debit()` method throws an exception if an attempt is made to withdraw too much money. That makes the `debit()` and `credit()` methods candidates for testing.

Now edit the `AccountManager` class to match this code listing:

```java
/**
 *
 */
package com.wiley.jfib.ch07;

/**
 * @author Chuck
 * The AccountManager class represents a system for handling transfers
 * between accounts.
 */
public class AccountManager
{
    /**
     * Transfer money from one account to another
     * @param fromAccount the account to transfer money from
     * @param toAccount the account to transfer money to
     * @param amount the amount to transfer
     */
    public void transfer(Account fromAccount, Account toAccount,
        double amount) throws Exception
    {
        System.out.println("Starting Balances:");
        System.out.println("From Account #"
            + fromAccount.getAccountNumber()
            + ": $" + fromAccount.getBalance());
        System.out.println("To Account #"
            + fromAccount.getAccountNumber()
            + ": $" + toAccount.getBalance());
        System.out.println("-------------------------------------"
            );
        fromAccount.debit(amount);
        toAccount.debit(amount);
        System.out.println("Ending Balances:");
        System.out.println("From Account #"
            + fromAccount.getAccountNumber()
            + ": $" + fromAccount.getBalance());
        System.out.println("To Account #"
    + fromAccount.getAccountNumber()
    + ": $" + toAccount.getBalance());
    }
}
```

The `AccountManager` class has a single method called `transfer()`. It takes two `Account` objects and an amount of money to transfer money from the first account to the second. It prints out the balances of each account before and after the transfer, something like a receipt for the person initiating the transfer. The `transfer()` method clearly does much more than simply set or return a value, so it's also a candidate for testing.

With the code in place, you can test it. First, you need to add the JUnit testing library to the project's build path. To add JUnit to the project's build path, follow these steps:

1. **Right-click the project in the Project Explorer view and then choose Build Path ⇨ Configure Build Path from the popup menu.** The Properties dialog box opens with the Java Build Path's Libraries tab selected, as shown in Figure 7.8.

FIGURE 7.8

The Properties dialog box with the Libraries tab selected

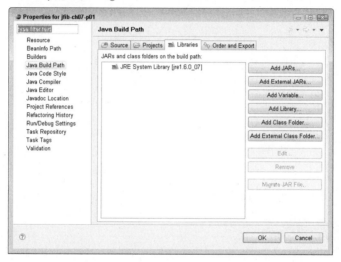

2. **Click Add Library.** The Add Library wizard, as shown in Figure 7.9, opens. This wizard allows you to add a number of libraries bundled with Eclipse, including JUnit, to your projects.

3. **Click JUnit in the Add Library list box and then click Next.** The JUnit Library screen, as shown in Figure 7.10, opens.

4. **Choose JUnit 4 from the JUnit library version dropdown list and then click Finish.** The Add Library wizard closes, and the JUnit 4 library is added to the Libraries tab of the Properties dialog box, as shown in Figure 7.11.

5. **Click OK.** The Properties dialog box closes, and the JUnit 4 library appears in the Project Explorer view, as shown in Figure 7.12.

FIGURE 7.9

The Add Library wizard

FIGURE 7.10

The JUnit Library screen

The JUnit 4 library appears in the Libraries tab once the Add Library wizard closes.

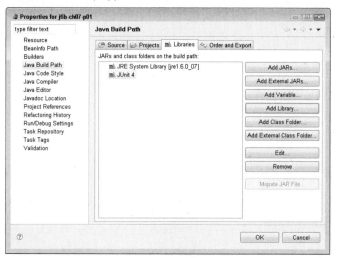

The JUnit 4 library in the Project Explorer view

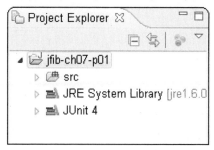

Building the testing suite

With JUnit 4 added to the project, you can begin writing tests. An examination of the methods in each class determines that the following methods need to be tested:

- The debit() and credit() methods in the Account class
- The transfer() method in the AccountManager class

One important thing to remember when writing unit tests is that you should strive to test all possible scenarios. For the credit() method, only one scenario exists: The deposit is either correctly added or not added to the balance. For the debit() method, there are multiple scenarios.

First, the withdrawal can either be correctly deducted or not deducted from the balance. Second, the method can throw an exception if the withdrawal amount is more than the balance. Both of these cases need to be tested. Similarly, the transfer method can correctly perform the transfer or not perform the transfer at all, but it can also throw an exception. Again, both of these scenarios must be tested.

When writing JUnit tests, it's customary to keep all the tests that test methods of the same class in a single JUnit test case. A *test case* in JUnit is a Java class containing one or more unit tests plus any configuration required for the tests. To test this balance transfer system, you need two test cases: one for the `Account` class and one for the `AccountManager` class.

To create the test case for the `Account` class, follow these steps:

1. **Right-click the `Account` class in the Project Explorer and then choose New ⇨ Other from the popup menu.** The Select a wizard dialog box, as shown in Figure 7.13, opens.

FIGURE 7.13

The Select a wizard dialog box

2. **Click the arrow next to Java to expand it.**
3. **Click the arrow next to the JUnit item below Java to expand it, select JUnit Test Case, and then click Next.** The New JUnit Test Case wizard, as shown in Figure 7.14, opens.

4. **Click the setUp() and tearDown() check boxes and then click Next.** The Test Methods screen, as shown in Figure 7.15, appears.

5. **Click the check boxes next to** `debit(double)` **and** `credit(double)` **and then click Finish.** The New JUnit Test Case wizard closes, and the new test case opens in the editor, as shown in Figure 7.16.

FIGURE 7.14

The New JUnit Test Case wizard

The test case that Eclipse generates for you contains methods named `testCredit()` and `testDebit()`, marked with the `@Test` annotation. An *annotation* in a Java class is a special piece of metadata that provides additional information about a method or class. In this case, the `@Test` annotation is recognized by JUnit to mean that the method contains a unit test for JUnit to run. The `testCredit()` and `testDebit()` methods are where you implement the unit tests for the `credit()` and `debit()` methods of the `Account` class. Eclipse adds only one unit test method per `Account` class method. Remember that the `debit()` method has two scenarios you want to test. Add the following method to the test case:

FIGURE 7.15

The Test Methods screen

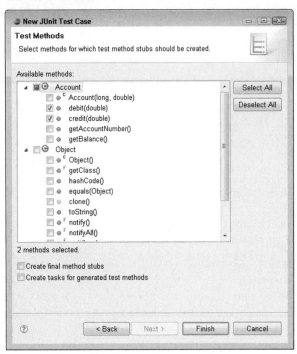

```
@Test
public void testDebitWithAmountGreaterThanBalance() {
    fail("Not yet implemented");
}
```

The name of the method is long, but it does an adequate job of describing what the test is supposed to assess.

The setUp() and tearDown() methods are marked with the @Before and @After annotations, respectively. The setUp() method is run before each unit test method is run. The tearDown() method is run after each unit test method is run. These methods can be used to set data used by the tests in the test case to a known state before each test is run.

When Eclipse generates a JUnit test case, each unit test method contains the line fail("Not yet implemented") by default. The fail() method is provided by the import static org.junit.Assert.* import statement and, as you might expect, causes the unit test to fail. Having your tests fail by default is a good strategy for testing because it ensures that you remember to implement every test. Any test that you forget to implement in a unit test method would fail, and you would notice immediately.

FIGURE 7.16

The new JUnit test case open in the editor

```
 1  package com.wiley.jfib.ch07;
 2
 3⊕ import static org.junit.Assert.*;□
 8
 9  public class AccountTest {
10
11⊖     @Before
12      public void setUp() throws Exception {
13      }
14
15⊖     @After
16      public void tearDown() throws Exception {
17      }
18
19⊖     @Test
20      public void testDebit() {
21          fail("Not yet implemented");
22      }
23
24⊖     @Test
25      public void testCredit() {
26          fail("Not yet implemented");
27      }
28
29  }
```

To run these unit tests and see them fail, you can right-click the `AccountTest` class in the Project Explorer and then choose Run As➪JUnit Test from the popup menu. The JUnit view opens, and you see the three unit tests that were run, along with a status bar with the results, as shown in Figure 7.17. The red bar on the status bar indicates that one or more of the unit tests that were run failed. You can click the name of each unit test method in the JUnit view to see the reason for the failure.

Now that you've seen the unit tests run and fail, you can start implementing them and getting them to pass. First, it's helpful to have a consistent set of data to use in each test. Add the following lines of code to the `AccountTest` class just before the `setUp()` method:

```
private final double startingBalance = 100.00;

private final double creditAmount = 20.00;
private final double postCreditBalance = 120.00;
```

```
private final double debitAmount = 20.00;
private final double postDebitBalance = 80.00;
private final double debitAmountGreaterThanBalance = 200.00;

private final long accountNumber = 123456789;

private Account account;
```

The JUnit view shows you the results of the unit tests that were run. Here, three unit tests were run, and they all failed. When Eclipse generates a JUnit test case, it sets up the unit test methods to fail by default.

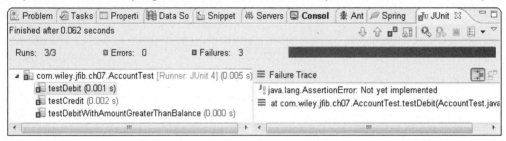

These variables set up some known amounts to work with. The starting balance of the account is 100.00. The test is working with a credit amount of 20.00, which should result in a post-credit amount of 120.00. The debit that's expected to work is also 20.00, which should result in a post-debit balance of 80.00. Finally, a test is run with an attempted debit of 200.00, which should throw an exception. All these variables, along with a made-up account number, are marked `final`, meaning that their values can't be modified. This ensures that the values are well-known throughout testing. An `Account` object is also set up to be used by all the unit tests.

Because the `Account` object is going to be used by all three tests, you need to reset it to its original state before each test is run. Edit the `setUp()` method so that it matches this code listing:

```
@Before
public void setUp() throws Exception {
    // start with a clean account with a $100.00 balance every time
    account = new Account(accountNumber, startingBalance);
}
```

The `setUp()` method runs before every test, which means that every test can safely assume that it's using an `Account` object with a starting balance of 100.00.

Now implement the `testCredit()` method. Edit the method so that it matches this code listing:

```
@Test
public void testCredit() {
    double newBalance = account.credit(creditAmount);
    assertEquals(postCreditBalance, newBalance);
}
```

This unit test is straightforward. Using the account that was initialized in the `setUp()` method to have a balance of 100.00, credit the account with the value of `creditAmount` (20.00). If the `credit()` method works correctly, this should return a new balance of 120.00, which is the value of `postCreditBalance`. Now the test asserts that the value that was expected (`postCredit Balance`) is equal to the actual value (`newBalance`). The expected value is always the first one in the `assertEquals()` method. If the two values are equal, the test passes. If not, it fails.

Save the test case and then run it again. You should still see the red bar because the other two tests still fail, but the failure count in the status bar is now two instead of three. Also, notice the green check mark next to the `testCredit()` method in the list of unit test methods. That indicates that the test passed and that the `credit()` method you tested works as expected.

Next, implement the `testDebit()` method. It should match this code listing when you're finished:

```
@Test
public void testDebit() {
    try
    {
        double newBalance = account.debit(debitAmount);
        assertEquals(postDebitBalance, newBalance);
    }
    catch(Exception e)
    {
        fail("Unexpected Exception encountered: " +
    e.getMessage());
    }
}
```

The test for `debit()` requires a little extra code. Because the `debit()` method throws an exception if the balance is less than the debit amount, that exception must be handled by the code. Because this test uses well-known values, it can assume that it should never encounter this exception. If it does, the test should fail because the `debit` method isn't working properly. If the `debit()` method runs as expected, then the `try` block completes as expected, and the `assertEquals()` statement determines whether the test passes.

Finally, implement the `testDebitWithAmountGreaterThanBalance()` method. It should match this code listing when you're finished:

```
@Test(expected = Exception.class)
public void testDebitWithAmountGreaterThanBalance() throws Exception
{
    double newBalance = account.debit(debitAmountGreaterThanBalance);
}
```

The big change here is that the annotation has changed from simply `@Test` to `@Test(expected = Exception.class)`. This addition to the annotation tells JUnit that this method expects an exception to be thrown. If it's not, the test fails. The method also adds a `throws Exception` clause. This eliminates the need for a try/catch block; you don't want a try/catch block here because you expect the exception to be thrown.

Save and run the test case again. This time, with all three tests passing, the colored bar on the status bar turns green, and there are no failures, as shown in Figure 7.18, indicating that all tests in this test case have run successfully.

FIGURE 7.18

When all the unit tests in a test case run successfully, the status bar changes from red to green.

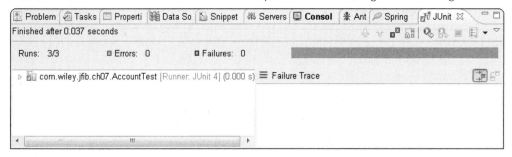

Now create the test case for the `AccountManager` class. To create the test case, follow these steps:

1. **Right-click the `AccountManager` class in the Project Explorer and then choose New ⇨ Other from the popup menu.** The Select a wizard dialog box opens.

2. **Click the arrow next to Java to expand it.**

3. **Click the arrow next to the JUnit item below Java to expand it, select JUnit Test Case, and then click Next.** The New JUnit Test Case wizard appears.

4. **Click Next.** The Test Methods screen, as shown in Figure 7.19, appears.

5. **Click the check box next to `transfer(Account, Account, double)` and then click Finish.** The New JUnit Test Case wizard closes, and the new test case opens in the editor.

FIGURE 7.19

The Test Methods screen

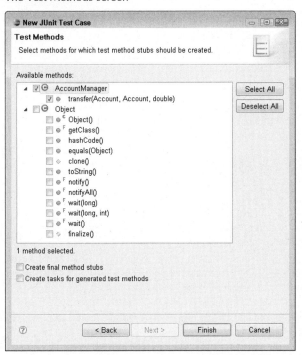

This test case is set up similarly to the one for `Account`. You add another unit test method to test for the case when an exception is expected, add some known values to use in the tests, and then initialize those objects in the `setUp()` method. Edit the `AccountManagerTest` class so that it matches this code listing:

```
package com.wiley.jfib.ch07;

import static org.junit.Assert.*;

import org.junit.After;
import org.junit.Before;
import org.junit.Test;

public class AccountManagerTest {
    private final long fromAccountNumber = 123456789;
    private final double fromAccountOriginalBalance = 100.00;
    private final long toAccountNumber = 987654321;
    private final double toAccountOriginalBalance = 100.00;
    private final double transferAmount = 20.00;
    private final double fromAccountNewBalance = 80.00;
```

```java
    private final double toAccountNewBalance = 120.00;
    private final double tooLargeAmount = 200.00;

    private AccountManager accountManager;
    private Account fromAccount;
    private Account toAccount;

    @Before
    public void setUp() throws Exception {
        accountManager = new AccountManager();
        fromAccount = new Account(fromAccountNumber,
fromAccountOriginalBalance);
        toAccount = new Account(toAccountNumber,
toAccountOriginalBalance);
    }

    @After
    public void tearDown() throws Exception {
    }

    @Test
    public void testTransfer() {
        try
        {
            accountManager.transfer(fromAccount, toAccount,
transferAmount);
            assertEquals(fromAccountNewBalance,
fromAccount.getBalance());
            assertEquals(toAccountNewBalance,
toAccount.getBalance());
        }
        catch(Exception e)
        {
            fail("Unexpected Exception encountered: " +
e.getMessage());
        }
    }

    @Test(expected = Exception.class)
    public void testTransferWithAmountGreaterThanFromBalance() throws
Exception
    {
        accountManager.transfer(fromAccount, toAccount,
tooLargeAmount);
    }

}
```

Save this test case and then run it. Because the `AccountManager` class outputs some information, the Console view opens to show that output, as shown in Figure 7.20. Click the JUnit tab to switch back to the JUnit view. You see that the second test passed, but the first test failed. Click `testTransfer()` in the JUnit view. An error message appears below the red failure bar on the right that says `java.lang.AssertionError: expected:<120.0> but was:<80.0>`. If you study the output, you may notice why the test has failed: After the transfer, both accounts have $20.00 less than before. The account the money was being transferred to should have $120.00, but it seems that both accounts were debited by mistake.

FIGURE 7.20

When the `AccountManagerTest` class invokes the transfer method on the `AccountManager` class, Eclipse switches to the Console view to display the method's output.

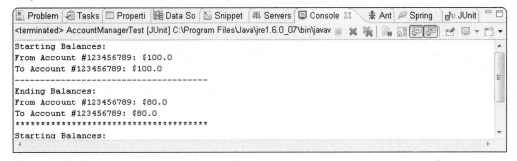

The mistake is in this line in the `AccountManager` class:

```
toAccount.debit(amount);
```

Change this line so that the `toAccount` is credited, not debited:

```
toAccount.credit(amount);
```

Save `AccountManager` and then run the `AccountManagerTest` test case again. This time, both tests pass.

To run all the tests at the same time, you can create a class that acts as a test suite. A *test suite* is a JUnit class that contains annotations that mark it as a test suite and tell JUnit which tests to run when the suite is run.

To create a test suite for the two test cases, follow these steps:

1. **Right-click the `com.wiley.jfib.ch07` package in the Project Explorer view and then choose New ⇨ Class from the popup menu.** The New Java Class dialog box opens.

2. **Type AccountTestSuite in the Name text field and then click Finish.** The new Java class is created and opens in the editor.

Now edit the `AccountTestSuite` class so that it matches this code listing:

```
package com.wiley.jfib.ch07;

import org.junit.runner.RunWith;
import org.junit.runners.Suite;

@RunWith(Suite.class)
@Suite.SuiteClasses({
  AccountTest.class,
  AccountManagerTest.class
})

public class AccountTestSuite {

}
```

The `AccountTestSuite` class contains no methods itself. It's simply a place to hold a couple of JUnit annotations. The `@RunWith` annotation tells JUnit that this class is for use by its `Suite` class. The `@Suite.SuiteClasses` annotation provides a list of all the test cases that should be run with this test suite. In this case, the `AccountTest` test case runs first, followed by the `AccountManagerTest`.

Save this class and then run it just like you run a regular JUnit test: Right-click the `AccountTestSuite` class and then choose Run As ⇨ JUnit Test from the popup menu. Eclipse switches to the Console view again to display the output of the `AccountManager` class. Click the JUnit tab to return to the JUnit view. You should see the green success bar. Notice that the Runs field in the status bar now says 5/5. The test suite ran the three tests in the `AccountTest` test case and the two tests in the `AccountManagerTest` test case, and all ran successfully in one suite.

Working with FlexUnit

In this section, you learn how to integrate and work with FlexUnit alongside your Flex development.

FlexUnit is an open-source framework created by Adobe for unit testing in Adobe Flex. This framework is based on JUnit, the popular Java unit testing framework.

FlexUnit allows you to develop an automated testing kit to easily debug advanced applications that have been developed in Flex. As you begin developing larger applications, you realize the need for more robust testing systems. Let's take a look at how FlexUnit can help you.

Using unit testing

A *unit test* is a portion of code that's meant to test the smallest piece of a class or package. A *unit* is this small piece of code — usually, a function or method.

You find unit testing in many of the popular programming languages because it allows developers to test their code without waiting until the entire application is developed. This is achieved by testing individual units of an application.

When a developer uses a unit test, the smallest portion of the project is tested. This is called *low-level* testing. It allows the developer to easily ensure that an application is functioning properly without a lot of setup and checking required.

Configuring FlexUnit

Now that you know what FlexUnit is and how it can help you, let's look at how to configure it to be used in your development process.

There are four steps to building a unit test:

1. **Download and add FlexUnit to your library.**
2. **Create the classes that are the unit tests.**
3. **Create a testing suite, which is a package of the required tests.**
4. **Create a test runner, which is the application to execute the tests.**

The first step is to download the FlexUnit framework from Adobe's open-source Web site. Adobe has created a very robust library of open-source tools and frameworks. Two of these tools covered in this book are BlazeDS and FlexUnit.

 For more on BlazeDS, see Chapter 11.

Downloading the FlexUnit framework

Go to `http://opensource.adobe.com/wiki/display/flexunit/Downloads` to download version 0.9 of the FlexUnit framework, as shown in Figure 7.21. Once the file is downloaded, locate it to unzip the archive to reveal the FlexUnit framework files.

 The FlexUnit framework is constantly being updated by Adobe and other developers. This section has been written using version 0.9 of the framework.

Adding the FlexUnit framework to a Flex project

Now that you have the FlexUnit framework downloaded, you need to add `flexunit.swc`, which is located in the `bin/` directory, to the `libs/` directory of your Flex project. This allows Flex to use the framework that's located within the SWC file.

FIGURE 7.21

The FlexUnit Web site displayed in a browser

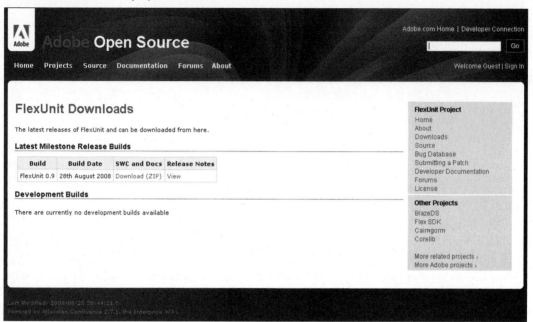

Flex 3 has made the process of adding new libraries a lot easier with the addition of the `libs/` directory to every new project. This also ensures that other developers on your team have all the necessary files.

You can drag the SWC file into the `libs/` directory, located in Flex, or you can locate the project directory on your machine to add the SWC file to that.

> **TIP** You can find the location of a project in Flex by right-clicking the project in the Project Navigator and then choosing Properties from the popup menu.

Developing the unit test

Once the framework is added to your project, you're ready to start building the unit test. However, before you start developing the unit test, let's take a look at the class the test will work with.

The sample class is named `School` and contains methods to manage students and then return the current total of students in the `School`. Create the class by right-clicking the `src/` directory of the project in Flex (see Figure 7.22), choose New ➪ ActionScript Class from the popup menu, and then name the class `School`.

FIGURE 7.22

Add a new class to the existing project by right-clicking the `src/` directory.

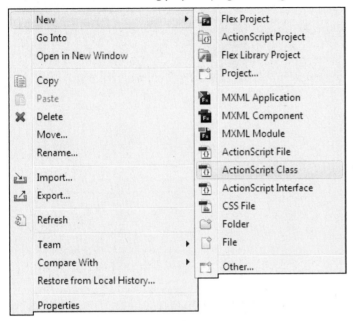

Here's the code for the `School` class:

```
Package com.example
{
    public class School
    {

        private var _students:Array;

        public function School()
        {
            _students = ['Tim', 'Susan', 'Nicole', 'Alex'];
        }

        public function addStudent(name:String):void
        {
            _students.push(name); // Add new student
        }

        public function removeStudent():void
        {
```

```
                _students.pop(); // Remove last student added
        }

        public function getStudents():Array
        {
                return _students;
        }

    }
}
```

Working with the unit test

Now that the sample class is written, the next step is developing the unit test class. The method names of the testing class need to start with `test` in order for the FlexUnit framework to automatically run the methods. If any of the methods in the unit test class don't begin with `test`, those methods aren't run. This is a quick way to hide a method from the testing suite without actually removing it from the unit test class.

A unit test is made up of assertions, which determine the result of the test. If an assertion is true, the test passes; if it's false, the test fails. FlexUnit offers various assertions depending on the test you need to perform. Table 7.1 shows the assertions that are available in FlexUnit.

TABLE 7.1

Assertion Methods Available in FlexUnit

assertEquals	Asserts that two values are equal
assertContained	Asserts that the first string is contained in the second one
assertFalse	Asserts that a condition is false
assertMatch	Asserts that a string matches a regexp
assertNoMatch	Asserts that a string doesn't match a regexp
assertNotContained	Asserts that the first string isn't contained in the second one
assertNotContained	Asserts that two objects are strictly identical
assertNotNull	Asserts that an object isn't null
assertNotUndefined	Asserts that an object isn't undefined
assertNull	Asserts that an object is null
assertTrue	Asserts that a condition is true
assertUndefined	Asserts that an object is undefined

The next step is to develop the test class. The complexity of this class is based on the amount of tests you need to run. In this example, you have only two tests. The first test is to add a student to the list of students, and the second test is to remove that student. You should have success as a result on both of these tests.

If you don't have success on both of the tests, you will know which method has a problem because the FlexUnit test tool displays the failed class/method name.

Create the class by right-clicking the `src/` directory of the project in Flex and then choosing New⇨ActionScript Class from the popup menu. Name the class `SchoolTest`.

This code is the example package to be used in this lesson:

```
package
{
    import flexunit.framework.TestCase;

    public class SchoolTest extends TestCase
    {
        .
        .
        .
    }
}
```

The first method adds a student to the list of students and then checks to see whether the total number of students has increased properly:

```
package
{
    import flexunit.framework.TestCase;

    public class SchoolTest extends TestCase
    {
        public function testAddStudent():void
        {
            var school:School = new School();
            school.addStudent('Julie');
            assertTrue("Student total should be 7",
                school.getStudents().length == 7);
        }
        .
        .
        .
    }
}
```

The second method is testing that when a student is removed from the list of students, the total is modified properly. This is achieved by accessing the `students` array and then removing the last entry in the array. If you've recently added a student, the total is different from the example:

```
package
{
    import flexunit.framework.TestCase;

    public class SchoolTest extends TestCase
    {
        public function testAddStudent():void
        {
            var school:School = new School();
            school.addStudent('Julie');
            assertEquals("Student total should be 5", 5,
                school.getStudents().length);
        }

        public function testRemoveStudent():void
        {
            var school:School = new School();
            school.removeStudent();
            assertEquals("Children count after remove should be 3",
                3, school.getStudents().length );
        }
    }
}
```

That's the completed testing class. Now that you have completed the test, the next step is developing the test suite. You can develop the test suite entirely in ActionScript or by using MXML. For this example, you develop it in MXML (Flex) to better understand how everything goes together.

Creating the testing suite

The FlexUnit framework ships with a few visual components that make testing a lot easier. One of these components is the `TestRunnerBase`, shown in Figure 7.23. In order to use the components, you need to ensure that the FlexUnit namespace is required. This is added to the `Application` tag at the top of the file:

```
<mx:Application ... xmlns="*" xmlns:flexunit="flexunit.flexui.*">
```

The next step is adding an event listener to the `Application` tag, which is called once the application has fully loaded. This event calls a method that's responsible for initializing the testing suite:

```
<mx:Application ... creationComplete="init()">
```

Now that the event is set up properly, let's add the visual component, which displays the results of the unit test. This component has been provided by the `flexunit` library. The component is set to take up the entire screen by setting the `width` and `height` properties. You could, of course, modify this if you want to place the test runner in your existing project:

```
<flexunit:TestRunnerBase id="test" width="100%" height="100%" />
```

That completes the visual portion of this application; the next portion is the code used to actually make the tests work. This example uses embedded ActionScript, but you could, of course, write it entirely in ActionScript if you preferred.

Start by importing the necessary classes. In this case, these are the `TestSuite` class provided by the FlexUnit framework and the `SchoolTest` that you developed earlier in this chapter:

```
<mx:Script>
    <![CDATA[
        import flexunit.framework.TestSuite;
    ]]>
</mx:Script>
```

FIGURE 7.23

The FlexUnit Runner application displayed in Flex

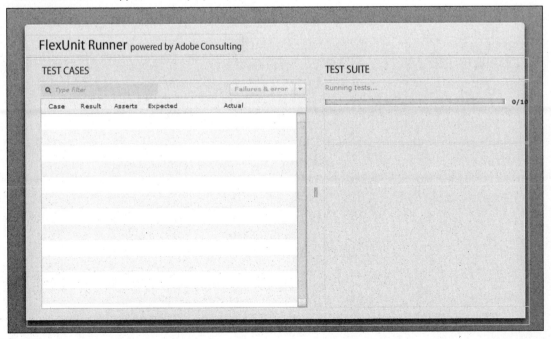

Once you have the classes and packages imported, the next step is creating the initialization method that's called by the event you added before. This method makes a call to the `initSuite()` method and assigns the result to the `test` property of the `TestRunner`. Then, once the new test suite is created, a call to `startTest()` is made to start the test:

```
<mx:Script>
    <![CDATA[
        import flexunit.framework.TestSuite;

        private function init():void
        {
            test.test = initSuite();
            test.startTest();
        }
    ]]>
</mx:Script>
```

In the previous method, you added a reference to a new method, `initSuite()`. This method is responsible for creating the testing suite based on the `SchoolTest` class. The testing suite is built dynamically by going through the `SchoolTest` class and looking for the methods that are assigned with the prefix `test`. The result of the `initSuite()` method is returned to the caller for reference:

```
<mx:Script>
    <![CDATA[

        import flexunit.framework.TestSuite;


        private function init():void
        {
            test.test = initSuite();
            test.startTest();
        }

        private function initSuite():TestSuite
        {
            var suite:TestSuite = new TestSuite();
            suite.addTestSuite(SchoolTest);

            return suite;
        }

    ]]>
</mx:Script>
```

That's the complete test runner application. You can test it by clicking the Debug icon in the tool-bar of Flex or by choosing Run ➪ Debug ➪ SchoolApp (substituting SchoolApp for the name of your application).

The application should open in your default browser with the unit test running, as shown in Figure 7.24. It's running automatically because the init() method was assigned to the creationComplete event, which is called automatically once the application has fully loaded and initialized.

FIGURE 7.24

Displaying the FlexUnit Runner application in the browser, with the results of a previously completed test

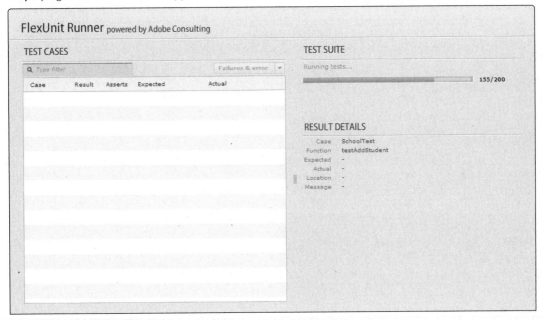

Working with the FlexUnit Runner

The FlexUnit Runner GUI is provided by Adobe as part of the FlexUnit framework. This tool allows you to quickly and visually see how your tests performed. Because this example is such a small application, by the time the GUI has loaded, the test has already been completed.

In a more advanced application, you would see the test running live. When the tests are running, the right panel displays a progress bar indicating how long it will be before the tests are complete.

Filtering results

The FlexUnit Runner allows you to search within the test results, which comes in handy if you have a long list of tests running.

Simply start typing in the search box, and the FlexUnit Runner automatically begins filtering the results. If you want to revert to the original list of tests, click the Close button that appears to the right of the search box.

The dropdown list to the far right of the search box is used to switch the view that's being displayed. The options contained in the dropdown list are:

- **All Results.** Display all the tests, whether they passed or failed
- **Empty Results.** Display only results that contained no data
- **Failures and Errors.** Display only results that failed or contained some type of error

You can simulate a long test by placing your testing code in a large loop.

 This is processor-intensive, but for demonstration purposes, it's fine.

Modify the `initSuite()` method to include a `for` loop that runs 100 times. On each pass through the loop, the `addTestSuite()` method is called. This creates a new test each time:

```
private function initSuite():TestSuite
{
    var suite:TestSuite = new TestSuite();

    for(var i:uint=0; i < 100; i++)
    {
        suite.addTestSuite(SchoolTest);
    }

    return suite;
}
```

Now when you run the test again, you have a chance to see the progress bar and the list of tests become populated. Once the tests are completed, the progress bar disappears, and the results are displayed, as shown in Figure 7.25.

 The previous code listing is for demonstration purposes only. It's not a good idea to place a test within a loop unless the application requires that type of testing.

You can now type various search terms to see the list update immediately based on what you type.

Gathering more specific information

The FlexUnit Runner provides information specific to each test. If you expand the test category and then choose one of the test names, the results displayed to the right now display specific information for that test, as shown in Figure 7.26.

Each test has a message assigned to it in the class you developed. This message is displayed when you drill down into the individual test.

The results of the previous test

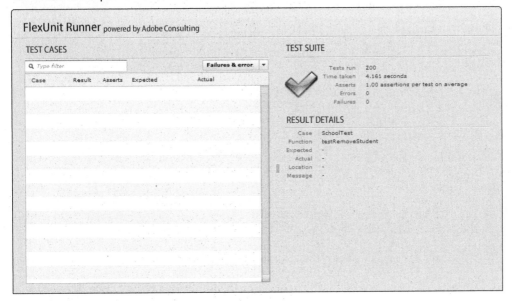

Specific information for each test

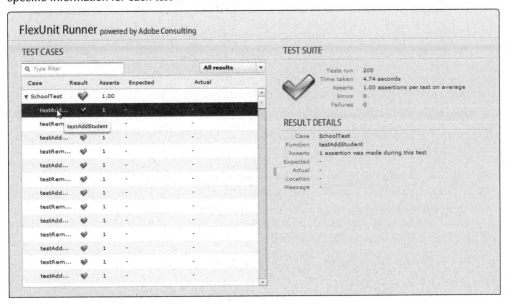

Forcing an error in the test

Sometimes during development, you may want to force a test to fail to ensure that your code handles it properly. You can do this by modifying the test case code to fail. One way to cause the test to fail is to modify the assertion test. For example, changing the addStudent() method to something like the following always creates an error because 1==2 will never be true:

```
public function testAddStudent():void
{
    var school:School = new School();
    school.addStudent('Julie');
    fail("Automatically Fail");
}
```

When you run the test suite once again, it fails instantly. However, the loop you placed in the previous section forces the tests to continue. At this point, you can remove that loop, as it's not needed anymore.

The FlexUnit Runner application displays the stack trace of the last error. This is a formatted trace that shows where the application failed and where it was called from.

Here's an example of a stack trace output:

```
    .
    .
    .

SchoolTest/testAddStudent()[/Library/WebServer/Documents/clients/
    Book/Java-Flex-Bible/source_code/ch07/src/SchoolTest.as:17]
  at SchoolApp/___SchoolApp_Application1_creationComplete() [/Library/
    WebServer/Documents/clients/Book/Java-Flex-Bible/source_code/
    ch07/src/SchoolApp.mxml:4]
  at flash.events::EventDispatcher/dispatchEventFunction()
  at flash.events::EventDispatcher/dispatchEvent()
  at mx.core::UIComponent/dispatchEvent()[E:\dev\3.0.x\frameworks\
    projects\framework\src\mx\core\UIComponent.as:9051]
  at mx.core::UIComponent/set initialized()[E:\dev\3.0.x\frameworks\
    projects\framework\src\mx\core\UIComponent.as:1167]
```

That output has been abbreviated, but you can basically see where the call fails. At this point, you can roll back the change you made to the SchoolTest class.

You should now understand how to work with the FlexUnit Runner and how to build a test suite to test your own code. You work with this framework later in this book, but feel free to refer to this chapter for a refresher.

Summary

In this chapter, you learned how to download and configure FlexUnit. You also learned how to do the same with JUnit for Java. Once you had the frameworks installed, you learned how to add them to your workflow.

While working with the FlexUnit framework, you learned how to use the FlexUnit Runner application to visually work with your test suites. This allowed you to dig deeper into the reasons why tests may have failed and allowed you to filter results by using the tools provided in the FlexUnit Runner application.

You should now have an understanding of unit testing and how it can help in your development process. Now take this information and start working with it during real-world development projects, and you will quickly create more robust, less error-prone code.

Chapter 8

Relational Databases

An application can have the most beautiful design or slick intuitive interface, but the fact remains that without the ability to retrieve, update, and store useful data, that application won't see much use. Most data-driven Web applications have a relational database on the back end to manage that data. In this chapter, you learn about key relational database concepts and work with MySQL, a popular open-source database server that powers many of today's Web applications.

IN THIS CHAPTER

Relational database concepts

The MySQL database server

Relational Database Concepts

The purpose of a relational database is to store data and allow for the retrieval and manipulation of stored data in response to a user's query. Data in a relational database is stored in structures called *tables*. Data is retrieved from the tables in a relational database by using a querying language called SQL. SQL can also be used to manipulate data stored in database tables. Complex data manipulation and retrieval operations can be grouped together in a stored procedure, which is a construct much like a Java method or ActionScript function. Let's look at these three relational database concepts in more detail.

Tables

Tables in a relational database are structured much like spreadsheets, composed of columns and rows. *Columns* describe each field of data being stored, and *rows* each contain a single unit of stored data.

Typically, a row in a database table represents a single entity. For example, look at the PERSON table in Figure 8.1. The columns each describe some attribute of a person, such as name or gender. Each row in this table represents one person's attributes. Row 1 contains only the information for John Smith.

203

FIGURE 8.1

A database table is structured much like a spreadsheet, with columns describing the data fields and rows representing a single unit of the data.

PERSON

PERSON_ID	FIRST_NAME	LAST_NAME	GENDER	HEIGHT_IN_INCHES	WEIGHT_IN_LB	AGE	DATE_OF_BIRTH
1	John	Smith	M	70	165	30	08-10-1978
2	Mary	Jones	F	63	120	25	04-01-1983
3	Sam	Taylor	F	65	130	35	11-24-1973

The concept of a database table can be related to the concept of a class in Java. A *class* in Java contains fields that describe the properties of an entity, much like the columns in a database table describe the properties of the entities stored in the table. Each row of the table represents a single entity, much like an instance of a class in Java represents a single entity.

 **For more on Java concepts, such as classes and class instances, see Chapter 1.**

Data types

Each column in a table is said to be of a specific data type. In the PERSON table, a few different datatypes are used:

- FIRST_NAME, LAST_NAME, and GENDER are all *variable character fields*, commonly referred to as *varchar* fields. These are fields containing text data of variable lengths. The maximum length of a varchar field is specific to the database system being used. For example, Oracle caps the length of varchar fields at 4,000 bytes, whereas MySQL allows varchar fields as long as 65,535 bytes.

- HEIGHT_IN_INCHES, WEIGHT_IN_LB, and AGE are all number fields. Number fields can hold integer values or decimal values.

- DATE_OF_BIRTH is a date field. Date fields store date information based on the Gregorian calendar. Implementations of date fields vary wildly between database systems. In Oracle, a date field contains both date and time information, whereas MySQL uses a separate datetime data type for fields that require both date and time information. When creating a database table, consult the documentation for the database system you're using to determine which data type best fits your needs.

When adding rows to a database table, these data types are checked to make sure the data being added conforms to the data types for each column. Attempting to set the value of a varchar field to a numeric value, for example, would cause the database to raise an error.

Keys

Database tables typically include one column or a set of columns used to uniquely identify each row in the table. This column or set of columns is referred to as the *primary key* of the table. Because the primary key is meant to identify the row, the following two conditions are always true of the primary key:

- **The primary key must be unique.** No two rows in a table can have identical primary keys.

- **The primary key must have a value.** Primary keys can't be *null*, a term used to describe a field with no value.

In the PERSON table, the PERSON_ID field is the primary key. Each row in the table can be identified by this field. The row containing John Smith's information has a PERSON_ID of 1. Asking the database for the row with a PERSON_ID of 1 will always return John Smith's information; no other row has the same PERSON_ID value.

Columns in other tables can refer to the primary key of a table to form a relationship with that table. Columns in a table that refer to primary keys in other tables are called *foreign keys*.

Figure 8.2 shows a table called PET. The PET table contains a PERSON_ID column that's a foreign key to the PERSON_ID primary key column in the PERSON table. You can see that Sam Taylor (PERSON_ID 3 in the PERSON table) has two cats: Fluffy and Mittens. John Smith (PERSON_ID 1 in the PERSON table) has a dog named Rocky. The foreign key column establishes the relationship between the pets in the PET table and the people in the PERSON table.

It's important to note that rows in a table with primary keys that are referred to by foreign key columns in other tables can't be deleted without the rows with the foreign key columns being deleted first. For example, if you needed to delete the Sam Taylor row (PERSON_ID 3) from the PERSON table, you would first need to delete the two rows in the PET table with foreign key relationships to that row (PET_ID 1 and PET_ID 3). The database raises an error if an attempt is made to delete Sam Taylor while these two rows exist in the PET table. On the other hand, Mary Jones (PERSON_ID 2) can be deleted freely because no corresponding foreign keys exist in the PET table.

FIGURE 8.2

The PET table contains a foreign key to the PERSON_ID column in the PERSON table.

PET

PET_ID	NAME	TYPE	PERSON_ID
1	Fluffy	cat	3
2	Rocky	dog	1
3	Mittens	cat	3

Similarly, a foreign key column can't contain a value that doesn't exist in the primary key column to which it refers. Attempting to insert a new row with a PERSON_ID value of 6, for example, would cause the database to raise an error because no row with a PERSON_ID of 6 exists in the PERSON table.

 In the MySQL relational database engine, tables can be created by using different types. The default type, known as MyISAM, doesn't enforce foreign keys as described above. When you're using MySQL, tables that use foreign keys should be created by using the InnoDB table type.

Constraints

The values stored in a particular column can be further controlled by the use of constraints. A *constraint* places limits or conditions on the data that a column accepts. A foreign key is a type of constraint in that it restricts the data being stored in a column to the set of values in the primary key to which it refers. There are a few other types of commonly used constraints:

- **A not-null constraint** requires each row to provide a value for this column. Any attempt to insert null into a column with a not-null constraint or to change a value in a not-null column to null causes the database to raise an error.

- **A unique constraint** requires all values in this column to be unique. Each row must contain a unique value in this column. A primary key is by definition also a unique constraint because all values in a primary key column must be unique. Any attempt to insert nonunique data into a column with a unique constraint or to update a unique column to a nonunique value causes the database to raise an error. A unique constraint doesn't prevent multiple nulls from being inserted into columns that allow nulls. Nulls are treated specially; two nulls when compared with each other are considered to be neither equal nor unequal. Therefore, having two nulls in a column with a unique constraint doesn't violate the constraint.

- **A check constraint** checks any added or modified data to see that it meets certain conditions. For example, if you add a check constraint to the AGE column of the PERSON table to ensure that any inserted values are less than or equal to 100, then any attempt to insert a row with an age value greater than 100 causes the database to raise an error.

All these constraints can be used in conjunction with one another. For example, a single column might not allow nulls, require uniqueness, and check for specific conditions for its data.

 Check constraints aren't supported in MySQL.

SQL queries

Once the structure of your data is defined by database tables and the permissible data further clarified through data types, keys, and constraints, you need a way to work with and manipulate the data. Relational databases typically retrieve and manipulate data in response to queries from a user or application. A *query* is simply a request to the database to retrieve or manipulate some data. The language used to make such a request is known as Structured Query Language, or SQL. SQL is a standardized language understood by relational databases.

The SQL language is quite expansive, and explaining it in detail could fill a book on its own. However, understanding the basics of SQL can give you a solid foundation to build upon later. Although SQL can be complex, it really boils down to only a few key query types, or *statements*.

Select statements

An SQL `select` statement tells the database to retrieve a specific set of information from one or more tables. A basic `select` statement to retrieve the data in the PERSON table would look like this:

```
SELECT * FROM PERSON;
```

This statement tells the database that you want to retrieve all columns and all rows of the PERSON table. The * is a wildcard character that means everything. You can limit the fields returned by the `select` statement by specifying the ones you want in a comma-delimited list in the query. For example, if you wanted only the first and last names of everyone in the PERSON table, you could modify the query to read like this:

```
SELECT LAST_NAME, FIRST_NAME FROM PERSON;
```

Similarly, you can filter the rows that are returned by adding specific search criteria by using a WHERE clause. The WHERE clause tells the database to retrieve only the rows that match the given criteria. For example, to retrieve only rows for people whose last name is Smith, the `select` statement would look like this:

```
SELECT * FROM PERSON WHERE LAST_NAME = 'Smith';
```

Insert statements

A SQL `insert` statement tells the database to add the given row of data to the given table. A basic `insert` statement to add a row of data to the PERSON table would look like this:

```
INSERT INTO PERSON (FIRST_NAME, LAST_NAME, GENDER, HEIGHT_IN_INCHES,
    WEIGHT_IN_LB, AGE, DATE_OF_BIRTH) VALUES ('Tom','Davis','M',72,
    180,35,'1973-07-24');
```

This statement tells the database that you want to insert a new row containing the given values into the PERSON table. Each column in the table is listed in a comma-delimited list, and each value for the row to be inserted is listed in a corresponding comma-delimited list. In this example, the new row contains the value Tom in the FIRST_NAME column, Davis in the LAST_NAME column, etc.

You can leave one or more columns out of the `insert` statement, and the database leaves those fields blank. For example, if you want to insert a new row into the table with only the first and last names filled in, your query might look like this:

```
INSERT INTO PERSON (FIRST_NAME, LAST_NAME) VALUES ('Tom', 'Davis');
```

If you're inserting values for every column, you can omit the column listing. The database inserts the values in the order in which the columns appear in the database:

```
INSERT INTO PERSON VALUES ('Tom','Davis','M',72,180,35,'1973-07-24');
```

However, it's recommended that you don't use this approach when using insert statements in application development. If the PERSON table is modified to add or remove columns, the last SQL statement no longer works. Also, explicitly listing the columns in your queries makes them easier to understand and maintain for others who might need to work with your code.

 For more on using SQL queries in your applications, see Chapter 9.

Update statements

A SQL update statement tells the database to update one or more existing rows in the database. A basic update statement for the PERSON table would look like this:

```
UPDATE PERSON SET AGE = 45;
```

This statement tells the database to set the value of the AGE column to 45 for every row in the PERSON table. You can add criteria by using the same WHERE clause syntax used for select statements to tell the database that only rows in the table that match the criteria should be updated. For example, to change the value in the AGE column for only those people under 30, the update statement would look like this:

```
UPDATE PERSON SET AGE = 45 WHERE AGE < 30;
```

This statement executes successfully even if no rows match the criteria. However, no rows are updated.

You can specify more than one column to be updated by separating the column name-value pairs with a comma:

```
UPDATE PERSON SET AGE = 45, WEIGHT_IN_LB = 150 WHERE LAST_NAME =
    'Smith';
```

Delete statements

A SQL delete statement tells the database to delete one or more existing rows in the database. A basic delete statement for the PERSON table would look like this:

```
DELETE FROM PERSON;
```

This statement tells the database to delete all rows from the PERSON table. You can add criteria by using the same WHERE clause syntax used for select and update statements to tell the database that only rows in the table that match the criteria should be deleted. For example, to delete everyone in the PERSON table under age 30, the delete statement would look like this:

```
DELETE FROM PERSON WHERE AGE < 30;
```

This statement executes successfully even if no rows match the criteria. However, no rows are deleted.

Stored procedures

Many databases allow you to create user-defined functions to group a set of database operations together into a single logical unit called a *stored procedure*. Stored procedures are typically written in a stored procedure language that incorporates SQL statements and proprietary language elements specific to the database system being used. The syntax for creating a stored procedure also varies from database to database.

A stored procedure is much like a method in a Java class. It can accept zero or more parameters for input, use those parameters in its operations along with any local variables it declares, and return some value or values to its caller.

There's some debate as to whether stored procedures should be used when developing applications. On the pro side, stored procedures are typically very fast to execute, thanks to optimizations and caching provided by the database. Using stored procedures to encapsulate your business logic also allows you to switch out the implementation of your application (for example, switching from Java to C#) more easily because the business logic in the database wouldn't need to change. On the con side, some argue that the database should be used only for data storage and not contain application logic, maintaining a separation of concerns that's one of the cornerstones of modular programming. Furthermore, because of the differences in stored procedure languages and implementations across different database systems, having application logic in the database makes the application dependent on one specific database, making it more difficult to port to other platforms.

In the end, the decision of whether to use stored procedures comes down to what best fits your application's requirements and your application's development roadmap.

The MySQL Database Server

MySQL is a free database server and is among the most widely used database servers for Web applications. MySQL is known for being lean and high-performing but also scalable for larger applications. One of the largest and most frequently accessed Web sites, Wikipedia, is powered by MySQL.

Installing and configuring MySQL

MySQL is available for many different platforms and processors. The MySQL download for 32-bit Windows operating systems can be found at `http://dev.mysql.com/downloads/mysql/5.0.html#win32`. As of this writing, the most stable version of MySQL is 5.0.67.

To download, install, and configure MySQL, follow these steps:

1. **Download the installer:**

   1. **Type the URL in a browser.** The MySQL 5.0 downloads page, as shown in Figure 8.3, opens. There are three installation packages to choose from for Windows. You should install the Windows Essentials (x86) package. This is a Windows installer package that contains everything you need to run MySQL on your development machine.

   2. **Click the Pick a mirror link to the right of the Windows Essentials (x86) package.** The Select a Mirror screen, as shown in Figure 8.4, opens. You're presented with the option of registering for an account on the MySQL Web site. Registering gives you a login that can be used for the MySQL user forums as well as other MySQL Web sites. You may also register at another time by visiting the main MySQL Web site at www.mysql.com. For now, proceed with the download.

FIGURE 8.3

The MySQL downloads page presents several packages for the Windows platform. The Windows Essentials (x86) package contains everything you need.

Windows downloads (platform notes)

Windows Essentials (x86)	5.0.67	23.3M	Pick a mirror
MD5: 6001ae41e1031e770c2cb576a4562e65 | Signature			
Windows ZIP/Setup.EXE (x86)	5.0.67	45.3M	Pick a mirror
MD5: ed76e5ad8b251ca643766c70926854d7 | Signature			
Without installer (unzip in C:\)	5.0.67	63.1M	Pick a mirror
MD5: aed74f2a9432e114d965ae52e5f36689 | Signature			

Windows x64 downloads (platform notes)

Windows Essentials (AMD64 / Intel EM64T)	5.0.67	27.4M	Pick a mirror
MD5: 28eaac91673d23d0f367f413565bb7fb | Signature			
Windows ZIP/Setup.EXE (AMD64 / Intel EM64T)	5.0.67	52.8M	Pick a mirror
MD5: 16f83ff572154f64e84226fc1c42c3a9 | Signature			
Without installer (AMD64 / Intel EM64T)	5.0.67	74.9M	Pick a mirror
MD5: f95c4724c2db81559900a9a75dd02d44 | Signature			

Linux (non RPM packages) downloads (platform notes)

Linux (x86, glibc-2.2, "standard" is static)	5.0.67	112.2M	Pick a mirror
MD5: 71f7281262f54d2674392e6ef7c7d18f | Signature			
Linux (x86)	5.0.67	99.1M	Pick a mirror
MD5: 3756f1b3580c65e1a9a1daf7a6ec9870 | Signature			

3. **Click the No thanks, just take me to the downloads! link.** The list of mirror sites appears.

4. **Click either the HTTP or FTP link for the mirror site that's geographically closest to you.** The Download File dialog box opens.

5. **Click Save, choose a location for the file in the Save File As dialog box, and then click the Save button.** The installer is downloaded to your machine.

2. **Double-click the installer.** The MySQL Server 5.0 Setup Wizard opens.

3. **Click Next.** The Setup Type screen, as shown in Figure 8.5, opens. The Setup Type screen presents you with three options: Typical, Complete, and Custom. Typical is the default selection and installs everything you need for typical MySQL development.

4. **Click the Typical radio button and then click Next.** The Ready to Install the Program screen, as shown in Figure 8.6, opens. Confirm that the settings are correct.

5. **Click Install.** MySQL is installed. When installation is complete, the MySQL Enterprise screen opens. This screen and the next one simply display the benefits of a MySQL Enterprise subscription. These benefits are more for corporate customers than individual customers.

FIGURE 8.4

On the Select a Mirror screen, you're given the opportunity to register for an account on the MySQL Web site if you choose. For now, simply proceed with the download.

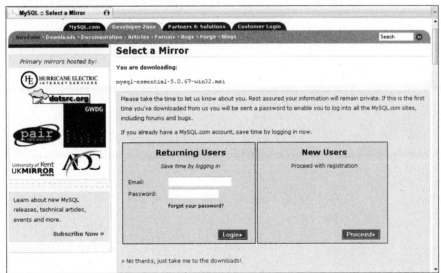

6. **Click Next on this screen and on the next screen.** The Wizard Completed screen, as shown in Figure 8.7, opens. The check box on this screen offers you the chance to configure MySQL now. This configuration generates a configuration file optimized for your MySQL usage, installs MySQL as a Windows service, and allows you to set a password for the MySQL root user.

7. **Click the check box next to Configure the MySQL Server now and then click Finish.** The MySQL Server 5.0 Setup Wizard closes, and the MySQL Server Instance Configuration Wizard opens.

FIGURE 8.5

The Setup Type screen offers three installation options. Typical is the default selection and is appropriate in most cases.

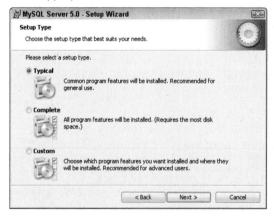

FIGURE 8.6

Confirm that the settings on the Ready to Install the Program screen are correct and then click the Install button to begin the installation.

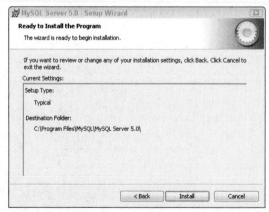

FIGURE 8.7

Once the installation has finished, the Wizard Completed screen offers you the chance to configure MySQL.

8. **Click Next.** The MySQL Server Instance Configuration Wizard screen, as shown in Figure 8.8, opens. This screen presents you with two options for configuration. The Detailed Configuration option contains options for optimizing and tuning the database for a variety of environments, from developer machines to large-scale data warehouses. The Standard Configuration option sets up sensible defaults without needing to go into that level of detail and is the more appropriate option in this case.

9. **Click the Standard Configuration radio button and then click Next.** The next screen of the wizard, as shown in Figure 8.9, opens. This screen contains two configuration settings. The first setting is whether to install the MySQL server as a Windows service. Installing as a service allows you to control the MySQL server from the Windows Services dialog box and also gives you the option of having MySQL start up when Windows starts up. As the dialog box explains, this is the recommended way of running MySQL on Windows. The second setting allows you to put the MySQL `bin` directory, where the MySQL executables are installed, into the PATH environment variable. This gives you access to the MySQL command-line tools from any directory.

10. **Click the check boxes for Install As Windows Service and Include Bin Directory in Windows PATH and then click Next.** The root account configuration screen, as shown in Figure 8.10, opens. On this screen, you're given the opportunity to set a password for the root user. By default, MySQL's root user doesn't have a password. Because the root user has access to all databases, this isn't very secure. Choose a password that's easy for you to remember but hard for someone else to guess. You can also click the Enable root access from remote machines check box. Unless you're doing development on multiple machines that need to access this MySQL installation, there's no need to enable this option. Similarly, leave the Create An Anonymous Account check box deselected, as it's not necessary.

FIGURE 8.8

The MySQL Server Instance Configuration Wizard screen offers two choices for configuration. The Standard Configuration option is more appropriate here.

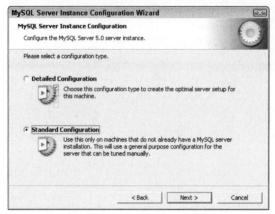

FIGURE 8.9

This screen allows you to install MySQL as a Windows service and add the path to the MySQL `bin` directory to the `PATH` environment variable. The defaults are fine for the first setting. The check box for the second setting isn't checked by default, but it's recommended that you also select this option.

FIGURE 8.10

On the root account configuration screen, you should set a password for the root user that's easy to remember but hard to guess. The default settings are fine for all other options on this screen.

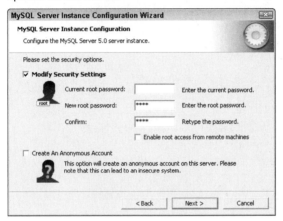

11. **Type a password for the root user in the New root password and Confirm boxes and then click Next.** The Ready to Execute screen opens.

12. **Click Execute.** The wizard performs the configuration steps. When it's finished, the wizard should look like Figure 8.11.

13. **Click Finish.** The wizard closes. The installation and configuration of MySQL are complete.

Out of the box, MySQL ships with a set of command-line tools for creating databases and tables and executing queries. For those who prefer working in a graphical user interface, MySQL offers a GUI tool set as a separate download. Although these tools aren't necessary for MySQL development, they provide a more convenient way of creating databases and tables without needing to type SQL statements by hand, and they also let you examine the SQL statements that MySQL runs behind the scenes. Because of this, it's worth taking the time to download the tool.

The MySQL GUI Tools installer for 32-bit Windows operating systems can be found at `http://dev.mysql.com/downloads/gui-tools/5.0.html`. As of this writing, the most stable version is 5.0-r14.

FIGURE 8.11

Once the wizard has performed the configuration steps, confirmation of success appears on the wizard screen.

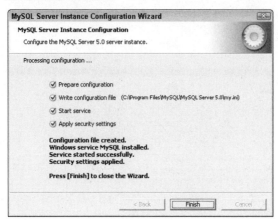

To download and install the MySQL GUI Tools, follow these steps:

1. **Download the installer:**

   1. **Type the URL in a browser.** The MySQL GUI Tools downloads page opens.

   2. **Scroll down to the Windows Downloads section and then click the Pick a mirror link to the right of the Windows (x86) item.** The Select a Mirror page opens. You're again presented with the option to register for an account on the MySQL Web site. For now, proceed with the download.

   3. **Click the No thanks, just take me to the downloads! link.** The list of mirror sites appears.

   4. **Click either the HTTP or FTP link for the mirror site that's geographically closest to you.** The File Download dialog box opens.

   5. **Click Save, choose a location for the file in the Save File As dialog box, and then click the Save button.** The installer is downloaded to your machine.

2. **Double-click the installer.** The MySQL Tools for 5.0 Installation Wizard opens.

3. **Click Next.** The license agreement screen opens.

4. **Read the license agreement, click the radio button to agree to the terms, and then click Next.** The destination folder screen opens. The default folder is appropriate for most installations.

5. **Click Next.** The Setup Type screen, as shown in Figure 8.12, opens.

6. **Click the Complete radio button and then click Next.** The Ready to Install the Program screen, as shown in Figure 8.13, opens.

7. **Verify the installation settings and then click Install.** The MySQL tools are installed. When installation is complete, the MySQL Enterprise screen opens. This screen and the next one simply display the benefits of a MySQL Enterprise subscription. These benefits are more for corporate customers than individual customers.

8. **Click Next on this screen and on the next screen.** The Wizard Completed screen opens.

9. **Click Finish.** The wizard closes.

FIGURE 8.12

The Setup Type screen for setting up the MySQL GUI Tools

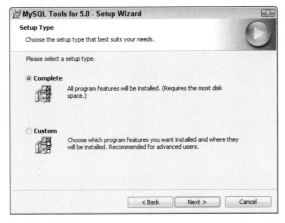

FIGURE 8.13

Confirm the installation settings on the Ready to Install the Program screen and then click the Install button to install the MySQL GUI Tools.

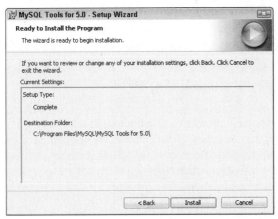

Creating a simple database in MySQL

Now that MySQL and the MySQL GUI Tools have been installed and configured, it's time to create a simple database that contains the PERSON and PET tables shown earlier in this chapter by using the MySQL Query Browser, one of the tools installed with the MySQL GUI Tools:

1. **Launch the MySQL Query Browser by choosing Start ⇨ All Programs ⇨ MySQL ⇨ MySQL Query Browser.** The Connect to MySQL Server Instance dialog box, as shown in Figure 8.14, opens.

FIGURE 8.14
_____

In the Connect to MySQL Server Instance dialog box, fill in the information for your installation of MySQL. Leave the Default Schema text field empty.

2. **Type the following values in the dialog box:**

   - **Server Host:** localhost

   - **Port:** 3306

   - **Username:** root

   - **Password:** Type the password you assigned the root user when installing MySQL.

   - **Default schema** should remain empty.

3. **Click OK.** A warning dialog box, as shown in Figure 8.15, appears, reminding you that you haven't selected a default schema. Click Ignore to dismiss this dialog box. The MySQL Query Browser launches. The term *schema* is essentially equivalent to *database*. A schema contains all the database objects, such as tables and stored procedures, that belong to a single database. A single MySQL server supports many databases at a time. Each database is separate from the others. You will create a new schema by using the tool, so you don't need to select a default schema here.

FIGURE 8.15

A warning dialog box appears to remind you that you've not selected a default schema. Click Ignore to dismiss this dialog box. You will create a new schema by using the tool.

The main interface of the MySQL Query Browser is shown in Figure 8.16. The interface is divided into several components:

- **The text field at the top of the screen is the query editor.** This is where you can type SQL queries and statements to execute.

- **The large area below the query editor contains a single tab labeled Resultset 1.** This is the results tab. It displays the results of any queries you execute in the query editor.

- **The tabbed area at the top right of the screen is the browser.** The Schemata tab allows you to browse the tables and stored procedures in each database. The Bookmarks tab stores queries that you have bookmarked. You can then load a query into the query editor by double-clicking it. This is very handy for queries you run frequently. Finally, the History tab stores every query run in the query editor. You can also load a query into the query editor by double-clicking it here, much like you can in the Bookmarks tab.

- **The tabbed area at the bottom right contains links to inline documentation.** The Syntax tab contains links to documentation about the syntax of SQL query statements and *data definition language* (DDL) statements for operations such as creating or modifying databases, tables, and stored procedures. The Functions tab contains links to documentation for MySQL's built-in data functions for operations such as string comparison or manipulation, date/time operations, and more. Finally, the Params and Trx tabs show any global parameters in use that affect all queries executed in the query editor and show the set of queries and statements that are executing within a single *transaction*, or single unit of work within a database.

As you can see in the Schemata browser tab, the MySQL server includes three databases by default:

- **The information_schema database** is where MySQL stores its *database metadata*, which is information about all the other databases running in the MySQL server and their objects. This metadata is also referred to by the term *data dictionary* because it contains the definitions of the structure of the data present in the system.

- **The mysql database** contains information about the user accounts in the MySQL server and their access privileges for databases running in the MySQL server.

- **The test database** is an empty database that can be used as a safe place to test SQL queries or stored procedures before using them on a real database.

FIGURE 8.16

The main interface of the MySQL Query Browser tool is divided into several components.

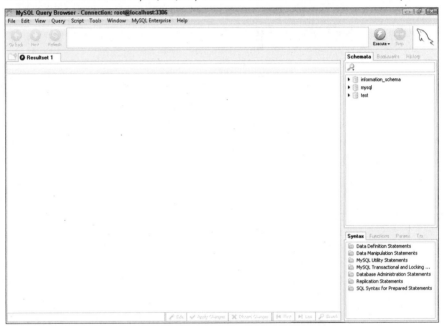

> **CAUTION**   It's possible to render your MySQL installation unusable by modifying or deleting data in the `information_schema` and `mysql` databases. It's strongly recommended that only experienced database administrators perform operations in these databases.

Using the MySQL Query Browser, you can create a new database called `petclub` and then create the PERSON and PET tables in that database:

1. **Right-click within the Schemata tab in the top-right corner and then choose Create New Schema from the popup menu.** Alternatively, you can press Ctrl+N. The Create new Schema dialog box, as shown in Figure 8.17, opens.

2. **Type PETCLUB in the Schema name text field and then click OK.** The `petclub` schema appears in the Schemata tab, as shown in Figure 8.18.

FIGURE 8.17

The Create new Schema dialog box

FIGURE 8.18

The newly created `petclub` database now appears in the Schemata tab.

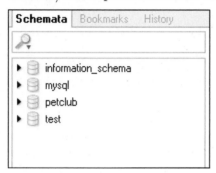

3. **Right-click the `petclub` database within the Schemata tab in the top-right corner and then choose Create New Table from the popup menu.** Alternatively, you can press Ctrl+T. The MySQL Table Editor dialog box, as shown in Figure 8.19, opens. This dialog box has a lot of fields and tabs, but for now, only the Table Name text field and the Columns and Indices tab are important. The Columns and Indices tab is where the columns for your table are defined.

4. **Type PERSON in the Table Name text field.**

5. **Double-click below the Column Name column in the Columns and Indices tab.** A text field appears.

6. **Type PERSON_ID in this text field, as shown in Figure 8.20, and then press the Tab key.** When you press Tab, the rest of the row for the new PERSON_ID column fills in with some default values, and a key icon appears next to PERSON_ID, as shown in Figure 8.21. The key icon indicates that the PERSON_ID field is used as the primary key for this table. The table editor makes the first column created for a table the primary key by default. Also by default, the table editor assigns some other attributes to the primary key column. It's given a data type of *integer*, given a *not null* constraint, set to *automatically increment*, and given an *unsigned* flag. The auto-increment option tells MySQL to

automatically assign this field an incrementing integer value, starting from 1. This is a commonly used attribute for primary keys, as it ensures that the same value isn't used twice. SQL insert statements that add data to this table won't include this field; the database automatically assigns it a value. The unsigned flag is an attribute of integer and other numeric data types that tells the database to use only non-negative values for this field. By default, an integer field can hold values ranging from –2147483648 to 2147483647. Using the unsigned flag changes this range from 0 to 4294967295.

FIGURE 8.19

The MySQL Table Editor dialog box

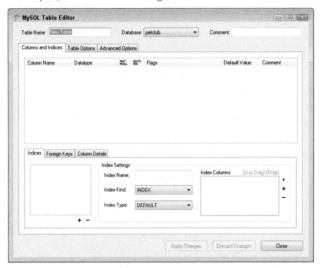

7. **Continue adding the columns for the** PERSON **table as specified by double-clicking below the previous column name to type the column name and then using the Tab key to move between the other settings.** When you've finished, the MySQL Table Editor should look like Figure 8.22, with the following columns:

- Column Name: FIRST_NAME; Datatype: VARCHAR(45); check NOT NULL. The data type VARCHAR(45) creates a variable-length character data field with a maximum length of 45 bytes.

- Column Name: LAST_NAME; Datatype: VARCHAR(45); check NOT NULL

- Column Name: GENDER; Datatype: VARCHAR(1); check NOT NULL.

- For this column, only a 1-byte field is needed because gender is stored as either M or F.

- Column Name: HEIGHT_IN_INCHES; Datatype: TINYINT; check NOT NULL; check UNSIGNED. TINYINT is a MySQL-specific datatype. An unsigned TINYINT column can range in value from 0 to 255.

- Column Name: WEIGHT_IN_LB; Datatype: SMALLINT; check NOT NULL; check UNSIGNED. SMALLINT is a MySQL-specific datatype. An unsigned SMALLINT column can range in value from 0 to 65,535. SMALLINT is more appropriate than TINYINT for this column, as a person might weigh more than 255 pounds.

- Column Name: AGE; Datatype: TINYINT; check NOT NULL; check UNSIGNED

- Column Name: DATE_OF_BIRTH; Datatype: DATE; check NOT NULL

8. **Click Apply Changes.** The Confirm Table Edit dialog box, as shown in Figure 8.23, opens. This dialog box shows the actual SQL code that's executed to create the table.

9. **Click Execute.** The PERSON table is created, and the Confirm Table Edit dialog box closes.

10. **Click Close.** The MySQL Table Editor dialog box closes.

11. **Right-click the petclub database within the Schemata tab in the top-right corner and then choose Create New Table from the popup menu.** Alternatively, you can press Ctrl+T. The MySQL Table Editor dialog box opens.

FIGURE 8.20

Double-clicking below the Column Name column in the Columns and Indices tab creates a text field where a column name can be typed.

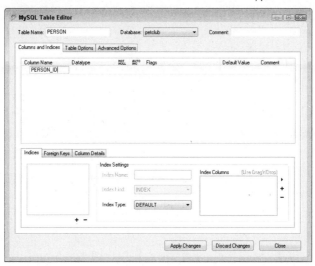

FIGURE 8.21

After you type the column name and pressing the Tab key, the MySQL Table Editor fills in some default values for the rest of the column attributes. Because PERSON_ID is the first column in the table, the MySQL Table Editor has made it the table's primary key.

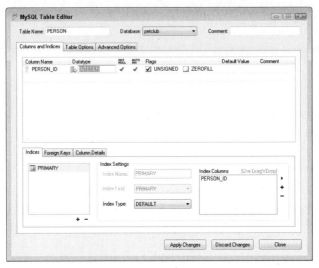

FIGURE 8.22

Once all the columns for the PERSON table have been added, the MySQL Table Editor dialog box should look like this.

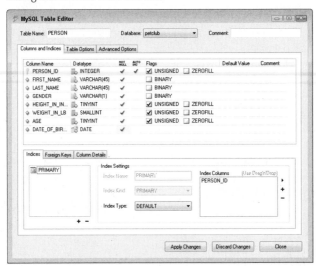

FIGURE 8.23

The Confirm Edit Table dialog box shows you the SQL statement that's executed in order to create the PERSON table.

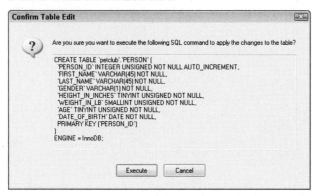

12. Type PET in the Table Name text field.

13. **Double-click below the Column Name column in the Columns and Indices tab.** A text field appears.

14. **Type PET_ID in the text field and then press the Tab key.** When you press Tab, the rest of the row for the new PET_ID column fills in with some default values, and a key icon appears next to PET_ID, indicating that the PET_ID field is used as the primary key for this table. It's given a data type of integer, given a not null constraint, set to automatically increment, and given an unsigned flag, similar to the PERSON_ID column in the PERSON table.

15. **Continue adding the columns for the PET table as specified by double-clicking below the previous column name to type the column name and then using the Tab key to move between the other settings.** When you've finished, the MySQL Table Editor should look like Figure 8.24, with the following columns:

    ▧ Column Name: NAME; Datatype: VARCHAR(45); check NOT NULL

    ▧ Column Name: TYPE; Datatype: VARCHAR(20); check NOT NULL

    ▧ Column Name: PERSON_ID; Datatype: INTEGER; check NOT NULL; check UNSIGNED

16. **Click the Foreign Keys tab next to the Indices tab in the bottom-right corner, click the PERSON_ID field in the Columns and Indices tab, and then click the + symbol below the Foreign Key tab.** The Add Foreign Key dialog box, as shown in Figure 8.25, opens.

17. **Click OK.** The new foreign key appears in the Foreign Keys tab, as shown in Figure 8.26.

FIGURE 8.24

Once all the columns for the PET table have been added, the MySQL Table Editor dialog box should look like this.

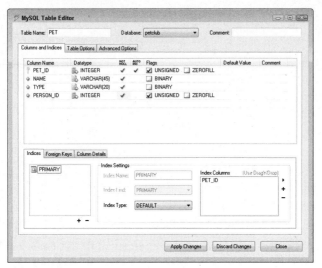

FIGURE 8.25

The Add Foreign Key dialog box provides an appropriate default name for a new foreign key.

18. **Choose** person **from the Ref Table dropdown list on the right side of the Foreign Keys tab.** The Column and Reference Column fields in the table below the dropdown list fill in with the value PERSON_ID, as shown in Figure 8.27. The Column and Reference Column fields refer to the table columns from the PET and PERSON tables, respectively. This foreign key establishes that the PERSON_ID column in the PET table references the PERSON_ID primary key column in the PERSON table. Now the PET table's PERSON_ID column can contain only values found in the PERSON_ID column of the PERSON table.

FIGURE 8.26

The new foreign key for the PET table appears in the Foreign Keys tab.

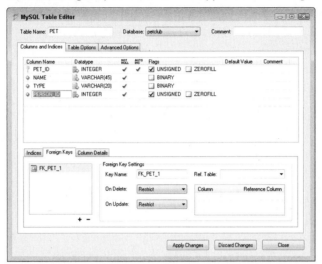

FIGURE 8.27

Choosing the PERSON table from the Ref Table dropdown list fills in the PERSON_ID columns from both the PET and PERSON tables into the Column and Reference Column fields, respectively.

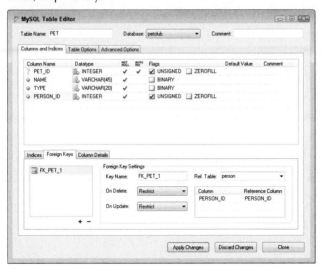

19. **Click Apply Changes.** The Confirm Table Edit dialog box, as shown in Figure 8.28, opens. This dialog box shows the actual SQL code that's executed to create the table. The code to create the foreign key is part of the table creation code that's executed.

FIGURE 8.28

The SQL code used to create the PET table contains the table creation code as well as code to create the foreign key that references the PERSON table.

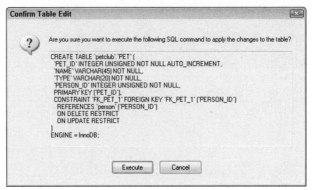

20. **Click Execute.** The PET table is created, and the Confirm Table Edit dialog box closes.
21. **Click Close.** The MySQL Table Editor dialog box closes.

Now that the tables have been created, the next step is to add some data to them. First, right-click the petclub database in the Schemata tab and then choose Make Default Schema from the popup menu to tell MySQL to use the petclub database for these operations. Next, type the following three SQL statements in the query editor, one at a time. After typing a statement in the query editor, click the Execute button to execute the statement. Once the statement has been executed, delete it from the query editor, type the next statement, and then click Execute. Continue until all three statements have been executed:

```
INSERT INTO PERSON (FIRST_NAME, LAST_NAME, GENDER, HEIGHT_IN_INCHES,
    WEIGHT_IN_LB, AGE, DATE_OF_BIRTH) VALUES ('John','Smith','M',70,
    165,30,'1978-08-10');

INSERT INTO PERSON (FIRST_NAME, LAST_NAME, GENDER, HEIGHT_IN_INCHES,
    WEIGHT_IN_LB, AGE, DATE_OF_BIRTH) VALUES ('Mary','Jones','F',63,
    120,25,'1983-04-01');
```

```
INSERT INTO PERSON (FIRST_NAME, LAST_NAME, GENDER, HEIGHT_IN_INCHES,
    WEIGHT_IN_LB, AGE, DATE_OF_BIRTH) VALUES ('Sam','Taylor','F',65,
    130,35,'1973-11-24');
```

These three records are now added to the PERSON table. You can see the data inside the PERSON table in a few different ways:

- Type **SELECT * FROM PERSON** in the query editor and then click the Execute button.
- Click the arrow next to the petclub database to expand it and then drag the PERSON table into the Resultset 1 tab.
- Click the arrow next to the petclub database to expand it and then double-click the PERSON table. The query SELECT * FROM petclub.person appears in the query editor. Click Execute to run the query.

Any of these operations results in the three rows of the PERSON table appearing in the Resultset 1 tab, as shown in Figure 8.29.

FIGURE 8.29

The results of querying the database for the records in the PERSON table are displayed in the Resultset 1 tab.

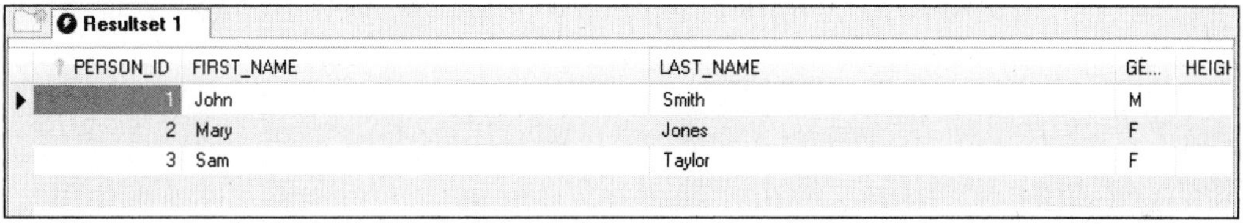

	PERSON_ID	FIRST_NAME	LAST_NAME	GE...	HEIGH
▶	1	John	Smith	M	
	2	Mary	Jones	F	
	3	Sam	Taylor	F	

Now add rows to the PET table by running each of the following SQL statements, one at a time, just as you did for the PERSON table:

```
INSERT INTO PET (NAME, TYPE, PERSON_ID) VALUES ('Fluffy', 'cat', 3);

INSERT INTO PET (NAME, TYPE, PERSON_ID) VALUES ('Rocky', 'dog', 1);

INSERT INTO PET (NAME, TYPE, PERSON_ID) VALUES ('Mittens', 'cat', 3);
```

You can verify that these three rows were added the same way you checked the rows in the PERSON table. Your data should look similar to that in Figure 8.30.

FIGURE 8.30

The results of querying the database for the records in the PET table are displayed in the Resultset 1 tab.

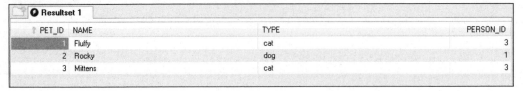

If you try to add a new record to the PET table with a PERSON_ID that doesn't exist in the PERSON table, you see an error. Try executing the following statement in the query editor:

```
INSERT INTO PET (NAME, TYPE, PERSON_ID) VALUES ('Aquaman', 'fish', 9);
```

When you click the Execute button, an error message appears at the bottom of the screen, telling you that the foreign key FK_PET_1 has been violated, as shown in Figure 8.31.

FIGURE 8.31

An error results if you try to add a row to the PET table with a PERSON_ID that doesn't exist in the PERSON table.

Finally, SQL allows you to select data from multiple related tables at a time in a single query. This type of query is said to contain a *join*. There are many types of joins. The simplest is called an *inner join*. An inner join selects values from each table where one or more related rows exist in each table being joined.

Suppose that you want to retrieve a list of people's first and last names alongside their pets' names. Type this query in the query editor and then click the Execute button:

```
SELECT person.first_name, person.last_name, pet.name
FROM person, pet
WHERE person.person_id = pet.person_id;
```

The WHERE clause of this query specifies that the PERSON_ID column in the PERSON table is related to the PERSON_ID column in the PET table. The results returned are shown in Figure 8.32. Notice that Mary Jones (PERSON_ID 2) doesn't appear in this list. That's because the

PERSON table and the PET table were joined, and there's no row with a PERSON_ID of 2 in the PET table. Sam Taylor (PERSON_ID 3) appears twice because she has two pets.

FIGURE 8.32

Using an inner join, you can return values from multiple related tables.

first_name	last_name	name
Sam	Taylor	Fluffy
John	Smith	Rocky
Sam	Taylor	Mittens

A more formal way of writing the same query is:

```
SELECT person.first_name, person.last_name, pet.name
FROM person
JOIN pet on pet.person_id = person.person_id;
```

The JOIN keyword is the ANSI standard syntax for joining tables in a select statement. The on keyword is used in conjunction with JOIN to define the column in each table used in the join. Both this version of the query and the previous version produce the same results. Which version you use largely comes down to personal preference and any coding standards your development team uses.

ANSI Join is the current syntax for joins:

```
SELECT person.first_name, person.last_name, pet.name
FROM person
JOIN pet on pet.person_id = person.person_id;
```

Summary

In this chapter, you learned about relational databases and some of the key concepts involved with them, such as tables, structured query language (SQL), and stored procedures. Then, you downloaded, installed, and configured MySQL, a popular and robust open-source database server. You also downloaded and installed a suite of GUI tools for working with MySQL databases. Finally, you built a simple database by using the GUI tools and then ran some queries against it to get a feel for how relational databases in general and MySQL specifically operate. This introduction to relational databases gives you a solid foundation upon which to build when working with MySQL to develop your Java and Flex applications.

Chapter 9

Java and Databases

J ava has a wide variety of libraries available for working with databases. This chapter discusses two of the most widely used methods of working with databases in Java. The first, Java Database Connectivity, is included with the Java Development Kit. The second, Hibernate, is a separate open-source library.

IN THIS CHAPTER

Java database connectivity

The Hibernate framework

Java Database Connectivity

Java Database Connectivity (JDBC) has been a standard component of the JDK almost since the beginning. JDK version 6 includes JDBC 4.0. It provides a set of classes that allow you to execute SQL statements and queries against a database and then work with the results. Because it uses standard SQL, developers who are familiar with SQL and running queries against a database are able to pick it up fairly quickly.

CROSS-REF For more on databases and SQL, see Chapter 8.

Overview of JDBC

The JDBC classes included with the JDK are part of the `java.sql` and `javax.sql` packages. There are a number of classes and interfaces in this package. These include the following:

■ **The Connection interface** represents a connection to a database. `Connection` is used to create the statements and queries that are run against the database as well as to retrieve information about the database itself.

- **The Statement interface** represents the SQL statement to be run against the database.

- **The PreparedStatement interface** is much like the `Statement` interface, but it also allows the addition of parameters. This allows you to execute the same query multiple times by using different values.

- **The ResultSet interface** represents the results of a `select` statement in SQL.

To support databases from different vendors, connections to databases using JDBC require a special class called a *JDBC driver*. The JDBC driver is responsible for managing communication and translation between the standard JDBC classes and the database. JDBC drivers aren't included with the JDK. They're usually provided by the database vendor or third-party developers.

Typically, code that uses JDBC to work with a database follows this pattern:

- Get a connection to the database and make sure it's valid.

- Create a SQL statement to execute.

- Execute the statement.

- If the statement was a `select` statement, retrieve and manipulate the results.

- If the statement was an `insert`, `update`, or `delete` statement, retrieve the number of rows affected by the query.

Using JDBC with MySQL

MySQL provides an open-source JDBC driver called MySQL Connector/J for use with MySQL databases. You need to download this JDBC driver in order to use JDBC with the MySQL database. MySQL Connector/J is available for download on the MySQL Web site at `http://dev.mysql.com/downloads/connector/j/5.1.html`. As of this writing, the most recent version of MySQL Connector/J is 5.1.6.

 Updates to MySQL Connector/J are likely, so use the current version available.

CROSS-REF For more on MySQL, see Chapter 8.

To download MySQL Connector/J, follow these steps:

1. **Click the Download link to the right of Source and Binaries (zip) on the download page.** The File Download dialog box opens.

2. **Choose Save and then choose a directory to save the ZIP file to your computer.**

3. **Open the ZIP file and then extract it to a location of your choice.** The ZIP file has a single folder that contains the MySQL Connector/J JDBC driver JAR file as well as the Java source code for the driver and documentation.

With MySQL Connector/J downloaded, you can create a simple stand-alone JDBC application by using the `petclub` database you created previously. This very basic application displays a list of pet names, their types, and which person they belong to. You use Eclipse to create a project, write the application, and run it.

CROSS-REF For a review of the sample `petclub` database, see Chapter 8. For more on Eclipse, see Chapter 1.

To create the MySQL JDBC application by using Eclipse, follow these steps:

1. **Right-click inside the Project Explorer view and then choose New ⇨ Project from the popup menu.** The Select a wizard dialog box, as shown in Figure 9.1, opens.

FIGURE 9.1

The Select a wizard dialog box allows you to choose a project type.

2. **Click the arrow next to Java to expand it, choose Java Project, and then click Next.** The Create a Java Project wizard, as shown in Figure 9.2, opens.

3. **Type a name for your project and then click Next.** The default values are appropriate for the rest of the options on this screen. The Java Settings screen, as shown in Figure 9.3, opens.

4. **Click the Libraries tab and then click the Add External JARs button.** The JAR Selection dialog box opens.

FIGURE 9.2

When the Create a Java Project wizard opens, you can type a name for your project. The default values for the other settings are appropriate.

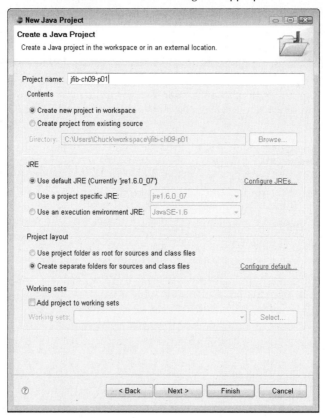

5. **Navigate to the location where you extracted MySQL Connector/J, choose the** `mysql-connector-java-5.1.6-bin.jar` **file, and then click Open.** The JAR Selection dialog box closes, and the `mysql-connector-java-5.1.6-bin.jar` file appears in the Libraries tab, as shown in Figure 9.4. JAR files listed in the Libraries tab for the project are added to the classpath used by the Java compiler and Eclipse.

6. **Click Finish.** The wizard closes, and the new project appears in the Project Explorer view, as shown in Figure 9.5.

FIGURE 9.3

The Java Settings screen

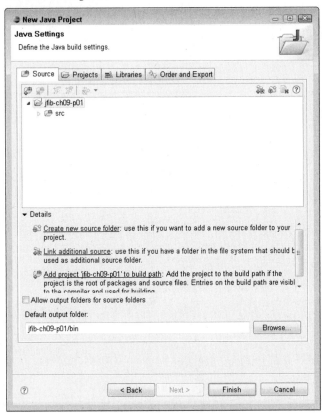

The application itself can't directly use any classes from the MySQL Connector/J library. Instead, the `DriverManager` class in the JDK searches for an appropriate JDBC driver on the classpath based on the connection information provided by the application. By adding the MySQL Connector/J JAR file to the libraries available to this project, when the application is run within Eclipse, the JDK can load the correct JDBC driver to talk to the database.

FIGURE 9.4

After choosing the `mysql-connector-java-5.1.6-bin.jar` file in the JAR Selection dialog box and clicking Open, the JAR file appears in the Libraries tab and is on the classpath used by the Java compiler and Eclipse.

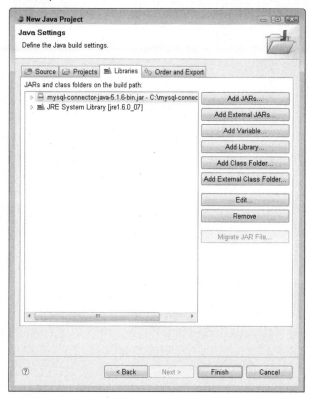

FIGURE 9.5

The newly created project appears in the Project Explorer view once the wizard is complete.

Now that the Eclipse project has been configured, the application can be coded. Follow these steps to create the Java file for the application:

1. **Right-click the `src` folder under the project in the Project Explorer view and then choose New ➪ Package from the popup menu.** The New Java Package dialog box, as shown in Figure 9.6, opens.

FIGURE 9.6

Type a name for the new package in the New Java Package dialog box. The default value in the Source folder text field is appropriate.

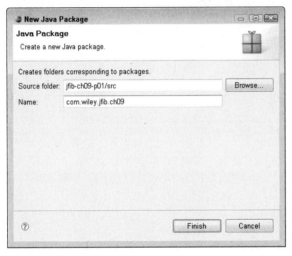

2. **Type** com.wiley.jfib.ch09 **for the package name and then click Finish.** The default value for the Source folder is appropriate. The new package appears in the `src` folder under the project, as shown in Figure 9.7.

3. **Right-click the `com.wiley.jfib.ch09` package in the Project Explorer view and then choose New ➪ Class from the popup menu.** The New Java Class dialog box, as shown in Figure 9.8, opens.

4. **Type** ListAllPets **in the Name text field, click the check boxes next to public static void main(String[ ] args) and Generate comments, and then click Finish.** The new Java class is created and opens in the editor, as shown in Figure 9.9.

Every stand-alone Java application includes a `main` method, which takes an array of string objects as a parameter. The array of strings corresponds to any arguments passed into the application, and the array is arranged in the order in which the arguments are passed. Arguments aren't required, and in this case, there won't be any arguments for the application, so the array of strings passed into the `main` method is null.

FIGURE 9.7

The newly created package appears in the `src` folder under the project in the Project Explorer view.

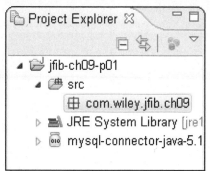

FIGURE 9.8

The New Java Class dialog box

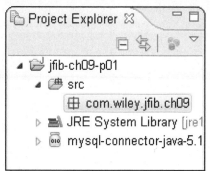

FIGURE 9.9

The newly created Java class opens in the editor. A stub of the `public static void main(String[] args)` method has been created for you.

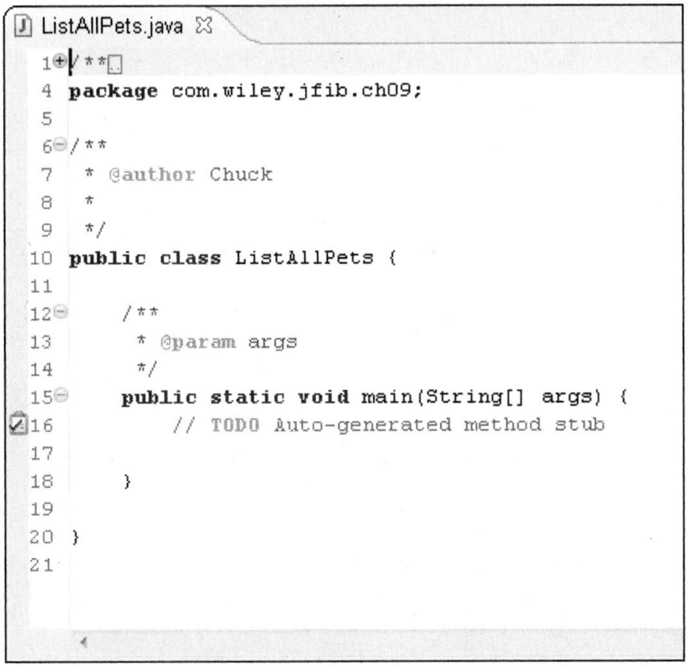

```
ListAllPets.java ⊠
  1⊕/**□
  4 package com.wiley.jfib.ch09;
  5
  6⊖/**
  7  * @author Chuck
  8  *
  9  */
 10 public class ListAllPets {
 11
 12⊖    /**
 13      * @param args
 14      */
 15⊖    public static void main(String[] args) {
 16        // TODO Auto-generated method stub
 17
 18    }
 19
 20 }
 21
```

The `main` method is where the main functionality of the application appears. Change the `main` method to match the following code listing:

```
public static void main(String[] args)
{
        String jdbcUrl = "jdbc:mysql://localhost:3306/petclub";
        String username = "root";
        String password = "toor";
        Connection conn = null;
        Statement stmt = null;
        ResultSet rs = null;
        String sql = "SELECT pet_id, name, type,"
            + "person_id FROM pet";

        try
        {
                conn = DriverManager.getConnection(jdbcUrl,username,
password);
                stmt = conn.createStatement();
```

241

```
                        rs = stmt.executeQuery(sql);
                        while(rs.next())
                        {
                                System.out.println(rs.getString("name")
                                    + " is a "
                                    + rs.getString("type")
                                    + " belonging to person id "
                                    + rs.getInt("person_id"));
                        }
                }

                catch(SQLException sqle)
                {
                        sqle.printStackTrace();
                }

                finally
                {
                        try
                        {
                                rs.close();
                                stmt.close();
                                conn.close();
                        }
                        catch(SQLException e)
                        {

                        }
                }
        }
}
```

The first three lines inside the `main` method define the three parameters needed to establish a connection to the database. The `username` and `password` parameters are fairly self-explanatory, but `jdbcUrl` needs clarifying. Each JDBC driver, such as MySQL Connector/J, defines a URL that tells the Java virtual machine (JVM) where to connect to the database. In this case, the URL `jdbc:mysql://localhost:3306/petclub` tells the JVM that this is a MySQL database that runs on the machine `localhost` on port 3306 and that the name of the database being connected to is `petclub`. The basic format of this URL is the same for all applications that use the MySQL Connector/J JDBC driver. If the database were located on a different server or running on a different port, those values could be changed to reflect that.

The next three lines define variables named `conn`, `stmt`, and `rs`. These variables hold implementations of the `Connection`, `Statement`, and `ResultSet` interfaces discussed earlier. Finally, a string variable named `sql` holds the actual SQL query that's used to get the data from the database.

The next section of code is enclosed in a try/catch block. A *try/catch block* is used to enclose code that might encounter an error that needs to be handled. The code in the try block is run, and if an error is encountered, it's caught and dealt with gracefully within the catch block. In this case, the JDBC classes and methods throw an SQLException if an error occurs, such as being unable to connect to the database or attempting to execute an invalid SQL statement. If a SQLException is thrown, execution of the code inside the try block ceases and the catch block then executes.

The first thing that happens inside the try block is that the JDBC DriverManager class attempts to connect to the MySQL database by using the connection information provided. You didn't have to tell the application that you're using the MySQL Connector/J driver. Using the jdbcUrl you provided, the JVM attempts to load an appropriate driver from the classpath.

Once the connection has been established, it's used to create a Statement object to be run against the database. Then, the sql string variable is passed into the Statement's execute() method, which runs that SQL against the database and returns the results of the query in a ResultSet object. The ResultSet object is a collection of rows returned from a database query. Finally, the code loops through the ResultSet as long as its next() method returns true, indicating it has more data. Each time next() is called, it moves an internal pointer to the next row in the ResultSet and returns true if it's pointing to a valid row or false if it has no more data. For each iteration of the loop, a message is printed out with the name and type of the pet along with the pet owner's person_id. The fields are referred to here by name explicitly, but they can also be retrieved by index. For example, because name is the first field in the results, calling rs.getString(1) has the same effect as rs.getString("name"). The advantage of using the field names rather than indexes is that if the query ever changes, you need to double-check that all your indexes are still appropriate.

CAUTION Although most things in Java are zero-indexed (meaning that the first item is index 0, the second item is index 1, etc.), ResultSet fields are one-indexed. It's easy to forget this and get a runtime error for using an invalid index of 0.

At the very end of the method is a finally block. The *finally block* contains code that's always executed at the end of the method, whether or not an error occurred. In this case, the finally block contains code that closes out all the database objects previously opened. This code is also contained in a try/catch block because the close() methods on all these objects throw SQLExceptions if something goes wrong (the connection is already closed, for example).

Eclipse has marked a number of lines of code with red underlines, which indicate that there's some error with the code. Mousing over each of these errors provides you with a description of the error and some possible solutions. In all these cases, the errors occur because the classes needed from the java.sql package can't be found. Add this line of code to the top of the class, just below the package declaration:

```
import java.sql.*;
```

This line tells the Java compiler to import all the classes in the java.sql package into this application. After you add this line and save the file, Eclipse knows to look for the needed classes in the java.sql package, and the errors then are cleared.

Run the application inside Eclipse by right-clicking the ListAllPets.java file in the Project Explorer and choosing Run As⇨Java Application from the popup menu. You should see the program's output in the Console view, as shown in Figure 9.10.

FIGURE 9.10

The output from running the application in Eclipse appears in the Console view.

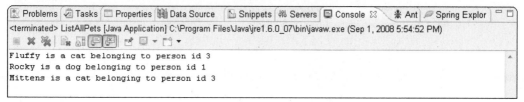

```
Fluffy is a cat belonging to person id 3
Rocky is a dog belonging to person id 1
Mittens is a cat belonging to person id 3
```

The Hibernate Framework

Although JDBC is fairly straightforward to use, it does have a few disadvantages. First, it requires a fair bit of code to perform a set of database operations. In addition to running the actual SQL query you want to run and processing the results, you must establish the database connection and create the statement, and you must remember to close all the database resources you open to avoid database connection and memory leaks in your application. Second, because different databases add their own functions and extensions to standard SQL, code written in pure JDBC may not be portable to another database without extensive modifications. Finally, it requires you to mix SQL code in with your Java code, meaning that you're using two very different programming methodologies in the same program. If another developer with a limited understanding of SQL needs to work with your code, it might be more difficult and time-consuming.

Working with JDBC also brings another issue to the forefront — namely, that relational databases, such as MySQL and Java, work with data much differently. A database stores data in rows and columns composed of simple types like VARCHAR and INTEGER. Java objects typically contain both simple types like String and int as well as other objects. In Java, it's easy to build an object composed of a mix of simple types and other objects. In SQL, complex table joins are usually required to represent this mix of data. Using JDBC to save data from a complex Java object to a relational database or to load data from many tables into a single Java object can be cumbersome.

One solution to this problem is a technique known as *object-relational mapping (ORM)*. This technique involves using a translation layer to allow Java objects to be stored in and retrieved from a database without actually needing to directly use SQL or JDBC. The objects themselves are simply passed into the ORM code, which does the work of translating the objects into SQL that the database understands. Similarly, objects can be retrieved from the database by asking for them from the ORM layer without having to write a SQL query. The code you write by using an ORM library is typically more portable than JDBC because you're not writing any SQL that's specific to a particular database; the ORM library translation generates appropriate SQL code for the database you're using.

One of the most popular ORM libraries for Java is Hibernate. Hibernate has all the features just mentioned but is also flexible enough to allow you to write your own custom SQL if you have complex or nonstandard data needs that don't quite fit what Hibernate does on its own.

Hibernate's flexibility and power can make its learning curve somewhat steep. This section covers the basics of Hibernate and provides a foundation upon which you can build.

 For more advanced Hibernate configuration and use, see Chapter 12.

Overview of Hibernate

Hibernate makes use of a number of XML configuration files. A global configuration file, usually named `hibernate.cfg.xml`, contains properties about the database being used by the application, such as the connection URL, username, and password (the same properties the JDBC example used). In addition to the global configuration file, each Java object that's saved to the database has a corresponding Hibernate mapping file. The *mapping file* tells Hibernate how the properties of the Java object should be translated to columns in the database table.

Hibernate uses the information in the global configuration file to create a Hibernate session. The Hibernate *session* is used to handle the translation between the objects and the database tables. Hibernate can also group multiple database operations into a single unit of work called a *transaction*. Using transactions is important when it's imperative that all database operations either succeed or fail as a group. Consider the example of a bank account transfer. A transfer involves withdrawing money from one account and depositing it in another account. These two operations should either succeed or fail as a group. Without a transaction, if the withdrawal succeeds but the deposit fails, the withdrawn money just disappears. With a transaction, the failure of the deposit causes the withdrawal to roll back so that both accounts are in the same state as before the transaction started.

Using Hibernate with MySQL

To use Hibernate with MySQL, you need the MySQL Connector/J JDBC driver you previously downloaded. You also need a JAR file included with your Spring Framework distribution, and you need to download Hibernate and SLF4J, which Hibernate depends on.

 For instructions on downloading the Spring Framework, see Chapter 6.

The most recent version of Hibernate is available for download on the Hibernate Web site at `www.hibernate.org/30.html`. As of this writing, the most recent version of Hibernate is 3.3.1.GA.

There are a number of packages available for download on this Web site. As its name implies, the Hibernate Core package contains all the core functionality of Hibernate. This is the package you need to download.

To download Hibernate Core, follow these steps:

1. **Click the Download link to the right of Hibernate Core on the download page.** The Hibernate Core file listing page opens.

2. Click the `hibernate-distribution-3.3.1.GA-dist.zip` **link.** The File Download dialog box opens.

3. **Choose Save and then choose a directory to save the ZIP file to your computer.**

4. **Open the ZIP file and then extract it to a location of your choice.** The ZIP file has a single folder that contains the Hibernate JAR file, other libraries used by Hibernate, and the Hibernate documentation.

Hibernate depends upon Simple Logging Façade for Java (SLF4J), which is a library that provides a single interface for many different Java logging mechanisms. This allows Hibernate to be used in applications that use any one of many different Java logging libraries, such as Apache's log4j, rather than requiring a specific logging library. This makes it easier to add Hibernate to an application with an established logging implementation.

The most recent version of SLF4J is available for download on the SLF4J Web site at `www.slf4j.org/download.html`. As of this writing, the most recent version of SLF4J is 1.5.6.

To download SLF4J, follow these steps:

1. **Click the** `slf4j-1.5.6.zip` **link on the download page.** The File Download dialog box opens.

2. **Choose Save and then choose a directory to save the ZIP file to your computer.**

3. **Open the ZIP file and then extract it to a location of your choice.** The ZIP file has a single folder that contains the SLF4J JAR files as well as the source code and build files for each one of the SLF4J JAR files.

The JDBC version of the `petclub` sample consisted of one Java class. The Hibernate version uses three Java classes and four configuration files. On the surface, this seems to contradict the idea that using Hibernate reduces the amount of code needed to work with a database. However, much of the work involved here is reusable, and when you compare the actual application class with that in the JDBC example, the amount of code is smaller and much easier to read.

Launch Eclipse again if it's not already running. First, you need to create a new project in Eclipse for this version of the sample. To create a new Eclipse project, follow these steps:

1. **Right-click inside the Project Explorer view.** The Select a wizard dialog box opens.

2. **Click the arrow next to Java to expand it, choose Java Project, and then click Next.** The Create a Java Project wizard opens.

3. **Type a name for your project and then click Next.** The default values are appropriate for the rest of the options on this screen. The Java Settings screen opens.

4. **Click the Libraries tab and then click the Add External JARs button.** The JAR Selection dialog box opens.

5. **Navigate to the location where you extracted Hibernate, choose the** `hibernate3.jar` **file, and then click Open.** The JAR Selection dialog box closes, and the `hibernate3.jar` file appears in the Libraries tab.

6. **Click Add External JARs again.** The JAR Selection dialog box opens.

7. **Navigate to the location where you extracted Hibernate, go into the `lib\required` folder, click all the JAR files in that folder, and then click Open.** The JAR Selection dialog box closes, and the six JAR files appear in the Libraries tab. Figure 9.11 shows the JAR Selection dialog box with the six JAR files in this folder.

8. **Navigate to the location where you extracted MySQL Connector/J, choose the `mysql-connector-java-5.1.6-bin.jar` file, and then click Open.** The JAR Selection dialog box closes, and the `mysql-connector-java-5.1.6-bin.jar` file appears in the Libraries tab.

9. **Click Add External JARs again.** The JAR Selection dialog box opens.

10. **Navigate to the location where you extracted SLF4J, choose the `slf4j-log4j12-1.5.6.jar` file, and then click Open.** The JAR Selection dialog box closes, and the `slf4j-log4j12-1.5.6.jar` file appears in the Libraries tab.

11. **Click Add External JARs again.** The JAR Selection dialog box opens.

12. **Navigate to the location where you extracted the Spring Framework, go into the `lib` folder, choose the `log4j-1.2.15.jar` file, and then click Open.** The JAR Selection dialog box closes, and the `log4j-1.2.15.jar` file appears in the Libraries tab. Once this JAR file has been added, the Libraries tab should contain all the JAR files shown in Figure 9.12.

13. **Click OK.** The wizard closes, and the new project appears in the Project Explorer view.

FIGURE 9.11

Click all six JAR files in the `lib\required` folder in the Hibernate folder you previously extracted. As the folder name implies, these libraries are required by Hibernate.

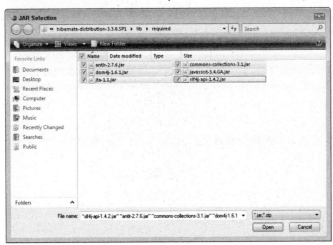

Because one of the main features of Hibernate is to map Java objects to database tables, the first thing to do is create objects to represent the data in the tables in the `petclub` database. Figure 9.13 shows the two tables in the database. Using the information in the tables, you can create a `Person` class and a `Pet` class to represent the data.

FIGURE 9.12

Once all the necessary JAR files have been added, the Libraries tab should look like this.

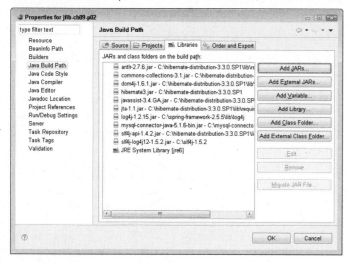

FIGURE 9.13

The PERSON and PET tables in the `petclub` database. Using the information here, you can create classes to represent the data in these tables.

PERSON

PERSON_ID	FIRST_NAME	LAST_NAME	GENDER	HEIGHT_IN_INCHES	WEIGHT_IN_LB	AGE	DATE_OF_BIRTH
1	John	Smith	M	70	165	30	08-10-1978
2	Mary	Jones	F	63	120	25	04-01-1983
3	Sam	Taylor	F	65	130	35	11-24-1973

PET

PET_ID	NAME	TYPE	PERSON_ID
1	Fluffy	cat	3
2	Rocky	dog	1
3	Mittens	cat	3

To create the `Person` and `Pet` classes, follow these steps:

1. **Right-click the `src` folder under the project in the Project Explorer view and then choose New ⇨ Package from the popup menu.** The New Java Package dialog box opens.

2. **Type com.wiley.jfib.ch09 for the package name and then click Finish.** The default value for the Source folder is appropriate. The new package appears in the `src` folder under the project.

3. **Right-click the `com.wiley.jfib.ch09` package in the Project Explorer view and then choose New ⇨ Class from the popup menu.** The New Java Class dialog box opens.

4. **Click the Add button to the right of the Interfaces box.** The Implemented Interfaces Selection dialog box, as shown in Figure 9.14, opens.

The Implemented Interfaces Selection dialog box

5. **Type Serializable in the Choose interfaces text field, choose `Serializable - java.io` from the Matching items list, and then click OK.** The Implemented Interfaces Selection dialog box closes, and the `java.io.Serializable` interface appears in the Interfaces box in the New Java Class dialog box.

6. **Type Person in the Name text field, click the check boxes next to Constructors from superclass and Generate comments, as shown in Figure 9.15, and then click Finish.** The new Java class is created and opens in the editor.

7. **Right-click the `com.wiley.jfib.ch09` package in the Project Explorer view and then choose New ⇨ Class from the popup menu.** The New Java Class dialog box opens.

8. **Click the Add button to the right of the Interfaces box.** The Implemented Interfaces Selection dialog box opens.

9. **Type** Serializable **in the Choose interfaces text field, choose** `Serializable - java.io` **from the Matching items list, and then click OK.** The Implemented Interfaces Selection dialog box closes, and the `java.io.Serializable` interface appears in the Interfaces box in the New Java Class dialog box.

10. **Type** Pet **in the Name text field, click the check boxes next to Constructors from superclass and Generate comments, and then click Finish.** The new Java class is created and opens in the editor.

Clicking the Constructors from superclass check box in the New Java Class dialog box causes Eclipse to generate the `Person` and `Pet` classes with constructors that don't take parameters. One of the requirements for objects that Hibernate handles is that they have a default constructor like this. Hibernate uses this constructor to instantiate objects when it retrieves data from the database.

FIGURE 9.15

The New Java Class dialog box

The classes have been created, but they have no properties in which to hold values from the database. Click the tab for the `Person.java` file in the editor and then add the properties for the Person class just below the opening curly brace for the class definition so that it matches this code listing:

```
/**
 *
 */
package com.wiley.jfib.ch09;

import java.io.Serializable;
import java.util.Calendar;

/**
 * @author Chuck
 *
 */
public class Person implements Serializable
{
    private int personId;
    private String firstName;
    private String lastName;
    private String gender;
    private int heightInInches;
    private int weightInPounds;
    private int age;
    private Calendar dateOfBirth;

    /**
     *
     */
    public Person()
    {
    }
}
```

The Person class has a property for each column in the database. The types of these properties match the data types of the database columns. For example, the `personId` property is an `int`, corresponding to the `PERSON_ID` column of type `INTEGER` in the database. The `dateOfBirth` property is a `java.util.Calendar` object, which maps to the `DATE` type in MySQL.

The Person class also implements the `Serializable` interface. `Serializable` is a special interface that has no methods to implement. Although this practice isn't required, having your objects implement `Serializable` is a good practice. The `Serializable` interface tells the JVM that the current state of this object can be saved and restored as necessary.

Although it's not particularly important for this simple example, more complicated applications that use caching mechanisms or share objects across multiple application servers make use of this functionality frequently. It's good to get into the habit of implementing this interface.

All the properties in this class are marked `private`. Remember that this means they can't be accessed outside this class. A standard convention for writing Java objects is to mark the properties of the objects as `private` and allow them to be manipulated only by using sets of *accessor methods*, sometimes referred to as *getters* and *setters*. Getters and setters follow a standard naming convention: the word *get* or *set* followed by the name of the property. For example, the getter and setter for the `personId` property would be called `getPersonId()` and `setPersonId()`, respectively. A Java class that has a no-argument constructor, implements the `Serializable` interface, and uses the standard naming convention for getters and setters is called a *Java bean*.

NOTE   The naming convention for getters for properties of type boolean (true/false) is slightly different. Rather than using `getProperty()`, the convention for boolean types is `isProperty()`.

CROSS-REF   For more on about Java syntax and keywords, such as private and public, see Chapter 1.

Eclipse makes it easy to create getters and setters for all the properties in an object. To create the getters and setters for the `Person` class, follow these steps:

1. **Right-click the `Person` class in the editor and then choose Source ⇨ Generate Getters and Setters from the popup menu.** The Generate Getters and Setters dialog box, as shown in Figure 9.16, opens.

2. **Click Select All and then click OK.** The Generate Getters and Setters dialog box closes, and the getters and setters for all properties of the `Person` class are added to the class after the constructor.

Now add the properties of the `Pet` object. When finished, the `Pet` object should look like this code listing:

```
/**
 *
 */
package com.wiley.jfib.ch09;

import java.io.Serializable;

/**
 * @author Chuck
```

```
     *
     */
    public class Pet implements Serializable
    {
        private int petId;
        private String name;
        private String type;
        private Person person;

        /**
         *
         */
        public Pet()
        {
        }
    }
```

The Pet class is structured much like the Person class. It implements the Serializable interface and has a property for each field in the database. However, there's one big difference: The PET table in the database has a PERSON_ID field of type INTEGER. Rather than include a personId property of type int, however, the Pet class has a person property, which is a Person object. In the database, the relationship between Pet and Person is established by the PERSON_ID column. In a Hibernate mapping file, this relationship is used to provide the full Person object to the Pet class.

Generate the getters and setters for the Pet class the same way you did for the Person class. Now that these two classes are complete, you can create the Hibernate mapping files for them.

Hibernate mapping files are XML files that describe the relationship between the properties in Java classes and fields in database tables. Hibernate uses these mappings at runtime to save and retrieve the objects to and from the database. The mapping files need to be on the application's classpath at runtime for Hibernate to be able to locate them.

To create the Hibernate mapping files for the Person and Pet classes, follow these steps:

1. **Right-click the project in the Project Explorer view and then choose New ⇨ Folder from the popup menu.** The New Folder dialog box, as shown in Figure 9.17, opens.

2. **Type cfg in the Folder name text field and then click Finish.** The New Folder dialog box closes, and the newly created folder appears in the Project Explorer view.

3. **Right-click the cfg folder in the Project Explorer view and then choose New ⇨ File from the popup menu.** The New File dialog box, as shown in Figure 9.18, opens.

FIGURE 9.16

The Generate Getters and Setters dialog box allows you to choose properties for which getters and setters are generated.

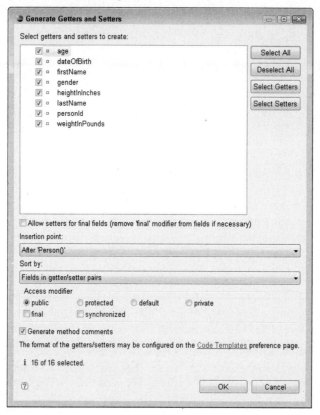

4. **Type** Person.hbm.xml **in the File name text field and then click Finish.** The New File dialog box closes, and the `Person.hbm.xml` file appears in the Project Explorer view and opens in the editor.

5. **Right-click the** `cfg` **folder in the Project Explorer view and then choose New ⇨ File from the popup menu.** The New File dialog box opens.

6. **Type** Pet.hbm.xml **in the File name text field and then click Finish.** The New File dialog box closes, and the `Pet.hbm.xml` file appears in the Project Explorer view and opens in the editor.

FIGURE 9.17

The New Folder dialog box

Click the `Person.hbm.xml` tab in the editor to switch to it. The file opens in the Eclipse XML editor, as shown in Figure 9.19. The Eclipse XML editor has two different views, represented by tabs at the bottom of the editor window. By default, the editor opens in the Design view, which shows a tabular representation of the XML structure or instructions for adding content to the document if the document is empty, as your `Person.hbm.xml` file is to begin with. Most of the time, however, it's easier to understand the structure of an XML document by examining the source directly. To switch the editor to Source view, click the Source tab in the bottom-left section of the editor window. All the instructions for editing XML files in this chapter assume that you have the Eclipse XML editor in Source view.

FIGURE 9.18

The New File dialog box

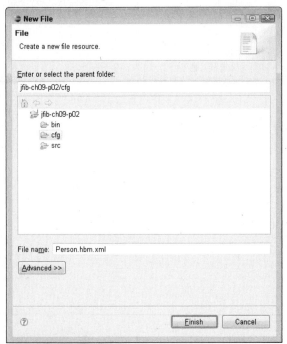

FIGURE 9.19

When editing an XML file in Eclipse, the Eclipse XML editor is used. By default, it opens in the Design view shown here. To switch to Source view, which is used in this chapter, click the Source tab in the bottom-left section of the editor window.

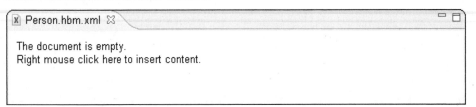

Switch the editor for `Person.hbm.xml` to Source view and then edit the file so that it matches this code listing:

```
<?xml version="1.0" encoding="UTF-8"?>
```

```
<!DOCTYPE hibernate-mapping PUBLIC "-//Hibernate/Hibernate Mapping
    DTD 3.0//EN" "http://hibernate.sourceforge.net/hibernate-mapping-
    3.0.dtd" >
<hibernate-mapping>
    <class name="com.wiley.jfib.ch09.Person" table="PERSON">
        <id name="personId" column="person_id"
            type="java.lang.Integer">
          <generator class="increment"/>
        </id>
        <property name="firstName" column="first_name"
            type="java.lang.String" />
        <property name="lastName" column="last_name"
            type="java.lang.String" />
        <property name="gender" column="gender"
            type="java.lang.String" />
        <property name="heightInInches" column="height_in_inches"
            type="java.lang.Integer" />
        <property name="weightInPounds" column="weight_in_lb"
            type="java.lang.Integer" />
        <property name="age" column="age"
            type="java.lang.Integer" />
        <property name="dateOfBirth" column="date_of_birth"
            type="java.util.Calendar"/>
    </class>
</hibernate-mapping>
```

The Person class is very basic, and the Hibernate mapping file for the Person class is also quite basic. The `<class>` tag relates the Person class in the `com.wiley.jfib.ch09` package to the PERSON table in the database. Inside the `<class>` tag are an `<id>` tag and a number of `<property>` tags. The `<id>` tag tells Hibernate what the primary key of the PERSON table is (person_id) and what property it maps to in the Person class (personId). Inside the `<id>` tag, the `<generator>` tag tells Hibernate that the values for this field are generated by an auto-incrementing function in the database. Each `<property>` tag maps one of the properties in the Person class to a column in the database and gives the data type of each one.

Now switch the editor for Pet.hbm.xml to Source view and then edit the file so that it matches this code listing:

```
<?xml version="1.0" encoding="UTF-8"?>
<!DOCTYPE hibernate-mapping PUBLIC "-//Hibernate/Hibernate Mapping
    DTD 3.0//EN" "http://hibernate.sourceforge.net/hibernate-mapping-
    3.0.dtd" >
<hibernate-mapping>
    <class name="com.wiley.jfib.ch09.Pet" table="PET">
        <id name="petId" column="pet_id" type="java.lang.Integer">
            <generator class="increment"/>
        </id>
```

```
            <property name="name" column="name" type="java.lang.String"
     />
            <property name="type" column="type" type="java.lang.String"
     />
            <many-to-one name="person" column="person_id" class="com.
     wiley.jfib.ch09.Person"/>
        </class>
     </hibernate-mapping>
```

This mapping file is largely similar to the `Person.hbm.xml` mapping file, but it also contains a `<many-to-one>` tag. The `<many-to-one>` tag describes a relationship between the `Pet` class and the `Person` class. It says that many Pets can belong to one Person and that they're related through the `person_id` column. Hibernate uses this relationship and the value in the `person_id` column to set the `person` property of each `Pet` object with the appropriate `Person` object.

The Java classes are configured with their own Hibernate mapping files, but Hibernate itself also needs a configuration file. This file gives Hibernate information about the database and also sets up the Hibernate *session*, which is used to perform all interactions with the database.

To create the Hibernate configuration file, follow these steps:

1. **Right-click the `cfg` folder in the Project Explorer view and then choose New ⇨ File from the popup menu.** The New File dialog box opens.

2. **Type hibernate.cfg.xml in the File name text field and then click Finish.** The New File dialog box closes, and the `hibernate.cfg.xml` file appears in the Project Explorer view.

Switch the editor for `hibernate.cfg.xml` to Source view and then edit the file so that it matches this code listing:

```
     <?xml version='1.0' encoding='utf-8'?>
     <!DOCTYPE hibernate-configuration PUBLIC
             "-//Hibernate/Hibernate Configuration DTD 3.0//EN"

       "http://hibernate.sourceforge.net/
       hibernate-configuration-3.0.dtd">

     <hibernate-configuration>
        <session-factory>

            <!-- Database connection settings -->

            <property name="connection.driver_class">com.mysql.jdbc.Driver
            </property>
            <property name="connection.url">jdbc:mysql://localhost:3306/petclub
            </property>
            <property name="connection.username">root</property>
            <property name="connection.password">toor</property>
```

```
        <!-- SQL dialect -->
        <property name="dialect">org.hibernate.dialect.MySQLDialect
        </property>

        <!-- Hibernate session -->
        <property name="current_session_context_class">thread
        </property>

        <!-- Write SQL to log or console -->
        <property name="show_sql">false</property>

        <mapping resource="Person.hbm.xml"/>
        <mapping resource="Pet.hbm.xml"/>

    </session-factory>
</hibernate-configuration>
```

> **NOTE** Be sure to use the correct password for your MySQL database's root user in your configuration file's `connection.password` property.

The Hibernate configuration file contains a `<session-factory>` tag. Much as a real-world factory's purpose is the construction or assembly of things, a *factory class* in object-oriented programming is a class responsible for the construction or assembly of other classes. Hibernate uses a `SessionFactory` class to create the Hibernate session. The configuration in this file is used by the `SessionFactory` when it creates the Hibernate session. There are quite a number of configuration options possible in this file. This example uses the bare minimum of required configuration options. The Hibernate documentation provides details on all the available options.

The first four `<property>` tags here provide the information needed to connect to the database. The `connection.driver_class` property tells Hibernate to use the MySQL Connector/J JDBC driver class to connect to the database. The next three properties contain the same information you used in the JDBC example: the connection URL, username, and password for the database.

The next property tells Hibernate which SQL *dialect* to use. Because most databases add their own proprietary keywords or structures to standard SQL, Hibernate needs to know what kind of database is being used so that it can generate SQL that the database understands. This is quite a powerful feature. For example, if your MySQL application ever needs to also run on Oracle, you can simply edit the Hibernate configuration file with the connection information and Oracle dialect. Little, if any, of your Hibernate Java code would need to change because the Java code doesn't contain anything database-specific.

The next property, `current_session_context_class`, tells Hibernate how the current session should be managed. The value `thread` means that the current session is tied to the running program thread. A *thread* is simply a set of running tasks within a program. Some programs split their operations into multiple threads so that more than one operation can be run in parallel. This program has only a single thread and uses only a single Hibernate session.

The last property tells Hibernate whether it should output the SQL it generates. Examining the SQL that Hibernate produces can be useful for understanding how Hibernate translates your Java classes into SQL by using the mapping files.

Finally, the two <mapping> tags simply list the Hibernate mapping files for your application. There's no path information for these files because they're in the same folder as the Hibernate configuration file, but if they were located in different folders, the file path would also need to be included.

The final configuration file is the log4j.properties file. Log4j is a Java logging library. Hibernate uses this library to output information either to a log file or to the console. Log4j supports several different levels of logging — such as info, warn, and error — allowing you control over how much information and what type of information is output to the log.

To create the log4j.properties file, follow these steps:

1. **Right-click the cfg folder in the Project Explorer view and then choose New ⇨ File from the popup menu.** The New File dialog box opens.

2. **Type log4j.properties in the File name text field and then click Finish.** The New File dialog box closes, and the log4j.properties file appears in the Project Explorer view.

Here's the code listing for the log4j.properties file:

```
log4j.appender.stdout=org.apache.log4j.ConsoleAppender
log4j.appender.stdout.layout=org.apache.log4j.PatternLayout

log4j.rootLogger=debug, stdout

log4j.logger.org.hibernate=error
log4j.logger.org.hibernate.SQL=error
log4j.logger.org.hibernate.type=error
log4j.logger.org.hibernate.cache=error
```

The important properties here are the four at the end that start with log4j.logger. Each of these properties tells what level of logging should be used for particular packages. In this configuration, code in the org.hibernate, org.hibernate.SQL, org.hibernate.type, and org.hibernate.cache package write to the log only in case of error.

Now that all the configuration files are written, you need to add them to the project's build path so that they can be found at runtime. To add the configuration files to the build path, follow these steps:

1. **Right-click the project in the Project Explorer view and then choose Build Path ⇨ Configure Build Path from the popup menu.** The Properties dialog box opens with the Java Build Path's Libraries tab selected.

2. **Click Add Class Folder.** The Class Folder Selection dialog box, as shown in Figure 9.20, opens.

3. **Click the check box next to the `cfg` folder and then click OK.** The Class Folder Selection dialog box closes, and the `cfg` folder appears in the Libraries list.

4. **Click OK.** The Properties dialog box closes.

The final step is to write the main application class. This application is much like the ListAllPets application you wrote in the JDBC portion of this chapter but uses Hibernate instead. To create the main application class, follow these steps:

1. **Right-click the `com.wiley.jfib.ch09` package in the Project Explorer view and then choose New⇨Class from the popup menu.** The New Java Class dialog box opens.

2. **Type ListAllPetsUsingHibernate in the Name text field, click the check boxes next to public static void main(String[] args) and Generate comments, and then click Finish.** The new Java class is created and opens in the editor.

FIGURE 9.20

The Class Folder Selection dialog box

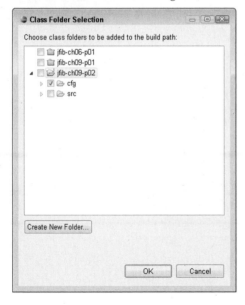

Here's the code listing for the `ListAllPetsUsingHibernate` class:

```
/**
 *
 */
```

```java
package com.wiley.jfib.ch09;

import java.util.List;

import org.hibernate.HibernateException;
import org.hibernate.SessionFactory;
import org.hibernate.Transaction;
import org.hibernate.cfg.Configuration;
import org.hibernate.classic.Session;

/**
 * @author Chuck
 * The ListAllPetsUsingHibernate class retrieves all of the pets from the
 * PETS table in the database and lists the name, type, and
 * owner's name for each one.
 */
public class ListAllPetsUsingHibernate {
    /**
     * @param args Any arguments passed to this application.
     * This application expects and uses no arguments.
     */
    public static void main(String[] args)
    {
        try
        {
            // Set up the Hibernate session
            Configuration config = new Configuration();
            config.configure("hibernate.cfg.xml");
            SessionFactory sessionFactory = config.
buildSessionFactory();
            Session session = sessionFactory.
getCurrentSession();
            Transaction tx = session.beginTransaction();

            // get the current list of pets and owners
            List<Pet> allPets = session.createCriteria(Pet.
class).list();
            for(Pet pet : allPets)
            {
                // print out each pet in the list
                System.out.println(pet.getName()
                        + " is a " + pet.getType()
                        + " belonging to "
                        + pet.getPerson().
getFirstName() + " " + pet.getPerson().getLastName());
            }
```

```
                    tx.commit();
          }

          catch (HibernateException e)
          {
                    e.printStackTrace();
          }
     }
}
```

At the beginning of this class, a number of Hibernate classes are imported. `Configuration` is used to read the configuration from the `hibernate.cfg.xml` file. `SessionFactory` uses this configuration to create a Session class. `Transaction` is a class that Hibernate provides for transaction management, which is a way of grouping operations into a single unit so that they all succeed or fail as one. Finally, any errors that occur within Hibernate code result in a `HibernateException` being thrown.

In the main method of this class, the Hibernate session is created by the `SessionFactory` by using the information from the Configuration object `config`. A transaction is started by the session — although, in reality, a session doesn't serve much purpose here with only a single operation being run; Hibernate requires some sort of transaction management to be in place.

This line of code does the bulk of the work:

```
List<Pet> allPets = session.createCriteria(Pet.class).list();
```

The Hibernate Session object has a variety of methods for retrieving objects. For retrieving single objects whose primary key value (for example, PET_ID) is known, you would use the `load()` method and supply it with the class of the `Pet` object and the primary key value. To retrieve a list of all objects of a given class, you would use a line like the one just presented. This line says to get a list of every `Pet` object from the database. Hibernate goes to the database and retrieves not only all the pets, but because of the many-to-one relationship you set up in the Hibernate mapping file between `Pet` and `Person`, it also populates the `Person` object property in the `Pet` object. The type `List<Pet>` indicates that this List object contains only Pets. The loop takes each `Pet` object in the list and prints out the pet's name and type, but thanks to the many-to-one relationship, it can also print out the owner's first and last names.

To run the application, right-click the `ListAllPetsUsingHibernate.java` file in the Project Explorer and then choose Run As ⇨ Java Application from the popup menu. You should see the program's output in the Console view, as shown in Figure 9.21.

Hibernate also makes it easy to limit the results by using criteria. Change the line that retrieves the list of pets so that it looks like this:

```
List<Pet> allPets = session.createCriteria(Pet.class).
     add(Restrictions.eq("type", "dog")).list();
```

FIGURE 9.21

Running the application results in this output in the Console view. The `Person` property of each `Pet` was populated just by retrieving the `Pet`.

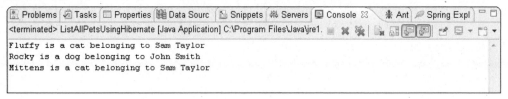

```
Fluffy is a cat belonging to Sam Taylor
Rocky is a dog belonging to John Smith
Mittens is a cat belonging to Sam Taylor
```

You also need to add an `import` statement at the top for `org.hibernate.criterion.Restrictions`. The `Restrictions` class functions much like a `WHERE` clause in a SQL statement, allowing you to place limits on the results of a database operation. In this case, the `eq` method of the `Restrictions` class is used to limit the list to those pets for which the type equals `dog`. Save the application and then run it again. This time, only one pet is retrieved because there's only one dog in the database.

> **TIP** If you're curious to see the SQL that Hibernate uses behind the scenes, click the `hibernate.cfg.xml` tab in the editor to switch to that file and then change the value of the `show_sql` property near the bottom of the file from `false` to `true`. You can run the SQL that Hibernate generates directly against your database. Just substitute any parameter placeholders (the ? character) with real values.

Summary

In this chapter, you learned about two common methods of working with databases in Java. First, you learned about JDBC, which uses classes from the `java.sql` package to allow you to write and run standard SQL queries within your Java code, and you saw an example that used JDBC to work with data in a MySQL database. Next, you learned about some of the disadvantages of working directly with JDBC and how using an object-relational mapping library can help. From there, you learned about and downloaded Hibernate, one of the most popular object-relational mapping libraries for Java database development. Finally, you saw an example that used Hibernate together with MySQL, and that showed how Hibernate lets you directly work with objects instead of having to write SQL code inside your Java code.

JDBC and Hibernate are both very deep topics. These examples provide a good starting point for more in-depth work with JDBC and Hibernate.

Chapter 10

Building a Basic Database-Powered Flex Application

In this chapter, you learn how to develop a basic database-powered application. This basic application is an admin panel for a Flex store, which is developed in Chapter 13. The code from that chapter is used so that you can focus on the Flex front-end development.

Once you complete this chapter, you should have a clear understanding of how to interact with a MySQL database by using Flex as the front end, which talks to Java on the server side (back end).

The last section of this chapter highlights testing the completed application to ensure that everything is working properly.

IN THIS CHAPTER

Understanding the database application

Building the database application

Developing the database communication with Java

Connecting the database application

Understanding the Database Application

The process of understanding your application is where you make sure that the proper tools, services, and abilities have been clearly defined.

Defining the application

Before beginning development on any project, you should take a moment to clearly define the purpose of that application. This is to ensure that important features aren't left out. For example, in a book project, the author is responsible for defining the steps required for completion. In a real-world project, the development team would sit down with the client and define the purpose of the application.

The following list contains key points to keep in mind when building the application:

- Adding and removing categories
- Managing products, which would include editing, adding, and deleting
- Testing the individual sections by using unit testing

Once you have defined what the application should do, you can start coming up with design ideas. At this point, a piece of paper and a pencil are probably all you need. For this application, the design phase has been completed for you.

File outline

A file outline clearly shows the required files for an application, ensuring that none are left out. Table 10.1 shows the class outline for this application. This table contains the list of classes for the store editor application. The forward slash (/) is relative to the `src/` directory.

TABLE 10.1

Classes and Package Paths

`JavaServiceHandler`	`/com.wiley.jfib.store.data`
`JavaFlexStoreEvent`	`/com.wiley.jfib.store.events`
`JavaFlexStoreAdmin`	`/`
`ManageRenderer`	`/`
`ProductEditor`	`/`

Now that you have an understanding of what the application will do and how it should be constructed, you can begin building it.

Building the Database Application

In this section, you focus on the design elements of the application, which include the product editor popup and the `ItemRenderer` for the product `DataGrid`.

Designing the application

Now that you have established what the application will do, it's time to start designing the various elements by using MXML.

Start by following these steps to create a new Flex project:

1. **Right-click in the Flex Navigator and then choose New ⇨ Flex Project from the popup menu**. The New Flex Project dialog box, as shown in Figure 10.1, opens.

2. In the Project name text field, type `JavaFlexStoreAdmin`.

3. Click Finish to build the project with all the default options set.

FIGURE 10.1

The New Flex Project dialog box

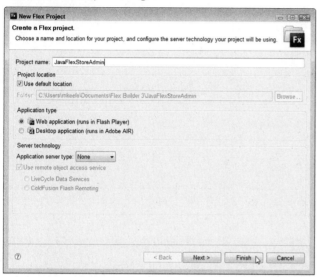

Once the new project is built, you can begin adding the design components for the main view. Start by opening the Source view and then type the following code:

JavaFlexStoreAdmin.mxml

```
<?xml version="1.0" encoding="utf-8"?>
<mx:Application xmlns:mx="http://www.adobe.com/2006/mxml"
    layout="absolute"
    creationComplete="init()"
>

    <mx:Label x="10" y="10" text="Java Flex Store Admin Panel"
    fontSize="16" color="#E9F3F5"/>
    <mx:DataGrid id="productGrid" dataProvider="{_productData}"
    bottom="10" right="10" top="68" left="10">
        <mx:columns>
            <mx:DataGridColumn width="70" headerText="ID"
    dataField="id"/>
            <mx:DataGridColumn width="200" headerText="Product"
    dataField="name"/>
            <mx:DataGridColumn headerText="Description"
    dataField="desc"/>
```

```
                    <mx:DataGridColumn width="100" headerText="Quantity"
        dataField="quantity"/>
                    <mx:DataGridColumn width="100" headerText="Price"
        dataField="price"/>
                    <mx:DataGridColumn width="100" headerText="Manage"
        itemRenderer="ManageRenderer"/>
            </mx:columns>
        </mx:DataGrid>
        <mx:Button click="displayNewHandler()" label="Add New Product"
        right="10" top="38"/>

    </mx:Application>
```

The product data is displayed in a DataGrid component, as shown in Figure 10.2, with a custom
ItemRenderer for the last column. This holds Edit and Delete buttons to manage the products.
The DataGrid is assigned a bindable data provider, which ensures that the grid is updated when-
ever the product list changes.

FIGURE 10.2

The DataGrid component displayed on the canvas in the Flex Builder Design view

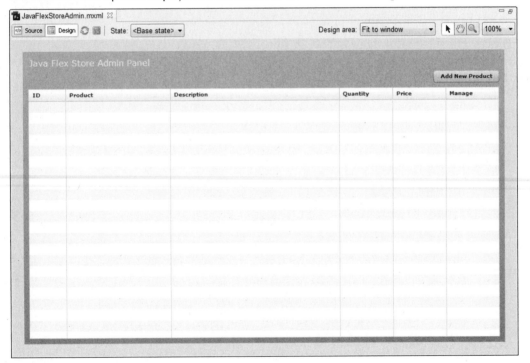

Creating the product editor popup

The next component to develop is the product editor popup. This component is used to edit and add products to the store.

 In a more complete application, you would give the user the ability to upload files and other common tasks, but as this is a basic database tutorial, that isn't covered here.

Start by following these steps to create a new Flex component:

1. **Right-click in the Flex Navigator and then choose New ⇨ MXML Component from the popup menu.** The New MXML Component dialog box, as shown in Figure 10.3, opens.

2. **In the Filename text field, type** `ProductEditor.mxml`.

3. **Set the Based On dropdown list to Panel.**

4. **Click Finish.**

FIGURE 10.3

The New MXML Component dialog box

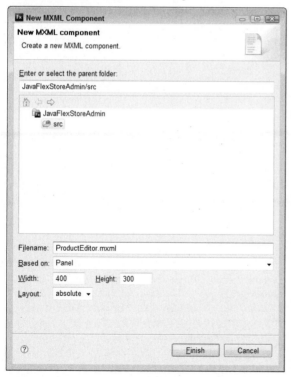

Once the new MXML component is created, add the following code within Source view:

ProductEditor.mxml

```
<?xml version="1.0" encoding="utf-8"?>
<mx:Panel xmlns:mx="http://www.adobe.com/2006/mxml" layout="absolute"
    width="400" height="300" title="Products">
    <mx:Script>
        <![CDATA[
            import mx.managers.PopUpManager;

            private function saveData():void
            {
                    parentApplication.save();
            }

            public function getXML():String
            {
                    var xml:String = "";
                    xml += "<product>";
                    xml += " <id>" + data.id + "</id>";
                    xml += " <name>" + data.name + "</name>";
                    xml += " <desc>" + data.desc + "</desc>";
                    xml += " <price>" + data.price + "</price>";
                    xml += " <quantity>" + data.quantity + "</quantity>";
                    xml += "</product>";

                    return xml;
            }

                    var xml:XML = <product>
                    <id>{data.id}</id>
                    <name>{data.name}</name>
                    <desc>{data.desc}</desc>
                    <price>{data.price}</price>
                    <quantity>{data.quantity}</quantity>
            </product>

                    return xml.toXMLString();

        ]]>
    </mx:Script>

    <mx:Label x="20" y="20" text="Name" fontWeight="bold"/>
    <mx:Label x="20" y="50" text="Quantity" fontWeight="bold"/>
    <mx:Label x="20" y="110" text="Description" fontWeight="bold"/>
    <mx:TextInput x="95" y="18" text="{data.name}"/>
    <mx:TextInput x="95" y="48" text="{data.quantity}"/>
    <mx:Label x="20" y="80" text="Price" fontWeight="bold"/>
```

```
<mx:TextInput x="95" y="78" text="{data.price}"/>
<mx:TextArea x="20" y="136" width="350" height="84" text="{data.
desc}"/>

<mx:Button click="saveData()" x="273" y="228" label="Add/
Update"/>
<mx:Button click="PopUpManager.removePopUp(this)" x="209" y="228"
label="Close"/>

</mx:Panel>
```

The majority of the previous code should be familiar to you from previous exercises in this book. The design is composed of multiple `Label` and `TextInput` components whose default values are automatically filled whenever the user clicks the edit button in the product grid.

> **NOTE** The above code uses `parentApplication`, which works, as you have seen. However, it's not best practice and should be used sparingly. The proper approach would be to use an event handler and dispatch an event rather than calling the function directly.

The only function that's specific to this application is `getXML()`. This function captures the data from the current product, creates an XML node, and returns that as a string. The string that's generated in the `getXML()` function is created by concatenating the individual XML elements to complete the whole node:

```
public function getXML():String
{
        var xml:String = "";
        xml += "<product>";
        xml += " <id>" + data.id + "</id>";
        xml += " <name>" + data.name + "</name>";
        xml += " <desc>" + data.desc + "</desc>";
        xml += " <price>" + data.price + "</price>";
        xml += " <quantity>" +data.quantity+ "</quantity>";
        xml += "</product>";

        return xml;
}
```

This XML is used to pass information back to the Java server.

Here's an example of the XML that's passed:

```
<product>
    <id>4</id>
    <name>DVD Player</name>
    <desc>A state of the art movie player</desc>
    <quantity>50</quantity>
    <price>89.99</price>
</product>
```

NOTE   In a more advanced application, such as a complete store application that would be deployed to millions of users, you would use a more secure or stable method of transporting data rather than passing everything as a GET method by using HTTP. One option is to use BlazeDS, which is covered in Chapter 11.

Creating the product grid ItemRenderer

The product grid has a manage column that's meant to hold button components to edit and delete the products. The default `DataGrid` doesn't allow other components to be placed in a column. However, with the use of an `ItemRenderer`, as shown in Figure 10.4, you can indeed achieve the custom result.

FIGURE 10.4

The `ItemRenderer` in the Design view of Flex

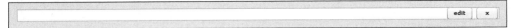

CROSS-REF   For more on ItemRenderers, see Chapter 13.

In order to create the `ItemRenderer`, follow these steps:

1. **Right-click in the Flex Navigator and then choose New⇨MXML Component from the popup menu.** The MXML Component editor opens.

2. **In the Filename text field, type** `ManageRenderer.mxml`.

3. **Set the Based On dropdown list to HBox.**

4. **Type** 100% **for the Width and** 22 **for the Height.**

5. **Click Finish.**

Once the new MXML component is created, add the following code that draws the `ItemRenderer` with events in place to handle the clicks from the Edit and Delete buttons:

ManageRenderer.mxml

```
<?xml version="1.0" encoding="utf-8"?>
<mx:HBox xmlns:mx="http://www.adobe.com/2006/mxml"
    width="100%"
    height="22"
    horizontalAlign="right"
    paddingRight="3"
>

    <mx:Script>
```

```
        <![CDATA[

                private function editHandler():void
                {
                        parentApplication.displayEditorHandler();
                }

                private function deleteHandler():void
                {
                        parentApplication.deleteProduct();
                }

        ]]>
    </mx:Script>

    <mx:Button click="editHandler()" label="edit" width="47"/>
    <mx:Button click="deleteHandler()" label="x"/>

</mx:HBox>
```

Both of the `Button` events make use of the `parentApplication` property in order to reference the main application file. These components don't contain any of the logic from the product grid because they don't need it.

When you're developing your applications, it's a best practice to ensure that each element is completing its task without too much fluff included. For example, you could have passed the product ID into this component and then returned it to the main application when the user clicked the button. However, this would require extra code and testing steps with no gain in performance or usability.

The product `DataGrid` knows which product is selected, and the product editor is a modal popup, so you can ensure that the selected product isn't going to change during the process.

You have now completed all the components and design for the application. In the next section, you start building the class, which communicates with the Java back end, and then connect everything.

Developing the Database Communication with Java

In this section, you learn how to communicate with the Java back end to load the product data and then add the ability to update the product data and listing.

The communication with Java is used at least three times: when loading the products when the application starts, when saving edited product information, and when a new product is added. Considering that these processes have similarities, building a custom class and reusing that class is a very good approach, so that's exactly how the application is built.

Start by creating a new ActionScript class:

1. **Right-click the** `src/` **directory in the Flex Navigator and then choose New ⇨ ActionScript Class from the popup menu.** The new ActionScript Class editor opens.

2. **In the Package text field, type** `package com.wiley.jfib.store.data`.

3. **In the Name text field, type** `JavaServiceHandler`.

4. **In the Superclass text field, type** `flash.events.EventDispatcher`.

5. **Click Finish.**

A new ActionScript class is created that should look like this:

```
package com.wiley.jfib.store.data
{
    import flash.events.EventDispatcher;
    import flash.events.IEventDispatcher;

    public class JavaServiceHandler extends EventDispatcher
    {
    public function JavaServiceHandler(target:IEventDispatcher=null)
        {
                super(target);
        }
    }
}
```

Building a custom data class

The class you just created is extending the `EventDispatcher`. This is because once the server responds with data, a custom event is dispatched. This is covered later in this chapter.

Now that the class is started, you need to add the variables that store the service path to load and the response data once it's returned.

The response is stored in the XML format so that the proper nodes can still be retrieved:

NOTE In a larger application, you would most likely load the data from the server, modify it, and then store it by using a simpler format, such as an Object.

```
package com.wiley.jfib.store.data
{
    .
    .
    .

    public class JavaServiceHandler extends EventDispatcher
    {
```

```
        public var serviceURL:String = "";
        public var response:XML;

        public function JavaServiceHandler()
        {
        }
    }
}
```

Adding the class methods

The next piece of code is used to add the methods that handle the loading and response of the server calls. The first method to add is `callServer()`. This method is called after the `serviceURL` has been properly defined:

```
    .
    .
    .

public function callServer():void
{
    if(serviceURL == "")
    {
        throw new Error("serviceURL is a required parameter");
        return;
    }

    var loader:URLLoader = new URLLoader();
    loader.addEventListener(Event.COMPLETE, handleResponse);
    loader.load(new URLRequest(serviceURL));
}
    .
    .
    .
```

The first part of this method checks for a valid `serviceURL` because if this variable is missing, the call to the server would immediately fail. If a proper URL is found, a new instance of the `URLLoader` class is created to handle the loading of server call.

When the data is fully loaded, an `Event.COMPLETE` is dispatched automatically. In this code, this is where the `handleResponse()` method is called, ensuring that the data is loaded before parsing it.

The last line actually makes the call to the server by using the `load()` method that's part of the `URLLoader` class. This method accepts a parameter that's an instance of the `URLRequest` class. A shorthand approach is to create the instance directly in the method call.

NOTE   When creating the instance directly within the method call limits, you're unable to change the `"send data"` or request method.

Handling the response from the server

The last method for this class is `handleResponse()`, which is called when the server responds with data. This method captures the data from the server and then stores it within the `response` property:

```
      .
      .
      .
private function handleResponse(event:Event):void
{
    var loader:URLLoader = URLLoader(event.currentTarget);
    response = XML(loader.data);

    dispatchEvent
    (
        new JavaFlexStoreEvent(JavaFlexStoreEvent.DATA_LOADED)
    );
}
```

The last step in this method is to dispatch a custom event that notifies any items listening to it that the server data is fully loaded and ready to be parsed. That completes the Java service handler class.

Here's the Java service handler class in its entirety:

JavaServiceClass.as

```
package com.wiley.jfib.store.data
{
    import com.wiley.jfib.store.events.JavaFlexStoreEvent;

    import flash.events.Event;
    import flash.events.EventDispatcher;
    import flash.net.URLLoader;
    import flash.net.URLRequest;

    public class JavaServiceHandler extends EventDispatcher
    {

        public var serviceURL:String = "";
        public var response:XML;

        public function JavaServiceHandler()
        {

        }

        public function callServer():void
        {
            if(serviceURL == "")
```

```
                {
                        throw new Error
                        (
                                "serviceURL is a required parameter"
                        );
                        return;
                }

                var loader:URLLoader = new URLLoader();
                loader.addEventListener(Event.COMPLETE,
        handleResponse);
                loader.load(new URLRequest(serviceURL));
        }

        private function handleResponse(e:Event):void
        {
                var loader:URLLoader = URLLoader(e.currentTarget);
                response = XML(loader.data);

                dispatchEvent
                (
                        new JavaFlexStoreEvent(
                                JavaFlexStoreEvent.DATA_LOADED)
                );
        }

    }
  }
```

The last custom class to develop is the custom event. This is dispatched when the data is loaded.

Start by creating a new ActionScript class:

1. **Right-click the `src/` directory in the Flex Navigator and then choose New ⇨ ActionScript Class from the popup menu.** The new ActionScript Class editor opens.
2. **In the Package text field, type `package com.wiley.jfib.store.events`.**
3. **In the Name text field, type `JavaFlexStoreEvent`.**
4. **In the Superclass text field, type `flash.events.Event`.**
5. **Click Finish.**

Now that the class is created, you add the following code to the Code editor to complete the custom event:

JavaFlexStoreEvent.as

```
        package com.wiley.jfib.store.events
        {
            import flash.events.Event;
```

```
public class JavaFlexStoreEvent extends Event
{

        public static const DATA_LOADED:String = "onDataLoaded";

        public function JavaFlexStoreEvent(
                type:String,
                bubbles:Boolean=false,
                cancelable:Boolean=false)
        {
                super(type, bubbles, cancelable);
        }

}
}
```

This custom event is referenced in the Java Service handler and in the main application, which is completed in the next section.

Connecting the Database Application

In the last section of the design and development phase, you add the code for the main application, which connects everything . The MXML design elements were added at the beginning of this process, but now you have to add the ActionScript.

Main application code

The code for the main application is responsible for loading the product data, saving new product data, and managing the editor popups.

The first part of the code contains the class imports and variable definitions and needs to be placed within a mx:Script block:

```
import mx.controls.Alert;
import mx.collections.ArrayCollection;
import mx.core.IFlexDisplayObject;
import mx.managers.PopUpManager;

import com.wiley.jfib.store.events.JavaFlexStoreEvent;
import com.wiley.jfib.store.data.JavaServiceHandler;

[Bindable]
private var _productData:ArrayCollection;

private var popup:IFlexDisplayObject;

private var javaServiceHandler:JavaServiceHandler;
```

Adding the methods

The next step is to add the methods for this application. The overall purpose of each function has been covered at this point, with the exception of the popup manager. The PopupManager is a unique popup handler that allows you to display nonmodal and modal popup windows.

Here are all the functions:

```
private function init():void
{
    javaServiceHandler = new JavaServiceHandler();
    javaServiceHandler.addEventListener(JavaFlexStoreEvent.DATA_LOADED,
        productListHandler);
    javaServiceHandler.serviceURL =
        "http://localhost:8080/store/product-list.htm";
    javaServiceHandler.callServer();
}

private function productListHandler(event:JavaFlexStoreEvent):void
{
    _productData = new ArrayCollection();

    for each(var item:* in
    JavaServiceHandler(event.currentTarget).response..product)
    {
        _productData.addItem({
                id:item.id,
                name:item.name,
                price:item.price,
                desc:item.desc,
                quantity:item.quantity
        });
    }
}

public function displayEditorHandler():void
{
    popup = PopUpManager.createPopUp(this, ProductEditor, true);
    ProductEditor(popup).data = productGrid.selectedItem;
    ProductEditor(popup).data.update = true;
    PopUpManager.centerPopUp(popup);
}

public function displayNewHandler():void
{
    popup = PopUpManager.createPopUp(this, ProductEditor, true);
    ProductEditor(popup).data = new Object();
    PopUpManager.centerPopUp(popup);
}
```

```
public function save():void
{
    var xml:String = ProductEditor(popup).getXML();
    javaServiceHandler = new JavaServiceHandler();
    javaServiceHandler.addEventListener(JavaFlexStoreEvent.DATA_LOADED,
        saveResponse);
    javaServiceHandler.serviceURL = "http://localhost:8080/store/
        + add-product.htm" + "?data=" + xml;
    javaServiceHandler.callServer();
}
private function saveResponse(event:JavaFlexStoreEvent):void
{
    if(event.currentTarget.response == "SUCCESS")
    {
        if(ProductEditor(popup).data.update == true)
        {
            var data:Object = event.currentTarget.data;
        _productData.addItemAt(data, productGrid.selectedIndex);
        }
        else
        {
            _productData.addItem(ProductEditor(popup).data);
        }
    }
    else
    {
        Alert.show("Error: while attempting to save product");
    }
}

public function deleteProduct():void
{
    var productID:int = productGrid.selectedItem.id;
    javaServiceHandler = new JavaServiceHandler();
    javaServiceHandler.addEventListener(
        JavaFlexStoreEvent.DATA_LOADED, deleteProductResponse);
    javaServiceHandler.serviceURL = "http://localhost:8080/store/" +
        "delete-product.htm" + "?id=" + productID;
    javaServiceHandler.callServer();
}
private function deleteProductResponse(event:JavaFlexStoreEvent):void
{
    if(event.currentTarget.response == "SUCCESS")
    {
        _productData.removeItemAt(e.currentTarget.data.id);
    }
```

```
         else
         {
                 Alert.show("Error: while attempting to delete product");
         }
    }
```

At this point, you have completed the code for the example; you can now test it, as shown in Figure 10.5, and then move on to adding more features with your newfound knowledge from this chapter.

FIGURE 10.5

The complete application running in a browser

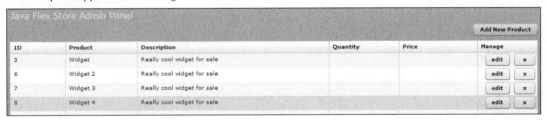

Here's the complete code for the main application:

JavaFlexStoreAdmin

```
<?xml version="1.0" encoding="utf-8"?>
<mx:Application xmlns:mx="http://www.adobe.com/2006/mxml"
    layout="absolute"
    creationComplete="init()"
>

    <mx:Script>
     <![CDATA[
       import mx.controls.Alert;
       import mx.collections.ArrayCollection;
       import mx.core.IFlexDisplayObject;
       import mx.managers.PopUpManager;

       import com.wiley.jfib.store.events.JavaFlexStoreEvent;
       import com.wiley.jfib.store.data.JavaServiceHandler;

       [Bindable]
       private var _productData:ArrayCollection;

       private var popup:IFlexDisplayObject;
```

```
    private var javaServiceHandler:JavaServiceHandler;

    private function init():void
    {
      javaServiceHandler = new JavaServiceHandler();
      javaServiceHandler.addEventListener(JavaFlexStoreEvent.DATA_LOADED,
      productListHandler);
      javaServiceHandler.serviceURL = "http://localhost:8080/store/product-
list.htm";
      javaServiceHandler.callServer();
    }

    private function productListHandler(event:JavaFlexStoreEvent):void
    {
      _productData = new ArrayCollection();
      for each(var item:* in event.currentTarget.response..product)
      {
      _        productData.addItem({
                  id:item.id,
                  name:item.name,
                  price:item.price,
                  desc:item.desc,
                  quantity:item.quantity
              });
      }
    }

    public function displayEditorHandler():void
    {
      popup = PopUpManager.createPopUp(this, ProductEditor, true);
      ProductEditor(popup).data = productGrid.selectedItem;
      ProductEditor(popup).data.update = true;
      PopUpManager.centerPopUp(popup);
    }

    public function displayNewHandler():void
    {
      popup = PopUpManager.createPopUp(this, ProductEditor, true);
      ProductEditor(popup).data = new Object();
      PopUpManager.centerPopUp(popup);
    }

    public function save():void
    {
      var xml:String = ProductEditor(popup).getXML();
      javaServiceHandler = new JavaServiceHandler();
      javaServiceHandler.addEventListener(JavaFlexStoreEvent.DATA_LOADED,
              saveResponse);
      javaServiceHandler.serviceURL = "http://localhost:8080/store/add"
              + "-product.htm" + "?data=" + xml;
```

```
    javaServiceHandler.callServer();
  }
  private function saveResponse(event:JavaFlexStoreEvent):void
  {
    if(event.currentTarget.response == "SUCCESS")
    {
          if(ProductEditor(popup).data.update == true)
          {
                var data:Object = event.currentTarget.data;
                _productData.addItemAt(data,
                productGrid.selectedIndex);
          }
          else
          {
                _productData.addItem(ProductEditor(popup).data);
          }
    }
    else
    {
          Alert.show("Error: while attempting to save the product");
    }
  }

  public function deleteProduct():void
  {
    var productID:int = productGrid.selectedItem.id;
    javaServiceHandler = new JavaServiceHandler();
    javaServiceHandler.addEventListener(JavaFlexStoreEvent.DATA_LOADED,
          deleteProductResponse);
    javaServiceHandler.serviceURL = "http://localhost:8080/store/"
    + "delete-product.htm" + "?id=" + productID;
    javaServiceHandler.callServer();
  }
  private function deleteProductResponse(event:JavaFlexStoreEvent):void
  {
    if(event.currentTarget.response == "SUCCESS")
    {
          _productData.removeItemAt(event.currentTarget.data.id);
    }
    else
    {
          Alert.show("Error: while attempting to delete product");
    }
  }
]]>
</mx:Script>

<mx:Label x="10" y="10" text="Java Flex Store Admin Panel"
fontSize="16" color="#E9F3F5"/>
```

```
<mx:DataGrid id="productGrid" dataProvider="{_productData}"
bottom="10" right="10" top="68" left="10">
<mx:columns>
<mx:DataGridColumn width="70" headerText="ID"
dataField="id"/>
<mx:DataGridColumn width="200" headerText="Product"
dataField="name"/>
<mx:DataGridColumn headerText="Description"
dataField="desc"/>
<mx:DataGridColumn width="100" headerText="Quantity"
dataField="quantity"/>
<mx:DataGridColumn width="100" headerText="Price"
dataField="price"/>
<mx:DataGridColumn width="100" headerText="Manage"
itemRenderer="ManageRenderer"/>
</mx:columns>
</mx:DataGrid>
<mx:Button click="displayNewHandler()" label="Add New Product"
right="10" top="38"/>
</mx:Application>
```

Summary

In this chapter, you learned how to build a simple database-powered application. You first designed the application by using standard MXML components and then, by adding ActionScript, added the functionality to add, remove, and update store products. You should now have an understanding of how to work with the Java back end for database use. This allows you to develop more advanced applications by using the same basic techniques.

Chapter 11

Developing a Stock Ticker with BlazeDS

In this chapter, you learn how to install, configure, and develop applications by using Flex and BlazeDS. Once the BlazeDS service is properly working, you create a complete stock ticker with real-time capabilities.

You also learn how to work with the messaging components in Flex, which allow applications to be more responsive and stable.

Developing Flex applications can require many different tools and libraries, even when related to Java development specifically. As you have probably seen in previous chapters, Java offers various tools and libraries, each having a proper use. You often stick to the tools that work, but the goal of learning is to gain a well-rounded view of all the various options.

Once you have completed this chapter, you should have a firm understanding of what BlazeDS has to offer and how you can implement it into your existing development toolkit.

BlazeDS has been available from Adobe for only a very short time, but it has already been adopted by many of the leading development agencies. Customers are already using BlazeDS to develop complete enterprise-level applications. The name *BlazeDS* is short for *Blaze Data Services*.

Here's what BlazeDS has to offer:

- Turnkey development options for rapid development and testing
- Robust code libraries for integrated development
- Testing suite with unit tests

IN THIS CHAPTER

Installing BlazeDS

Understanding messaging in Flex

Developing a stock ticker application

Installing BlazeDS

BlazeDS allows you to deploy a turnkey Web server on your local machine, and all you need to have installed is the JDK (Java Development Kit). You can download a copy of BlazeDS from `http://opensource.adobe.com/wiki/display/blazeds/Downloads`. The installation process is very simple. You start off by unzipping the archive file you downloaded. Once the files are unpacked, you move them to the root of your machine: `C:\blazeds`.

Now that the installation is complete, the next step is to start the database by using the following command:

```
$ \blazeds\sampledb\startdb.bat
```

Now that the database is started, the final installation step is to start the Web server. Issue a command that matches the path you chose in the installation process.

The Web server and database are now ready to use. You can verify this by visiting the following URL: `http://localhost:8400/`. You should be presented with a simple welcome screen and links to some sample applications. For now, you can skip over the samples and dive in to create your own.

Understanding Messaging in Flex

Now that BlazeDS is properly installed, let's take a look at how this application functions before you dive right into coding. The stock ticker application uses messaging to send data to and receive data from the Java code located on the server.

Flex applications use a client-side messaging API to send and receive messages from a server-side destination. The messaging process is based primarily on two components: the `Producer` and the `Consumer`.

Producer and Consumer messaging components

The `Producer` component sends messaging to the server-side destination. The `Consumer` component subscribes to the server side and is a message receiver. The `Producer` is the message sender. Both of these components can be built by using pure ActionScript or an MXML and ActionScript mixture. For this application, you use the pure ActionScript option, but you also learn how the MXML alternative works.

Both the `Producer` and `Consumer` require a valid message destination, which is defined in the `services-config.xml` file, explained later in this chapter.

Creating the Producer

The `Producer` handles the sending of data to the server-side code. Start off by importing the necessary packages and classes:

```
<mx:Script>
<![CDATA[

    import mx.messaging.*;
    import mx.messaging.messages.*;
    import mx.messaging.events.*;

]]>
</mx:Script>
```

These classes are used to create event listeners, message objects, and handlers. Next, you want to create a variable that's the reference to the `Producer` instance. You need only one `Producer` for this application, so the name `producer` is perfectly okay for the variable name. In a larger application, you may want to name it something more specific, such as `NameOfServiceProducer` or `MessageHandler`:

```
import mx.messaging.*;
import mx.messaging.messages.*;
import mx.messaging.events.*;

private var producer:Producer;
```

The `Producer` component offers a few event listener options; two of those options are the fault and acknowledge handlers. The fault handler is dispatched whenever an error occurs during the process of sending to the server. A fault handler method looks something like this:

```
private function faultHandler(event:MessageFaultEvent):void
{

}
```

This would be the place to display proper error messages to users so that they don't think the application has locked up. The acknowledge handler is called whenever the `Producer` is notified that the sending process was successful:

```
private function ackHandler(event:MessageAckEvent):void
{

}
```

This is the place to display messages in the client, stating that the message was received by the server — similar to the fault handler. You could also use these events to place flood control on an application, such as chat. Basically, you create a timer in the sending process, and depending on whether the message was successful, you update or delete the timer. This is, of course, only one use of those event listeners.

Now that you have everything loaded and the proper event handlers created, the next step is to generate the `Producer` call. For this example, this code is placed within the `init()` method:

```
private function init():void
{
    producer = new Producer();
    producer.destination = "stockticker";
}
```

The `destination` property is a reference to the value defined in the `services-config.xml` file. This ensures that the proper messaging service is being used. This unique name is especially important if your application has more than one messaging service.

The event handlers you defined in the previous section need to be assigned to some listener, so the best place to do this is in the `init()` method to ensure that they're configured immediately:

```
private function init():void
{
    producer = new Producer();
    producer.destination = "stockticker";

    producer.addEventListener(MessageAckEvent.ACKNOWLEDGE,
    ackHandler);
    producer.addEventListener(MessageFaultEvent.FAULT, faultHandler);
}
```

Sending a message

You have completed the `Producer` setup, but you probably realized that nothing is being sent to it. Well, it's a pretty good guess that you would want to actually send something to the server. This is done by using the `AsyncMessage` class. You start off by creating a new `AsyncMessage` object, fill it with your data, and then call the `Producer` component's `send()` method, passing in the `AsyncMessage` object:

```
private function getStockData():void
{
    var msg:AsyncMessage = new AsyncMessage();
    msg.body = "adbe";
    producer.send(msg);
}
```

That code creates a new `AsyncMessage` object, assigns the stock ticker for Adobe (`"adbe"`) to the body of the message, and finally makes a call to the `Producer` by using the `send()` method. Once this application is complete, that code alerts the server to load the stock data for Adobe or whichever stock ticker you request.

Creating the Consumer

The `Consumer` component has many similarities with the `Producer`. You start off by creating a variable to hold the instance of the `Consumer`, as you did in the previous code for the `Producer`:

```
<mx:Script>
<![CDATA[

    import mx.messaging.*;
    import mx.messaging.messages.*;
    import mx.messaging.events.*;

    private var producer:Producer;
    private var consumer:Consumer;

]]>
</mx:Script>
```

The Consumer also makes use of the fault and acknowledge handlers, but for this example, you can simply reuse the ones defined for the Producer:

```
private function init():void
{
    .
    .
    .

    consumer = new Consumer();
    consumer.destination = "stockticker";
    consumer.addEventListener(MessageAckEvent.ACKNOWLEDGE,
    ackHandler);
    consumer.addEventListener(MessageFaultEvent.FAULT, faultHandler);
}
```

The destination property is assigned to the same value as the Producer, as defined in the services-config.xml file.

Managing the destination service

The process of managing the destination service is where you set up the unsubscribe and subscribe methods. These are used to stop and start the service connection.

Subscribing to the destination service

In order to start the Consumer, you must make a call to the subscribe() method:

```
private function init():void
{
    .
    .
    .

    consumer = new Consumer();
    consumer.destination = "stockticker";
```

```
consumer.addEventListener(MessageAckEvent.ACKNOWLEDGE,
ackHandler);
consumer.addEventListener(MessageFaultEvent.FAULT, faultHandler);

consumer.subscribe();
}
```

Unsubscribing from the destination service

You can unsubscribe a Consumer component at any time by calling the unsubscribe()
method. If you unsubscribe for an active messaging process, you may get an error, which should
be captured in the faultHandler handler function:

```
consumer.unsubscribe();
```

Developing a Stock Ticker Application

Now that you have an understanding of how the messaging service works in Flex, let's move on to
the stock ticker application.

The stock ticker application consists of Java and Flex portions. A stock ticker application would
normally use a live feed to the stock exchange, but for this example, fake stock data is used. If you
want to create a live ticker, which means that it would update almost instantly, you would need to
purchase a service.

When writing the application, you can develop the Flex or Java first, but it's a best practice to outline what the back-end and overall data processes are supposed to accomplish. On larger projects,
you would probably have multiple developers and designers, but in this book, it's only you.

Setting up the messaging config file

You need to add the unique messaging object to the messaging-config.xml file located on
the BlazeDS server. If you installed by using the default directions, the config file can be found by
using the following path:

```
/blazeds/tomcat/webapps/blazeds/WEB-INF/flex/messaging-config.xml
```

Open that XML file in your favorite text editor and then add the unique service destination ticker,
as shown below. Once you have added that line, save and quit the XML file:

```
<?xml version="1.0" encoding="UTF-8"?>
<service id="message-service"
  class="flex.messaging.services.MessageService">

  <adapters>
   <adapter-definition id="actionscript"
   class="flex.messaging.services.messaging.adapters.ActionScriptAdapter"
        default="true" />
```

```
<!-- <adapter-definition id="jms" class="flex.messaging.services.
messaging.adapters.JMSAdapter"/> -->
 </adapters>

<default-channels>
    <channel ref="my-polling-amf"/>
</default-channels>

<destination id="stockticker"/>

</service>
```

NOTE If for some reason the server throws a connection error, restart the server. That normally isn't needed, but at other times, restarting the server is needed when the service can't be properly reached.

Developing the Java back end

The Java portion of this application consists of two Java classes. The first returns the stock ticker information to the client. The second is a Java object containing properties for the stock ticker data that mirror the properties that are displayed in the Flex application. This example application uses randomized static data rather than fetching real financial data from an external service.

The first thing to do is set up an Eclipse project for the stock application. The Eclipse project includes only the two Java class files. Eclipse automatically builds the class files for you. For this application, you only need to copy the compiled class files to the BlazeDS Web application's WEB-INF/classes directory.

Open Eclipse by navigating to the Eclipse install directory in Windows Explorer and then double-click eclipse.exe. To create and configure the Eclipse project, follow these steps:

1. **Right-click in the Project Explorer view and then choose New⇨Project from the popup menu.** The New Project selection dialog box opens.

2. **Click the arrow next to Java to expand it, click the Java Project item below Java, and then click Next.** The Create a Java Project wizard opens.

3. **Type jfib-ch11-p01 in the Name text field and then click Next.** The Java Settings screen opens.

4. **Click the Libraries tab.** The Library list is displayed.

5. **Click the Add External JARs button.** The JAR Selection dialog box opens.

6. **Navigate to the folder where you unzipped BlazeDS, double-click the lib folder, choose flex-messaging-core.jar and flex-messaging-common.jar in that lib folder, and then click Open.** These two JAR files are added to the Library list.

7. **Click Finish.** The Create a Java Project wizard closes, and the newly created project appears in the Project Explorer view.

The Eclipse project is now set up, allowing you to start creating your Java classes. First, create the Java class that represents the stock ticker information. This class has three public properties: `ticker`, `value`, and `change`. These three property names also appear in the `Flex DataGrid` control that displays the stock ticker information.

To create the ticker information class, follow these steps:

1. **Right-click the `src` folder under the `jfib-ch11-p01` project in the Project Explorer view and then choose New ⇨ Class from the popup menu.** The New Java Class dialog box opens.

2. **Type com.wiley.jfib.ch11 in the Package text field, type TickerValue in the Name text field, and then click the check box next to Generate comments.**

3. **Click Finish.** The New Java Class dialog box closes, and the newly created `com.wiley.jfib.ch11` package and `TickerValue` class appear in the `src` folder under the `jfib-ch11-p01` project. The `TickerValue` class opens in the editor.

Now edit the `TickerValue` class so that it matches this code listing:

```
/**
 *
 */
package com.wiley.jfib.ch11;

/**
 * A class representing a stock ticker value
 * @author Chuck
 *
 */
public class TickerValue {
    public String ticker = "";
    public String value = "";
    public String change = "";
}
```

Now you can create the Java class that will communicate with the Flex client and provide stock information. The Java class extends BlazeDS's `ServiceAdapter` class. The `ServiceAdapter` class is an abstract class that requires you to implement a single method called `invoke()`. The `invoke()` method receives messages from publishers in the Flex application and sends messages back to any subscribing Flex clients. In this case, the invoke method sends a `TickerValue` object back to the Flex client as the body of the message. The Flex client can then use this object in the data provider of its `DataGrid` control.

To create the Java stock ticker server class, follow these steps:

1. **Right-click the `com.wiley.jfib.ch11` package under the `jfib-ch11-p01` project in the Project Explorer view and then choose New ⇨ Class from the popup menu.** The New Java Class dialog box opens.

2. **Click the Browse button next to the Superclass text field**. The Superclass Selection dialog box opens.

3. **Type** ServiceAdapter **in the Choose a type text field**. The Matching items list box fills in with classes whose names match your entry.

4. **Choose** ServiceAdapter – flex.messaging.services **from the list and then click OK**. The Superclass Selection dialog box closes, and the Superclass text field in the New Java Class dialog box is filled in with the ServiceAdapter class.

5. **Type** StockTickerServer **in the Name text field and then click the check box next to Generate comments**.

6. **Click Finish**. The New Java Class dialog box closes, and the newly created StockTickerServer class appears in the src folder under the com.wiley.jfib. ch11 package. The StockTickerServer class opens in the editor.

Now edit the StockTickerServer class so that it matches this code listing:

```java
/**
 *
 */
package com.wiley.jfib.ch11;

import java.util.ArrayList;
import java.util.Collection;
import java.util.Random;

import flex.messaging.messages.AsyncMessage;
import flex.messaging.messages.Message;
import flex.messaging.services.MessageService;
import flex.messaging.services.ServiceAdapter;

/**
 * @author Chuck
 * The StockTickerServer class creates some random stock ticker data and returns
 * it to a Flex consumer.
 */
public class StockTickerServer extends ServiceAdapter {
    @Override
    public Object invoke(Message arg0) {
            AsyncMessage stockMessage = (AsyncMessage)arg0;

            TickerValue tickerValue = new TickerValue();
            tickerValue.ticker = "abde";
            tickerValue.value = String.valueOf(
                            new Random().nextDouble() * 100.0);
            tickerValue.change = "+" + String.valueOf(
                            new Random().nextDouble() * 9.0);

            TickerValue tickerValue2 = new TickerValue();
```

```
        tickerValue2.ticker = "siri";
        tickerValue2.value = String.valueOf(
                                new Random().nextDouble() * 100.0);
        tickerValue2.change = "+" + String.valueOf(
                                new Random().nextDouble() * 9.0);

        TickerValue tickerValue3 = new TickerValue();
        tickerValue3.ticker = "xmsr";
        tickerValue3.value = String.valueOf(
                                new Random().nextDouble() * 100.0);
        tickerValue3.change = "+" + String.valueOf(
                                new Random().nextDouble() * 9.0);

        Collection<TickerValue> tickerValues = new ArrayList<TickerValue>();
        tickerValues.add(tickerValue);
        tickerValues.add(tickerValue2);
        tickerValues.add(tickerValue3);
        stockMessage.setBody(tickerValues);
        MessageService messageService =
                (MessageService)getDestination().getService();
        messageService.pushMessageToClients(stockMessage, false);
        return null;
    }
}
```

The import statements import some BlazeDS messaging classes necessary for the
`StockTickerServer` class to receive and republish messages. In the `invoke()` method, a
`TickerValue` object is created, and its properties are set using a string for the ticker property
and random double-precision decimal values converted to strings for the value and change properties. This process is repeated three times, once for each stock to be displayed in the Flex client.
Each of these `TickerValue` objects is added to a Java `ArrayList` collection, which is then set
as the body of the message. Finally, the message is pushed out to any Flex clients subscribing to
the stock ticker destination in the messaging configuration.

By default, Eclipse automatically compiles the Java files in this project. Once these files have been
created, you can simply copy the compiled classes from the project directory into the BlazeDS Web
application. Eclipse outputs the class files into a folder named `bin` inside the project directory.
The project directory is located in the directory you specified for your Eclipse workspace. If you
forget where that is, you can also find the location of the project directory by choosing Project ⇨
Properties from the menu and then clicking the Resource item on the left side of the project properties dialog box. Go into the `bin` directory inside the project directory. You see a single directory
here, named com. This name corresponds to the first part of the package name of the two Java
classes. You need to copy the com folder into the `WEB-INF`/classes folder inside the BlazeDS Web
application folder (`/blazeds/tomcat/webapps/blazeds/`, for example). Once you've done
that, the classes are available for use by the Flex code in the Web application.

Building the Flex user interface

Now that the Java back end is developed, the next step is to design and integrate the Flex user interface (UI). You can start with the provided sample files and then skip ahead to the ActionScript or create the application from scratch.

All Flex applications start at the same place: setting up the workspace and creating the project. Follow these steps:

1. **Choose File ➪ New Flex Project.** The New Flex Project dialog box, as shown in Figure 11.1, opens.

2. **Type a name for the application, such as** BlazeDSStockTicker.

3. **Ensure that the Application type is set to Web Application and that the server technology is set to J2EE.**

4. **Click Next.**

Setting the J2EE Server options

The next screen is where you configure the Flex application to use the BlazeDS server that you installed. Start by clicking Browse to choose your root folder. The path is wherever you placed the `blazeds` directory; within that, choose `tomcat/webapps/blazeds`. If your BlazeDS installation was at `/blazeds`, the full Root folder path would become:

`/blazeds/tomcat/webapps/blazeds/`

FIGURE 11.1

The Configure J2EE Server screen

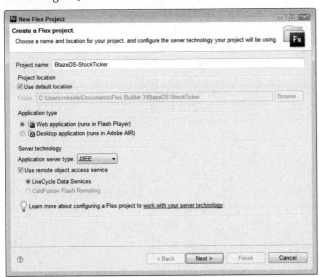

The Root URL is the Web path to the BlazeDS server. A default installation would place the server at the following location:

```
http://localhost:8400/blazeds/
```

The Context root defines the root directory of the application, which in this case is `blazeds/`. Now that the server variables are configured, click Validate Configuration to ensure that everything was set up properly.

If the validation is successful, you can click Finish to complete the project creation process. You should now see your new project sitting in the Flex Navigator pane on the left side of the screen. If you don't, make sure you that created and loaded the new project properly.

Building the user interface

Now that the project is created, you can move on to creating the Flex UI. The UI consists of a `DataGrid` component and a label, which in the overall scheme of applications isn't big, but the idea is to learn about BlazeDS integration, not to develop an award-winning application — for the time being. Figure 11.2 shows a sample application in Flex.

FIGURE 11.2

A sample application shown in the Flex Design view

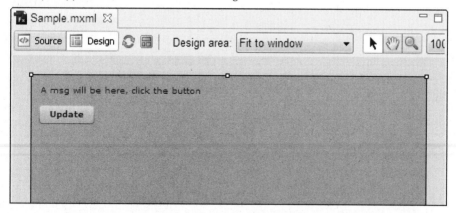

Make sure that you're in the Design view and then drag out the components from the Components pane to build the application. Once the components are on the canvas, you can either add the unique IDs by selecting the components and editing them in the Property panel to the right or you can move into Source view to add them by using pure code.

Developing the ActionScript

Switch to Source view, if you're not already there, to begin developing the ActionScript necessary to request and update the stock tickers. All the code is located within the <mx:Script> tags. In most applications, the first part of the code is where your imports and variable definitions are located:

```
import mx.controls.dataGridClasses.DataGridColumn;
import mx.controls.DataGrid;
import mx.controls.Alert;
import mx.collections.ArrayCollection;
import mx.utils.ArrayUtil;
import mx.utils.ObjectUtil;

import mx.messaging.*;
import mx.messaging.messages.*;
import mx.messaging.events.*;

private var consumer:Consumer;
private var producer:Producer;

[Bindable]
private var tickers:ArrayCollection;
```

Bindable variables

The variables for this application are straightforward. First off, you have a `Bindable Array Collection`, which holds the stock ticker object data. A `Bindable` variable offers the ability to auto-update, which means that whenever the value changes, anything watching that variable is also updated and notified. When you're working in MXML code, anything within { } is a reference to a bindable expression.

You can also assign change watchers by using pure ActionScript, but that's beyond the scope of this book. You can check out the help material that ships with Flex for more information about `Bindable` variables.

Now that the packages are loaded and the variables are defined, the next step in the code is an event handler that's called once the Flex application is loaded. This is the preferred way to initialize code so that you can ensure the code is executed at startup:

```
creationComplete="init()"
```

Flex offers many different events that allow you to develop more solid code and ensure that your application acts the way you intended. Previous versions of ActionScript allowed you to use event handlers for some tasks, but ActionScript is the first to truly allow common application development practices and abilities.

The `init()` method in this example has been assigned to the `creationComplete` event, which is called once the application has fully loaded and has been drawn to the display list.

This `init()` method handles the data loading and events associated with this application. The `init()` method is also where you would initialize the `ArrayCollection`, which holds the ticker object data once it's been properly loaded:

```
private function init():void
{
    tickers = new ArrayCollection();
}
```

The next step is to initialize a new instance of the `Consumer` component, assign event listeners, and set the `destination` property:

```
private function init():void
{
    tickers = new ArrayCollection();

    consumer = new Consumer();
    consumer.destination = "stockticker";
    consumer.addEventListener(MessageAckEvent.ACKNOWLEDGE,
    ackHandler);
    consumer.addEventListener(MessageFaultEvent.FAULT, faultHandler);
}
```

Once the message is sent to the server, a response is returned. The `ackHandler` is set up to handle that response. This method basically takes the message response and converts it to an `ArrayCollection` object so that it can be placed in the `DataGrid`:

```
private function ackHandler(event:MessageAckEvent):void
{
    tickers = ArrayCollection(event.message);
}
```

Now that the data handler has been completed, the next step is to modify the default `DataGrid` that you added to the canvas. First off, as exemplified in Figure 11.3, here's the default code for the `DataGrid`:

```
<mx:DataGrid x="82" y="107">
    <mx:columns>
            <mx:DataGridColumn headerText="Column 1" dataField="col1"/>
            <mx:DataGridColumn headerText="Column 2" dataField="col2"/>
            <mx:DataGridColumn headerText="Column 3" dataField="col3"/>
    </mx:columns>
</mx:DataGrid>
```

Start by adding the `Bindable` string to automatically load the latest stock data as it's returned from the server. This is achieved by using the `dataProvider` property and assigning it to the `ticker` variable:

```
<mx:DataGrid ... dataProvider="{tickers}">
```

FIGURE 11.3

The default `DataGrid`

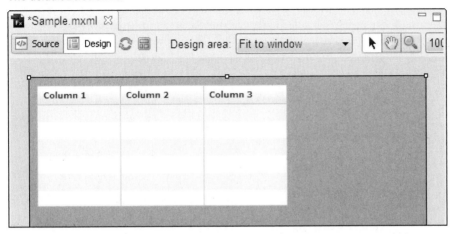

For this example, you can also change the default column names by modifying the `headerText` property, but that's purely for visual purposes. The `dataField` property, on the other hand, is the link to the `ArrayCollection` data and is also used when modifying the column data, which is covered later in this chapter:

```
<mx:DataGrid ...>
   <mx:columns>
        <mx:DataGridColumn headerText="Ticker" dataField="ticker"/>
        <mx:DataGridColumn headerText="Value" dataField="value"/>
        <mx:DataGridColumn headerText="Change" dataField="change"/>
   </mx:columns>
</mx:DataGrid>
```

Using the labelFunction

The `DataGrid` component has a special property being used in this example. That property is `labelFunction`, which is called for each column in the grid as the `dataProvider` is looped through. In this example, this property is used to assign a method that's responsible for ensuring that the ticker name is in all caps. You can also perform many other actions, such as converting currency and adding values.

The `labelFunction` property is defined on the `DataGridColumn` item as follows:

```
<mx:DataGridColumn labelFunction="strToUpper" .../>
```

The `labelFunction` property accepts a method name as a value and automatically passes in two arguments. The structure of the method is as follows:

```
private function strToUpper(item:Object,column:DataGridColumn):String
{
}
```

The first argument is the object that's contained within the `ArrayCollection`. The second argument is a reference to the `DataGridColumn`. In order to get the proper value, you must use the following code, which grabs the object value based on the column name:

```
item[column.dataField]
```

That code returns `'ticker'` in the above code. In a larger application, you would probably create a `switch` statement to handle various `labelFunction` actions, similar to the following example:

```
switch(String(item[column.dataField]))
{
    case 'ticker' :
            // handle ticker code
            break;
    case 'option-2' :
            // handle other option here
            break;
}
```

Now that the value has been discovered, you need to datatype it as a string, just as a precaution. Then, you convert the string to all uppercase characters and return it to the `DataGrid` column for display:

```
private function strToUpper(item:Object,column:DataGridColumn):String
{
    return String(item[column.dataField]).toUpperCase();
}
```

The remaining display process happens automatically at this point because Flex is able to bind to that ticker variable. You could certainly assign more `labelFunction` calls if you required more data modification.

 **Even though you can modify the data on the Flex side, it's best to make all changes possible on the server side for memory and responsiveness concerns for the client.**

You may be asking yourself whether it's possible to test the `labelFunction` and overall `ArrayCollection` process that was just developed. Well, the answer is yes, you can. You don't even need to involve the server to do so.

Start by commenting out the `Consumer` code in the `init()` function and then prefill the `ArrayCollection` with some fake data:

```
private function init():void
{
    tickers = new ArrayCollection();
```

```
//consumer = new Consumer();
//consumer.destination = "stockticker";
//consumer.addEventListener(MessageAckEvent.ACKNOWLEDGE,
ackHandler);
//consumer.addEventListener(MessageFaultEvent.FAULT,faultHandler);

tickers.addItem({ticker:'adbe', value:'24.0', change:'+ 0.6'});
tickers.addItem({ticker:'siri', value:'10.0', change:'- 0.8'});
tickers.addItem({ticker:'xmsr', value:'12.0', change:'- 0.1'});
}
```

Now when you run the application, you see the `DataGrid` fill instantly, and the `labelFunction` has properly capitalized all the tickers. Figure 11.4 shows an application with `DataGrid` data.

FIGURE 11.4

The application with fake `DataGrid` data

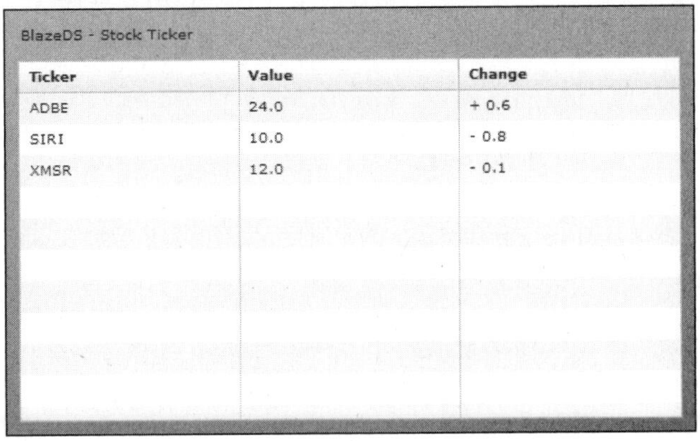

At this point, you have completed both the Java and Flex portions of this stock ticker application. Feel free to expand upon it to dig deeper into the abilities of BlazeDS and messaging.

The complete Flex (MXML) code has been provided for easy viewing, but you can also find the original source on this book's Web site:

```
<?xml version="1.0" encoding="utf-8"?>
<mx:Application xmlns:mx="http://www.adobe.com/2006/mxml"
   layout="absolute"
   width="500"
   height="300"
   creationComplete="init()">

<mx:Script>
<![CDATA[
```

```
import mx.controls.dataGridClasses.DataGridColumn;
import mx.controls.DataGrid;
import mx.collections.ArrayCollection;
import mx.utils.ArrayUtil;
import mx.controls.Alert;
import mx.utils.ObjectUtil;

import mx.messaging.*;
import mx.messaging.messages.*;
import mx.messaging.events.*;

private var consumer:Consumer;

[Bindable]
private var tickers:ArrayCollection;

private function init():void
{
        tickers = new ArrayCollection();

        consumer = new Consumer();
        consumer.destination = "stockticker";
        consumer.addEventListener(MessageAckEvent.ACKNOWLEDGE, ackHandler);
        consumer.addEventListener(MessageFaultEvent.FAULT, faultHandler);
        consumer.subscribe();

        producer = new Producer();
        producer.destination = "stockticker";

        producer.addEventListener(MessageAckEvent.ACKNOWLEDGE, ackHandler);
        producer.addEventListener(MessageFaultEvent.FAULT, faultHandler);

}

private function getStockData():void
{
        var msg:AsyncMessage = new AsyncMessage();
        msg.body = "adbe";
        producer.send(msg);
}

private function faultHandler(e:MessageFaultEvent):void
{
        Alert.show(ObjectUtil.toString(e.message));
}

private function ackHandler(e:MessageAckEvent):void
{
        tickers = ArrayCollection(e.message);
```

```
        }

        private function strToUpper(item:Object,c:DataGridColumn):String
        {
                return String(item[c.dataField]).toUpperCase();
        }

]]>
</mx:Script>

    <mx:Label x="10" y="10" text="BlazeDS - Stock Ticker"/>
    <mx:DataGrid x="10" y="36" width="480" height="254" dataProvider="{tickers}">
            <mx:columns>
                        <mx:DataGridColumn labelFunction="strToUpper"
    headerText="Ticker" dataField="ticker"/>
                        <mx:DataGridColumn headerText="Value" dataField="value"/>
                        <mx:DataGridColumn headerText="Change" dataField="change"/>
            </mx:columns>
    </mx:DataGrid>

</mx:Application>
```

Summary

In this chapter, you learned how to install and configure BlazeDS. Then, you learned about messaging in Flex and how it helps you develop more responsive applications by using less code. In the last part of the chapter, you built a complete messaging-based stock ticker application.

The complete application should have allowed you to grasp the concepts of BlazeDS and how you can use them in your own development. At this point, you can move on to developing much larger and more robust applications, which are covered in later chapters of this book.

Part III

Building Advanced Applications

IN THIS PART

Chapter 12
Developing a Storefront Server Application with Java

Chapter 13
Developing a Storefront Server Application with Flex

Chapter 14
Building a Real-Time Messaging System

Chapter 15
Extending Java and Flex Development

Chapter 16
Advanced Development

Chapter 12

Developing a Storefront Server Application with Java

I n this chapter, you write a basic Web store back-end application by using Java. The Java Web application accepts incoming requests for data, communicates with a MySQL database by using Hibernate to save and retrieve data, and finally presents the data to the Flex client as blocks of XML. The Flex client application you develop in Chapter 13 takes that XML, parses it, and then renders the information into a user interface that presents the store to the user. Users can then see a set of products filtered by category and click to add products to their shopping cart.

CROSS-REF For the complete Flex front end for the Web store application, see Chapter 13.

IN THIS CHAPTER

Application best practices

Developing the Java

Deploying and testing the Web application

Application Best Practices

Application development doesn't end when the first version is released to the world. There are bugs that need to be fixed and features that your users will clamor for. In the world of Web applications, users have come to expect that exciting new features, performance improvements, and bug fixes will continuously roll out throughout the life of the application.

Following a few development best practices can make all these things easier for you to provide to your users. Code modularity makes it easier to fix or upgrade portions of your applications with minimal impact on other parts. Separation of interface and implementation makes your code reusable by allowing you to write your application logic by using interfaces and then use different implementations for different program modules.

Code modularity

Making your code *modular* means separating it into units of code that provide distinct functionality with little or no overlap between modules. Separating your code into distinct modules means that if changes need to be made to one area of functionality in your application, they can be made with little or no impact on other areas of your application.

In a storefront, one of the functions used frequently is calculating shipping for an order. Shipping costs are typically based on the carrier used, the location of the purchaser, and the type of delivery desired.

One way to approach calculating shipping is to have the shopping cart code tally the shipping costs along the way. The cart knows what products are being shipped and has information about the user, so it should be able to use that information to calculate shipping. However, this approach isn't modular because the shopping cart code now contains code for two unrelated functions: storing products from a user's shopping session and managing shipping information. If, in the future, the store switches to another shipping company, the shopping cart code would need to be updated to accommodate this change. Thus, the chances that some of the shopping cart functionality is inadvertently changed and bugs are introduced into your application increase.

A better approach would be to separate the shipping code into its own module. The shopping cart code would provide the shipping module information about the products being shipped and the customer's address, and the shipping module would return shipping costs for the various delivery types offered. Now, if the store were to change shipping companies, the shopping cart code wouldn't need to change. Instead, the shipping code would change, and the shopping cart code could continue to use it as though nothing had changed.

Separation of interface and implementation

One of the most important development practices, especially for those building large or complex applications, is to write code that's reusable across many areas of an application or even across different applications.

Consider this example: The application you build in this chapter is a storefront, which allows customers to view products, add them to a shopping cart, and purchase them. The data about the products is stored in a database. Suppose that this store is just one of many owned by a parent company. Each store has its own database, and a scheduled nightly job collects data about the products and sales for each day into a data warehouse so that the sales and marketing departments at the parent company can determine which products are selling well, which prices may need to be adjusted, etc.

The sales department might ask you to build a Web application to help it visualize and work with the data in the data warehouse. Many of the operations and objects, such as lists of products and contents of shopping carts, used by the storefront are relevant to the data the sales department would want to analyze. By writing these modules of code in a way that's reusable, you can create a set of objects that's useable in both the storefront and the data warehouse applications.

Part of the process of writing modular code, and one way to write reusable code, is to separate the interface from the implementation. In simple terms, the *interface* is what something does, and the *implementation* is how it does that something. The interface defines what methods are available, what parameters they require, and what values they return. It's the contract between code that calls into your application and the implementation code within your application. Code that calls into the application rarely cares about how something is done; it just wants to receive some value based on parameters it provides.

The code that talks to the database when writing the storefront has an interface that defines methods to obtain a list of products, see details of a specific product, and retrieve a user's shopping cart. The implementation contains code that performs these functions. In the previous example, if the store front application had been written without interfaces, much of it would not be reusable. The service code that requests information from the database access module would need to be changed to request information from a different module that works with the data warehouse instead of the store database. By using interfaces, the service would just be calling a function on the interface, and the code would work the same way for both the store application and the data warehouse. When deploying the data warehouse application, you would only need to swap out the implementation of the database access code with the correct version for the data warehouse. Application code dealing with the interface wouldn't need to change.

Developing the Java

The back end of the storefront application is a standard Spring MVC Web application that uses Hibernate to access data in a MySQL database. The service layer exposes the following services by using Spring controllers and URL mappings to the Flex user interface:

- `LogInService` provides a `User` object based on the username and password provided.

- `ProductListService` provides a collection of `Product` objects. The Flex client can optionally provide a category parameter to filter the product list by category.

- `ProductDetailsService` provides a `Product` object based on the product ID provided.

- `AddProductToCartService` adds some number of a given product to the given user's shopping cart and returns the updated cart.

- `RetrieveCartService` retrieves the current shopping cart for a given user.

CROSS-REF For more on Hibernate, see Chapter 9. For more on Spring MVC, controllers, and URL mappings, see Chapter 6.

The model contains the value objects needed by this application. These objects are:

- A `User` object to represent the customer user of this Web storefront application

- A `Product` object to represent the products offered for sale

- A `CartItem` object to represent products in a specific shopping cart
- A `Cart` object to represent the shopping cart of a specific user

Finally, the data access layer contains a single interface and a data access object (DAO) class that extends that interface. It communicates with the MySQL database to save and retrieve the value objects. The DAO class contains one method for each of the five services exposed to the Flex client. The MySQL database contains one table for each of the four value objects.

The MySQL database

The MySQL database consists of four tables, one for each of the value objects in the application. These tables are related to one another through foreign key relationships. The `cart` table contains a `user_id` field that maps to the `user` table so that each cart is owned by a user. The `cart_item` table contains a `product_id` field that maps to the `product` table and a `cart_id` field that maps to the `cart` table.

 **CROSS-REF** For more on MySQL, foreign keys, and the MySQL Query Browser tool, see Chapter 8.

To create the MySQL database and the `product` table for the storefront application, follow these steps:

1. **Launch the MySQL Query Browser tool by choosing Start ➪ All Programs ➪ MySQL ➪ MySQL Query Browser.** The MySQL Query Browser connection dialog box, as shown in Figure 12.1, opens.

FIGURE 12.1

The MySQL Query Browser connection dialog box is where you provide connection information for your MySQL server. Some of the values may have already been filled in for you.

2. **Type** localhost **in the Server Host text field, type** 3306 **in the Port text field, type** root **in the Username text field, type** toor **in the Password text field, and then click OK.** Some of these values may have already been filled in for you. The MySQL Query Browser application, as shown in Figure 12.2, opens.

FIGURE 12.2

The MySQL Query Browser's main interface is where the database for the storefront application is created.

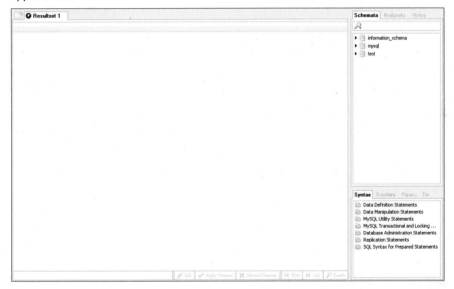

3. **Right-click inside the Schemata tab and then choose Create New Schema from the popup menu.** The Create New Schema dialog box opens.

4. **Type** store **in the schema name text field and then click OK.** The store schema appears in the Schemata tab.

5. **Right-click the store schema in the Schemata tab and then choose Create New Table from the popup menu.** The MySQL Table Editor dialog box, as shown in Figure 12.3, opens.

6. **Type** product **in the Table Name text field.**

7. **Double-click below the Column Name header in the Columns and Indices tab.** A text field appears.

8. **Type** id **in the text field and then press the Tab key.** The rest of the columns in this row fill in with acceptable default values, as shown in Figure 12.4. This text field is the primary key of the `product` table, which is referenced by a foreign key in the `cart_item` table. The MySQL Table Editor fills in a value of INTEGER for Datatype and checks

the NOT NULL, AUTO INC, and UNSIGNED check boxes. This means that the field is populated with positive integer values that are automatically incremented by the database. The id column is added to the Index Columns box in the bottom-right corner, and PRIMARY appears in the Indices tab in the bottom-left corner, indicating that the id column is the primary key.

9. **Add the information for the rest of the columns in the table as specified below.** Start by double-clicking below the column name for the previous column and then typing the column name in the text field that appears. Press the Tab key to move from field to field in the row. When you're finished, the MySQL Table Editor dialog box should look like Figure 12.5.

   ■ Column Name: name; Datatype: VARCHAR(100); NOT NULL checked

   ■ Column Name: description; Datatype: VARCHAR(4000); NOT NULL checked

   ■ Column Name: category; Datatype: VARCHAR(100); NOT NULL checked

   ■ Column Name: price; Datatype: DOUBLE; NOT NULL and UNSIGNED checked

10. **Click Apply Changes.** The Confirm Table Edit dialog box, as shown in Figure 12.6, opens. This dialog box displays the SQL statement that's executed to create the `product` table.

11. **Click Execute.** The Confirm Table Edit dialog box closes, and you return to the MySQL Table Editor dialog box.

12. **Click Close.** The MySQL Table Editor dialog box closes.

FIGURE 12.3

The MySQL Table Editor dialog box is where the tables for the application are created.

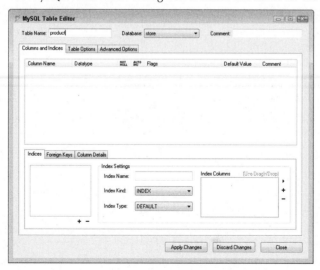

FIGURE 12.4

Once you type **id** as the name of the first column and press the Tab key, the rest of the columns in this row of the Columns and Indices tab are populated with appropriate default values, and the column is set as the primary key of the table.

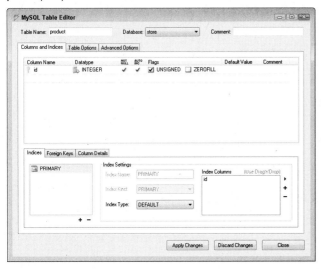

FIGURE 12.5

The MySQL Table Editor dialog box should look like this once all the columns have been added to the product table.

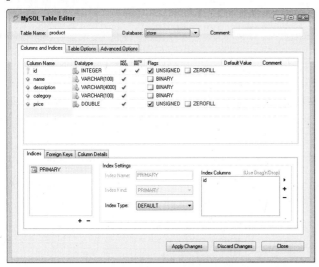

You can see the newly created table by clicking the arrow next to the store database to expand it in the Schemata tab. Clicking the arrow next to the `product` table expands it to display the set of columns that make up the table.

The Confirm Table Edit dialog box shows the SQL statement that's used to create the `product` table.

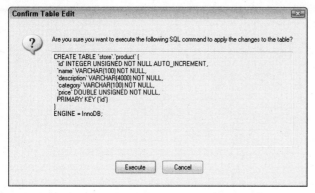

Now create the `user` table by following these steps:

1. **Right-click the store schema in the Schemata tab and then choose Create New Table from the popup menu.** The MySQL Table Editor dialog box opens.

2. **Type** user **in the Table Name text field.**

3. **Double-click below the Column Name header in the Columns and Indices tab.** A text field appears.

4. **Type** id **in the text field and then press the Tab key.** The rest of the columns in this row fill in with acceptable default values. This text field is the primary key of the `user` table, which is referenced by a foreign key in the `cart` table. As with the `product` table, the MySQL Table Editor fills in a value of INTEGER for Datatype and checks the NOT NULL, AUTO INC, and UNSIGNED check boxes; the id column is added to the Index Columns box in the bottom-right corner, and PRIMARY appears in the Indices tab in the bottom-left corner, indicating that the id column is the primary key.

5. **Add the information for the rest of the columns in the table as specified below.** Start by double-clicking below the column name for the previous column and then typing the column name in the text field that appears. Press the Tab key to move from field to field in the row. When you're finished, the MySQL Table Editor dialog box should look like Figure 12.7.

- Column Name: first_name; Datatype: VARCHAR(45); NOT NULL checked
- Column Name: last_name; Datatype: VARCHAR(45); NOT NULL checked
- Column Name: user_name; Datatype: VARCHAR(45); NOT NULL checked
- Column Name: password; Datatype: VARCHAR(45); NOT NULL checked

6. **Click Apply Changes.** The Confirm Table Edit dialog box opens. This dialog box displays the SQL statement that's executed to create the product table.

7. **Click Execute.** The Confirm Table Edit dialog box closes, and you return to the MySQL Table Editor dialog box.

8. **Click Close.** The MySQL Table Editor dialog box closes.

FIGURE 12.7

The MySQL Table Editor dialog box should look like this once all the columns have been added to the user table.

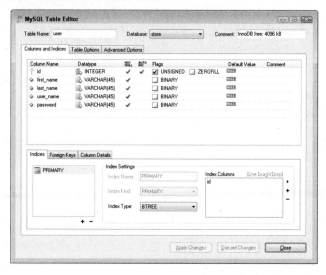

Next is the cart table. A couple of extra steps are required for this table to create the foreign key from the cart table to the user table. Follow these steps to create the cart table:

1. **Right-click the store schema in the Schemata tab and then choose Create New Table.** The MySQL Table Editor dialog box opens.

2. **Type cart in the Table Name text field.**

3. **Double-click below the Column Name header in the Columns and Indices tab.** A text field appears.

4. **Type id in the text field and then press the Tab key.** The rest of the columns in this row fill in with acceptable default values. This text field is the primary key of the `cart` table, which is referenced by a foreign key in the `cart_item` table you create next. As with the `product` table, the MySQL Table Editor fills in a value of INTEGER for Datatype and checks the NOT NULL, AUTO INC, and UNSIGNED check boxes; the id column is added to the Index Columns box in the bottom-right corner; and PRIMARY appears in the Indices tab in the bottom-left corner, indicating that the id column is the primary key.

5. **Add the information for the user_id column as specified below.** Start by double-clicking below the column name for the previous column and then typing the column name in the text field that appears. Press the Tab key to move from field to field in the row.

   ■ Column Name: user_id; Datatype: INTEGER; NOT NULL and UNSIGNED checked

6. **Click the Foreign Keys tab in the bottom-left corner and then click the + button below the Foreign Keys box.** The Add Foreign Key dialog box opens.

7. **Type FK_cart_1 in the Foreign Key Name text field and then click OK.** The FK_cart_1 foreign key is added to the Foreign Keys box.

8. **Choose user from the Ref. Table dropdown list, double-click id in the Column column, and then choose user_id from the dropdown list.** When you're finished, the MySQL Table Editor dialog box should look like Figure 12.8.

FIGURE 12.8

After the columns have been added and the foreign key to the user table has been created, the MySQL Table Editor dialog box should look like this.

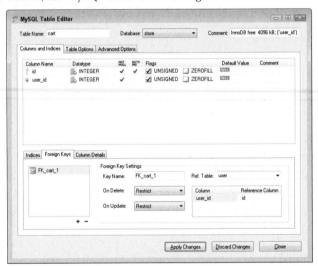

9. **Click Apply Changes.** The Confirm Table Edit dialog box opens. This dialog box displays the SQL statement that's executed to create the `product` table.

10. **Click Execute.** The Confirm Table Edit dialog box closes, and you return to the MySQL Table Editor dialog box.

11. **Click Close.** The MySQL Table Editor dialog box closes.

Finally, the `cart_item` table contains foreign keys to both the `cart` table and the `product` table. Follow these steps to create the `cart_item` table:

1. **Right-click the store schema in the Schemata tab and then choose Create New Table from the popup menu.** The MySQL Table Editor dialog box opens.

2. **Type** cart_item **in the Table Name text field.**

3. **Double-click below the Column Name header in the Columns and Indices tab.** A text field appears.

4. **Type** id **in the text field and then press the Tab key.** The rest of the columns in this row fill in with acceptable default values. This text field is the primary key of the `cart_item` table. As with the `product` table, the MySQL Table Editor fills in a value of INTEGER for Datatype and checks the NOT NULL, AUTO INC, and UNSIGNED check boxes; the id column is added to the Index Columns box in the bottom-right corner; and PRIMARY appears in the Indices tab in the bottom-left corner, indicating that the id column is the primary key.

5. **Add the information for the rest of the columns in the table as specified below.** Start by double-clicking below the column name for the previous column and then typing the column name in the text field that appears. Press the Tab key to move from field to field in the row.

   - Column Name: product_id; Datatype: INTEGER; NOT NULL and UNSIGNED checked
   - Column Name: quantity; Datatype: INTEGER; NOT NULL and UNSIGNED checked
   - Column Name: cart_id; Datatype: INTEGER; NOT NULL and UNSIGNED checked

6. **Click the Foreign Keys tab in the bottom-left corner and then click the + button below the Foreign Keys box.** The Add Foreign Key dialog box opens.

7. **Type** FK_cart_item_1 **in the Foreign Key Name text field and then click OK.** The FK_cart_item_1 foreign key is added to the Foreign Keys box.

8. **Choose product from the Ref. Table dropdown list, double-click id in the Column column, and then choose product_id from the dropdown list.**

9. **Click the Foreign Keys tab in the bottom-left corner and then click the + button below the Foreign Keys box.** The Add Foreign Key dialog box opens.

10. **Type** FK_cart_item_2 **in the Foreign Key Name text field and then click OK.** The FK_cart_item_2 foreign key is added to the Foreign Keys box.

11. **Click the FK_cart_item_2 foreign key.**

12. **Choose cart from the Ref. Table dropdown list, double-click id in the Column column, and then choose cart_id from the dropdown list.** When you're finished, the MySQL Table Editor dialog box should look like Figure 12.9.

13. **Click Apply Changes.** The Confirm Table Edit dialog box opens. This dialog box displays the SQL statement that's executed to create the `product` table.

14. **Click Execute.** The Confirm Table Edit dialog box closes, and you return to the MySQL Table Editor dialog box.

15. **Click Close.** The MySQL Table Editor dialog box closes.

FIGURE 12.9

After the columns have been added and the foreign keys to the `cart` and `product` tables have been created, the MySQL Table Editor dialog box should look like this.

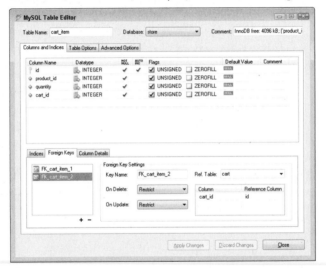

The database is now ready to be used by the application, but it won't be of much use without any data in it. You can use the MySQL Query Browser tool to write a SQL script to add some data to the database. Choose File ➪ New Script Tab to open a tab where you can type a set of SQL queries. Type the following code in the text area on this tab:

```
INSERT INTO store.USER(first_name, last_name, user_name, password)
VALUES('Charles','Christiansen','charles','selrahc');

INSERT INTO store.USER(first_name, last_name, user_name, password)
VALUES('Matthew','Keefe','matthew','wehttam');

INSERT INTO store.PRODUCT(name, description, category, price)
```

```
VALUES('Plasma Television','65 inch screen with
    1080p','electronics',3000.00);

INSERT INTO store.PRODUCT(name, description, category, price)
VALUES('Surround Sound Stereo','7.1 surround sound receiver with
    wireless speakers','electronics',1000.00);

INSERT INTO store.PRODUCT(name, description, category, price)
VALUES('Refrigerator','Bottom drawer freezer with water and ice on
    the door','appliances',1200.00);

INSERT INTO store.PRODUCT(name, description, category, price)
VALUES('Dishwasher','Large capacity with water saver
    setting','appliances',500.00);

INSERT INTO store.PRODUCT(name, description, category, price)
VALUES('Leather Sectional','Plush leather with room for 6
    people','furniture',1500.00);
```

Click the green Execute button in the top-right corner of the MySQL Query Browser. The script runs, and the sample data is added to the database. No sample data is added to the `cart` or `cart_item` tables. These tables don't need sample data because they're populated by adding items to the cart by using the application. You can verify that the data was inserted by clicking the X on the Script tab to close it and then dragging the `user` and `product` tables onto the Resultset tab. Dragging these tables onto the Resultset tab displays all the data in the table, as shown for the `product` table in Figure 12.10.

FIGURE 12.10

Dragging the `product` table onto the Resultset tab displays all the data in the table. You can see that all the sample data from your SQL script has been added.

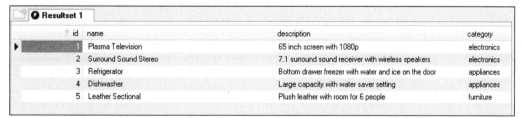

The Eclipse project

Before starting to develop the application, you need to set up a new project in Eclipse that contains the code, configuration files, and build scripts for the Web application. The project contains the standard folder structure for a Java Web application. After creating the project, you must add all the libraries that the project depends on to compile and run. These libraries are:

- Hibernate and all its required libraries

- The MySQL Connector/J JDBC driver

- The SLF4J and log4j logging libraries used by Hibernate

- Spring Framework's Web MVC and ORM modules

- JSTL and Jakarta standard tag libraries

CROSS-REF For more on Hibernate, MySQL Connector/J, and SLF4J, see Chapter 9. For more on the Spring Framework and tag libraries, see Chapter 6.

Finally, once the libraries have been added to the project, you must configure the project's build path to use some of those libraries when compiling the code for the project.

Open Eclipse, and create a new Spring project. When entering the project properties in the New Spring Project dialog box, change the output folder for the project to `web/WEB-INF/classes`. When you change the output directory to `web/WEB-INF/classes`, Eclipse outputs the compiled Java class files to that directory. This directory is where Web applications typically look for the Java files they need to run. When the application is bundled up as a WAR file, the class files are already in the correct location.

CROSS-REF For more on creating a Spring project in Eclipse, see Chapter 6.

Once the project is created, you need to add all the libraries that the Web application needs to run to a `lib` folder beneath the `WEB-INF` folder. There are a number of steps below, but the same pattern of steps is repeated throughout. Use the Eclipse Import from File system dialog box to navigate to a folder containing some library JAR files, select them, and then repeat for other library locations.

You will open the Import from File system dialog box several times. Each time, the steps are the same. To open the Import from File system dialog box, follow these steps:

1. **Right-click the `jfib-ch12-p01` project in the Project Explorer view and then choose New ➪ Folder from the popup menu.** The New Folder dialog box, as shown in Figure 12.11, opens.

2. **Type web\WEB-INF\lib in the Folder name text field and then click Finish.** The New Folder dialog box closes, and the newly created folder structure is added to the project.

FIGURE 12.11

The New Folder dialog box allows you to add new folders to your project. You can type nested folder paths here (for example, `web\WEB-INF\lib`), and Eclipse creates the entire structure for you.

3. **Right-click the `lib` folder and then choose Import from the popup menu.** The Import Select dialog box, as shown in Figure 12.12, opens.

4. **Click the arrow next to the General item to expand it, choose File System from the list, and then click the Next button.** The Import from File system dialog box, as shown in Figure 12.13, opens.

Use these steps any time you need to open the Import from File system dialog box to add libraries to the `web/WEB-INF/lib` folder.

FIGURE 12.12

The Import Select dialog box allows you to import resources for your project from a variety of sources.

Six sets of libraries need to be added to the project. First, add the Spring Framework core library and the Spring ORM and Spring Web MVC libraries by following these steps:

1. **Open the Import from File system dialog box as previously described.**

2. **Click the Browse button next to the From directory text field.** The Import from directory dialog box, as shown in Figure 12.14, opens.

3. **Navigate to the dist directory below your extracted Spring Framework directory, select it, and then click OK.** The directory appears in the left pane of the Import from File system dialog box, as shown in Figure 12.15. Clicking the dist directory displays its contents in the right pane of the dialog box. Clicking the arrow next to the directory name on the left expands it to displays its subfolders.

4. **Click the dist folder in the left pane and then click the check box next to spring.jar in the right pane.**

5. **Click Finish.** The spring.jar file you just added appears beneath the web\ WEB-INF\lib folder.

FIGURE 12.13

The Import from File system dialog box lets you bring resources located on your computer's file system into your project. Resources are copied from their original locations into your project's directory structure.

FIGURE 12.14

The Import from directory dialog box allows you to choose resources to import into your project from your computer's file system.

FIGURE 12.15

Once you've selected the `dist` directory, it appears in the left pane of the Import from File system dialog box, and its contents appear in the right pane. Clicking the arrow next to the directory in the left pane expands it to displays its subfolders.

6. **Open the Import from File system dialog box.**

7. **Click the Browse button next to the From directory text field.** The Import from directory dialog box opens.

8. **Navigate to the `dist\modules` directory below your extracted Spring Framework directory, select it, and then click OK.** The directory appears in the left pane of the Import from directory dialog box. Clicking the `modules` directory displays its contents in the right pane of the dialog box.

9. **Click the `modules` folder in the left pane and then click the check boxes next to `spring-orm.jar` and `spring-webmvc.jar` in the right pane.**

10. **Click Finish.** The `spring-orm.jar` and `spring-webmvc.jar` files you just added appear beneath the `web\WEB-INF\lib` folder.

Next, import the MySQL Connector/J JDBC Driver JAR file by following these steps:

1. **Open the Import from File system dialog box.**

2. **Click the Browse button next to the From directory text field.** The Import from directory dialog box opens.

3. **Navigate to your extracted `mysql-connector-java-5.1.6` directory, select it, and then click OK.** The directory appears in the left pane of the Import from directory dialog box. Clicking the `mysql-connector-java-5.1.6` directory displays its contents in the right pane of the dialog box.

4. **Click the `mysql-connector-java-5.1.6` folder in the left pane and then click the check box next to `mysql-connector-java-5.1.6-bin.jar` in the right pane.**

5. **Click Finish.** The `mysql-connector-java-5.1.6-bin.jar` file you just added appears beneath the `web\WEB-INF\lib` folder.

Next, import the Hibernate JAR file and the libraries required by Hibernate:

1. **Open the Import from File system dialog box.**

2. **Click the Browse button next to the From directory text field.** The Import from directory dialog box opens.

3. **Navigate to your extracted Hibernate distribution directory, select it, and then click OK.** The directory appears in the left pane of the Import from directory dialog box. Clicking the `hibernate-distribution-3.3.0.SP1` directory displays its contents in the right pane of the dialog box.

4. **Click the `hibernate-distribution-3.3.0.SP1` folder in the left pane and then click the check box next to `hibernate3.jar` in the right pane.**

5. **Click Finish.** The `hibernate3.jar` file you just added appears beneath the `web\WEB-INF\lib` folder.

6. **Open the Import from File system dialog box.**

7. **Click the Browse button next to the From directory text field.** The Import from directory dialog box opens.

8. **Navigate to the `lib/required` directory below your extracted Hibernate distribution directory, select it, and then click OK.** The directory appears in the left pane of the Import from directory dialog box. Clicking the required directory displays its contents in the right pane of the dialog box.

9. **Click the `required` folder in the left pane and then click the check boxes next to each of the six JAR files in the right pane.**

10. **Click Finish.** The six files you just added appear beneath the `web\WEB-INF\lib` folder.

Next, import the Jakarta standard and JSTL tag library files by following these steps:

1. **Open the Import from File system dialog box.**

2. **Click the Browse button next to the From directory text field.** The Import from directory dialog box opens.

3. **Navigate to the `lib/jakarta-taglibs` directory below your extracted Spring Framework distribution directory, select it, and then click OK.** The directory appears in the left pane of the Import from directory dialog box. Clicking the `jakarta-taglibs` directory displays its contents in the right pane of the dialog box.

4. **Click the `jakarta-taglibs` folder in the left pane and then click the check box next to `standard.jar` in the right pane.**

5. **Click Finish.** The `standard.jar` file you just added appears beneath the `web\WEB-INF\lib` folder.

6. **Open the Import from File system dialog box.**

7. **Click the Browse button next to the From directory text field.** The Import from directory dialog box opens.

8. **Navigate to the `lib/j2ee` directory below your extracted Spring Framework distribution directory, select it, and then click OK.** The directory appears in the left pane of the Import from directory dialog box. Clicking the `j2ee` directory displays its contents in the right pane of the dialog box.

9. **Click the `j2ee` folder in the left pane and then click the check box next to the `jstl.jar` file in the right pane.**

10. **Click Finish.** The `jstl.jar` file you just added appears beneath the `web\WEB-INF\lib` folder.

Finally, import the SLF4J libraries:

1. **Open the Import from File system dialog box.**

2. **Click the Browse button next to the From directory text field.** The Import from directory dialog box opens.

3. **Navigate to your extracted SLF4J distribution directory, select it, and then click OK.** The directory appears in the left pane of the Import from directory dialog box. Clicking the `slf4j-1.5.2` directory displays its contents in the right pane of the dialog box.

4. **Click the `slf4j-1.5.2` folder in the left pane and then click the check box next to `slf4j-log4j12-1.5.2.jar` in the right pane.**

5. **Click Finish.** The `slf4j-log4j12-1.5.2.jar` file you just added appears beneath the `web\WEB-INF\lib` folder.

When you have finished importing all the libraries, the Project Explorer view should look like Figure 12.16.

FIGURE 12.16

Once all the required libraries have been added to the web/WEB-INF/lib folder, the Project Explorer view should look like this.

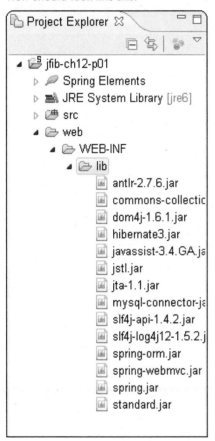

```
Project Explorer ⊠

▲ jfib-ch12-p01
   ▷ Spring Elements
   ▷ JRE System Library [jre6]
   ▷ src
   ▲ web
      ▲ WEB-INF
         ▲ lib
            antlr-2.7.6.jar
            commons-collectic
            dom4j-1.6.1.jar
            hibernate3.jar
            javassist-3.4.GA.ja
            jstl.jar
            jta-1.1.jar
            mysql-connector-ja
            slf4j-api-1.4.2.jar
            slf4j-log4j12-1.5.2.j
            spring-orm.jar
            spring-webmvc.jar
            spring.jar
            standard.jar
```

These libraries are now available to the Web application at runtime, but Eclipse can't use them to compile your Java classes until you add them to the build path for the project. Once they're added to the build path, the Eclipse project configuration is complete.

To configure the Java build path for your project, follow these steps:

1. **Right-click the project in the Project Explorer view and then choose Properties from the popup menu.** The Properties dialog box opens.

2. **Choose Java Build Path from the left navigation pane of the Properties dialog box.** The Java Build Path tabbed dialog box opens in the right pane, as shown in Figure 12.17.

3. **Click the Libraries tab.** The list of library JAR files and class folders appears. The JRE System Library from the installed JDK is already included in this list.

4. **Click the Add JARs button.** The JAR Selection dialog box opens.

5. **Click** `spring.jar`, `spring-webmvc.jar`, `spring-orm.jar`, **and** `hibernate3.jar` **under** `web/WEB-INF/lib` **and then click OK.** The JARs are added to the library list, as shown in Figure 12.18.

6. **Click the Add External JARs button.** The JAR Selection dialog box opens.

7. **Navigate to the client folder within your JBoss installation, click the** `servlet-api.jar` **file, and then click OK.** The `servlet-api.jar` library is added to the library list.

8. **Click OK.** The Properties dialog box closes. The build path libraries appear in the Project Explorer view.

FIGURE 12.17

Choosing Java Build Path from the left pane of the Properties dialog box opens the Java Build Path tabbed dialog box in the right pane.

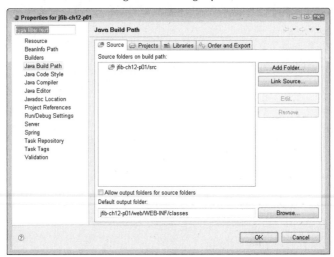

FIGURE 12.18

Click `spring.jar`, `spring-webmvc.jar`, `spring-orm.jar`, and `hibernate3.jar` under `web/WEB-INF/lib` in the JAR Selection dialog box to add them to the build library path for your project.

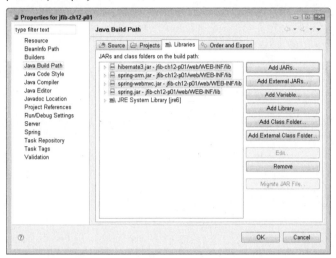

The model layer

The model is the part of the Model-View-Controller (MVC) application that contains the value objects and business logic that compose the application. For this Web application, there are four objects that correspond to the four tables in the MySQL database previously created.

Because the Flex client is expecting XML from the Web application, each of these objects should provide a method that returns an XML representation of the object. Because this functionality is common to all the objects and is required, you can create an interface that each object implements. The interface has a single `toXml()` method. Classes that implement this interface provide an implementation for the `toXml()` method that returns the XML representation of that object.

CROSS-REF   For more on interfaces in Java, see Chapter 6.

To create the `IXmlSerializable` interface, follow these steps:

1. **Right-click the `src` folder under the `jfib-ch12-p01` project in the Project Explorer view and then choose New ➪ Interface from the popup menu.** The New Java Interface dialog box, as shown in Figure 12.19, opens.

FIGURE 12.19

In the New Java Interface dialog box, fill in the Package and Name text fields for the `IXmlSerializable` interface.

2. **Click the Add button next to the Extended interfaces list box.** The Extended Interfaces Selection dialog box, as shown in Figure 12.20, opens.

3. **Type** Serializable **in the Choose interfaces text field, choose** `Serializable-java.io-[jre6]` **from the Matching items list box, and then click OK.** The Extended Interfaces Selection dialog box closes, and the `Serializable` interface appears in the Extended interfaces list box.

4. **Type** com.wiley.jfib.ch12.store.vo **in the Package text field, type** IXmlSerializable **in the Name text field, and then click Finish.** The newly created package and interface appear in the Project Explorer view.

Remember that implementing the `Serializable` interface is a best practice when using Hibernate to store and retrieve objects from a database. Because the `IXmlSerializable` interface extends the `Serializable` interface, any class that implements `IXmlSerializable` is also considered to have implemented `Serializable`. Therefore, the value object classes you create only need to implement `IXmlSerializable`.

FIGURE 12.20

The Extended Interfaces Selection dialog box allows you to choose an interface to extend.

Edit the `IXmlSerializable` interface to match this code listing:

```java
/**
 *
 */
package com.wiley.jfib.ch12.store.vo;

import java.io.Serializable;

/**
 * @author Chuck
 *
 */
public interface IXmlSerializable extends Serializable {

    /**
     * Return this object as an XML string
     * @return an XML string representing this object
     */
    public String toXml();

}
```

Now you can create the four value object classes that implement the `IXmlSerializable` interface. Use the New Java Class dialog box to create each of the four value object classes used by this application: `User`, `Product`, `Cart`, and `CartItem`. The same steps are used to create each of these classes. To create the value objects, follow these steps for each of the four classes:

1. **Right-click the** `com.wiley.jfib.ch12.store.vo` **package below the** `src` **folder under the** `jfib-ch12-p01` **project in the Project Explorer view and then choose New ⇨ Class from the popup menu.** The New Java Class dialog box, as shown in Figure 12.21, opens.

2. **Click the Add button next to the Interfaces list box.** The Implemented Interfaces Selection dialog box, as shown in Figure 12.22, opens.

3. **Type IXmlSerializable in the Choose interfaces text field, choose** `IXmlSerializable-com.wiley.jfib.ch12.store.vo` **from the Matching items list box, and then click OK.** The Implemented Interfaces Selection dialog box closes, and the `IXmlSerializable` interface appears in the Interfaces list box.

4. **Type** `com.wiley.jfib.ch12.store.vo` **in the Package text field, type the class name** (User, Product, Cart, or CartItem) **in the Name text field, click the Constructors from superclass and Inherited abstract methods check boxes, and then click Finish.** The newly created class appears in the Project Explorer view.

5. **Repeat steps 1–4 for each of the remaining classes.**

FIGURE 12.21

In the New Java Class dialog box, type the name for the value object class you're creating. The package name is filled in for you.

The Implemented Interfaces Selection dialog box allows you to choose an interface to implement.

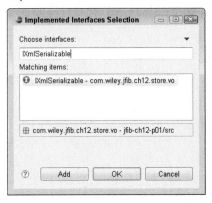

Here are the code listings for each of these objects:

User.java

```java
/**
 *
 */
package com.wiley.jfib.ch12.store.vo;


/**
 * @author Chuck
 *
 */
public class User implements IXmlSerializable {

    private static final long serialVersionUID = 1L;
    private int id;
    private String firstName;
    private String lastName;
    private String userName;
    private String password;

    /**
     *
     */
    public User() {
    }

    /**
```

```
 * @return the userId
 */
public int getId() {
    return id;
}

/**
 * @param userId the userId to set
 */
public void setId(int id) {
    this.id = id;
}

/**
 * @return the firstName
 */
public String getFirstName() {
    return firstName;
}

/**
 * @param firstName the firstName to set
 */
public void setFirstName(String firstName) {
    this.firstName = firstName;
}

/**
 * @return the lastName
 */
public String getLastName() {
    return lastName;
}

/**
 * @param lastName the lastName to set
 */
public void setLastName(String lastName) {
    this.lastName = lastName;
}

/**
 * @return the userName
 */
public String getUserName() {
    return userName;
}

/**
```

```java
     * @param userName the userName to set
     */
    public void setUserName(String userName) {
        this.userName = userName;
    }

    /**
     * @return the password
     */
    public String getPassword() {
        return password;
    }

    /**
     * @param password the password to set
     */
    public void setPassword(String password) {
        this.password = password;
    }

    /* (non-Javadoc)
     * @see com.wiley.jfib.ch12.store.vo.IXmlSerializable#toXml()
     */
    @Override
    public String toXml() {
        String xml = "<user>";
        xml += "<id>" + id + "</id>";
        xml += "<firstname>" + firstName + "</firstname>";
        xml += "<lastname>" + lastName + "</lastname>";
        xml += "</user>";
        return xml;
    }

}
```

Product.java
```java
/**
 *
 */
package com.wiley.jfib.ch12.store.vo;


/**
 * @author Chuck
 *
 */
public class Product implements IXmlSerializable {
```

```java
        private static final long serialVersionUID = 1L;
        private int id;
        private String category;
        private String name;
        private String description;
        private double price;

        public Product() {
        }

        /**
         * @return the id
         */
        public int getId() {
            return id;
        }

        /**
         * @param id the id to set
         */
        public void setId(int id) {
            this.id = id;
        }

        /**
         * @return the category
         */
        public String getCategory() {
            return category;
        }

        /**
         * @param category the category to set
         */
        public void setCategory(String category) {
            this.category = category;
        }

        /**
         * @return the name
         */
        public String getName() {
            return name;
        }

        /**
         * @param name the name to set
         */
        public void setName(String name) {
```

```
        this.name = name;
}

/**
 * @return the description
 */
public String getDescription() {
      return description;
}

/**
 * @param description the description to set
 */
public void setDescription(String description) {
      this.description = description;
}

/**
 * @return the price
 */
public double getPrice() {
      return price;
}

/**
 * @param price the price to set
 */
public void setPrice(double price) {
      this.price = price;
}

/* (non-Javadoc)
 * @see java.lang.Object#equals(java.lang.Object)
 */
@Override
public boolean equals(Object arg0) {
      return this.id == ((Product)arg0).getId();
}

/* (non-Javadoc)
 * @see com.wiley.jfib.ch12.store.vo.IXmlSerializable#toXml()
 */
@Override
public String toXml() {
      String xml = "<product>";
      xml += "<id>" + id + "</id>";
      xml += "<cat>" + category + "</cat>";
      xml += "<name>" + name + "</name>";
      xml += "<desc>" + description + "</desc>";
```

```
            xml += "<price>$" + price + "</price>";
            xml += "</product>";
            return xml;
        }
    }
```

CartItem.java

```java
/**
 *
 */
package com.wiley.jfib.ch12.store.vo;

/**
 * @author Chuck
 *
 */
public class CartItem implements IXmlSerializable {

    private static final long serialVersionUID = 1L;
    private int id;
    private int cartId;
    private Product product;
    private int quantity;

    /**
     *
     */
    public CartItem() {
    }

    /**
     * @return the id
     */
    public int getId() {
        return id;
    }

    /**
     * @param id the id to set
     */
    public void setId(int id) {
        this.id = id;
    }

    /**
     * @return the cartId
     */
    public int getCartId() {
```

```java
        return cartId;
}

/**
 * @param cartId the cartId to set
 */
public void setCartId(int cartId) {
      this.cartId = cartId;
}

/**
 * @return the product
 */
public Product getProduct() {
      return product;
}

/**
 * @param product the product to set
 */
public void setProduct(Product product) {
      this.product = product;
}

/**
 * @return the quantity
 */
public int getQuantity() {
      return quantity;
}

/**
 * @param quantity the quantity to set
 */
public void setQuantity(int quantity) {
      this.quantity = quantity;
}

/**
 * Retrieve the total cost for this cart item
 * @return
 */
public double getItemTotal()
{
      return product.getPrice() * quantity;
}


/**
```

```
         *
         */
        public boolean equals(Object obj)
        {
                CartItem item2 = (CartItem)obj;
                return cartId == item2.cartId
                                && product.getId() ==
                                item2.getProduct().getId();
        }


        /* (non-Javadoc)
         * @see com.wiley.jfib.ch12.store.vo.IXmlSerializable#toXml()
         */
        @Override
        public String toXml() {
                String xml = "<item>";
                xml += product.toXml();
                xml += "<quantity>" + quantity + "</quantity>";
                xml += "<item_total>$"
                        + this.getItemTotal()
                        + "</item_total>";
                xml += "</item>";
                return xml;
        }
    }
```

Cart.java

```
/**
 *
 */
package com.wiley.jfib.ch12.store.vo;

import java.util.Collection;
import java.util.HashSet;


/**
 * @author Chuck
 *
 */
public class Cart implements IXmlSerializable {
    private static final long serialVersionUID = 1L;
    private int id;
    private int userId;
    private Collection<CartItem> items;

    /**
     *
     */
    public Cart() {
```

```java
        items = new HashSet<CartItem>();
    }

    /**
     * @return the id
     */
    public int getId() {
        return id;
    }

    /**
     * @param id the id to set
     */
    public void setId(int id) {
        this.id = id;
    }

    /**
     * @return the userId
     */
    public int getUserId() {
        return userId;
    }

    /**
     * @param userId the userId to set
     */
    public void setUserId(int userId) {
        this.userId = userId;
    }

    /**
     * @return the items
     */
    public Collection<CartItem> getItems() {
        return items;
    }

    /**
     * @param items the items to set
     */
    public void setItems(Collection<CartItem> items) {
        this.items = items;
    }

    /**
     *
     * @param item
     */
```

```
public void addItem(CartItem item) {
    boolean itemExists = false;
    for(CartItem existingItem : items)
    {
        if(item.equals(existingItem))
        {
            existingItem.setQuantity
                (existingItem.getQuantity()
                + item.getQuantity());
            itemExists = true;
            break;
        }
    }
    if(!itemExists)
        items.add(item);
}

/* (non-Javadoc)
 * @see com.wiley.jfib.ch12.store.vo.IXmlSerializable#toXml()
 */
@Override
public String toXml() {
    double cartTotal = 0.0;
    String xml = "<cart>";
    xml += "<userid>" + userId + "</userid>";
    xml += "<items>";
    for (CartItem item : items)
    {
        xml += item.toXml();
        cartTotal += item.getItemTotal();
    }
    xml += "</items>";
    xml += "<total>$" + cartTotal + "</total>";
    xml += "</cart>";
    return xml;
}

}
```

As you can see, each of these four value objects has properties and getter and setter methods corresponding to the columns in each of the database tables. They also all implement the toXml() method from the IXmlSerializable interface. Each of the implementations of toXml() returns a string of XML representing that object. The CartItem class has one additional method, getItemTotal(), that calculates the total cost of the item by multiplying the unit price by the quantity. This value is returned to the Flex client in the XML created by the toXml() method.

To store and retrieve these objects by using Hibernate, you need to create a Hibernate mapping file for each of them. Remember that Hibernate mapping files are XML files that by convention have an `.hbm.xml` suffix and contain information mapping the properties of the object to columns in the database. The process for creating the Hibernate mapping file is the same for all four classes, aside from the filename. To create the Hibernate mapping files, follow these steps:

1. **Right-click the `com.wiley.jfib.ch12.store.vo` package in the Project Explorer view and then choose New ⇨ Other from the popup menu.** The Select a wizard dialog box, as shown in Figure 12.23, opens.

2. **Click the arrow next to General to expand it, click File, and then click Next.** The New File dialog box, as shown in Figure 12.24, opens.

3. **Type the name of the Hibernate mapping file to create in the File name text field and then click Finish.** The filename should be the name of the class followed by the suffix `.hbm.xml` (for example, `User.hbm.xml`). The New File dialog box closes, and the new Hibernate mapping file appears in the Project Explorer view.

4. **Repeat steps 1–3 for each of the Hibernate mapping files you need to create.**

FIGURE 12.23

The Select a wizard dialog box lets you choose the kind of object you want to create. Select File from below General in the list.

FIGURE 12.24

The New File dialog box lets you create a new empty file.

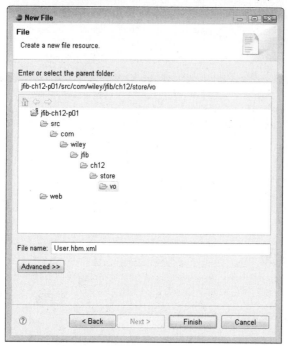

Here are the code listings for each of the Hibernate mapping files:

Cart.hbm.xml

```xml
<?xml version="1.0" encoding="UTF-8"?>
<!DOCTYPE hibernate-mapping PUBLIC "-//Hibernate/Hibernate Mapping
    DTD 3.0//EN" "http://hibernate.sourceforge.net/hibernate-mapping-
    3.0.dtd" >
<hibernate-mapping>
    <class name="com.wiley.jfib.ch12.store.vo.Cart" table="CART">
        <id name="id" column="id" type="java.lang.Integer">
            <generator class="increment"/>
        </id>
        <property name="userId" column="user_id"
                type="java.lang.Integer" />
        <set name="items" lazy="false" cascade="all-delete-orphan">
            <key column="cart_id" not-null="true"/>
            <one-to-many
                    class="com.wiley.jfib.ch12.store.vo.CartItem"/>
```

```
                    </set>
                </class>
            </hibernate-mapping>
```

CartItem.hbm.xml

```
<?xml version="1.0" encoding="UTF-8"?>
<!DOCTYPE hibernate-mapping PUBLIC "-//Hibernate/Hibernate Mapping
    DTD 3.0//EN" "http://hibernate.sourceforge.net/hibernate-mapping-
    3.0.dtd" >
<hibernate-mapping>
    <class name="com.wiley.jfib.ch12.store.vo.CartItem"
            table="CART_ITEM">
            <id name="id" column="id" type="java.lang.Integer">
                    <generator class="increment"/>
            </id>
            <property name="cartId" insert="false" update="false"
    column="cart_id" type="java.lang.Integer" />
            <many-to-one lazy="false" name="product"
                    class="com.wiley.jfib.ch12.store.vo.Product"
                    column="product_id"/>
            <property name="quantity" column="quantity"
                    type="java.lang.Integer" />
    </class>
</hibernate-mapping>
```

Product.hbm.xml

```
<?xml version="1.0" encoding="UTF-8"?>
<!DOCTYPE hibernate-mapping PUBLIC "-//Hibernate/Hibernate Mapping
    DTD 3.0//EN" "http://hibernate.sourceforge.net/hibernate-mapping-
    3.0.dtd" >
<hibernate-mapping>
    <class name="com.wiley.jfib.ch12.store.vo.Product"
    table="PRODUCT">
            <id name="id" column="id" type="java.lang.Integer">
                    <generator class="increment"/>
            </id>
            <property name="category" column="category"
                    type="java.lang.String" />
            <property name="name" column="name"
                    type="java.lang.String" />
            <property name="description" column="description"
                    type="java.lang.String" />
            <property name="price" column="price"
                    type="java.lang.Double" />
    </class>
</hibernate-mapping>
```

User.hbm.xml

```xml
<?xml version="1.0" encoding="UTF-8"?>
<!DOCTYPE hibernate-mapping PUBLIC "-//Hibernate/Hibernate Mapping
    DTD 3.0//EN" "http://hibernate.sourceforge.net/hibernate-mapping-
    3.0.dtd" >
<hibernate-mapping>
    <class name="com.wiley.jfib.ch12.store.vo.User" table="USER">
        <id name="id" column="id" type="java.lang.Integer">
            <generator class="increment"/>
        </id>
        <property name="firstName" column="first_name"
            type="java.lang.String" />
        <property name="lastName" column="last_name"
            type="java.lang.String" />
        <property name="userName" column="user_name"
            type="java.lang.String" />
        <property name="password" column="password"
            type="java.lang.String" />
    </class>
</hibernate-mapping>
```

The Hibernate mapping files contain <property> tags for each property in the object, mapping them to columns in the database table. The mapping file for the Cart class contains a <set> tag that establishes that a single Cart can contain a set of one or more CartItem objects. The mapping file for the CartItem class contains a <many-to-one> tag that establishes that many CartItem objects can contain the same Product class.

CROSS-REF For more on Hibernate mapping files, see Chapter 9.

Hibernate also needs a log4j.properties file to configure the logging that it does. To create the log4j.properties file, follow these steps:

1. **Right-click the** web/WEB-INF **folder in the Project Explorer view and then choose New ⇨ Other from the popup menu.** The Select a wizard dialog box opens.

2. **Click the arrow next to General to expand it, click File, and then click Next.** The New File dialog box opens.

3. **Type** log4j.properties **in the File name text field and then click Finish.** The New File dialog box closes, and the new log4j.properties file appears in the Project Explorer view.

Here's the code listing for the log4j.properties file:

```properties
log4j.appender.stdout=org.apache.log4j.ConsoleAppender
log4j.appender.stdout.layout=org.apache.log4j.PatternLayout

log4j.rootLogger=debug, stdout
```

```
log4j.logger.org.hibernate=error
log4j.logger.org.hibernate.SQL=error
log4j.logger.org.hibernate.type=error
log4j.logger.org.hibernate.cache=error
```

In this properties file, `log4j` is configured to output any logging messages to the JBoss console view, which is referred to as `stdout`, for standard output. Logging for Hibernate is set to output to the console only when an error occurs. This setting results in a minimal amount of information output to the console. To display more information, the logging level can be changed from `error` to `warn`, which displays both errors and warnings; `debug`, which displays errors, warnings, and any debugging information from Hibernate; and `info`, which is the most verbose level of output.

CROSS-REF For more on the `log4j.properties` file, see Chapter 9.

Finally, the application needs a Hibernate configuration file to allow it to set up communication between Hibernate and the database. The Hibernate configuration file should be named `hibernate.cfg.xml`. You create it in the root of the `src` folder. When the project is built, it's placed in the root of the `web/WEB-INF/classes` folder, where it's accessible on the classpath along with the compiled class files. The configuration is read in when JBoss is started, and the communication with the database is set up at that time.

To create the `hibernate.cfg.xml` configuration file, follow these steps:

1. **Right-click the `src` folder in the Project Explorer view and then choose New⇨ Other from the popup menu.** The Select a wizard dialog box opens.

2. **Click the arrow next to General to expand it, click File, and then click Next.** The New File dialog box opens.

3. **Type** hibernate.cfg.xml **in the File name text field and then click Finish.** The New File dialog box closes, and the new Hibernate configuration file appears in the Project Explorer view.

Here's the code listing for the `hibernate.cfg.xml` file:

```
<?xml version='1.0' encoding='utf-8'?>
<!DOCTYPE hibernate-configuration PUBLIC
"-//Hibernate/Hibernate Configuration DTD 3.0//EN"
"http://hibernate.sourceforge.net/hibernate-configuration-3.0.dtd">

<hibernate-configuration>
    <session-factory>

        <!-- Database connection settings -->
```

```
<property name="connection.driver_class">
   com.mysql.jdbc.Driver
</property>

<property name="connection.url">
   jdbc:mysql://localhost:3306/store
</property>

<property name="connection.username">root</property>
<property name="connection.password">toor</property>
<property name="connection.autocommit">true</property>
<!-- SQL dialect -->
<property name="dialect">
   org.hibernate.dialect.MySQLDialect
</property>
<!-- Enable Hibernate's automatic session context management -->
<property name="current_session_context_class">jta</property>

<!-- Echo all executed SQL to stdout -->
<property name="show_sql">true</property>
<mapping
   resource="com/wiley/jfib/ch12/store/vo/Cart.hbm.xml"/>
<mapping
   resource="com/wiley/jfib/ch12/store/vo/CartItem.hbm.xml"/>
<mapping
   resource="com/wiley/jfib/ch12/store/vo/Product.hbm.xml"/>
<mapping
   resource="com/wiley/jfib/ch12/store/vo/User.hbm.xml"/>
</session-factory>
</hibernate-configuration>
```

NOTE Make sure to use the correct root password for your MySQL database for the value of the "connection.password" property.

CROSS-REF For more on the structure and properties of the hibernate.cfg.xml file, see Chapter 9.

The data access layer

The *data access layer* is the part of the application that communicates with the database. For this application, an interface called IStoreDao defines the data access functions available to the service layer of the application. A class called StoreDao implements this interface and provides the implementations of these data access functions. Remember, when you separate the interface from the implementation, if the need ever arises to change the way the data for the application is accessed, the StoreDao implementation can be changed without needing to change any of the service layer code, which uses the interface and isn't dependent on the implementation of the interface behind the scenes.

The `IStoreDao` interface contains one method for each of the services in the application. To create the `IStoreDao` interface, follow these steps:

1. **Right-click the `src` folder under the `jfib-ch12-p01` project in the Project Explorer view and then choose New ⇨ Interface from the popup menu.** The New Java Interface dialog box opens.

2. **Type com.wiley.jfib.ch12.store.dao in the Package text field, type IStoreDao in the Name text field, and then click Finish.** The newly created package and interface appear in the Project Explorer view.

Edit the `IStoreDao` interface so that it matches this code listing:

```
/**
 *
 */
package com.wiley.jfib.ch12.store.dao;

import java.util.Collection;

import com.wiley.jfib.ch12.store.vo.Cart;
import com.wiley.jfib.ch12.store.vo.Product;
import com.wiley.jfib.ch12.store.vo.User;

/**
 * @author Chuck
 *
 */
public interface IStoreDao {
    /**
     *
     * @param category
     * @return
     */
    public Collection<Product> getProductList(String category);

    /**
     *
     * @param productId
     * @return
     */
    public Product getProductDetails(String productId);

    /**
     *
     * @param username
     * @param password
     * @return
     */
    public User logIn(String username, String password);
```

```
/**
 *
 * @param userId
 * @return
 */
public Cart retrieveCart(String userId);

/**
 *
 * @param userId
 * @param product
 */
public Cart addProductToCart(String userId, Product product,
String quantity);

/**
 *
 * @param userId
 * @param product
 */
public Cart addProductToCart(String userId, String productId,
String quantity);

/**
 *
 * @param product
 * @return
 */
public Product saveOrUpdateProduct(Product product);

/**
 *
 * @param productId
 * @return
 */
public void deleteProduct(int productId);
}
```

To create the `StoreDao` class, follow these steps:

1. **Right-click the** `com.wiley.jfib.ch12.store.dao` **package in the Project Explorer view and then choose New ⇨ Class from the popup menu.** The New Java Class dialog box opens.

2. **Click the Add button next to the Interfaces list box.** The Implemented Interfaces Selection dialog box opens.

3. **Type** IStoreDao **in the Choose interfaces text field, choose** IStoreDao-com.wiley. jfib.ch12.store.dao **from the Matching items list box, and then click OK.** The Implemented Interfaces Selection dialog box closes, and the IStoreDao interface appears in the Interfaces list box.

4. **Click the Browse button next to the Superclass text field.** The Superclass Selection dialog box, as shown in Figure 12.25, opens.

5. **Type** HibernateDaoSupport **in the Choose a type text field, choose** HibernateDaoSupport-org.springframework.orm.hibernate3.support **from the Matching items list box, and then click OK.** The Superclass Selection dialog box closes, and the HibernateDaoSupport class appears in the Superclass text field.

6. **Type** StoreDao **in the Name text field, click the Constructors from superclass and Inherited abstract methods check boxes, and then click Finish.** The New Java Class dialog box closes, and the newly created class appears in the Project Explorer view.

FIGURE 12.25
_____

The Superclass Selection dialog box lets you choose a superclass for your Java classes. The superclass for the StoreDao class is the HibernateDaoSupport class found in the Spring ORM library.

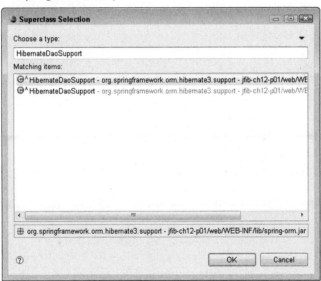

Edit the StoreDao class so that it matches this code listing:

```
/**
 *
 */
```

```
package com.wiley.jfib.ch12.store.dao;

import java.util.Collection;

import org.hibernate.criterion.DetachedCriteria;
import org.hibernate.criterion.Restrictions;
import org.springframework.orm.hibernate3.support.
    HibernateDaoSupport;

import com.wiley.jfib.ch12.store.vo.Cart;
import com.wiley.jfib.ch12.store.vo.CartItem;
import com.wiley.jfib.ch12.store.vo.Product;
import com.wiley.jfib.ch12.store.vo.User;

/**
 * @author Chuck
 *
 */
public class StoreDao extends HibernateDaoSupport implements
    IStoreDao {

    /**
     *
     */
    public StoreDao() {
    }

    /* (non-Javadoc)
     * @see com.wiley.jfib.ch12.store.dao.
    IStoreDao#addProductToCart(java.lang.String, com.wiley.jfib.ch12.
    store.vo.Product)
     */
    @Override
    @SuppressWarnings("unchecked")
    public Cart addProductToCart(String userId, Product product,
            String quantity) {
                DetachedCriteria criteria =
                    DetachedCriteria.forClass(Cart.class)
                    .add(Restrictions.eq("userId",
                            Integer.parseInt(userId)));
                Collection<Cart> carts = getHibernateTemplate().
                    findByCriteria(criteria, 0, 1);
                Cart cart = new Cart();
                cart.setUserId(Integer.parseInt(userId));
                if(carts.size() > 0)
                    cart = carts.iterator().next();
                CartItem item = new CartItem();
                item.setCartId(cart.getId());
                item.setProduct(product);
```

```
      item.setQuantity(Integer.parseInt(quantity));
      cart.addItem(item);
      getHibernateTemplate().saveOrUpdate(cart);
      return cart;
}


/* (non-Javadoc)
 * @see com.wiley.jfib.ch12.store.dao.
IStoreDao#addProductToCart(java.lang.String, com.wiley.jfib.ch12.
store.vo.Product)
 */
@Override
public Cart addProductToCart(String userId, String productId,
String quantity) {
      Product product = getProductDetails(productId);
      return addProductToCart(userId,product,quantity);
}


/* (non-Javadoc)
 * @see com.wiley.jfib.ch12.store.dao.IStoreDao#getProductDetails
(java.lang.String)
 */
@Override
public Product getProductDetails(String productId) {
      return (Product)getHibernateTemplate()
            .get(Product.class, Integer.parseInt(productId));
}


/* (non-Javadoc)
 * @see com.wiley.jfib.ch12.store.dao.
IStoreDao#getProductList(java.lang.String)
 */
@Override
@SuppressWarnings("unchecked")
public Collection<Product> getProductList(String category) {
      DetachedCriteria criteria =
            DetachedCriteria.forClass(Product.class);
      if(category != null)
         criteria = criteria.add(
            Restrictions.eq("category", category));
      return getHibernateTemplate().findByCriteria(criteria);
}


/* (non-Javadoc)
 * @see com.wiley.jfib.ch12.store.dao.IStoreDao#logIn(java.lang.
String, java.lang.String)
 */
@Override
@SuppressWarnings("unchecked")
```

```java
public User logIn(String username, String password) {
    DetachedCriteria criteria =
            DetachedCriteria.forClass(User.class)
            .add(Restrictions.eq("userName", username))
            .add(Restrictions.eq("password", password));
    Collection<User> user = getHibernateTemplate().
            findByCriteria(criteria, 0, 1);
    if(user.size() == 0)
        return null;
    else
        return user.iterator().next();
}


/* (non-Javadoc)
 * @see com.wiley.jfib.ch12.store.dao.IStoreDao#retrieveCart(java.
lang.String)
 */
@Override
@SuppressWarnings("unchecked")
public Cart retrieveCart(String userId) {
    DetachedCriteria criteria =
            DetachedCriteria.forClass(Cart.class)
            .add(Restrictions.eq("userId",
                    Integer.parseInt(userId)));
    Collection<Cart> carts =
            getHibernateTemplate().findByCriteria(criteria, 0, 1);
    Cart cart = new Cart();
    cart.setUserId(Integer.parseInt(userId));
    if(carts.size() > 0)
            cart = carts.iterator().next();
    return cart;
}


@Override
public Product saveOrUpdateProduct(Product product) {
    getHibernateTemplate().saveOrUpdate(product);
    return product;
}


/* (non-Javadoc)
 * @see com.wiley.jfib.ch12.store.dao.IStoreDao#deleteProduct(int)
 */
@Override
public void deleteProduct(int productId) {
    // TODO Auto-generated method stub
    Product product = (Product) getHibernateTemplate().
            get(Product.class, productId);
```

```
            if(product != null)
                getHibernateTemplate().delete(product);
    }


    }
```

The methods in the `StoreDao` class use Hibernate's `DetachedCriteria` class to define the criteria to be used when retrieving objects. For example, in the `getProductList()` method, first the `DetachedCriteria` is created by using the `Product` class. Then the category passed in is selected, and if it's not null, a restriction is added to the `DetachedCriteria` to retrieve only the Products in the given category. Finally, the Hibernate template is retrieved, and its `findBy Criteria` method is called by using the `DetachedCriteria` object to retrieve the Products that fit the criteria. The rest of the methods in the `StoreDao` class follow this same general pattern.

The service layer

The service layer contains five service classes that handle requests from the Flex client and return XML data that fits into a well-defined structure. The outermost tag is a `<result>` tag that contains a type attribute that indicates success or failure. Inside the `<result>` tag is the XML for the actual result of the operation. For successful operations, this is the XML representation of the object being retrieved. For failure, some well-defined error XML containing the error message is returned.

Because much of the XML structure is the same for all the services, you can separate that code out into its own class and then let each of the services extend that class. This base class is responsible for creating the `<result>` tag and the standard error XML. Each of the service classes that extend it is responsible for providing the XML from the objects it retrieves. The base class will be *abstract*, meaning that it can't be instantiated directly. An abstract class typically contains one or more abstract methods, which extending classes are required to provide implementations for. In this way, an abstract class acts much like an interface that provides some implementation code itself.

To create the abstract `StoreBaseService` class, follow these steps:

1. **Right-click the `com.wiley.jfib.ch12.store.dao` package in the Project Explorer view and then choose New ➪ Class from the popup menu.** The New Java Class dialog box opens.

2. **Click the Add button next to the Interfaces list box.** The Implemented Interfaces Selection dialog box opens.

3. **Type Controller in the Choose interfaces text field, choose `Controller-org. springframework.web.servlet.mvc` from the Matching items list box, and then click OK.** The Implemented Interfaces Selection dialog box closes, and the `Controller` interface appears in the Interfaces list box.

4. **Type StoreBaseService in the Name text field, click the Abstract and Constructors from superclass check boxes, and then click Finish.** The New Java Class dialog box closes, and the newly created class appears in the Project Explorer view.

Edit the `StoreBaseService` class so that it matches the following code listing:

```java
/**
 *
 */
package com.wiley.jfib.ch12.store.service;

import javax.servlet.http.HttpServletRequest;
import javax.servlet.http.HttpServletResponse;

import org.springframework.web.servlet.ModelAndView;
import org.springframework.web.servlet.mvc.Controller;

import com.wiley.jfib.ch12.store.dao.IStoreDao;

/**
 * @author Chuck
 *
 */
public abstract class StoreBaseService implements Controller {
    private IStoreDao storeDao;

    @Override
    public ModelAndView handleRequest(HttpServletRequest arg0,
                HttpServletResponse arg1) throws Exception
    {
        String xmlString = "";
        try {
                xmlString = getResultXmlHeader();
                xmlString += getXmlFromOperation(arg0,arg1);
                xmlString += getResultXmlFooter();
        } catch (Exception e) {
                xmlString = getErrorXml(e.getMessage());
        }
        return new ModelAndView("WEB-INF/jsp/xml.jsp",
                "xmlString",xmlString);
    }

    protected String getErrorXml(String message)
    {
        String errorXml = "<?xml version=\"1.0\"
encoding=\"ISO-8859-1\"?>";
        errorXml += "<result type=\"error\">";
        errorXml += "<message>";
        errorXml += message;
        errorXml += "</message>";
        errorXml += "</result>";
        return errorXml;
    }
```

```
        protected String getResultXmlHeader()
        {
                String resultXml = "<?xml version=\"1.0\""
                        + "encoding=\"ISO-8859-1\"?>";
                resultXml += "<result type=\"success\">";
                return resultXml;
        }

        protected abstract String getXmlFromOperation
                (HttpServletRequest request,
                HttpServletResponse response) throws Exception;

        protected String getResultXmlFooter()
        {
                return "</result>";
        }

        /**
         * @return the storeDao
         */
        public IStoreDao getStoreDao() {
                return storeDao;
        }

        /**
         * @param storeDao the storeDao to set
         */
        public void setStoreDao(IStoreDao storeDao) {
                this.storeDao = storeDao;
        }
}
```

The StoreBaseService class implements the Spring Framework's Controller interface, which is part of the Spring Web MVC module. Classes that implement the Controller interface handle requests dispatched to them from the Spring Dispatcher servlet. This class constructs some header XML and then calls an abstract method called getXmlFromOperation(). No implementation is provided for this method. The service classes that extend StoreBaseService are required to provide an implementation for it. This is where the services return the XML representations of the objects they retrieve.

You use the New Java Class dialog box to create each of the five service classes used by this application. These service classes are as follows:

- AddProductToCartService
- LogInService
- ProductDetailsService
- ProductListService
- RetrieveCartService

The same steps are used to create each of these classes. To create the services, follow these steps for each of the five classes:

1. Right-click the `com.wiley.jfib.ch12.store.service` **package below the** `src` **folder under the** `jfib-ch12-p01` **project in the Project Explorer view and then choose New ⇨ Class from the popup menu.** The New Java Class dialog box opens.

2. **Click the Add button next to the Interfaces list box.** The Implemented Interfaces Selection dialog box opens.

3. **Type IXmlSerializable in the Choose interfaces text field, choose** `IXmlSerializable-com.wiley.jfib.ch12.store.vo` **from the Matching items list box, and then click OK.** The Implemented Interfaces Selection dialog box closes, and the `IXmlSerializable` interface appears in the Interfaces list box.

4. **Click the Browse button next to the Superclass text field.** The Superclass Selection dialog box opens.

5. **Type StoreBaseService in the Choose a type text field, choose** `StoreBaseService-com.wiley.jfib.ch12.store.service` **from the Matching items list box, and then click OK.** The Superclass Selection dialog box closes, and the `StoreBaseService` class appears in the Superclass text field.

6. **Type the class name of the service in the Name text field, click the Constructors from superclass and Inherited abstract methods check boxes, and then click Finish.** The newly created class appears in the Project Explorer view.

7. **Repeat steps 1–6 for each of the remaining classes.**

Here are the code listings for each of these services:

AddProductToCartService.java

```
/**
 *
 */
package com.wiley.jfib.ch12.store.service;

import javax.servlet.http.HttpServletRequest;
import javax.servlet.http.HttpServletResponse;

import com.wiley.jfib.ch12.store.vo.Cart;

/**
 * @author Chuck
 *
 */
public class AddProductToCartService extends StoreBaseService {

    /* (non-Javadoc)
     * @see com.wiley.jfib.ch12.store.service.StoreBaseService#getXml
    FromOperation(javax.servlet.http.HttpServletRequest, javax.
    servlet.http.HttpServletResponse)
```

```
    */
    @Override
    protected String getXmlFromOperation(HttpServletRequest request,
            HttpServletResponse response) throws Exception {
        String productId = request.getParameter("productid");
        String userId = request.getParameter("userid");
        String quantity = request.getParameter("quantity");
        Cart cart = getStoreDao().addProductToCart(userId,
productId, quantity);
        return cart.toXml();
    }
}
```

LogInService.java

```
/**
 *
 */
package com.wiley.jfib.ch12.store.service;

import javax.servlet.http.HttpServletRequest;
import javax.servlet.http.HttpServletResponse;

import com.wiley.jfib.ch12.store.vo.User;

/**
 * @author Chuck
 *
 */
public class LogInService extends StoreBaseService {

    /* (non-Javadoc)
     * @see com.wiley.jfib.ch12.store.service.StoreBaseService#getXml
    FromOperation(javax.servlet.http.HttpServletRequest, javax.
    servlet.http.HttpServletResponse)
     */
    @Override
    protected String getXmlFromOperation(HttpServletRequest request,
            HttpServletResponse response) throws Exception {
        String username = request.getParameter("username");
        String password = request.getParameter("password");
        User user = getStoreDao().logIn(username, password);
        if(user == null)
                throw new Exception
                        ("Invalid credentials - login failed.");
        return user.toXml();
    }
}
```

ProductDetailsService.java

```
/**
 *
 */
package com.wiley.jfib.ch12.store.service;

import javax.servlet.http.HttpServletRequest;
import javax.servlet.http.HttpServletResponse;

import com.wiley.jfib.ch12.store.vo.Product;

/**
 * @author Chuck
 *
 */
public class ProductDetailsService extends StoreBaseService {
    /* (non-Javadoc)
     * @see com.wiley.jfib.ch12.store.service.StoreBaseService#getXml
    FromOperation(javax.servlet.http.HttpServletRequest, javax.
    servlet.http.HttpServletResponse)
     */
    @Override
    protected String getXmlFromOperation(HttpServletRequest request,
                HttpServletResponse response) throws Exception {
        String productId = request.getParameter("id");
        Product product = getStoreDao().
                getProductDetails(productId);
        return product.toXml();
    }
}
```

ProductListService.java

```
/**
 *
 */
package com.wiley.jfib.ch12.store.service;

import java.util.Collection;

import javax.servlet.http.HttpServletRequest;
import javax.servlet.http.HttpServletResponse;

import com.wiley.jfib.ch12.store.vo.Product;

/**
 * @author Chuck
 *
 */
public class ProductListService extends StoreBaseService {
```

```
    /* (non-Javadoc)
     * @see com.wiley.jfib.ch12.store.service.StoreBaseService#getXml
    FromOperation(javax.servlet.http.HttpServletRequest, javax.
    servlet.http.HttpServletResponse)
     */
    @Override
    protected String getXmlFromOperation(HttpServletRequest request,
                HttpServletResponse response) throws Exception {
            String xmlString = "";
            String category = request.getParameter("cat");
            Collection<Product> products = getStoreDao().
                getProductList(category);
            xmlString += "<products>";
            for(Product product : products)
                    xmlString += product.toXml();
            xmlString += "</products>";
            return xmlString;
    }
}
```

RetrieveCartService.java

```
/**
 *
 */
package com.wiley.jfib.ch12.store.service;

import javax.servlet.http.HttpServletRequest;
import javax.servlet.http.HttpServletResponse;

import com.wiley.jfib.ch12.store.vo.Cart;

/**
 * @author Chuck
 *
 */
public class RetrieveCartService extends StoreBaseService {
    /* (non-Javadoc)
     * @see com.wiley.jfib.ch12.store.service.StoreBaseService#getXml
    FromOperation(javax.servlet.http.HttpServletRequest, javax.
    servlet.http.HttpServletResponse)
     */
    @Override
    protected String getXmlFromOperation(HttpServletRequest request,
                HttpServletResponse response) throws Exception {
            String userId = request.getParameter("userid");
            Cart cart = getStoreDao().retrieveCart(userId);
            return cart.toXml();
    }
}
```

The only method implemented by the service classes is the abstract `getXmlFromOperation()` method in the `StoreBaseService` base class. Each service uses the `IStoreDao` interface provided by the base class to retrieve the data it needs and then calls the `toXml()` method on the returned object to get the XML representation of the object. The `StoreBaseService` class then places this XML inside the `<result>` tags, and this XML block is returned to the client.

As you saw in the `StoreBaseService` class, the view for all these services is a JSP file named `xml.jsp`. This JSP file simply outputs the XML string so that the Flex client can use it. To create the `xml.jsp` file, follow these steps:

1. **Right-click the** `web/WEB-INF` **folder in the Project Explorer view and then choose New⇨Other from the popup menu.** The Select a wizard dialog box opens.

2. **Click the arrow next to General to expand it, click File, and then click Next.** The New File dialog box opens.

3. **Type** /jsp **at the end of the path in the Enter or select the parent folder text field, type** xml.jsp **in the File name text field, and then click Finish.** The New File dialog box closes, and the new JSP file appears in the Project Explorer view.

The code listing for the `xml.jsp` file follows. The code should be entered on a single line and without breaks:

```
<?xml version="1.0" encoding="ISO-8859-1" ?><%@ page language="java"
   contentType="text/html; charset=ISO-8859-1"
   pageEncoding="ISO-8859-1"%><%@ taglib prefix="c" uri="http://
   java.sun.com/jsp/jstl/core" %><c:out value="${xmlString}"/>
```

The JSP page uses the JSTL tag library to output the value of the variable `xmlString` passed in from the `Controller`. The Flex client receives this block of XML, parses it, and displays the data to the user.

CROSS-REF For more on the JSTL tag library and JSP views, see Chapter 6.

There are two configuration files needed for a Spring Web MVC Web application. The first is `web.xml`, which is the standard configuration file for all Web applications. In the `web.xml` file, you set up a servlet registration and mapping for the Spring dispatcher servlet. This servlet handles all incoming requests to the Web application and delegates them to the appropriate service class based on the URL of the request. The mapping for each of the service classes as well as the Hibernate template configuration is handled in the second configuration file: `spring-dispatcher-servlet.xml`. In this file, each URL is mapped to a specific controller, and the Hibernate configuration for the Hibernate session and template is defined.

First, create `spring-dispatcher-servlet.xml` by following these steps:

1. **Right-click the `web/WEB-INF` folder in the Project Explorer view and then choose New ⇨ Other from the popup menu.** The Select a wizard dialog box opens.

2. **Click the arrow next to General to expand it, click File, and then click Next.** The New File dialog box opens.

3. **Type** spring-dispatcher-servlet.xml **in the File name text field and then click Finish.** The New File dialog box closes, and the new Spring configuration file appears in the Project Explorer view.

Here's the code listing for the `spring-dispatcher-servlet.xml` file:

```
<?xml version="1.0" encoding="UTF-8"?>
<beans xmlns="http://www.springframework.org/schema/beans"
      xmlns:xsi="http://www.w3.org/2001/XMLSchema-instance"
      xsi:schemaLocation="http://www.springframework.org/schema/beans
          http://www.springframework.org/schema/beans/spring-beans-2.5.xsd">
    <bean id="sessionFactory"
          class="org.springframework.orm.hibernate3.LocalSessionFactoryBean">
        <property name="configLocation">
            <value>classpath:/hibernate.cfg.xml</value>
        </property>
    </bean>
    <bean id="hibernateTemplate"
          class="org.springframework.orm.hibernate3.HibernateTemplate">
        <property name="sessionFactory" ref="sessionFactory"/>
    </bean>
    <bean name="storeDao"
          class="com.wiley.jfib.ch12.store.dao.StoreDao">
        <property name="hibernateTemplate"
                ref="hibernateTemplate"/>
    </bean>
    <bean name="/add-product.htm"
          class="com.wiley.jfib.ch12.store.service.AddProductToCartService">
        <property name="storeDao" ref="storeDao"/>
    </bean>
    <bean name="/cart.htm"
          class="com.wiley.jfib.ch12.store.service.RetrieveCartService">
        <property name="storeDao" ref="storeDao"/>
    </bean>
    <bean name="/product-list.htm"
          class="com.wiley.jfib.ch12.store.service.ProductListService">
        <property name="storeDao" ref="storeDao"/>
    </bean>
```

```
      <bean name="/product-details.htm"
            class="com.wiley.jfib.ch12.store.service.ProductDetailsService">
            <property name="storeDao" ref="storeDao"/>
      </bean>
      <bean name="/login.htm"
            class="com.wiley.jfib.ch12.store.service.LogInService">
            <property name="storeDao" ref="storeDao"/>
      </bean>
  </beans>
```

This configuration file defines the Spring beans for the Hibernate template and session by using the `hibernate.cfg.xml` file to provide them with the Hibernate configuration. It also maps a URL to each service class and then sets up the `StoreDao` property each service uses to retrieve the data it needs.

Now create the `web.xml` configuration file by following the same steps you used to create `spring-dispatcher-servlet.xml`. Here's the code listing for `web.xml`:

```
<?xml version="1.0" encoding="UTF-8"?>
<web-app version="2.4"
         xmlns="http://java.sun.com/xml/ns/j2ee"
         xmlns:xsi="http://www.w3.org/2001/XMLSchema-instance"
         xsi:schemaLocation="http://java.sun.com/xml/ns/j2ee
         http://java.sun.com/xml/ns/j2ee/web-app_2_4.xsd" >
    <servlet>
      <servlet-name>spring-dispatcher</servlet-name>
      <servlet-class>
            org.springframework.web.servlet.DispatcherServlet
      </servlet-class>
      <load-on-startup>1</load-on-startup>
    </servlet>

    <servlet-mapping>
      <servlet-name>spring-dispatcher</servlet-name>
      <url-pattern>*.htm</url-pattern>
    </servlet-mapping>
</web-app>
```

This configuration file defines the Spring `DispatcherServlet` and maps it to a URL pattern that says that any URL ending in `.htm` is handled by this servlet.

CROSS-REF   **For more on these Web application configuration files, see Chapter 6.**

The Ant build file

Now that the setup is finished, you can create the Ant build properties file and the `build.xml` file. To create these two files, follow these steps:

1. **Right-click the** `jfib-ch12-p01` **project in the Project Explorer view and then choose New⇨File from the popup menu.** The New File dialog box opens.

2. **Type** store-build.properties **in the File name text field and then click Finish.** The New File dialog box closes, and the newly created `store-build.properties` file appears below the `jfib-ch12-p01` project in the Project Explorer view.

3. **Right-click the** `jfib-ch12-p01` **project in the Project Explorer view and then choose New⇨File from the popup menu.** The New File dialog box opens.

4. **Type** build.xml **in the File name text field and then click Finish.** The New File dialog box closes, and the newly created `build.xml` file appears below the `jfib-ch12-p01` project in the Project Explorer view.

The properties contained in the `store-build.properties` file are used by the `build.xml` build file, so first edit the `store-build.properties` file to match this code listing:

```
# Ant build properties for store
src.dir=src
web.dir=web
build.dir=${web.dir}/WEB-INF/classes

name=store

appserver.home=${env.JBOSS_HOME}/server/default
appserver.lib=${appserver.home}/lib
deploy.path=${appserver.home}/deploy
```

CROSS-REF   For more on Ant build properties files, see Chapter 6.

This properties file contains properties for the Java source and Web file directories in the project, the build output directory, the application name, the JBoss home, and the application deployment path.

Now edit the `build.xml` file to match this code listing:

```
<?xml version="1.0" encoding="UTF-8"?>
<project name="store" basedir="." default="usage">
    <property environment="env"/>
     <property file="store-build.properties"/>

     <path id="cp">
```

```
            <fileset dir="${web.dir}/WEB-INF/lib">
                <include name="*.jar"/>
            </fileset>
            <fileset dir="${appserver.lib}">
                <include name="servlet*.jar"/>
            </fileset>
            <pathelement path="${build.dir}"/>
    </path>

    <target name="usage">
        <echo message=""/>
        <echo message="${name} build file"/>
        <echo message="-----------------------------------"/>
        <echo message=""/>
        <echo message="Available targets are:"/>
        <echo message=""/>
        <echo message="build     --> Build the application"/>
        <echo message="deploy   --> Deploy application as a WAR
    file"/>
        <echo message=""/>
    </target>

    <target name="build" description="Compile main source tree java
    files">
        <mkdir dir="${build.dir}"/>
        <javac destdir="${build.dir}" source="1.5" target="1.5"
         debug="true" deprecation="false" optimize="false"
         failonerror="true">
        <src path="${src.dir}"/>
        <classpath refid="cp"/>
        </javac>
    </target>

    <target name="deploy" depends="build" description="Deploy
    application as a WAR file">
        <war destfile="${name}.war"
            webxml="${web.dir}/WEB-INF/web.xml">
            <fileset dir="${web.dir}">
                <include name="**/*.*"/>
            </fileset>
        </war>
        <copy todir="${deploy.path}" preservelastmodified="true">
            <fileset dir=".">
                <include name="*.war"/>
            </fileset>
        </copy>
    </target>
</project>
```

 For more on the structure and functions of Ant `build.xml` files, see Chapter 6.

Deploying and Testing the Web Application

To run the Ant build script from within Eclipse, you need to add it to the Ant view in your project. To add the build script to the Ant view, follow these steps:

1. **Choose Window ⇨ Show View ⇨ Other.** The Show View dialog box, as shown in Figure 12.26, opens.

FIGURE 12.26

Choose the Ant view from the Show View dialog box.

2. **Click the arrow next to Ant to expand it, click Ant in the expanded menu, and then click OK.** The Ant view opens.

3. **Click the Add Buildfiles button (the leftmost button in the Ant view, containing a plus sign next to an ant icon) in the Ant view.** The Buildfile Selection dialog box opens.

4. **Click the arrow next to the project name to expand it, click the `build.xml` file, as shown in Figure 12.27, and then click OK.** The Buildfile Selection dialog box closes, and the build file is added to the Ant view, as shown in Figure 12.28.

FIGURE 12.27

Choose the `build.xml` file for your project in the Buildfile Selection dialog box to add it to the Ant view.

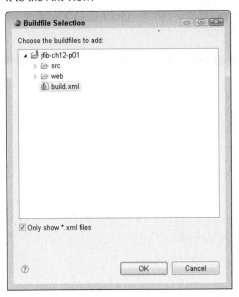

FIGURE 12.28

The build file appears in the Ant view using the name of the project as defined in `build.xml`.

Click the arrow next to the build file entry in the Ant view to expand it and see the available build targets. The three targets you saw in the `build.xml` file appear here. Now double-click the `deploy` target to run it. Because the `build` target has never been run, the `deploy` target first launches the `build` target to compile the code, runs the `deploy` target to package the application into a WAR file, and then deploys the WAR file to the JBoss server.

Once the application has been successfully deployed, you can start up JBoss to see the application in action. To start JBoss and test your application, follow these steps:

1. **Switch to the Servers view by clicking the Servers tab.**

2. **Click the Start the Server button (the green button with the white arrow in the Servers view).** Eclipse switches to the Console view while JBoss starts up. Once the server startup has completed, Eclipse switches back to the Servers view and then shows the state of the JBoss server as Started, as shown in Figure 12.29.

FIGURE 12.29

Once the JBoss server has started successfully, the Servers view shows its state as Started.

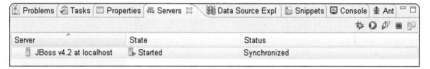

3. **Open your Web browser, type** http://localhost:8080/store/product-list.htm **in the address bar, and then press Enter.** You should see the screen shown in Figure 12.30.

FIGURE 12.30

This screen indicates that the Java storefront application has been successfully deployed to JBoss.

In a browser, this data is returned as an unformatted block of XML and is fairly unreadable. This Web application's data is meant to be parsed and displayed in the Flex client. For testing purposes, however, it can be useful to access each of the services directly in a Web browser to examine the XML that's returned for any mistakes that might cause problems for the Flex client.

Summary

In this chapter, you wrote the Java back end for a Web storefront application. First, you created a database to hold the data for the store. Next, you created the Java code, including all the objects to represent the store data, the data access code to communicate with the database, and the Spring controllers to receive requests from the front end. Finally, you wrote an Ant build script to build the application and then deployed it to the JBoss server.

The Java Web application is now finished and ready to provide data to a Flex client. In Chapter 13, you design and develop the Flex client, learn how to communicate with the Java server by using Flex, and parse the XML data returned from the Java server.

Chapter 13

Developing a Storefront Server Application with Flex

O ne of the most popular uses of the Web is commerce. Whether you're buying a new DVD player or auctioning off your old CDs, many products are bought and sold online. Of course, this means that a store must exist in order to handle the sales. Some companies go with turnkey solutions to start but quickly learn that a custom solution is a better option.

IN THIS CHAPTER

Designing and developing the Flex front end

As a developer or just someone who wants to build a store, you need to know how to properly develop the front end and the server side. The front end is what the end user interacts with, and the server side handles the behind-the-scenes processes.

In this chapter, you learn how to build a complete storefront end to connect to the Java back end you built in Chapter 12. By the end of this chapter, you will have the tools and knowledge necessary to build a custom store for yourself or your clients. The only piece you have to add is a payment process, which is covered at the end of this chapter.

CROSS-REF For the complete Java back end for the Web store application, see Chapter 12.

Designing and Developing the Flex Front End

In Chapter 12, you built the Java back end for the store application. In this chapter, you learn how to design and develop the Flex front end. The focus here is on scalability. The application should be able to handle a few thousand products just as effectively as it can handle one.

In order to build reusable code, you develop the application in various classes, allowing those classes to be reused in other aspects of the application when required.

Communicating with the Java back end

It shouldn't come as a surprise that the Flex front end talks to the Java back end to retrieve store-specific information. Some examples include lists of products, cart data, or even customers currently logged in.

This application has more than one task, which means a series of calls to the server are needed. This certainly won't be a problem, but it's a best practice to develop one service with multiple calls rather than one for each task.

Handling multiple server calls

The best way to handle multiple calls to a server is to build a class that handles all the heavy lifting and always returns the same format of data to the overall application.

Here's what this class would look like from a global perspective:

```
package com.wiley.jfib.store.data
{

    import com.wiley.jfib.ch13.store.events.*;
      import flash.events.*;

    public class ServerHandler extends EventDispatcher
    {
        private var _xmlResponse:XML;

        public function callServer(obj:Object):void
        {
            // make call to server here
        }

        private function responseHandler():void
        {
            _xmlResponse = response;
            dispatchEvent(new Event(StoreEvent.DATA_LOADED));
        }
    }

}
```

The previous class example has no specific store information contained within it. In fact, it has no application-specific code. The advantage to this simple but common approach is code reusability. This class (when complete) could now be used for any server calls in this project and could even be used in future projects, with no core changes.

The key line in the sample class is the `dispatchEvent()` call. This is called when the server data has been fully loaded, which is explained in more detail later in this chapter.

Explanation of application URLs

In Chapter 12, you created the Java back end, where each of the services has a unique URL. These URLs are used in the Flex code to communicate with the server.

Here's the URL list, assuming that your application is located at `http://localhost:8080/ store/`, for reference as you begin to develop the application:

- **http://localhost:8080/store/product-list.htm:** Returns a list of products in the store.
- **http://localhost:8080/store/product-details.htm:** Provides details for a single product, `productID`, that's sent along with this request.
- **http://localhost:8080/store/cart.htm:** Displays the current shopping cart for the logged-in user.
- **http://localhost:8080/store/add-product.htm:** Adds a new product to the store; this can be run only by an administrator.
- **http://localhost:8080/store/login.htm:** The log in to the store; this allows management and purchasing.

Setting up the Flex project

Now that you have an understanding of how the application communicates with the server, you can start building the Flex application.

First, create a new Flex project:

1. **Right-click in the Flex Navigator and then choose New ⇨ Flex Project from the popup menu.** The New Flex Project editor opens, as shown in Figure 13.1.
2. **In the Project name text field, type** JavaFlexStoreAdmin.
3. **Click Finish to build the project with all the default options set.**

Once the new Flex project is created, the default MXML file opens, as shown in Figure 13.2. You're now ready to start building the application.

Start by adding the MXML for the display. The store needs a product view, shopping cart, category filter, and login and logout buttons. The category and login components are for display purposes only — as a way for you to expand the example.

The New Flex Project dialog box, where you create a new project

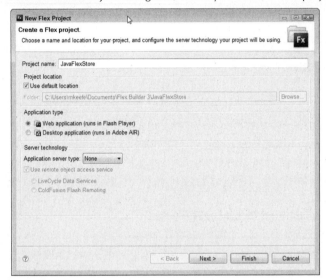

The default MXML file that displays when a new Flex project is completed and loaded

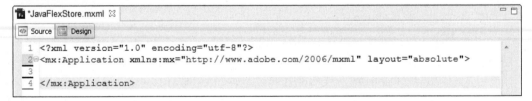

Here's the complete example:

```
<?xml version="1.0" encoding="utf-8"?>
<mx:Application xmlns:mx="http://www.adobe.com/2006/mxml"
    layout="absolute" creationComplete="init()">
```

```
<mx:TileList
      dataProvider="{_productData}"
      right="268"
      left="10"
      top="40"
      bottom="10"
      id="products"
      itemRenderer="ProductItem"
/>

<mx:List
      dataProvider="{_shoppingCartData}"
      width="250"
      height="360"
      right="10"
      top="40"
      id="shoppingCart"
      itemRenderer="ShoppingCartListItem"
/>

<mx:Label x="10" y="14" text="Products" fontSize="14"/>
<mx:Label text="Shopping Cart" fontSize="14" top="10"
right="10"/>
<mx:ComboBox y="12" right="269" id="category"/>
<mx:Label y="14" text="Category:" right="437"/>
<mx:Label y="412" text="Total: ${total}" right="10" width="250"
fontWeight="bold" color="#FAFAFA" fontSize="12" id="totalTxt"/>
<mx:Button id="checkoutBtn" click="checkoutHandler()" y="438"
label="Checkout" width="250" height="30" right="10"/>

</mx:Application>
```

The majority of this MXML consists of standard components used for displaying the product and shopping cart data, as shown in Figure 13.3. The important variables and events for this application have been placed in bold text in the above code block. These concepts have been covered in previous chapters, but basically, the idea is to build `Bindable` data objects that automatically update the display when the values change.

An example of a `Bindable` value in the above example is `total`. This value displays the total that's determined when a product is added to or removed from the shopping cart.

The next step is to build the classes required for this application.

FIGURE 13.3

The design of the store application as displayed in the Design view in Flex

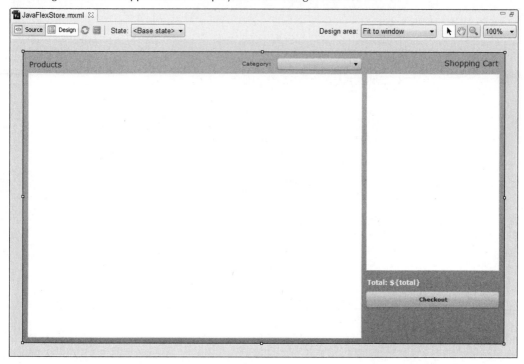

Creating the Java Service Handler

The order in which you develop the classes doesn't really matter until you start testing the application. In this application, the service classes are built before the main application so that you have something with which to test.

The Java Service Handler handles the communication with the Java back end that you developed in Chapter 12. The reason for developing a custom handler is to separate the response logic and calling to keep the code modular.

Follow these steps to create the service handler class:

1. **Right-click the `src/` directory in the Flex Navigator and then choose New ⇨ ActionScript Class from the popup menu.** The New ActionScript Class dialog box, as shown in Figure 13.4, opens.

2. **Type** com.wiley.jfib.store.data **in the Package text field and then type** JavaServiceHandler **in the Name text field.**

3. **Type** flash.events.EventDispatcher **in the Superclass text field and then click Finish**. A new class file is created and automatically opened. In the Flex Navigator, the com/wiley/jfib/store/data class package has been created.

The New ActionScript Class dialog box, where you create the service handler class

You should see the following code, which is the start of the Java Service Handler code, displayed in the script editor:

```
package com.wiley.jfib.store.data
{
    import flash.events.EventDispatcher;

    public class JavaServiceHandler extends EventDispatcher
    {
        public function JavaServiceHandler()
        {

        }
    }
}
```

You need to import a few packages for the service handler, one of which is a custom event for this application, which you create later in this chapter. In order to keep all the code in order, you should add the new import statements directly below the EventDispatcher line that's automatically added when the class is built:

```
import flash.events.EventDispatcher;
import flash.events.Event;
import flash.net.URLLoader;
import flash.net.URLRequest;

import com.wiley.jfib.store.events.JavaFlexStoreEvent;
```

The next portion of code contains the functions that call the server and handle the response once the server processes the request:

```
package com.wiley.jfib.store.data
{
    ...

    public class JavaServiceHandler extends EventDispatcher
    {

        ...

        public function callServer():void
        {
            if(serviceURL == "")
            {
                throw new Error
                (
                        "serviceURL is a required parameter"
                );
                return;
            }

            var loader:URLLoader = new URLLoader();
            loader.addEventListener(Event.COMPLETE,
                handleResponse);
            loader.load(new URLRequest(serviceURL));
        }

        private function handleResponse(event:Event):void
        {
            var loader:URLLoader = URLLoader
                (event.currentTarget);
            response = XML(loader.data);

            dispatchEvent(
                new JavaFlexStoreEvent
                (
```

```
                                          JavaFlexStoreEvent.DATA_LOADED
                              )
                    );
            }

        }
    }
```

The `callServer()` function is executed from the calling script, which in this case is the main application. This function throws an error if the `serviceURL` isn't defined because the service call would throw its own error if that URL were empty. The `Error()` class allows the developer to create custom events, which the debug version of Flash Player displays in an error.

The `handleResponse()` function is called once the server responds. This function simply grabs the response, stores it in an internal variable, and then dispatches a custom event, which is defined in the main application. One of the advantages to this approach is code reuse. This class can easily be used for other applications because no application-specific logic is found in the class until it's running.

At this point, the last task for this class is to add the variables that handle the server response and help the service URL load:

```
package com.wiley.jfib.store.data
{
    ...

    public class JavaServiceHandler extends EventDispatcher
    {

        public var serviceURL:String = "";

        public var response:XML;

        public function JavaServiceHandler()
        {

        }
    }
}
```

The `JavaServiceHandler` class is now complete. Here's the whole class:

JavaServiceHandler.as
```
package com.wiley.jfib.store.data
{
    import com.wiley.jfib.store.events.JavaFlexStoreEvent;

    import flash.events.Event;
    import flash.events.EventDispatcher;
    import flash.net.URLLoader;
```

```
import flash.net.URLRequest;

public class JavaServiceHandler extends EventDispatcher
{

       public var serviceURL:String = "";

       public var response:XML;

       public function JavaServiceHandler()
       {

       }

       public function callServer():void
       {
              if(serviceURL == "")
              {
                     throw new Error(
                        "serviceURL is a required parameter");
                     return;
              }

              var loader:URLLoader = new URLLoader();
              loader.addEventListener(Event.COMPLETE,
handleResponse);
              loader.load(new URLRequest(serviceURL));
       }

       private function handleResponse(e:Event):void
       {
              var loader:URLLoader = URLLoader(e.currentTarget);
              response = XML(loader.data);

              dispatchEvent(
                new JavaFlexStoreEvent
                   (JavaFlexStoreEvent.DATA_LOADED));
       }

       }
}
```

Adding custom events

Custom events have many uses, some of which include knowing when data is loaded, knowing when a task is complete, or extending the standard abilities of the events found in Flex.

For this application, a custom event class is being used to dispatch events when the server data is loaded. This makes it so the loading and response can be asynchronous. In a larger application, this would mean that the data-loading process isn't a blocking process. A *blocking process* occurs when an event or task prevents other actions until that one process is completed. This is known as a *synchronous* event, which isn't possible in Flex.

An *asynchronous* event is dispatched and completed on its own, letting the application continue as normal. The one drawback is that there's no way to create an `if/else` to determine when the data has been loaded. This is where events come in.

Flex works in the manner that a service is called and an event is assigned. This event is called when the server responds, allowing you to continue processing. If you're coming from a pure Java background, this may be a new concept to you, but once you understand the fundamentals, you should be all set.

Now that you know what an event is and how it's important for this application, it's time to build one:

1. **Right-click the `store/` directory in the Flex Navigator and then choose New ⇨ ActionScript Class from the popup menu.** The New ActionScript Class dialog box, as shown in Figure 13.5, opens.

2. **Type com.wiley.jfib.store.events in the Package text field and then type JavaFlexStoreEvent in the Name text field.**

3. **Type flash.events.Event in the Superclass text field and then click Finish.** In the Flex Navigator, the `/events` class package has been created below the `data/` package that was previously created.

The only line you need to add is the constant. All the remaining code is added automatically by Flex when the class is created:

JavaFlexStoreEvent.as

```
package com.wiley.jfib.store.events
{
    import flash.events.Event;

    public class JavaFlexStoreEvent extends Event
    {

        public static const DATA_LOADED:String = "onDataLoaded";

        public function JavaFlexStoreEvent(
                type:String,
                bubbles:Boolean=false,
                cancelable:Boolean=false)
        {
            super(type, bubbles, cancelable);
        }
    }
}
```

FIGURE 13.5

The New ActionScript Class dialog box, where you create a new event

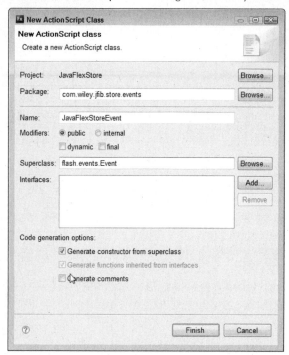

Developing the product viewer

In the previous section, you built the classes necessary to communicate with the Java back end. In this section, you learn how to develop and design the product viewer, which is the portion that the user interacts with.

The overall product viewer consists of a `TileList`, which is located in the main application. A custom `ItemRenderer` is used to build a display box for each product in the display.

 For more on the `ItemRenderer`, see Chapter 10.

Creating the ItemRenderers

Follow these steps to create the `ProductList ItemRenderer`:

1. **Right-click the `src/` directory in the Flex Navigator and then choose New ⇨ MXML Component from the popup menu.** The New MXML Component dialog box, as shown in Figure 13.6, opens.

2. Type `ProductItem.mxml` in the Filename text field.

3. Set the Based on dropdown list to VBox.

4. Type 150 as the Width and 190 as the Height.

5. Click Finish to create the new MXML component.

FIGURE 13.6

The New MXML Component dialog box, where you create the `ProductList ItemRenderer`

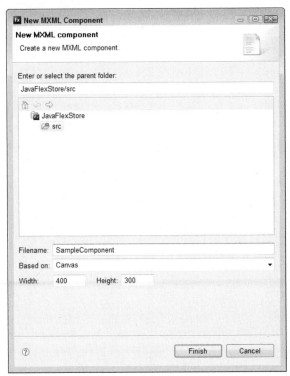

The product list component consists of two buttons, `Label` and `Canvas` components, which are displayed here:

ProductItem.mxml

```
<?xml version="1.0" encoding="utf-8"?>
<mx:VBox paddingTop="3" paddingLeft="3" xmlns:mx="http://www.adobe.
    com/2006/mxml"
    width="150"
    height="190"
```

```
verticalAlign="middle"
horizontalAlign="center">

<mx:Canvas width="120" height="100" backgroundColor="#E4D9D9">
<mx:Label text="No Img" x="10" y="21" textAlign="center"
width="100"/>
</mx:Canvas>
<mx:Label text="{data.item}"/>

<mx:Button click="parentApplication.productAdded()"
       label="Add To Cart" id="addBtn"/>
<mx:Button click="parentApplication.viewProductInfo()"
       label="More Info..." id="addBtn0"/>

    </mx:VBox>
```

At this point, this code should look standard, aside from the `parentApplication` reference. Rather than creating a custom event for each button component, you use the `parentApplication` property. This property returns a reference to the main application so that you can access public properties and methods.

The second `ItemRenderer` that needs to be created is used in the shopping cart list. Start by creating a new MXML component:

1. **Right-click the `src/` directory in the Flex Navigator and then choose New ➪ MXML Component from the popup menu.** The New MXML Component dialog box opens.

2. **Type ShoppingCartListItem.mxml in the Filename text field.**

3. **Set the Based on dropdown list to HBox.**

4. **Type 100 as the Width and 24 as the Height.**

5. **Click Finish to create the new MXML component.**

Once the new component is created, you can begin adding the design elements, which in this file are three text boxes and a `Button` component.

The `Button` is assigned an event to remove the shopping cart item and recalculate the total. This event makes use of the `parentApplication`, as the previous code did, to reference a function that's located in the main application:

ShoppingCartListItem.mxml

```
<?xml version="1.0" encoding="utf-8"?>
<mx:HBox xmlns:mx="http://www.adobe.com/2006/mxml"
    paddingLeft="3"
    paddingRight="3"
    height="24"
    verticalAlign="middle"
```

```
                horizontalAlign="right"
                width="100%"
    >

                <mx:Script>
                        <![CDATA[

                                private function remove():void
                                {
                                        parentApplication.removeItemFromCart();
                                }

                        ]]>
                </mx:Script>

                <mx:Text text="{data.quantity}" width="20%"/>
                <mx:Text text="{data.name}" width="50%"/>
                <mx:Text text="${data.price}" width="30%" textAlign="center"/>
                <mx:Button click="remove()" label="x" width="30"/>

        </mx:HBox>
```

The above code is the complete `ItemRenderer` for the shopping cart list. The `Text` components display item data that's automatically assigned inside the main application.

Creating the product description popup

The last design element to build is the product description popup. This is visible whenever the user clicks the More Info button located in the product boxes. This description popup has the ability to add the item to the cart or update an existing cart entry automatically.

The calling of the popup is placed in the main application file, but the actual popup is a `Panel` component that allows a title and structured layout.

Follow these steps to create a new component:

1. **Right-click the `src/` directory in the Flex Navigator and then choose New⇨MXML Component from the popup menu.** The New MXML Component dialog box opens.

2. **Type** ProductDetailsPopup.mxml **in the Filename text field.**

3. **Set the Based on dropdown list to Panel.**

4. **Type** 400 **as the Width and** 300 **as the Height.**

5. **Click Finish to create the new MXML component.**

Once the new MXML component is created, place the following code and design components in the script editor to complete the component:

ProductDetailsPopup

```
<?xml version="1.0" encoding="utf-8"?>
<mx:Panel xmlns:mx="http://www.adobe.com/2006/mxml"
    layout="absolute"
    width="400"
    height="300"
    title="Product Information"
>
    <mx:Script>
        <![CDATA[
            import mx.managers.PopUpManager;

            private function addHandler():void
            {
                parentApplication.productAdded();
                PopUpManager.removePopUp(this);
            }
        ]]>
    </mx:Script>

    <mx:Label x="220" y="10" text="Product ID: {data.id}"
        width="150" textAlign="right"/>

    <mx:Label x="10" y="10" text="{data.item}" width="202"
color="#3D7581"
        fontWeight="bold" fontSize="12"/>

    <mx:Text x="10" y="48" text="{data.description}" height="130"
        width="232"/>

    <mx:Text x="10" y="228" text="Price: ${data.price}" height="22"
        width="232" fontSize="11" fontWeight="bold"/>

    <mx:Button click="addHandler()" x="250" y="156" label="Add To
Cart"
        id="addBtn" width="120"/>

    <mx:Button click="PopUpManager.removePopUp(this)" label="Close"
        id="closeBtn" x="314" y="228"/>

    <mx:Canvas width="120" height="100" backgroundColor="#E4D9D9"
x="250"
        y="48">
        <mx:Label text="No Image" x="10" y="21" textAlign="center"
```

```
                               width="100" color="#747676"/>

            </mx:Canvas>

        </mx:Panel>
```

At this point, you have completed all the ItemRenderers, data handlers, events, and custom components required for this application. The final steps are to add the code for the main application, which ties everything together, and then test the complete application.

Adding the code to the main application

The code for the main application handles most of the functionality of this store application. In a larger project, you may even split this process up. However, to keep it simpler and easier to understand, I have opted to keep all the core application code in one place.

Earlier in this process, you created the start of the main application, which is displayed here in example form (most of the code has been removed for brevity):

```
        <?xml version="1.0" encoding="utf-8"?>
        <mx:Application xmlns:mx="http://www.adobe.com/2006/mxml"
            layout="absolute"
            creationComplete="init()"
        >
            .
            .
            .

        </mx:Application>
```

The design portion of this application has already been created, so start by adding the <mx:Script> and then adding the package imports:

```
        <mx:Script>
            <![CDATA[
                    import com.wiley.jfib.store.events.JavaFlexStoreEvent;
                    import com.wiley.jfib.store.data.JavaServiceHandler;
                    import com.wiley.jfib.store.ShoppingCartItem;

                    import mx.controls.Alert;
                    import mx.containers.Panel;
                    import mx.core.IFlexDisplayObject;
                    import mx.managers.PopUpManager;
                    import mx.utils.ObjectProxy;
```

```
                  import mx.collections.ArrayCollection;
          ]]>
      </mx:Script>
```

The first three imports are specific to this project and have the custom package namespace that was defined earlier. The other packages are from the core Flex library that any application would have access to.

The next portion to add is the `Bindable` variables and custom event definition that are called whenever an Add to Cart button is clicked:

```
<mx:Script>
    <![CDATA[
          ...


        private var javaServiceHandler:JavaServiceHandler;

        [Bindable]
        private var total:Number = 0;

        [Bindable]
        private var _shoppingCartData:ArrayCollection =
                new ArrayCollection([]);

        [Bindable]
        private var _productData:ArrayCollection;

    ]]>
</mx:Script>
```

Now that the variables are defined, the next step is to add the methods (functions). The first method is `init()`, which is called when the application has been fully loaded and displayed. This code is used to set up the service for the Java back end. An event is defined based on the custom `JavaFlexStoreEvent` event class, which is dispatched when the server has returned the results:

```
private function init():void
{
    addEventListener("addProduct", productAdded);
    checkoutBtn.enabled = false;

    javaServiceHandler = new JavaServiceHandler();
    javaServiceHandler.addEventListener(JavaFlexStoreEvent.DATA_LOADED,
            productListHandler);

    javaServiceHandler.serviceURL =
```

```
                  "http://localhost:8080/store/product-list.htm";

         javaServiceHandler.callServer();
    }
```

The next method, `productListHandler()`, is called when the custom event defined in the `init()` method has been dispatched. This method loops through the `resultset` and adds items to the `_productData ArrayCollection`, which is ultimately displayed in the `TileList` component:

```
    private function productListHandler(e:JavaFlexStoreEvent):void
    {
        _productData = new ArrayCollection();

        for each(var item:* in
                JavaServiceHandler(e.currentTarget).response..product)
        {
                _productData.addItem({
                        id:item.id,
                        item:item.name,
                        price:item.price,
                        description:item.desc
                });
        }
    }
```

> **NOTE** The * data type is a wildcard, which means that the data type of this property can be anything. This isn't a best-case process because you won't know what data type you get during processing.

When a product's Add to Cart button is clicked, a method is called to add the specified item to the cart or update the quantity if it's already in the cart. This method is `productAdded()`. It first grabs the selected item data, checks to see if the item is already in the shopping cart, deselects the active item, and then finally makes a call to the `calculateTotal()` method:

```
    public function productAdded():void
    {
        var cartData:* = products.selectedItem;

        if(checkForExistingItems(cartData.id) == false)
        {
                var shoppingItem:ShoppingCartItem = new ShoppingCartItem();
                shoppingItem.id = cartData.id;
                shoppingItem.name = cartData.item;
                shoppingItem.price = cartData.price;
```

```
        _shoppingCartData.addItem(shoppingItem);
    }

    products.selectedIndex = -1;

    calculateTotal();
}
```

 Any methods that you want to call from external classes or components by using the `parentApplication` property must be set as public.

The next method to create is `viewProductInfo()`. This handles the product information popup by creating a new `PopupManager` call, which is a static class because there's only one popup manager:

```
public function viewProductInfo():void
{
    var popup:IFlexDisplayObject = PopUpManager.createPopUp(this,
        ProductDetailsPopup, true);
    ProductDetailsPopup(popup).data = products.selectedItem;
    PopUpManager.centerPopUp(popup);
}
```

The active data from the product's `TileList` is assigned to the `data` property of the product details popup. This is a way to feed the product information into the popup without requiring any special code in the actual popup to complete that task.

Even though you would love to force users to buy everything in the store, they probably want the ability to remove items from the cart. This is accomplished with the `removeItemFromCart()` method. This method takes the `selectedIndex` of the shopping cart list and then uses the `remove ItemAt()` method on the `_shoppingCartData ArrayCollection`. The last task is to make a call to the `calculateTotal()` method to ensure that the displayed total is always up to date:

```
public function removeItemFromCart():void
{
    _shoppingCartData.removeItemAt(shoppingCart.selectedIndex);
    calculateTotal();
}
```

The next method is `checkForExistingItems()`, which loops through the shopping cart items and increments the quantity if the item already exists:

```
private function checkForExistingItems(id:int):Boolean
{
    var i:uint=0;
    for each(var item:Object in _shoppingCartData)
    {
```

```
        if(item.id == id)
        {
                var oldData:* = item;
                oldData.quantity = oldData.quantity++;

                _shoppingCartData.setItemAt(oldData, i);

                return true;
        }
        i++;
    }
    return false;
}
```

You have seen the `calculateTotal()` method in previous portions of the code, and here's the actual code for it:

```
private function calculateTotal():void
{
    var newTotal:Number = 0;
    for each(var item:Object in _shoppingCartData)
    {
            newTotal += (Number(item.price) * Number(item.quantity));
    }

    total = round2d.format(newTotal);

    checkoutBtn.enabled = (_shoppingCartData.length==0) ? false : true;
}
```

This method loops through each shopping cart item and then calculates the total cost, multiplying the quantity account for multiple requests of the same item.

To ensure that the dollar value is properly represented, you must round the decimals off to a whole value. This is accomplished by using the `NumberFormatter` found in the Flex framework. Place this code below the `mx:Script` block:

```
<mx:NumberFormatter id="round2d" precision="2" rounding="nearest" />
```

The last method, `checkoutHandler()`, is called when the user clicks the Checkout button component. In this application, it displays an Alert box notifying the user of the total and the fact that the payment processing isn't included in this code:

```
private function checkoutHandler():void
{
    Alert.show("Your total is $" + total
            + "\nCheckout is not active in this example");
```

```
        }
```

Here's the completed code for the main application:

JavaFlexStore.mxml

```
<?xml version="1.0" encoding="utf-8"?>
<mx:Application xmlns:mx="http://www.adobe.com/2006/mxml" layout="absolute"
    creationComplete="init()">

    <mx:Script>
        <![CDATA[
        import com.wiley.jfib.store.events.JavaFlexStoreEvent;
        import com.wiley.jfib.store.data.JavaServiceHandler;
        import mx.controls.Alert;
        import mx.containers.Panel;
        import mx.core.IFlexDisplayObject;
        import mx.managers.PopUpManager;
        import com.wiley.jfib.store.ShoppingCartItem;
        import mx.utils.ObjectProxy;
        import mx.collections.ArrayCollection;

        [Event(name="addProduct", type="mx.events.MouseEvent")]

        private var javaServiceHandler:JavaServiceHandler;

        [Bindable]
        private var total:Number = 0;

        [Bindable]
        private var _shoppingCartData:ArrayCollection = new ArrayCollection([]);

        [Bindable]
        private var _productData:ArrayCollection;

        private function init():void
        {
          addEventListener("addProduct", productAdded);
          checkoutBtn.enabled = false;
          javaServiceHandler = new JavaServiceHandler();
          javaServiceHandler.addEventListener
          (
               JavaFlexStoreEvent.DATA_LOADED, productListHandler
          );
          javaServiceHandler.serviceURL ="http://localhost:8080/store/+
               product-list.htm";
```

```
    javaServiceHandler.callServer();
}

private function productListHandler(e:JavaFlexStoreEvent):void
  {
  _productData = new ArrayCollection();
  for each(var item:* in
  JavaServiceHandler(e.currentTarget).response..product)
  {
_       productData.addItem({
              id:item.id,
              item:item.name,
              price:item.price,
              description:item.desc
        });
  }
}

public function productAdded():void
{
  trace("Add a product");
  var cartData:* = products.selectedItem;
  if(checkForExistingItems(cartData.id) == false)
  {
        var shoppingCartItem:ShoppingCartItem = new
              ShoppingCartItem();
  shoppingCartItem.id = cartData.id;
  shoppingCartItem.name = cartData.item;
  shoppingCartItem.price = cartData.price;
  _shoppingCartData.addItem(shoppingCartItem);
  }
  products.selectedIndex = -1;
  calculateTotal();
}
public function viewProductInfo():void
{
  var popup:IFlexDisplayObject =
  PopUpManager.createPopUp(this,
  ProductDetailsPopup, true);
  ProductDetailsPopup(popup).data = products.selectedItem;
  PopUpManager.centerPopUp(popup);
}

public function removeItemFromCart():void
{
  _shoppingCartData.removeItemAt(shoppingCart.selectedIndex);
```

```
    calculateTotal();
  }

  private function checkForExistingItems(id:int):Boolean
  {
    var i:uint=0;
    for each(var item:Object in _shoppingCartData)
    {
        if(item.id == id)
        {
                var oldData:* = item;
                oldData.quantity = oldData['quantity'] + 1;
                _shoppingCartData.setItemAt(oldData,i);
                return true;
        }
        i++;
    }
    return false;
  }

  private function calculateTotal():void
  {
    var newTotal:Number = 0;
    for each(var item:Object in _shoppingCartData)
    {
        newTotal += (Number(item.price) * Number(item.quantity));
    }
    total = round2D(newTotal);
    checkoutBtn.enabled = (_shoppingCartData.length == 0) ? false :

    true;
  }

  private function round2D(n:Number):Number
  {
    return Math.round(n * Math.pow(10, 2)) / Math.pow(10, 2);
  }

  private function checkoutHandler():void
  {
    Alert.show("Your total is $" + total +
    "\nCheckout is not active in this example");
  }
]]>
</mx:Script>
<mx:TileList
  dataProvider="{_productData}"
  right="268"
```

```
          left="10"
          top="40"
          bottom="10"
          id="products"
          itemRenderer="ProductItem"
      />
      <mx:List
        dataProvider="{_shoppingCartData}"
        width="250"
        height="360"
        right="10"
        top="40"
        id="shoppingCart"
        itemRenderer="ShoppingCartListItem"
      />
      <mx:Label x="10" y="14" text="Products" fontSize="14"/>
      <mx:Label text="Shopping Cart" fontSize="14" top="10" right="10"/>
      <mx:ComboBox y="12" right="269" id="category"></mx:ComboBox>
      <mx:Label y="14" text="Category:" right="437"/>
      <mx:Label y="412" text="Total: ${total}" right="10" width="250"
      fontWeight="bold" color="#FAFAFA" fontSize="12" id="totalTxt"/>
      <mx:Button id="checkoutBtn" click="checkoutHandler()" y="438"
      label="Checkout" width="250" height="30" right="10"/>
      </mx:Application>
```

Testing the application

You have now completed all the code for this example. In fact, you have completed the entire application and are now ready to test it.

In order to test the application, choose Run ⇨ Debug JavaFlexStore, which opens the application in a browser. You should see products displayed in the `TileList`.

Developing the payment solution

Now that the application is completed, the final step is to develop the payment solution. This is the business logic that handles the actual purchasing from the store.

This was omitted from this application because it's a rather complex topic — one that shouldn't be rushed because of the requirements for strict security. I highlight a few points and services to work with in this section, and that should get you started.

Choosing a credit card processing solution

The first thing to do when developing the payment processing for the store is to make sure you never actually have the credit card data on your server. This is for security and legal reasons. If your server's security is somehow compromised and your customers' data is exposed, you could be held accountable.

The best approach here is to sign up with a reputable credit card processing service. Here's a list of some good companies to use. This isn't a complete list, but it does include some companies that other developers and I have worked with:

- **www.authorize.net**: API for various programming languages; offers services for merchants
- **www.linkpoint.com**: Offers easy setup with an advanced testing system and documentation
- **www.paypal.com**: Trusted payment solution, made popular with eBay.com but also offers a robust library for developers to use
- **www.google.com/checkout**: New payment solution by Google; also offers a great library
- **www.2checkout.com**: One of the most popular payment processors used on large-scale Web sites

When choosing a payment processor, it's a good idea to check for a proper testing solution and an API that seamlessly connects to your programming language. In this case, it would be Java.

Developing and testing

Once you've decided on a payment processor and have begun developing the code to connect with those companies' services, you need to start testing. Most of the popular companies have test modes, and some even have testing accounts. In the test region, you can work with data, process test transactions, and make sure all your application logic is set up properly.

The goal is to develop the complete application in testing mode or with the test account and then "flip the switch" to the live system with little or no changes required. Depending on the complexity of the store, you may want to run a few real transactions. You can use an American Express card to run actual transactions through the system. Historically, American Express allows you to revert any charges for free.

 The abilities of American Express cardholders may change at some point, so please check with your credit card company before running live transactions.

Once everything is working properly, you're ready to deploy the store to your customers. While the store is live for the first couple of weeks, make sure that someone keeps watch over the store process to ensure that everything's working properly.

You should now have a good understanding of how to develop a complete store application, including direction for the payment processor. The next step is to develop the store and start selling some products.

Summary

In this chapter, you learned how to build a complete Flex storefront end that uses the Java back end application built in Chapter 12. The Flex front end was built by using custom components and events. `ItemRenderers` were used to enhance the functionality of the application while maintaining overall usability for the end user.

You should now have a good understanding of how the whole application is built and be able to create a more advanced store application.

Chapter 14

Building a Real-Time Messaging System

A real-time messaging system allows users to talk with one another in real time as though they were in the same room. This functionality can be used in such diverse applications as chat or instant messaging programs, customer support systems, and multiplayer games.

Understanding the Application Process

This simple chat application allows users to type a username to use during the chat or generates a random username for the user. Once the username has been typed, a note is sent saying that the user has entered the chat. The user types messages in a text input field. When the user clicks the Send button or presses the Enter key while the text input field has focus, the message is sent to the chat server. When the chat server receives the message, it publishes the message to all clients connected to the chat server.

The Flex client for this application consists of text input fields to type a username and the messages to be sent during the chat, a list control to display all the messages in the chat room, and buttons for saving the username and sending the chat message.

On the Java side, a single Java class acts as a message receiver and sender. It takes any messages it receives from a single chat client and broadcasts them to every chat client connected to the server.

IN THIS CHAPTER

Understanding the application process

Writing the Java code

Writing the Flex code

Connecting the Java and Flex pieces

This application uses BlazeDS as its messaging system. On the Flex side, the MXML file includes a publisher and consumer to send and receive messages, respectively. On the Java side, a custom BlazeDS message adapter handles all the receipt and repackaging of the messages.

CROSS-REF   For more on downloading, installing, and configuring BlazeDS, see Chapter 11.

Writing the Java Code

The Java portion of this application consists of a single Java file that acts as the chat server, the Web application configuration, and the BlazeDS configuration.

Setting up the Eclipse project

The first thing to do is to set up an Eclipse project for the chat application. The Eclipse project includes the Java class file, all the Web application and BlazeDS configuration files, and the MXML and HTML files for the Flex application itself. You can build the MXML file into an SWF file by using a combination of Ant and the Flex SDK.

Before creating the Eclipse project, you need to unzip the `blazeds.war` file found inside your BlazeDS distribution. You'll use a number of JAR files found inside this WAR file in the build path of your Eclipse project. Because WAR files are essentially just ZIP files containing a Web application structure, you can use any ZIP utility to unzip the `blazeds.war` file to a location of your choosing (for example, `c:\blazeds.war`).

CROSS-REF   For more on installing and configuring Ant, see Chapter 1. For more on creating an Ant build file, see Chapter 6. For more information on BlazeDS, see Chapter 11.

Open Eclipse by navigating to the Eclipse install directory in Windows Explorer and double-clicking `eclipse.exe`. To create and configure an Eclipse project, follow these steps:

1. **Right-click inside the Project Explorer view and then choose New ⇨ Project from the popup menu.** The New Project dialog box, as shown in Figure 14.1, opens.

2. **Click the arrow next to Java to expand it, click the Java Project item below Java, and then click Next.** The Create a Java Project wizard, as shown in Figure 14.2, opens.

3. **Type** jfib-ch14-p01 **in the Project name text field and then click Next.** The Java Settings screen opens.

4. **Click the Libraries tab.** The Library list appears.

5. **Click the Add External JARs button.** The JAR Selection dialog box, as shown in Figure 14.3, opens.

FIGURE 14.1

The New Project dialog box

FIGURE 14.2

The Create a Java Project wizard contains options and settings for new Java projects.

6. **Navigate to the folder where you unzipped the `blazeds.war` file, double-click the `WEB-INF` folder, double-click the `lib` folder, select all the JAR files in that `lib` folder, and then click Open.** The 12 JAR files are added to the Library list, as shown in Figure 14.4.

7. **Click Finish.** The Create a Java Project wizard closes, and the newly created project appears in the Project Explorer view.

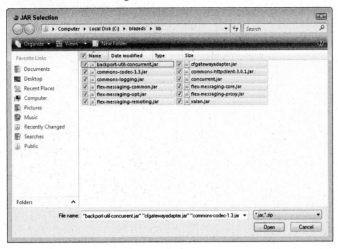

FIGURE 14.3

The JAR Selection dialog box

Only two of the BlazeDS JAR files that you added to the Library list — `flex-messaging-core.jar` and `flex-messaging-common.jar` — are needed to compile the project. Adding all of them now means that the others are immediately available should you need them in the future when expanding on the project.

The chat server

Now you can create the Java class that acts as the chat server for this application. The Java class extends BlazeDS's `ServiceAdapter` class. The `ServiceAdapter` class is an abstract class that requires you to implement a single method called `invoke()`. The `invoke()` method receives messages from publishers in the Flex application. For this application, you want the chat server to take the message it receives and republish it so that every chat client connected to the chat server can display the message.

The 12 JAR files are added to the Library list when you select them in the JAR Selection dialog box.

To create the Java chat server class, follow these steps:

1. **Right-click the `src` folder under the `jfib-ch14-p01` project in the Project Explorer view and then choose New ⇨ Class from the popup menu.** The New Java Class dialog box opens.

2. **Click the Browse button next to the Superclass text field.** The Superclass Selection dialog box, as shown in Figure 14.5, opens.

The Superclass Selection dialog box allows you to choose the class that you want your class to extend.

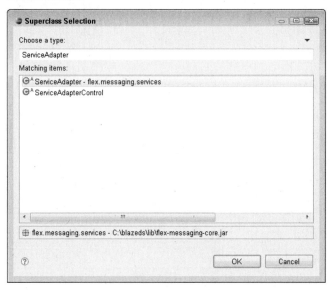

3. **Type** ServiceAdapter **in the Choose a type text field.** The Matching items list box fills in with classes whose names match your entry.

4. **Choose** ServiceAdapter-flex.messaging.services **from the list box and then click OK.** The Superclass Selection dialog box closes, and the Superclass text field in the New Java Class dialog box is filled in with the ServiceAdapter class.

5. **Type** com.wiley.jfib.ch14 **in the Package text field, type** ChatServer **in the Name text field, and then click the check box next to Generate comments, as shown in Figure 14.6.**

6. **Click Finish.** The New Java Class dialog box closes, and the newly created com.wiley.jfib.ch14 package and ChatServer class appear in the src folder under the jfib-ch14-p01 project. The ChatServer class opens in the editor, as shown in Figure 14.7.

FIGURE 14.6

The New Java Class dialog box as it appears once all the appropriate values have been filled in for the Package and Name text fields and the Generate comments check box has been selected.

FIGURE 14.7

The ChatServer class opens in the editor once the New Java Class dialog box closes. The inherited invoke() method has been created for you.

```
ChatServer.java
  1 /**
  4 package com.wiley.jfib.ch14;
  5
  6 import flex.messaging.messages.Message;
  8
  9 /**
 10  * @author Chuck
 11  *
 12  */
 13 public class ChatServer extends ServiceAdapter {
 14
 15     /* (non-Javadoc)
 16      * @see flex.messaging.services.ServiceAdapter#invoke(flex.messaging.messages.Mess
 17      */
 18     @Override
 19     public Object invoke(Message arg0) {
 20         // TODO Auto-generated method stub
 21         return null;
 22     }
 23
```

Now edit the `ChatServer` class so that it matches this code listing:

```
/**
 *
 */
package com.wiley.jfib.ch14;

import flex.messaging.messages.AsyncMessage;
import flex.messaging.messages.Message;
import flex.messaging.services.MessageService;
import flex.messaging.services.ServiceAdapter;

/**
 * @author Chuck
 * The ChatServer class implements a very basic chat
 * server using a custom BlazeDS* service adapter. The ChatServer class receives
 * a message from a Flex publisher
 * and republishes that message to any Flex consumer
 * that subscribes to this service.
 */
public class ChatServer extends ServiceAdapter {

    /* (non-Javadoc)
     * @see flex.messaging.services.ServiceAdapter#invoke(flex.messaging.
    messages.Message)
     */
    @Override
    public Object invoke(Message arg0) {
            AsyncMessage chatMessage = (AsyncMessage)arg0;
            chatMessage.setBody(arg0.getBody());
            MessageService messageService =
                    (MessageService)getDestination().getService();
            messageService.pushMessageToClients(chatMessage, false);
            return null;
    }


}
```

The import statements import some BlazeDS messaging classes necessary for the `ChatServer` class to receive and republish messages. The `invoke()` method is where the entirety of the chat server functionality is found. Take a look at each line of the `invoke()` method. The first line casts the incoming message to a variable of type `AsyncMessage`. The `AsyncMessage` class is the Flex asynchronous message used for publish-and-subscribe messaging. In *asynchronous messaging*, publishers of messages don't wait for responses to each message before continuing with other tasks. This is the opposite of *synchronous messaging*, in which publishers take no further action after sending a message until a response is received. In the case of a chat client and server, it's necessary for the server to be able to process messages from many clients without waiting for each one.

Similarly, the chat client should be able to receive many messages from the chat server without waiting for a response to a specific message it sends. In the Flex code for this application, there's an equivalent type in the MXML code that's sent to this Java class.

The second line sets the message body of this `AsyncMessage` to the value of the body of the incoming message. Remember, the chat server is simply taking the incoming message and republishing it to all chat clients.

The next line of the `invoke()` method establishes the `MessageService` class that's used to republish the message. The `MessageService` class is retrieved from the BlazeDS configuration file you create later. This code doesn't know anything about the specifics of the configuration being used. If the BlazeDS destination that this class publishes to needs to change, only the configuration file needs to change, not the chat server code itself.

The fourth line of the `invoke()` method publishes the message to all subscribing clients. The second parameter (`false`) is the `evalSelector` value. In addition to the message body text, a message can include one or more headers that subscribers can use to filter out messages they're not interested in. For example, if your chat application includes multiple chat rooms, clients currently logged into one chat room can use these message headers to publish messages to the correct room and to ignore messages from rooms they're not currently logged into. The server can check each client to see whether it needs to receive each message by setting this `evalSelector` value to `true`. In this case, your chat application includes only a single chat room; thus, the `evalSelector` value is set to `false`. Every client, therefore, receives every message from the chat server without checking.

Finally, the `invoke()` method returns `null`. Because the only actual data of value coming from this application is the messages being published, the return value of the method itself isn't used.

Writing the Flex Code

The client for this chat application is a single MXML application file that's compiled into an SWF file and an HTML file that embeds the SWF file. As discussed previously, the MXML file contains the following elements:

- A `TextInput` control and a Button control for typing a username for the chat. These are hidden once the user has chosen a username.

- A List control for displaying each chat message as it arrives from the server.

- A `TextInput` control and a Button control for typing messages to send to the chat server.

Figure 14.8 shows what the user interface for the chat application looks like when run in a browser.

FIGURE 14.8

The user interface for the chat application. It consists of two Flex `TextInput` controls, two Flex Button controls, and a Flex List control.

To add the MXML and HTML file for the chat application client to the Eclipse project, follow these steps:

1. **Right-click the** `jfib-ch14-p01` **project in the Project Explorer view and then choose New ➪ Folder from the popup menu.** The New Folder dialog box, as shown in Figure 14.9, opens.

2. **Type** web\WEB-INF\lib **in the Folder name text field and then click Finish.** The New Folder dialog box closes, and the newly created folder structure appears expanded beneath the `jfib-ch14-p01` project in the Project Explorer view.

3. **Right-click the** `lib` **folder you just created and then choose Import from the popup menu.** The Import wizard, as shown in Figure 14.10, opens.

4. **Click the arrow next to General in the Select an import source list box to expand it, click the File System item below General, and then click Next.** The Import from File system screen, as shown in Figure 14.11, opens.

5. **Click the Browse button next to the From directory text field.** The Import from directory dialog box, as shown in Figure 14.12, opens.

FIGURE 14.9

The New Folder dialog box allows you to create new folders to hold files for the Web application.

6. **Navigate to the `lib` directory below your BlazeDS installation directory, click it to select it, and then click OK.** The Import from directory dialog box closes. The `lib` directory appears in the left pane of the File System screen, and the JAR files within the `lib` directory appear in the right pane, as shown in Figure 14.13. Adding the BlazeDS JAR files to the Web application's `WEB-INF\lib` directory makes them available to the Web application at runtime. The Flex chat client uses these BlazeDS JAR files to create and send messages to the Java chat server.

FIGURE 14.10

The Import wizard allows you to bring external resources into your project.

FIGURE 14.11

The File System screen lets you select resources from your computer's file system to bring into your project.

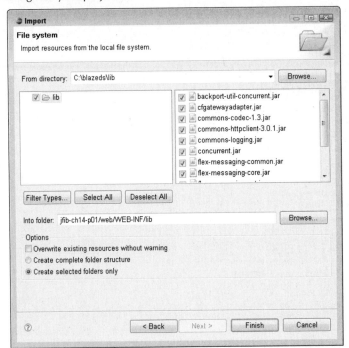

FIGURE 14.12

The Import from directory dialog box lets you choose a directory on your file system from which to import resources.

FIGURE 14.13

After you select the BlazeDS distribution's `lib` folder in the Import from directory dialog box, it appears in the left pane of the File System screen, and its contents appear in the right pane.

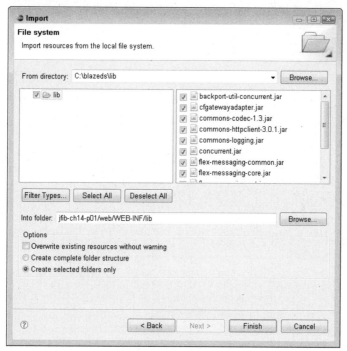

7. **Click the check box next to the `lib` folder in the left pane of the Import from Directory screen and then click Finish.** The Import from File system screen closes, and the JAR files appear below the `web\WEB-INF\lib` directory in the Project Explorer view, as shown in Figure 14.14.

8. **Right-click the `web` folder and then choose New ⇨ File from the popup menu.** The New File dialog box, as shown in Figure 14.15, opens.

9. **Type Chat.mxml in the File name text field and then click Finish.** The New File dialog box closes, and the `Chat.mxml` file appears below the `web` folder in the Project Explorer view.

FIGURE 14.14

After you select the BlazeDS JAR files in the File System screen, they are copied into the `web\WEB-INF\lib` folder of your project.

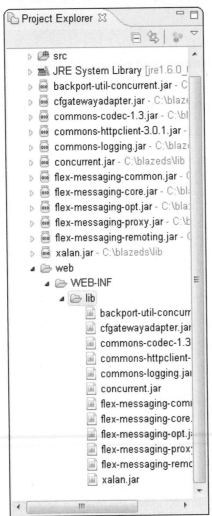

10. **Right-click the `web` folder and then choose New ⇨ File from the popup menu.** The New File dialog box opens.

11. **Type `chat.html` in the File name text field and then click Finish.** The New File dialog box closes, and the `chat.html` file appears below the `web` folder in the Project Explorer view.

The New File dialog box lets you create a new empty file of any type.

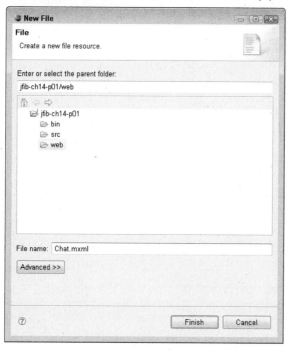

First, edit the Chat.mxml file to match this code listing:

```
<?xml version="1.0" encoding="utf-8"?>
<mx:Application xmlns:mx="http://www.adobe.com/2006/mxml"
   creationComplete="subscribeToChat();">
<mx:Script>
      <![CDATA[
         import flash.events.MouseEvent;
         import mx.collections.ArrayCollection;
         import mx.events.FlexEvent;
         import mx.messaging.events.MessageAckEvent;
         import mx.messaging.messages.AsyncMessage;
         import mx.messaging.events.MessageEvent;
         import mx.messaging.events.MessageFaultEvent;
         import mx.controls.Alert;
         import mx.rpc.events.FaultEvent;

         [Bindable]
         private var dp:ArrayCollection = new ArrayCollection();
```

```
[Bindable]
private var uname:String = "";

private function setUserName():void
{
        if(username.text == "")
        {
                uname = randomName();
        }
        else
        {
                uname = username.text;
        }
        unhb.visible = false;
        var msg:AsyncMessage = new AsyncMessage();
        msg.body = uname + " has entered the chat!";
        producer.send(msg);
        chatEntry.enabled = true;
        chatEntry.setFocus();
        sendMessageButton.enabled = true;

}

private function randomName():String
{
        var letters:String =
"abcdefghijklmnopqrstuvwxyzABCDEFGHIJKLMNOPQRSTUVWXYZ";
        var alphabetArray:Array = letters.split("");
        var name:String = "";
        for (var x:Number = 0; x < 8; x++)
        {
            name += alphabetArray[Math.floor(Math.random()
                * alphabetArray.length)];
        }
        return name;
}

private function subscribeToChat():void
{
        consumer.subscribe();
}

private function receiveChatMessages(event:MessageEvent):void
{
        dp.addItem(event.message.body.toString());
        statusLabel.text = "";
}

private function sendChatMessage():void
{
```

```
                     var msg:AsyncMessage = new AsyncMessage();
                     msg.body = uname + ":  " + chatEntry.text;
                     producer.send(msg);
                     chatEntry.text = "";
             }

             private function handleFault(event:MessageFaultEvent):void
             {
                     Alert.show(event.faultString);
             }

             private function acknowledgeSend(event:MessageAckEvent):void
             {
                     statusLabel.text = "Sending . . .";
             }

             private function acknowledgeRec(event:MessageAckEvent):void
             {
                     statusLabel.text = "";
             }
        ]]>
</mx:Script>
<mx:Producer id="producer"
    destination="ChatAdapter"
    acknowledge="acknowledgeSend(event);"
    fault="handleFault(event);"
/>

<mx:Consumer id="consumer"
    destination="ChatAdapter"
    message="receiveChatMessages(event);"
    acknowledge="acknowledgeRec(event);"
    fault="handleFault(event);"
/>

<mx:Panel width="80%" height="80%" title="Chatroom"
    paddingTop="10"
    paddingBottom="10"
    paddingLeft="10"
    paddingRight="10">
  <mx:HBox id="unhb" width="100%">
        <mx:Label id="unl"
                text="User Name (leave empty for a random name): "/>
        <mx:TextInput id="username" width="50%"/>
        <mx:Button label="Set Name" click="setUserName()"/>
  </mx:HBox>
  <mx:List dataProvider="{dp}" id="chatTranscript"
        width="100%" height="80%"/>
  <mx:TextInput enabled="false" enter="sendChatMessage()"
```

```
                    id="chatEntry" width="100%"/>
        <mx:Button id="sendMessageButton" enabled="false"
                click="sendChatMessage()" label="Send"/>
        <mx:Label id="statusLabel" text=""/>
        </mx:Panel>
    </mx:Application>
```

CROSS-REF For more on Flex syntax and programming constructs, see Chapter 4.

Much of this code listing consists of ActionScript functions contained inside `<mx:Script>` tags. Most of these ActionScript functions are handlers for various events fired by the user interface controls, such as button clicks. Take a look at these functions one by one:

- The `setUserName()` function handles the event fired when the user either clicks the Set Name button or presses the Enter key within the username `TextInput` control. This function takes the current value of the username text field and stores it in a variable. If the username text field has no value, another function is called to generate a random name, and that value is stored in the variable instead. Once the username is stored, the `TextInput` and Button controls are hidden, and the chat entry `TextInput` and Button controls are enabled, allowing the user to start chatting. A message is sent to the server to let everyone know that the user has logged in to the chat room.

- The `randomName()` function is used to generate a random username if the user doesn't type one.

- The `subscribeToChat()` function is called once the application has finished loading. The value of the `creationComplete` attribute of the `<mx:Application>` tag is set to this function. This function is what actually subscribes this client to receive messages from the chat server. The `consumer` variable name refers to the `id` attribute of the `<mx:Consumer>` tag.

- The `receiveChatMessages()` function receives messages from the server and then adds them to the `dp ArrayCollection` variable. This variable is set as the `dataProvider` of the List control defined by the `<mx:List>` tag. Each time an item is added to this `Array Collection`, the List control updates to display the new item along with the other items in the `ArrayCollection`.

- The `sendChatMessage()` function sends the current value of the `chatEntry TextInput` control to the server. The type of the message that's created and sent to the server is `AsyncMessage`, just as it was on the Java side. The message is sent by using the `producer` variable, which refers to the `id` attribute of the `<mx:Producer>` tag. The Flex `AsyncMessage` and the Java `AsyncMessage` are structured similarly so that translation between the Java and Flex versions is seamless.

- The `handleFault()` function is called if an error occurs when sending or receiving a message. This error might be displayed, for instance, if the connection to the chat server is lost.

- The `acknowledgeSend()` function is called whenever a message is successfully sent to the chat server from the client. This function sets a status message to let the user know that the message has been sent successfully.

- The `acknowledgeRec()` function is called whenever a message is received from the client. This function simply clears the status message. This function is called in addition to the `receiveChatMessage()` function. The `acknowledgeRec()` function simply indicates that something has been received from the client, whereas `receiveChat Message()` processes what was received.

The publish and subscribe functionality of the chat client is set up by the `<mx:Producer>` and `<mx:Consumer>` tags, respectively. These two tags both contain a `destination` attribute with a value of `ChatAdapter`. This destination is part of the BlazeDS configuration. It provides a gateway between the Java code and the Flex code. The producer sends messages to the destination and defines which functions handle the success and failure of sending a message. The consumer defines which functions handle the success and failure of receiving a message as well as a function for processing any message received from the chat server.

Finally, edit the `chat.html` file to match this code listing:

```
<html>
<head>
<title>Flex/Java/BlazeDS Chat Room</title>
</head>
<body>
<object classid="clsid:D27CDB6E-AE6D-11cf-96B8-444553540000" codebase="http://
    download.macromedia.com/pub/shockwave/cabs/flash/swflash.
    cab#version=9,0,124,0" width="100%" height="100%"
id="Chat.swf">
  <param name="flashvars" value="versionChecked=true">
  <param name="src" value="Chat.swf">
  <embed pluginspage="http://www.macromedia.com/go/getflashplayer"
          width="100%" height="100%"
          flashvars="versionChecked=true"
          src="Chat.swf"
          name="Chat Room"
  />
</object>
</body>
</html>
```

The HTML file is a standard wrapper for an SWF file. It contains `<object>` and `<embed>` tags that define the source of the embedded SWF file as well as the URL for users to download the Flash Player browser plug-in if they don't already have it.

Connecting the Java and Flex Pieces

The Java chat server and Flex chat client are finished, but they still can't communicate with each other yet. First, you need to write Web application and BlazeDS configuration files to wire everything together. After the configuration files are written, you need an Ant build script to compile the Java source code into a class file and the Flex MXML file into an SWF file, and then package the compiled code and configuration together into a Web application archive (WAR) file.

 For more on Java WAR files and Web application configuration, see Chapter 6.

The Web application configuration

The configuration for the Web application lives in the web.xml file. This file sets up a servlet and some other code that BlazeDS uses to perform its messaging tasks. To create the web.xml configuration file, follow these steps:

1. **Right-click the** web\WEB-INF **folder below the** jfib-ch14-p01 **project in the Project Explorer view and then choose New ➪ File from the popup menu.** The New File dialog box opens.

2. **Type** web.xml **in the File name text field and then click Finish.** The New File dialog box closes, and the newly created web.xml file appears below the web\WEB-INF folder in the Project Explorer view.

Edit the web.xml file to match this code listing:

```
<?xml version="1.0" encoding="UTF-8"?>
<!DOCTYPE web-app PUBLIC "-//Sun Microsystems, Inc.//DTD Web Application 2.3//
    EN" "http://java.sun.com/dtd/web-app_2_3.dtd">
<web-app>

    <display-name>BlazeDS Chat</display-name>
    <description>BlazeDS chat application</description>

    <!-- Http Flex Session attribute and binding listener support -->
    <listener>
        <listener-class>flex.messaging.HttpFlexSession</listener-class>
    </listener>

    <!-- MessageBroker Servlet -->
    <servlet>
        <servlet-name>MessageBrokerServlet</servlet-name>
        <display-name>MessageBrokerServlet</display-name>
        <servlet-class>flex.messaging.MessageBrokerServlet</servlet-class>
        <init-param>
            <param-name>services.configuration.file</param-name>
```

```
                <param-value>/WEB-INF/services-config.xml</param-value>
            </init-param>
            <load-on-startup>1</load-on-startup>
        </servlet>

        <servlet-mapping>
            <servlet-name>MessageBrokerServlet</servlet-name>
            <url-pattern>/messagebroker/*</url-pattern>
        </servlet-mapping>

        <welcome-file-list>
            <welcome-file>chat.html</welcome-file>
        </welcome-file-list>
    </web-app>
```

This is a fairly standard web.xml file. The <listener> tag sets up a FlexHttpSession object that listens for messaging requests on BlazeDS HTTP channels and keeps track of sessions between the clients and server. The <servlet> tag registers the Flex MessageBrokerServlet. The MessageBrokerServlet provides message destination endpoints for the various BlazeDS channels in the BlazeDS configuration. The value of the services.configuration.file parameter points to the location of this BlazeDS configuration. The <load-on-startup> tag's value of 1 indicates that this servlet is loaded when JBoss starts. The <servlet-mapping> tag maps the MessageBrokerServlet class to the URL pattern /messagebroker/*, meaning that any URL that matches this pattern is handled by the MessageBrokerServlet. The endpoint URLs in the BlazeDS configuration file match this URL pattern. Finally, the <welcome-file-list> tag contains one entry that specifies the default file to load when accessing this application if no file is specified. This application has only one HTML file — chat.html — so it's the default welcome file.

 **For more on BlazeDS channels, see Chapter 11.**

The BlazeDS configuration

The web.xml file contains a reference to the BlazeDS configuration file services-config.xml. This configuration file defines the BlazeDS channels available for the chat application and the messaging service for the chat server.

To create the services-config.xml file, follow these steps:

1. **Right-click the** web\WEB-INF **folder below the** jfib-ch14-p01 **project in the Project Explorer view and then choose New ⇨ File from the popup menu.** The New File dialog box opens.

2. **Type** services-config.xml **in the File name text field and then click Finish.** The New File dialog box closes, and the newly created services-config.xml file appears below the web\WEB-INF folder in the Project Explorer view.

Edit the `services-config.xml` file so that it matches this code listing:

```
<?xml version="1.0" encoding="UTF-8"?>
<services-config>
    <services>
        <default-channels>
            <channel ref="my-http"/>
        </default-channels>
        <service id="message-service"
                class="flex.messaging.services.MessageService">
            <adapters>
                    <adapter-definition id="Ch14ChatAdapter"
                            class="com.wiley.jfib.ch14.ChatServer"/>
            </adapters>
            <destination id="ChatAdapter">
                    <adapter ref="Ch14ChatAdapter"/>
            </destination>
        </service>
    </services>
    <channels>
            <!-- Simple HTTP -->
            <channel-definition id="my-http"
                class="mx.messaging.channels.HTTPChannel">
                <endpoint uri="http://localhost:8080/chat/messagebroker/http"
                        class="flex.messaging.endpoints.HTTPEndpoint"/>
            </channel-definition>
    </channels>
</services-config>
```

This configuration file defines two things: services and channels. The `<services>` tag defines the message service that's used to send and receive messages as well as a set of default channels that those messages are sent and received on. For the chat application, there's only a single message service. It uses an adapter provided by the `ChatServer` class you wrote and makes that adapter available at the `ChatAdapter` destination. Remember that this is the same destination specified by the `<mx:Producer>` and `<mx:Consumer>` tags in the MXML file. The `<channels>` tag defines the set of channels that are available to all services in this application. This application has only one service and uses only one channel, which is a standard HTTP channel.

Configuring Ant and Eclipse to build the application

The final task in tying everything together is creating an Ant build script that can compile both the Java file and the MXML file, package the application up, and deploy it to the JBoss server. Before writing the build file, you need to provide Ant a JAR file, `flexTasks.jar`, from your Flex SDK. This JAR file defines Ant tasks for compiling Flex MXML files into SWF files.

The `flexTasks.jar` file can be found in the `ant\lib` subfolder of your Flex SDK installation. Copy the `flexTasks.jar` file from the `ant\lib` subfolder of your Flex SDK installation into the `lib` subfolder of your Ant installation directory.

NOTE The Flex Ant Tasks are available only in Flex SDK version 3 and later. Older versions of the SDK don't include these Ant tasks.

CROSS-REF For more on installing the Flex SDK, see Appendix A.

To run the Ant build from within Eclipse, you also need to add the `flexTasks.jar` file to your Eclipse Ant configuration. To modify the Eclipse Ant configuration to include this file, follow these steps:

1. **Choose Window ➪ Preferences in Eclipse.** The Preferences dialog box, as shown in Figure 14.16, opens.

2. **Click the arrow next to Ant in the left pane to expand it and then click the Runtime item below Ant.** The Runtime dialog box opens in the right pane with the Classpath tab selected, as shown in Figure 14.17.

FIGURE 14.16

The Preferences dialog box allows you to configure a variety of preferences for Eclipse.

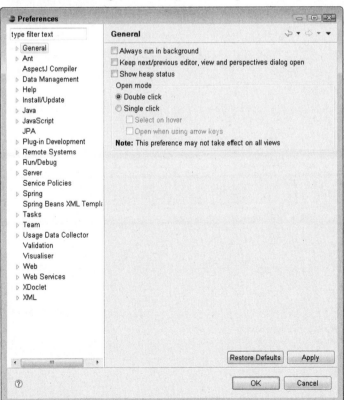

3. **Click the Ant Home Entries item in the Classpath tab and then click Add External JARs.** The Open JAR dialog box opens.

4. **Navigate to the `lib` folder in the `ant\lib` directory below your Flex SDK installation directory, click the `flexTasks.jar` file, and then click Open.** The Open JAR dialog box closes, and the `flexTasks.jar` file appears with the rest of the Ant JARs in the Classpath tab, as shown in Figure 14.18.

5. **Click OK.** The Preferences dialog box closes.

FIGURE 14.17

The Runtime dialog box lets you set runtime properties for Ant. On the Classpath tab, JAR files used by Ant can be added.

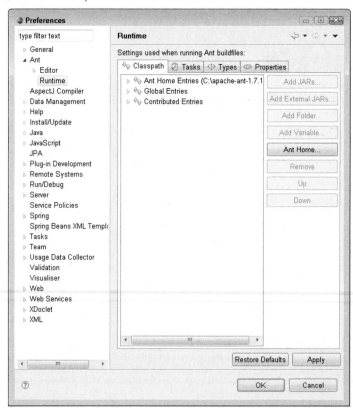

FIGURE 14.18

The `flexTasks.jar` file appears with the rest of the Ant JAR files once it has been selected in the Open JAR dialog box.

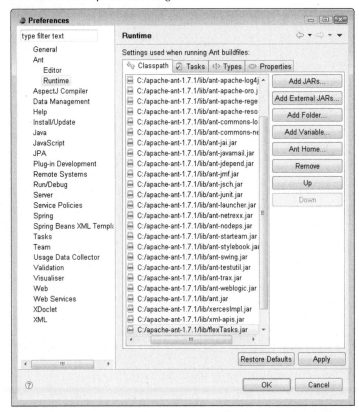

Now that the setup is finished, you can create the Ant build properties file and the `build.xml` file. To create these two files, follow these steps:

1. **Right-click the** `jfib-ch14-p01` **project in the Project Explorer view and then choose New ➪ File from the popup menu.** The New File dialog box opens.

2. **Type** chat-build.properties **in the File name text field and then click Finish.** The New File dialog box closes, and the newly created `chat-build.properties` file appears below the `jfib-ch14-p01` project in the Project Explorer view.

3. **Right-click the** `jfib-ch14-p01` **project in the Project Explorer view and then choose New ➪ File.** The New File dialog box opens.

4. **Type** build.xml **in the File name text field and then click Finish.** The New File dialog box closes, and the newly created `build.xml` file appears below the `jfib-ch14-p01` project in the Project Explorer view.

The properties contained in the `chat-build.properties` file are used by the `build.xml` build file, so first edit the `chat-build.properties` file to match this code listing:

```
# Ant build properties for chat
src.dir=src
web.dir=web
build.dir=${web.dir}/WEB-INF/classes

name=chat

appserver.home=${env.JBOSS_HOME}/server/default
deploy.path=${appserver.home}/deploy

APP_ROOT=web
FLEX_HOME=c:/flex/sdk
```

 Make sure that you set the value of the **FLEX_HOME** property to the location of the Flex SDK on your machine.

CROSS-REF For more on Ant build properties files, see Chapter 6.

This properties file contains properties for the Java source and Web file directories in the project, the build output directory, the application name, the JBoss home and application deployment path, and the Web application root and Flex SDK home for compiling the Flex MXML file.

Now edit the `build.xml` file to match this code listing:

```
<?xml version="1.0" encoding="UTF-8"?>
<project name="chat" basedir="." default="usage">
    <property environment="env"/>
     <property file="chat-build.properties"/>

    <path id="cp">
        <fileset dir="${web.dir}/WEB-INF/lib">
            <include name="*.jar"/>
        </fileset>
        <pathelement path="${build.dir}"/>
    </path>

    <taskdef resource="flexTasks.tasks"
        classpath="${FLEX_HOME}/ant/lib/flexTasks.jar"/>

    <target name="usage">
        <echo message=""/>
```

```
            <echo message="${name} build file"/>
            <echo message="---------------------------------"/>
            <echo message=""/>
            <echo message="Available targets are:"/>
            <echo message=""/>
            <echo message="build        --> Build the Java code and the Flex app"/>
            <echo message="deploy          --> Deploy application as a WAR file"/>
            <echo message=""/>
    </target>

    <target name="build" description="Compile main source tree java files">
        <mkdir dir="${build.dir}"/>
        <javac destdir="${build.dir}"
                    source="1.5"
                    target="1.5"
                    debug="true"
                    deprecation="false"
                    optimize="false"
                    failonerror="true">
            <src path="${src.dir}"/>
            <classpath refid="cp"/>
        </javac>
        <mxmlc file="${APP_ROOT}/Chat.mxml"
                    keep-generated-actionscript="false">
            <load-config filename="${FLEX_HOME}/frameworks/flex-config.xml"/>
            <source-path path-element="${FLEX_HOME}/frameworks"/>
            <services>web/WEB-INF/services-config.xml</services>
        </mxmlc>
    </target>
    <target name="build-and-deploy"
            depends="build"
            description="Deploy application as a WAR file">
        <war destfile="${name}.war"
            webxml="${web.dir}/WEB-INF/web.xml">
            <fileset dir="${web.dir}">
                <include name="**/*.*"/>
            </fileset>
        </war>
        <copy todir="${deploy.path}" preservelastmodified="true">
            <fileset dir=".">
                <include name="*.war"/>
            </fileset>
        </copy>
    </target>
</project>
```

CROSS-REF For more on the structure of Ant `build.xml` files, see Chapter 6.

Much of this build.xml file is like others you've seen in previous chapters. There are two elements of this file that are new. First, the <taskdef> tag near the top of the file imports the Flex Ant tasks contained in the flexTasks.jar file for use in this build file. Second, the <mxmlc> tag makes use of that imported Flex Ant task to compile the MXML file into an SWF file. It uses the standard flex-config.xml file that's included with the Flex SDK and loads the Flex framework files to use during compilation. The <services> tag inside the <mxmlc> tag points the compiler to the BlazeDS configuration file. The compiler includes the information in the configuration file about messaging services and destinations in the compiled SWF file so that the SWF knows how to call into the messaging services on the server. Without this tag, the compiled SWF file wouldn't know how to communicate with the Java server.

The final piece of setup to perform is adding the Ant build.xml file to the Eclipse Ant view. To add the build.xml file to the Ant view, follow these steps:

1. **Choose Window ⇨ Show View ⇨ Other in Eclipse.** The Show View dialog box, as shown in Figure 14.19, opens.

2. **Click the arrow next to Ant to expand it, click the Ant item below the expanded Ant item, and then click OK.** The Ant view, as shown in Figure 14.20, opens.

3. **Click the Add Buildfiles button in the Ant view.** The Add Buildfiles button is the left-most button in the Ant view and has a + sign next to an ant. The Buildfile Selection dialog box, as shown in Figure 14.21, opens.

4. **Click the arrow next to the jfib-ch14-p01 project to expand it, click the build.xml file, and then click OK.** The Buildfile Selection dialog box closes, and the build file appears in the Ant view, as shown in Figure 14.22.

FIGURE 14.19

The Show View dialog box lets you select an Eclipse view to open.

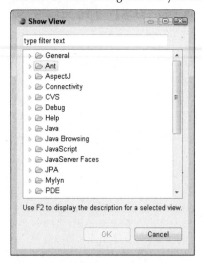

FIGURE 14.20

The Ant view opens with no build files available until you add one.

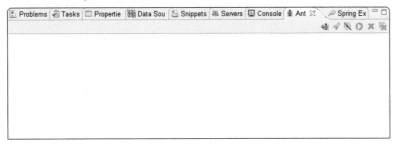

FIGURE 14.21

The Buildfile Selection dialog box allows you to choose build files to add to the Ant view.

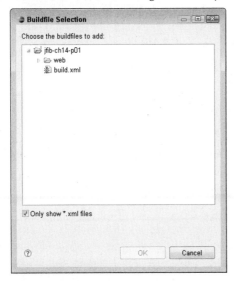

FIGURE 14.22

The build file appears in the Ant view once it's selected in the Buildfile Selection dialog box. Each of the targets in the build file is displayed.

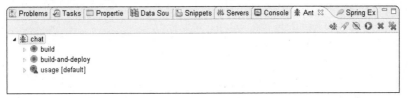

To compile, package, and deploy the application, double-click the `build-and-deploy` target in the Ant view. Eclipse switches to the Console view, and you can see the output from the Ant tasks as they run. When the build-and-deploy process is complete, Ant displays the message BUILD SUCCESSFUL, as shown in Figure 14.23.

FIGURE 14.23

When the Ant build has run successfully, you see a BUILD SUCCESSFUL message in the Console view.

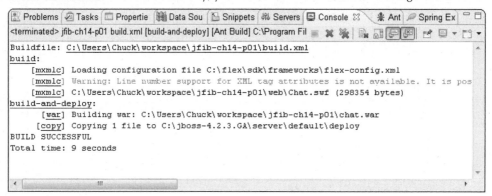

> **CAUTION** As of this writing, an incompatibility between the Flex SDK 3.1 Ant tasks and Ant 1.7.1 may result in the build's failing. If Ant displays errors and finishes with BUILD FAILED, it may be due to this incompatibility. A workaround for this problem is to navigate to the `lib` folder below your Flex SDK installation and rename the file `xercesPatch.jar` to `xercesPatch.backup`. Once you rename this file, double-click the `build-and-deploy` target again. The build should run successfully.

Connecting to the chat server

The chat Web application is now deployed to the JBoss server as `chat.war`, which means that it's available on JBoss in the `/chat` Web application context. To test the chat application, first start up JBoss and then open the chat application in a browser to send and receive messages from the server.

> **CROSS-REF** For more on installing JBoss and configuring it to run inside Eclipse, see Chapter 1. For more on Web application contexts, see Chapter 6.

To start JBoss inside Eclipse, follow these steps:

1. Choose Window ⇨ Show View ⇨ Servers in Eclipse. The Servers view, as shown in Figure 14.24, opens.

2. **Click the Start the Server button.** Eclipse switches to the Console view, and JBoss startup information appears there, as shown in Figure 14.25. Once JBoss has started up, Eclipse switches back to the Servers view.

FIGURE 14.24

The Servers view shows a list of the application servers that have been configured in Eclipse and their current state (Stopped or Started).

FIGURE 14.25

When starting JBoss, Eclipse switches to the Console view so that you can see the JBoss startup information. Once JBoss has started up, Eclipse switches back to the Servers view.

```
22:34:19,019 INFO  [Server] Patch URL: null
22:34:19,020 INFO  [Server] Server Name: default
22:34:19,020 INFO  [Server] Server Home Dir: C:\jboss-4.2.3.GA\server\default
22:34:19,020 INFO  [Server] Server Home URL: file:/C:/jboss-4.2.3.GA/server/default/
22:34:19,020 INFO  [Server] Server Log Dir: C:\jboss-4.2.3.GA\server\default\log
22:34:19,020 INFO  [Server] Server Temp Dir: C:\jboss-4.2.3.GA\server\default\tmp
22:34:19,020 INFO  [Server] Root Deployment Filename: jboss-service.xml
22:34:19,619 INFO  [ServerInfo] Java version: 1.6.0_10,Sun Microsystems Inc.
22:34:19,620 INFO  [ServerInfo] Java VM: Java HotSpot(TM) Client VM 11.0-b15,Sun Microsyste
22:34:19,620 INFO  [ServerInfo] OS-System: Windows Vista 6.0,x86
```

Testing the chat application

A chat application is hard to test alone, but it can be done by opening two browser windows and switching between them to type messages. To test the chat application, follow these steps:

1. **Open your favorite browser.** This example uses Internet Explorer.

2. **Press Ctrl+N.** A second Internet Explorer window opens.

3. **Type** http://localhost:8080/chat **in the address bar of the first window and then press Enter.** The chat application opens.

4. **Type** http://localhost:8080/chat **in the address bar of the second window and then press Enter.** The chat application opens.

5. **Type a name in the username text field of the first chat window and then either press Enter or click the Set Name button.** The username text field and Set Name button disappear, and the chat text field and Send button become available. A message appears in the list control stating that you've entered the chat.

6. **Switch to the second browser window.** Notice that the same message about entering the chat is displayed here.

7. **Type a name in the username text field of the second chat window and then either press Enter or click the Set Name button.** The username text field and Set Name button disappear, and the chat text field and Send button become available. A message appears in the list control stating that you've entered the chat.

8. **Type a message in the chat text field and then press Enter or click Send.** The Sending message appears briefly in the status area and then the message appears in the list control, preceded by the username you typed in this window.

9. **Switch back to the first browser window.** The message you sent in the second browser window has appeared in the list control in this window.

10. **Type a message in the chat text field and then press Enter or click Send.** The Sending message appears briefly in the status area and then the message appears in the list control, preceded by the username you typed in this window.

11. **Switch back to the second browser window.** The message from the user in the first browser window appears here.

Figure 14.26 shows what a chat session in two browsers might look like. If this application were deployed to a public JBoss server, people on different machines could open Web browsers and also chat across different machines.

This application is a great starting point for future expansion. For example, it could be expanded to use different chat rooms and filter messages based on header information. The back end could be enhanced to require the user to log in before chatting or to keep a friends list for each user so that only messages from friends are accepted. Use this application as a reference for building your own communications applications with Java and Flex.

FIGURE 14.26

A demonstration of two browser windows open to a chat application

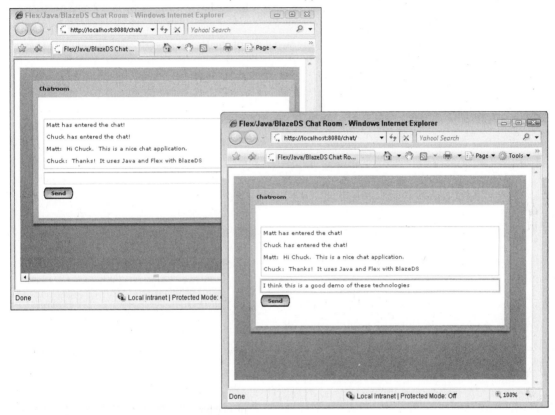

Summary

In this chapter, you wrote a basic chat application to demonstrate the real-time messaging capabilities of Java and Flex connected by BlazeDS. First, you set up an Eclipse project for developing the application and then configured it to use the BlazeDS Java libraries. Next, you extended the BlazeDS ServiceAdapter Java class to create the simple ChatServer Java class. After that, you set up the structure of the Web application archive (WAR) file in Eclipse and then wrote the MXML chat client, which used the <mx:Producer> and <mx:Consumer> MXML tags to set up publish and subscribe relationships with the chat server code. Next, you wired together the communication lines between the Java code and the Flex code by creating some Web application and BlazeDS configuration files. To package up the application, you configured Ant in Eclipse to use the Flex Ant tasks included with the Flex SDK and then wrote an Ant build script to compile, package, and deploy the application to JBoss. Finally, you tested the application by running JBoss in Eclipse and then used two browser windows to simulate multiple users chatting.

Chapter 15

Extending Java and Flex Development

T he combination of Java and Flex can create some very powerful Web applications. Data coming from a Java back end can be given life with the dynamic visuals that a Flex front end can provide. Similarly, a rich Flex user interface can become even more engaging by receiving live data from a Java back end.

Often, data that might be useful for your applications resides outside your control. Data such as mapping coordinates, product ratings from online stores, etc., can add another dimension to your Web application that sets it apart from other similar applications. In this chapter, you learn how to combine data from multiple locations and then use it to deliver something entirely new.

IN THIS CHAPTER

Building mashups

Overview of developing custom Flex interfaces

Building Mashups

In the world of Web applications, a *mashup* is an application that uses data or functionality from two or more disparate services and then combines it into a new service that's different from any of the original data sources or functions. For example, a Web application might pull in a list of open houses within 10 miles of a certain ZIP code within a certain date range from a real estate listing site and then use a mapping API (application programming interface) from another site to display those open houses on a map. The mapping site alone doesn't show open houses, and the real estate site doesn't have a mapping feature, but the combination of data from the real estate site and the functionality of the mapping site creates something new: an open house mapping site.

There are multiple approaches to creating a mashup. First, the mashup can be created on the client side. This typically involves using an `XmlHttpRequest` in JavaScript to retrieve XML or JavaScript Object Notation (JSON) data from multiple Web services and then combining that data on the client side. Second, the mashup can be created on the server side. This involves requests being made to the various Web services from the server. The server receives all the necessary data, combines it in a format expected by the client application, and then sends that data back in response. Finally, a mashup can be created by using one of a variety of online mashup builder tools, such as:

- Yahoo! Pipes (`http://pipes.yahoo.com`)
- Google Mashup Editor (`http://editor.googlemashups.com`)
- Microsoft PopFly (`www.popfly.com`)

Most mashups make use of publicly accessible Web services provided by Web sites to allow access to their data. The mashup requests data by using HTTP calls and then receives the requested data back. Most of these public APIs require that developers register with the site owners in order to receive an application ID that must be sent with each Web service request. This is so that abuse of their services can be prevented and use of the services by each application can be measured. In most cases, application IDs are free for personal or noncommercial use.

Libraries for mashups

In addition to simply using plain HTTP requests to access data and functionality from other sites, you can use third-party libraries made specifically for the purpose of accessing Web service APIs. These libraries make it easier to work with a Web application's Web services API in a language more familiar to the developer. For example, the flickrj library is a Java implementation of the Web service API for the online photo-sharing service Flickr. It contains Java object implementations of a number of Flickr API calls and presents the data returned from those calls in an object model that's easy to use and understand.

Advanced example

This example mashup uses both standard HTTP requests and a third-party library, both on the server side, to create a Web application called `ArtWeather`. The application asks the user to input a five-digit ZIP code. When the ZIP code is submitted to the server, an HTTP request is first made to the Yahoo! Weather RSS service to retrieve the forecast for the next two days for that ZIP code. The XML for this RSS feed is parsed to extract the city and state along with the conditions and high and low temperatures for each day. The text of the conditions (for example, Sunny or Showers) is then used as search criteria in the Flickr photo-sharing service's public API. The XML returned from the photo search is then used to build a URL pointing to each image on the Flickr servers. Finally, the city, state, forecast details, and image URLs are placed into a HashMap and then delivered to a JSP view. The JSP view renders the data. The end result can be seen in Figure 15.1.

FIGURE 15.1

The JSP rendering of the `ArtWeather` mashup. The weather data on this page comes from Yahoo! Weather; the images are retrieved from Flickr based on the text of the weather forecast. For example, the image on the right was retrieved from Flickr by using the search term PM Thunderstorms.

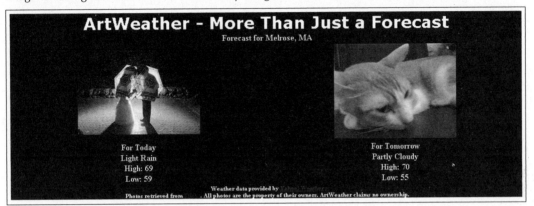

Obtaining a Flickr API key

Before you can access the Flickr API from your Java code, you need to register for a Flickr API key. Requests for data to the Flickr API require you to pass your API key as a parameter. The Flickr development team uses these API keys to keep track of how often their APIs are being used and for what purposes. Flickr API keys are provided free for noncommercial use, including internal development and testing. If you plan to use your Flickr API key for a commercial project, the Flickr team provides you a key after reviewing your application's intended functionality and use of their data, usually within a few weeks of your application.

Along with the API Key, you receive a key known as the Shared Secret. This key is typically used for Flickr services that require some sort of authentication.

To obtain a Flickr API key, follow these steps:

1. **Open your Web browser, type** www.flickr.com/services/api/keys/apply/ **in the address bar, and then press Enter.** The Flickr API Key application page, as shown in Figure 15.2, opens.

2. **Type the information required by the registration form.** Be sure to fill in a description of your application or just a general description of what you plan to do with the API key (for example, build mashups by using the Flickr API) if you don't have a specific application in mind. Be sure that you click the Non-commercial use radio button and that you click the check boxes to acknowledge the ownership rights of photos from Flickr and to agree to the Flickr Terms of Service.

3. **Click Apply.** The next screen, as shown in Figure 15.3, opens, showing you your API key.

4. **Highlight this API key and then press Ctrl+C to copy it to the Clipboard.**

5. **Open Notepad by choosing Start ➪ All Programs ➪ Accessories ➪ Notepad.**

6. **Press Ctrl+V.** Your API key is pasted into Notepad. Add some text, such as Flickr API key, to help you remember that this is your Flickr API key.

FIGURE 15.2

The Flickr API Key application page lets you register for your own Flickr API key.

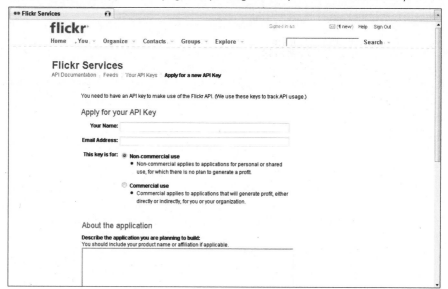

FIGURE 15.3

Your API key is shown on the screen following the registration information page. Copy this key and then save it to a text file. Don't share this key with anyone, as any abuse of the Flickr API caused by your key is your responsibility and may result in your key's being revoked.

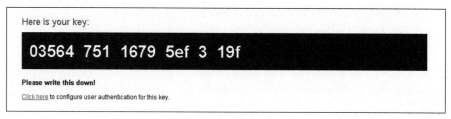

7. **On the API key page in your browser, click the Click here link below your API key.** The API Key Authentication Setup page, as shown in Figure 15.4, opens.

8. **Highlight the string of letters and numbers next to Shared Secret and then press Ctrl+C to copy the string to the Clipboard.**

9. **In the Notepad file where you pasted your API key, press Ctrl+V.** The Shared Secret string is pasted into the document. Add some text, such as Flickr API Shared Secret, to help you remember that this is the Shared Secret.

10. **In Notepad, choose File ➪ Save and then save the file to a location you can easily find again.** Consider giving it a meaningful name, such as `flickr-api-key-and-shared-secret.txt`.

FIGURE 15.4

On the API Key Authentication Setup page, copy your Shared Secret and then save it in the text file where you saved your API key. You need to use the Flickr API in your applications.

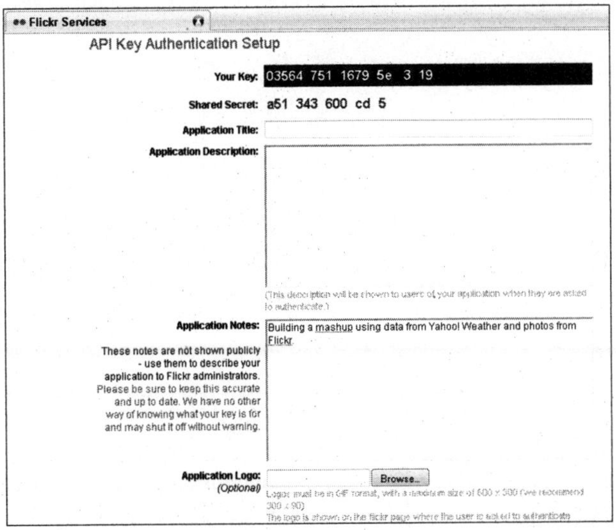

Downloading the flickrj library

As mentioned previously, the flickrj Java library contains a set of Java classes that map to the Flickr API. The `ArtWeather` mashup uses this API to search for photos on the Flickr Web site.

You can download flickrj at `http://sourceforge.net/projects/flickrj/`. As of this writing, the most recent version of flickrj is 1.1. To download flickrj, follow these steps:

1. **Open your Web browser, type** sourceforge.net/projects/flickrj/ **in the address bar, and then press Enter.** The flickrj project page, as shown in Figure 15.5, opens.

2. **Click the green arrow.** The screen showing versions available for download, as shown in Figure 15.6, opens. As of this writing, only one version of flickrj is available for download.

3. **Click the download link for flickrj-1.1.** The file download screen, as shown in Figure 15.7, opens.

4. **Click the `flickrapi-1.1.zip` link.** The Download File dialog box opens.

5. **Click Save to save the file to your desktop.**

6. **Extract the contents of the `flickrapi-1.1.zip` file to a location of your choice (for example, `c:\flickrapi-1.1`).** The flickrj library is now available to include in your Eclipse projects and applications.

FIGURE 15.5

The flickrj project page on the SourceForge Web site

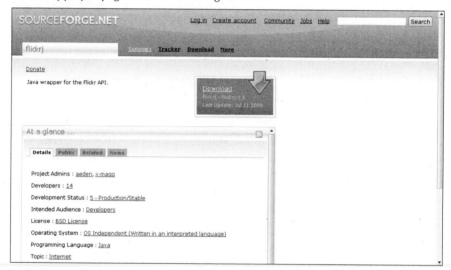

FIGURE 15.6

Currently, there's only one version of flickrj available to download: flickrj 1.1.

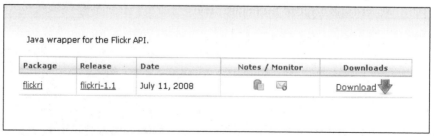

FIGURE 15.7

The flickrj 1.1 release is available to download in a couple of different formats on the download page.

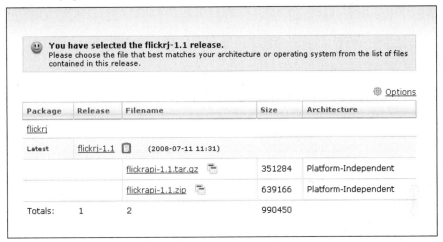

😊 **You have selected the flickrj-1.1 release.**
Please choose the file that best matches your architecture or operating system from the list of files contained in this release.

⚙ Options

Package	Release	Filename	Size	Architecture
flickrj				
Latest	flickrj-1.1 🗋 (2008-07-11 11:31)			
		flickrapi-1.1.tar.gz 📄	351284	Platform-Independent
		flickrapi-1.1.zip 📄	639166	Platform-Independent
Totals:	1	2	990450	

Creating the Eclipse project

The weather mashup is configured as a typical Spring Web MVC project in Eclipse. You create all the source code as well as the configuration files and Ant build files used to build and deploy the application to JBoss within this Eclipse project. In the weather mashup application, a single Spring controller receives the ZIP code parameter from the client, retrieves the Yahoo! Weather RSS data and the Flickr photo data, packages it all up, and then returns the needed information to the client in a JSP view.

To create the Eclipse project, follow these steps:

1. **Open Windows Explorer by choosing Start ⇨ All Programs ⇨ Accessories ⇨ Windows Explorer.**

2. **Navigate to the Eclipse install directory and then double-click** `eclipse.exe`. Eclipse starts. If you didn't click the Use this as the default and don't ask again check box the first time you ran Eclipse, Eclipse again asks you to choose a workspace directory. Leave the default value in place and then click the OK button.

3. **Create a new project by choosing File ⇨ New ⇨ Project or right-clicking within the Project Explorer view and then choosing New ⇨ Project from the popup menu.** The New Project selection screen, as shown in Figure 15.8, opens.

4. **Click the arrow next to Spring to expand it, choose Spring Project, and then click the Next button.** The New Spring Project dialog box, as shown in Figure 15.9, opens.

5. **Type** `jfib-ch15-p01` **for the project name, change the output folder to** `web/WEB-INF/classes`, **and then click Finish.** The dialog box closes, and the newly created project appears in the Project Explorer view.

FIGURE 15.8

The New Project selection screen in Eclipse is the first step in creating a new project.

FIGURE 15.9

The New Spring Project dialog box contains settings for creating a new Spring project.

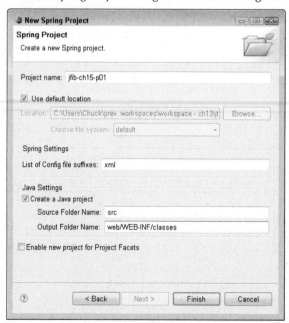

CROSS-REF For more on the folder structure of a Java Web application, see Chapter 6.

The libraries needed by this Web application need to be placed in a `lib` folder below the `web/WEB-INF` folder. There are five library JAR files that need to be added to the `lib` folder by using Eclipse's Import from File system dialog box:

- The Spring Core and Spring Web MVC modules from the Spring Framework distribution
- The JSTL and Jakarta tag libraries, also found in the Spring Framework distribution
- The Flickr API JAR file

You will open the Import from File system dialog box several times. Each time, the steps are the same. To open the Import from File system dialog box, follow these steps:

1. **Right-click the `web/WEB-INF` folder under the `jfib-ch15-p01` project in the Project Explorer view and then choose New⇨ Folder from the popup menu.** The New Folder dialog box, as shown in Figure 15.10, opens.

2. **Type lib in the Folder name text field and then click Finish.** The New Folder dialog box closes, and the newly created folder is added to the project.

FIGURE 15.10

The New Folder dialog box allows you to add new folders to your project.

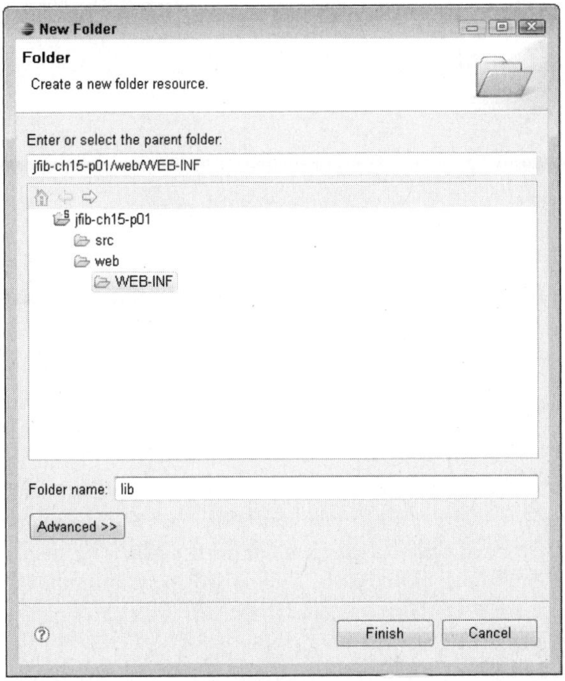

3. **Right-click the** `lib` **folder and then choose Import from the popup menu.** The Import Select dialog box, as shown in Figure 15.11, opens.

4. **Click the arrow next to the General item to expand it, choose File System from the list, and then click the Next button.** The Import from File system dialog box, as shown in Figure 15.12, opens.

FIGURE 15.11

The Import Select dialog box allows you to import resources for your project from a variety of sources.

Use the previous steps whenever you need to open the Import File system dialog box to add libraries to the `web/WEB-INF/lib` folder. First, add the Spring Framework core library and the Spring Web MVC library by following these steps:

1. **Open the Import File system dialog box.**

2. **Click the Browse button next to the From directory text field.** The Import from directory dialog box opens.

3. **Navigate to the** `dist` **directory below your extracted Spring Framework directory, select it, and then click OK.** The directory appears in the left pane of the Import from directory dialog box. Clicking the `dist` directory displays its contents in the right pane of the dialog box. Clicking the arrow next to the directory name on the left expands it to display its subfolders.

4. Click the `dist` **folder in the left pane and then click the check box next to** `spring.jar` **in the right pane.**

5. **Click Finish.** The `spring.jar` file you just added appears beneath the `web/WEB-INF/lib` folder.

6. **Open the Import from File system dialog box.**

7. **Click the Browse button next to the From directory text field.** The Import from directory dialog box opens.

8. **Navigate to the** `dist/modules` **directory below your extracted Spring Framework directory, select it, and then click OK.** The directory appears in the left pane of the Import from directory dialog box. Clicking the `modules` directory displays its contents in the right pane of the dialog box.

9. **Click the** `modules` **folder in the left pane and then click the check box next to** `spring-webmvc.jar` **in the right pane.**

10. **Click Finish.** The `spring-webmvc.jar` file you just added appears beneath the `web/WEB-INF/lib` folder.

FIGURE 15.12

The Import File system dialog box lets you bring resources located on your computer into your project. Resources are copied from their original locations into your project's directory structure.

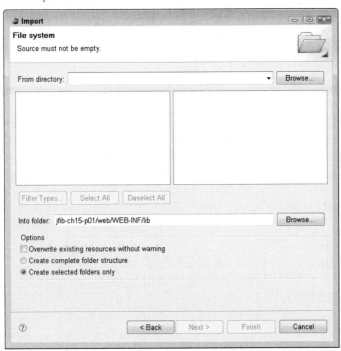

Next, add the JSTL and Jakarta tag library JAR files by following these steps:

1. **Open the Import from File system dialog box.**

2. **Click the Browse button next to the From directory text field.** The Import from directory dialog box opens.

3. **Navigate to the `lib/j2ee` directory below your extracted Spring Framework directory, select it, and then click OK.** The directory appears in the left pane of the Import from directory dialog box. Clicking the `j2ee` directory displays its contents in the right pane of the dialog box. Clicking the arrow next to the directory name on the left expands it to display its subfolders.

4. **Click the `j2ee` folder in the left pane and then click the check box next to `jstl.jar` in the right pane.**

5. **Click Finish.** The `jstl.jar` file you just added appears beneath the `web/WEB-INF/lib` folder.

6. **Open the Import from File system dialog box.**

7. **Click the Browse button next to the From directory text field.** The Import from directory dialog box opens.

8. **Navigate to the `lib/jakarta-taglibs` directory below your extracted Spring Framework directory, select it, and then click OK.** The directory appears in the left pane of the Import from directory dialog box. Clicking the `jakarta-taglibs` directory displays its contents in the right pane of the dialog box.

9. **Click the `jakarta-taglibs` folder in the left pane and then click the check box next to `standard.jar` in the right pane.**

10. **Click Finish.** The `standard.jar` file you just added appears beneath the `web/WEB-INF/lib` folder.

Finally, add the Flickr API JAR file by following these steps:

1. **Open the Import from File system dialog box.**

2. **Click the Browse button next to the From directory text field.** The Import from directory dialog box opens.

3. **Navigate to your extracted Flickr API directory, select it, and then click OK.** The directory appears in the left pane of the Import from directory dialog box. Clicking the `flickrapi-1.1` directory displays its contents in the right pane of the dialog box. Clicking the arrow next to the directory name on the left expands it to display its subfolders.

4. **Click the `flickrapi-1.1` folder in the left pane and then click the check box next to `flickrapi-1.1.jar` in the right pane.**

5. **Click Finish.** The `flickrapi-1.1.jar` file you just added appears beneath the `web/WEB-INF/lib` folder.

The libraries used by the Web application are now in place. Eclipse also needs to have some of these libraries and one other library on the project's build path to compile the code for the application. To add the required libraries to the build path, follow these steps:

1. **Right-click the** `jfib-ch15-p01` **project in the Project Explorer view and then choose Build Path ⇨ Configure Build Path from the popup menu.** The Java Build Properties dialog box opens with the Libraries tab selected.

2. **Click the Add JARs button.** The JAR Selection dialog box, as shown in Figure 15.13, opens.

3. **Click the arrow next to the** `jfib-ch15-p01` **project to expand it.**

4. **Click the arrow next to** `web` **to expand it.**

5. **Click the arrow next to** `WEB-INF` **to expand it and then click the arrow next to** `lib` **to expand it.**

6. **Click** `flickrapi-1.1.jar`, `spring.jar`, **and** `spring-webmvc.jar` **and then click OK.** The JAR Selection dialog box closes, and the three JAR files are added to the list in the Library tab.

7. **Click the Add External JARs button.** The JAR Selection dialog box, as shown in Figure 15.14, opens.

FIGURE 15.13

The JAR Selection dialog box

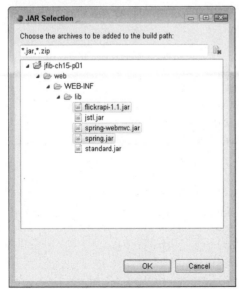

8. Navigate to the `jboss-4.2.3.GA/lib` directory, click the `commons-httpclient.jar` file, and then click Open. The `commons-httpclient.jar` file is added to the list in the Library tab.

9. Click the **Add External JARs button.** The JAR Selection dialog box opens.

10. Navigate to the `jboss-4.2.3.GA/client` directory, click the `servlet-api.jar` file, and then click Open. The `servlet-api.jar` file is added to the list in the Library tab.

11. Click OK. The Java Build Properties dialog box closes.

The `commons-httpclient.jar` file contains the `HttpClient` Java class, which the controller uses to call the Yahoo! Weather RSS service to retrieve the weather data. Because this JAR file is part of the JBoss distribution, it's not necessary to bundle it in the `web/WEB-INF/lib` directory of your Web application, but Eclipse does need to reference it on the project's build path.

FIGURE 15.14

The JAR Selection dialog box lets you select JARs that are external to your Eclipse project to add to the build path. This is useful for adding JARs that are needed only at compile time, not runtime.

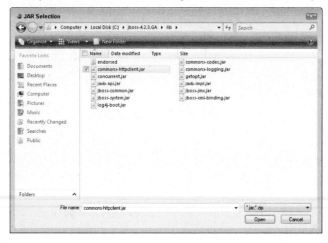

Writing the mashup

The application consists of a single service and a utility class. The utility class is used in parsing the XML retrieved from the Yahoo! Weather RSS feed. The service receives an XML block from this Web service. You can find the XML format of the Yahoo! Weather RSS feed on the Yahoo! developers' site at `http://developer.yahoo.com/weather/`. This XML structure contains a number of tags, but this application uses information from only a few of them.

To traverse the XML block returned from the RSS call, the application uses XPath expressions. *XPath expressions* are a way of traversing an XML block by using a language that looks much like a directory path in Windows. The JDK includes classes that allow you to construct XML documents and then construct XPath expressions to find values in those documents. Because the structure of the XML returned from the RSS request has a known structure, XPath expressions are a great way to get to specific values in the XML.

The first class needed by the application is a class that implements one of the XML interfaces in the JDK: `NamespaceContext`. One of the tags in the RSS XML that contains information needed by the application is `<yweather:forecast>`. The `yweather` portion of this tag is known as the prefix that stands for an XML namespace. A *namespace* is a way of grouping XML that belongs to a specific area of functionality. You've already seen examples of namespaces in use in some of the JSP views in this book. The JSTL core tag library uses the namespace prefix `c`. When you see the tag `<c:out>` in a JSP page, it means the `out` tag of the `c` namespace. Namespaces are defined by *uniform resource identifiers,* or URIs, in the XML file — typically, by using another XML namespace prefix, `xmlns`, as an attribute of the opening XML tag. A URI is used to specify a location or name for some resource on the Internet. A URL used to navigate to a Web page is one example of a URI. For example, in the Yahoo! Weather RSS feed, the `yweather` namespace is defined by using the attribute `xmlns:yweather=http://xml.weather.yahoo.com/ns/rss/1.0` in the outermost tag in the file, `<rss>`.

By default, the XPath classes in the JDK use the default empty namespace when evaluating XPath expressions. If you want the XPath classes in the JDK to know about other namespaces, you need to provide them a class that implements the `NamespaceContext` interface, which provides methods for the retrieval of XML namespace prefixes and URIs. The XPath classes search all the namespaces they're aware of when evaluating XPath expressions.

To create a `YWeatherNamespaceContext` class that implements the `NamespaceContext` controller, follow these steps:

1. **Right-click the `src` folder in the Project Explorer view and then choose New ⇨ Class from the popup menu.** The New Java Class dialog box, as shown in Figure 15.15, opens.

2. **Click the Add button next to the Interfaces list box.** The Implemented Interfaces Selection dialog box, as shown in Figure 15.16, opens.

3. **Type** NamespaceContext **in the Choose interfaces text field, choose** `NamespaceContext - javax.xml.namespace [jre6]` **from the Matching items list box, and then click OK.** The Implemented Interfaces Selection dialog box closes, and the `NamespaceContext` interface appears in the Interfaces list box.

4. **Type** com.wiley.jfib.ch15.mashup.util **in the Package text field, type** YWeatherNamespaceContext **in the Name text field, click the Constructors from superclass and Inherited abstract methods check boxes, and then click Finish.** The New Java Class dialog box closes, and the newly created class appears in the Project Explorer view.

449

FIGURE 15.15

The New Java Class dialog box walks you through the creation of a new Java class that implements the NamespaceContext interface.

FIGURE 15.16

The Implemented Interfaces Selection dialog box

Here's the code listing for the `YWeatherNamespaceContext` class:

```java
package com.wiley.jfib.ch15.mashup.util;
import java.util.Iterator;

import javax.xml.XMLConstants;
import javax.xml.namespace.NamespaceContext;

/**
 *
 */

/**
 * @author Chuck
 *
 */
public class YWeatherNamespaceContext implements NamespaceContext {

    private String namespaceUri;
    private String prefix;

    /**
     *
     */
    public YWeatherNamespaceContext(String namespaceUri, String
    prefix) {
            this.namespaceUri = namespaceUri;
            this.prefix = prefix;
    }

    /* (non-Javadoc)
     * @see javax.xml.namespace.NamespaceContext#getNamespaceURI(jav
    a.lang.String)
     */
    @Override
    public String getNamespaceURI(String prefix) {
            if(this.prefix.equals(prefix))
                    return namespaceUri;
            else
                    return XMLConstants.NULL_NS_URI;
    }

    /* (non-Javadoc)
     * @see javax.xml.namespace.NamespaceContext#getPrefix(java.lang.
    String)
     */
    @Override
    public String getPrefix(String namespaceURI) {
            if(this.namespaceUri.equals(namespaceURI))
```

```
                        return prefix;
            else
                        return XMLConstants.DEFAULT_NS_PREFIX;
        }

        /* (non-Javadoc)
         * @see javax.xml.namespace.NamespaceContext#getPrefixes(java.
        lang.String)
         */
        @Override
        public Iterator getPrefixes(String namespaceURI) {
            // Useful to implement if you have more
            // than one namespace prefix
            return null;
        }


    }
```

The `YWeatherNamespaceContext` class defines a URI field and a prefix field that are set in the constructor when the class is instantiated. These are set in the service class at the time when the XPath classes are created.

To create the `ArtWeatherService` class, follow these steps:

1. **Right-click the `src` folder in the Project Explorer view and then choose New⇨ Class from the popup menu.** The New Java Class dialog box opens.
2. **Click the Add button next to the Interfaces list box.** The Implemented Interfaces Selection dialog box opens.
3. **Type Controller in the Choose interfaces text field, choose `Controller - org. springframework.web.servlet.mvc` in the Matching items list box, and then click OK.** The Implemented Interfaces Selection dialog box closes, and the Controller interface appears in the Interfaces list box.
4. **Type com.wiley.jfib.ch15.mashup.service in the Package text field, type ArtWeather Service in the Name text field, click the Constructors from superclass and Inherited abstract methods check boxes, and then click Finish.** The New Java Class dialog box closes, and the newly created class appears in the Project Explorer view.

Here's the code listing for the `ArtWeatherService` class:

```
/**
 *
 */
package com.wiley.jfib.ch15.mashup.service;

import java.io.InputStream;
import java.util.HashMap;
import java.util.Map;
```

```java
import javax.servlet.http.HttpServletRequest;
import javax.servlet.http.HttpServletResponse;

import javax.xml.parsers.DocumentBuilderFactory;
import javax.xml.xpath.XPath;
import javax.xml.xpath.XPathConstants;
import javax.xml.xpath.XPathFactory;

import org.apache.commons.httpclient.HttpClient;
import org.apache.commons.httpclient.HttpStatus;
import org.apache.commons.httpclient.methods.GetMethod;
import org.springframework.web.servlet.ModelAndView;
import org.springframework.web.servlet.mvc.Controller;
import org.w3c.dom.Document;

import com.aetrion.flickr.Flickr;
import com.aetrion.flickr.photos.Photo;
import com.aetrion.flickr.photos.PhotoList;
import com.aetrion.flickr.photos.SearchParameters;
import com.wiley.jfib.ch15.mashup.util.YWeatherNamespaceContext;

/**
 * @author Chuck
 *
 */
public class ArtWeatherService implements Controller {
    private String apiKey = "abcdefghijkl";
    private String sharedSecret = "mnopqrst";
    private Flickr flickr;
    private final static String YAHOO_STRING = "Yahoo! Weather - ";

    @Override
    public ModelAndView handleRequest(HttpServletRequest arg0,
                HttpServletResponse arg1) throws Exception {
        String zipCode = arg0.getParameter("zip");
        // if a zip code is not given, send this back to the view
        // so that it knows not to display the non-existent forecast
        if(zipCode == null || zipCode.length() != 5)
                return new ModelAndView(
                        "WEB-INF/jsp/artweather.jsp",
                        "entry",
                        "true");
        else
        {
                Map<String,String> model = buildModelForZipCode(zipCode);
                return new ModelAndView("WEB-INF/jsp/artweather.jsp",
                        "model",model);
        }
```

```
        }

    public Map<String,String> buildModelForZipCode(String zipCode)
        throws Exception {
        Map<String,String> model = new HashMap<String,String>();
        String request = "http://weather.yahooapis.com/forecastrss?p=" + zipCode;

        HttpClient client = new HttpClient();
        GetMethod method = new GetMethod(request);

        // Send GET request
        int statusCode = client.executeMethod(method);

        if (statusCode != HttpStatus.SC_OK) {
                System.err.println("Method failed: " + method.getStatusLine());
        }
        InputStream rstream = null;

        // Get the response body
        rstream = method.getResponseBodyAsStream();

        //Process response

Document response = DocumentBuilderFactory.newInstance()
                .newDocumentBuilder().parse(rstream);

        XPathFactory factory = XPathFactory.newInstance();
        XPath xPath=factory.newXPath();

xPath.setNamespaceContext(
                new YWeatherNamespaceContext(
                        "http://xml.weather.yahoo.com/ns/rss/1.0","yweather"));
        //Get each xpath expression as a string

String cityState = (String)xPath.evaluate("/rss/channel/title",
                response, XPathConstants.STRING);
        if(cityState != null && cityState.indexOf(YAHOO_STRING) == 0)
        {
                cityState = cityState.replaceAll(YAHOO_STRING, "");
        }
        String todayCondition = (String)xPath.evaluate(
                "/rss/channel/item/forecast[1]/@text",
                response, XPathConstants.STRING);

        String todayHigh = (String)xPath.evaluate(
                "/rss/channel/item/forecast[1]/@high",
                response, XPathConstants.STRING);

        String todayLow = (String)xPath.evaluate(
                "/rss/channel/item/forecast[1]/@low",
                response, XPathConstants.STRING);
```

```
            String tomorrowCondition = (String)xPath.evaluate(
                    "/rss/channel/item/forecast[2]/@text",
                    response, XPathConstants.STRING);

            String tomorrowHigh = (String)xPath.evaluate(
                    "/rss/channel/item/forecast[2]/@high",
                    response, XPathConstants.STRING);

            String tomorrowLow = (String)xPath.evaluate(
                    "/rss/channel/item/forecast[2]/@low",
                    response, XPathConstants.STRING);

            model.put("cityState", cityState);
            model.put("todayCondition", todayCondition);
            model.put("todayHigh", todayHigh);
            model.put("todayLow", todayLow);
            model.put("todayPhotoUrl", getFlickrPhotoUrl(todayCondition));

            model.put("tomorrowCondition", tomorrowCondition);
            model.put("tomorrowHigh", tomorrowHigh);
            model.put("tomorrowLow", tomorrowLow);
            model.put("tomorrowPhotoUrl", getFlickrPhotoUrl(tomorrowCondition));

            return model;
    }

        /**
         *
         * @param weatherCondition
         * @return
         * @throws Exception
         */
        private String getFlickrPhotoUrl(String weatherCondition) throws Exception
        {
            // now get a Flickr image for each of the condition strings
                String photoUrl = "";
            flickr = new Flickr(apiKey);
                flickr.setSharedSecret(sharedSecret);
                SearchParameters params = new SearchParameters();
                params.setText(weatherCondition);
                PhotoList photos = flickr.getPhotosInterface().search(params, 10, 1);
                for(Object p : photos)
                {
                        Photo photo = (Photo)p;
                        if(photo.isPublicFlag())
                        {
                                photoUrl = "http://farm"
                                        + photo.getFarm()
                                        + ".static.flickr.com/"
                                        + photo.getServer()
                                        + "/"
```

```
                                        + photo.getId() + "_"
                                        + photo.getSecret()
                                        + "_m.jpg";
                        break;
                }
            }

        return photoUrl;
    }
}
```

In this class, the `handleRequest()` method receives the `zip` parameter from the client request. It passes off the `zip` parameter to a method called `buildModelForZipCode()`. This method does a few things:

- It creates an `HttpClient` object and gives it the URL to the Yahoo! Weather RSS service. The request is sent, and an `InputStream` is returned that contains the XML result of the request.

- The `InputStream` is parsed into an XML document.

- An XPath object is created by using the `YWeatherNamespaceContext` object to register the `yweather` namespace with the XPath object so that it's used in expression lookups.

- The XML document is parsed by using XPath expressions, and the values relevant to the application are put into a `Map` object as name-value pairs of strings.

- When all the values are retrieved, the map is returned to the `handleRequest()` method, which in turn adds it to the `ModelAndView` object that's returned to the client.

The view for the `ArtWeatherService` is a JSP file named `artweather.jsp`. This JSP file extracts the values from the model map and then uses them to construct the application interface. To create the `artweather.jsp` file, follow these steps:

1. **Right-click the `web/WEB-INF` folder in the Project Explorer view and then choose New ➪ Other from the popup menu.** The Select a wizard dialog box opens.

2. **Click the arrow next to General to expand it, click File, and then click Next.** The New File dialog box opens.

3. **Type /jsp at the end of the parent folder text field, type artweather.jsp in the File name text field, and then click Finish.** The New File dialog box closes, and the new folder and JSP file appear in the Project Explorer view.

Here's the code listing for the `artweather.jsp` file:

```
<?xml version="1.0" encoding="ISO-8859-1" ?>
<%@ page language="java" contentType="text/html; charset=ISO-8859-1"
    pageEncoding="ISO-8859-1"%>
<%@ taglib prefix="c" uri="http://java.sun.com/jsp/jstl/core" %>
<!DOCTYPE html PUBLIC "-//W3C//DTD XHTML 1.0 Transitional//EN"
    "http://www.w3.org/TR/xhtml1/DTD/xhtml1-transitional.dtd">
<html xmlns="http://www.w3.org/1999/xhtml">
```

```html
<head>
        <meta http-equiv="Content-Type" content="text/html;
charset=ISO-8859-1" />
        <title>ArtWeather - More Than Just a Forecast</title>
</head>
<body>
        <div style="text-align: center; font-family: Verdana; font-
weight: bold; font-size: 24pt; width: 100%; background-color:
black; color: white">
                ArtWeather - More Than Just a Forecast
                <br/>
                <img src="blank.png" height="100px"/>
        </div>
        <div style="text-align: center; cwidth: 100%; background-
color: black; color: white">
                <c:if test="${empty param.entry}">
                <span style="font-weight: bold">Forecast for <c:out
value='${model["cityState"]}'/></span><br/>
                <table border="0" width="100%">
                        <tr>
<td>
    <img src="<c:out value='${model["todayPhotoUrl"]}'/>"/>
</td>
<td>
    <img src="<c:out value='${model["tomorrowPhotoUrl"]}'/>"/>
</td>
                        </tr>
                        <tr>
<td>For Today<br/>
<c:out value='${model["todayCondition"]}'/><br/>
High: <c:out value='${model["todayHigh"]}'/><br/>
Low: <c:out value='${model["todayLow"]}'/>
</td>
<td>For Tomorrow<br/>
<c:out value='${model["tomorrowCondition"]}'/><br/>
High: <c:out value='${model["tomorrowHigh"]}'/><br/>
Low: <c:out value='${model["tomorrowLow"]}'/>
</td>
                        </tr>
                </table>
                </c:if>
<form method="post"
    action="/artweather/artweather.htm">
    <input type="text" size="5" maxlength="5"
        name="zip" id="zip"
        style="font-family: Verdana;
        font-weight: bold; font-size: 18pt"/>
    <br/>
    <input type="submit"
        style="font-family: Verdana;
        font-weight: bold; font-size: 12pt"/>
```

```
</form>
<span style="font-size: 8pt">
   Weather data provided by
   <a href="http://weather.yahoo.com">
        Yahoo! Weather
   </a><br/>
   Photos retrieved from
   <a href="http://flickr.com">Flickr</a>.
   All photos are the property of their
   owners. ArtWeather claims no ownership.
</span>
        </div>
   </body>
</html>
```

This JSP page first checks for the existence of an `entry` parameter, which the controller places in the model in the case where no ZIP code is passed in; that means this is the initial visit to the application. If the `entry` parameter exists, the JSP page displays only the text field for typing the ZIP code and the button to submit it to the server. If the `entry` parameter isn't present, the JSP page renders the images and labels for the weather forecast and then uses JSTL `<c:out>` tags to retrieve the values from the model map to populate them with data.

The final development pieces are the two Web application configuration files: `web.xml` and `spring-dispatcher-servlet.xml`. These two files are a standard part of all Spring Web MVC applications.

First, create `spring-dispatcher-servlet.xml` by following these steps:

1. **Right-click the** `web/WEB-INF` **folder in the Project Explorer view and then choose New⇨Other from the popup menu.** The Select a wizard dialog box opens.

2. **Click the arrow next to General to expand it, click File, and then click Next.** The New File dialog box opens.

3. **Type** spring-dispatcher-servlet.xml **in the File name text field and then click Finish.** The New File dialog box closes, and the new Spring configuration file appears in the Project Explorer view.

Here's the code listing for the `spring-dispatcher-servlet.xml` file:

```
<?xml version="1.0" encoding="UTF-8"?>
<beans xmlns="http://www.springframework.org/schema/beans"
        xmlns:xsi="http://www.w3.org/2001/XMLSchema-instance"
        xsi:schemaLocation="http://www.springframework.org/schema/beans
        http://www.springframework.org/schema/beans/spring-beans-2.5.xsd">
   <bean name="/artweather.htm"
   class="com.wiley.jfib.ch15.mashup.service.ArtWeatherService"/>
</beans>
```

This configuration file simply creates the Spring bean definition for the `ArtWeatherService` class and then maps a URL to it.

Now create the `web.xml` configuration file by following these steps:

1. **Right-click the `web/WEB-INF` folder in the Project Explorer view and then choose New ⇨ Other from the popup menu.** The Select a wizard dialog box opens.

2. **Click the arrow next to General to expand it, click File, and then click Next.** The New File dialog box opens.

3. **Type web.xml in the File name text field and then click Finish.** The New File dialog box closes, and the new `web.xml` configuration file appears in the Project Explorer view.

Here's the code listing for `web.xml`:

```
<?xml version="1.0" encoding="UTF-8"?>
<web-app version="2.4"
        xmlns="http://java.sun.com/xml/ns/j2ee"
        xmlns:xsi="http://www.w3.org/2001/XMLSchema-instance"
        xsi:schemaLocation="http://java.sun.com/xml/ns/j2ee
        http://java.sun.com/xml/ns/j2ee/web-app_2_4.xsd" >
  <servlet>
   <servlet-name>spring-dispatcher</servlet-name>
   <servlet-class>
        org.springframework.web.servlet.DispatcherServlet
   </servlet-class>
   <load-on-startup>1</load-on-startup>
  </servlet>

  <servlet-mapping>
    <servlet-name>spring-dispatcher</servlet-name>
    <url-pattern>*.htm</url-pattern>
  </servlet-mapping>
</web-app>
```

This configuration file defines the Spring `DispatcherServlet` and then maps it to a URL pattern that says that any URL ending in `.htm` is handled by this servlet.

 For more on these Web application configuration files, see Chapter 6.

Writing the Ant build script

The application code is complete. Now you need to create the Ant build script and build properties files to build and deploy the application. To create these two files, follow these steps:

1. **Right-click the `jfib-ch15-p01` project in the Project Explorer view and then choose New ⇨ File from the popup menu.** The New File dialog box opens.

2. **Type artweather-build.properties in the File name text field and then click Finish.** The New File dialog box closes, and the newly created `artweather-build.properties` file appears below the `jfib-ch15-p01` project in the Project Explorer view.

3. **Right-click the** `jfib-ch15-p01` **project in the Project Explorer view and then choose New ⇨ File from the popup menu.** The New File dialog box opens.

4. **Type** build.xml **in the File name text field and then click Finish.** The New File dialog box closes, and the newly created `build.xml` file appears below the `jfib-ch15-p01` project in the Project Explorer view.

The properties contained in the `artweather-build.properties` file are used by the `build.xml` build file, so first edit the `artweather-build.properties` file to match this code listing:

```
# Ant build properties for artweather
src.dir=src
web.dir=web
build.dir=${web.dir}/WEB-INF/classes

name=artweather

appserver.home=${env.JBOSS_HOME}/server/default
appserver.lib=${appserver.home}/lib
deploy.path=${appserver.home}/deploy
```

CROSS-REF For more on Ant build properties files, see Chapter 6.

This properties file contains properties for the Java source and Web file directories in the project, the build output directory, the application name, the JBoss home, and the application deployment path.

Now edit the `build.xml` file to match this code listing:

```
<?xml version="1.0" encoding="UTF-8"?>
<project name="artweather" basedir="." default="usage">
    <property environment="env"/>
     <property file="artweather-build.properties"/>

    <path id="cp">
        <fileset dir="${web.dir}/WEB-INF/lib">
            <include name="*.jar"/>
        </fileset>
        <fileset dir="${appserver.lib}">
            <include name="servlet*.jar"/>
        </fileset>
        <pathelement path="${build.dir}"/>
    </path>

    <taskdef resource="flexTasks.tasks"
        classpath="${FLEX_HOME}/ant/lib/flexTasks.jar"/>

    <target name="usage">
        <echo message=""/>
```

```
        <echo message="${name} build file"/>
        <echo message="---------------------------------"/>
        <echo message=""/>
        <echo message="Available targets are:"/>
        <echo message=""/>
        <echo message="build        --> Build the Java code and the Flex
app"/>
        <echo message="build-and-deploy       --> Deploy application
as a WAR file"/>
        <echo message=""/>
 </target>

 <target name="build" description="Compile main source tree java
files">
        <mkdir dir="${build.dir}"/>
<javac destdir="${build.dir}" source="1.5" target="1.5"
   debug="true" deprecation="false" optimize="false"
   failonerror="true">
          <src path="${src.dir}"/>
          <classpath refid="cp"/>
        </javac>
        <mxmlc file="${APP_ROOT}/ArtWeather.mxml"
          keep-generated-actionscript="false">

<load-config
        filename="${FLEX_HOME}/frameworks/flex-config.xml"/>
<source-path path-element="${FLEX_HOME}/frameworks"/>
<services>web/WEB-INF/services-config.xml</services>
        </mxmlc>
 </target>
 <target name="build-and-deploy" depends="build"
description="Deploy application as a WAR file">
        <war destfile="${name}.war"
           webxml="${web.dir}/WEB-INF/web.xml">
          <fileset dir="${web.dir}">
              <include name="**/*.*"/>
          </fileset>
        </war>
        <copy todir="${deploy.path}" preservelastmodified="true">
          <fileset dir=".">
              <include name="*.war"/>
          </fileset>
        </copy>
    </target>
</project>
```

CROSS-REF   For more on the structure and functions of Ant `build.xml` files, see Chapter 6.

Deploying and running the mashup

The Ant build script builds the application and then deploys it to the JBoss server. You need to add the build script to the Ant view to run it. To add the build script to the Ant view, follow these steps:

1. **Choose Window ⇨ Show View ⇨ Other.** The Show View dialog box opens.

2. **Click the arrow next to Ant to expand it, click Ant in the expanded menu, and then click OK.** The Ant view opens.

3. **Click the Add Buildfiles button in the Ant view.** The Buildfile Selection dialog box opens.

4. **Click the arrow next to the project name to expand it, click the `build.xml` file, and then click OK.** The Buildfile Selection dialog box closes, and the build file is added to the Ant view.

Click the arrow next to the build file entry in the Ant view to expand it to see the available build targets. The three targets you saw in the `build.xml` file appear here. Now double-click the `build-and-deploy` target to run it. The `build-and-deploy` target first launches the `build` target to compile the code, packages the application into a WAR file, and then deploys it to the JBoss server.

Once the application has been deployed successfully, you can start up JBoss to see the application in action. To start JBoss and test your application, follow these steps:

1. **Switch to the Servers view by clicking the Servers tab.**

2. **Click the Start the Server button.** Eclipse switches to the Console view while JBoss starts up. Once the server startup has completed, Eclipse switches back to the Servers view and shows the state of the JBoss server as Started.

3. **Open your Web browser, type** http://localhost:8080/artweather/artweather.htm **in the address bar, and press Enter.** The application opens and displays the screen shown in Figure 15.17.

4. **Type your ZIP code in the text field and then click the Submit button.** The application loads the weather forecast for your area, accompanied by two photos from Flickr whose metadata (name, tag, or description) matches the weather conditions for that day (see Figure 15.1).

In the next section, you learn how to create a Flex version of this application. Not much changes about the Java code, but the front end is completely different. Leave this project open in Eclipse, as you will add to it in the next section.

FIGURE 15.17

The initial entry into the `ArtWeather` application shows only the title, text field, and form submission button. The other fields that hold the data returned from the server are hidden because the entry parameter was returned in the model.

Overview of Developing Custom Flex Interfaces

The standard look of Flex components can be changed by using graphics or ActionScript code to provide a different look. The process of changing the look and feel of the standard Flex components to create a custom interface is known as *skinning*. I discuss two methods of skinning a Flex application: CSS and ActionScript.

Custom interfaces using CSS

CSS is a standard language for describing the presentation properties of a document. CSS is most widely used when writing HTML documents to keep the presentation details of the document separate from the layout and data. However, CSS can also be applied to other XML-based user interfaces, including Flex.

CSS styles can be applied to all UI components of a specific type or can be used explicitly by name to style components individually. Each UI component can use a `styleName` attribute to select a specific style from the CSS available in the application.

If you're used to working with CSS in HTML applications, you find that the CSS support in Flex isn't as robust as it is in HTML. For example, Flex CSS doesn't support nesting element styles, such as using `div p` to style a paragraph inside a `div` in an HTML document. It's also worth noting that although styles in CSS used in HTML typically use dashes between words (for example, `font-family`), Flex CSS styles use camel case notation. *Camel case* means that the style is given as a single compound word made up of one or more distinct words, with the first in lowercase and the remaining words capitalized (for example, `fontFamily`).

CSS styles are defined in an MXML file by using the `<mx:Style>` tag. The CSS styles can be placed inline within this tag directly inside the MXML file, or they can be placed in an external CSS file and referenced by using the `source` attribute of the `<mx:Style>` tag.

In addition to changing things like colors, fonts, and text decoration as you would using CSS with HTML, Flex allows you to embed resources, such as image files or SWF files, and use them as parts of a custom skin. This allows you to do more advanced skinning of your applications without needing to do any advanced ActionScript programming. The following CSS code styles the scroll bars in an application by using image files for each of the scroll bar pieces:

```
ScrollBar {
    downArrowUpSkin: Embed(source="/images/sbDownArrowStd.png");
    downArrowOverSkin: Embed(source="/images/sbDownArrowHover.png");
    downArrowDownSkin: Embed(source="/images/sbDownArrowClick.png");
    upArrowUpSkin: Embed(source="/images/sbUpArrowStd.png");
    upArrowOverSkin: Embed(source="/images/sbUpArrowHover.png");
    upArrowDownSkin: Embed(source="/images/sbUpArrowClick.png");
    thumbUpSkin: Embed(source="/images/sbThumbStd.png");
    thumbOverSkin: Embed(source="/images/sbThumbHover.png");
    thumbDownSkin: Embed(source="/images/sbThumbClick.png");
    trackSkin: Embed(source="/images/sbTrack.png");
}
```

Notice the level of control you have over the images used to skin the various pieces of the scroll bar. The up and down arrows, the scroll bar thumb (the part that does the scrolling), and the scroll bar track are all skinnable. Furthermore, you can embed different images to use when the scroll bar part is clicked, hovered over with the mouse pointer, or used for the normal mouse-up state. The `Embed` keyword here is important. It means that these image resources are compiled into the SWF file rather than being referenced externally from the application server.

Using embedded resources requires more work than simply changing colors and fonts by using CSS styles because there's work involved in creating the resources to be embedded. However, using embedded resources is a great way to ensure that you get exactly the look you want in your Flex application.

Custom interfaces using ActionScript

In addition to simple styling by using CSS style and embedded resources, Flex allows you to perform a more detailed level of skinning by creating custom ActionScript classes that extend one of a number of skin classes provided by the Flex SDK and then applying these custom classes to your Flex components.

The skins provided by the Flex SDK can be found in the `mx.skins` package. They include the following:

- `ProgrammaticSkin` is the base class for skin classes that draw themselves entirely programmatically.

- `Border` extends `ProgrammaticSkin` and is the base class for skin classes that draw borders.

- `RectangularBorder` extends `Border` and is specifically used as a base class for skin classes that draw rectangular borders.

To skin a UI component by using ActionScript, you first create an ActionScript class that extends one of these ActionScript skin base classes. These classes have an `updateDisplayList()` method that must be overridden by the extending skin class to perform the drawing necessary to implement the skin.

CROSS-REF For more on ActionScript class structure and extending another ActionScript class, see Chapter 3.

In terms of complexity, CSS styles are much less difficult to implement. Programmatic style by using ActionScript requires a fairly deep understanding of the Drawing API of the Flash Player — specifically, the `Graphics` object. The upside of using ActionScript to skin your components is that it offers a much higher degree of control and flexibility to customizing your interfaces. The trade-off between ease of implementation and fine-grained control is something you must take into consideration when deciding which skinning method to use in your applications.

Creating the Flex mashup UI

To demonstrate each of these skinning techniques, you can create a Flex UI for the `ArtWeather` mashup application. You use the same BlazeDS messaging technique used in the chat application to send a message to the server and receive the mashup data back. Only a small addition to the `ArtWeatherService` class and some additions to the Eclipse project build path are required on the Java side. Some configuration files need to be added to the Web side in addition to the new MXML application and HTML container for the SWF file. Finally, a few additions to the Ant build and build properties files are needed.

CROSS-REF For more on using BlazeDS and step-by-step instructions on building the chat application, see Chapter 14.

First, import the Blaze DS libraries into your `WEB-INF/lib` directory. These libraries need to be deployed with the application to use BlazeDS. To import the BlazeDS libraries, follow these steps:

1. **Right-click the `lib` folder in the Project Explorer view and then choose Import from the popup menu.** The Import Select dialog box opens.

2. **Click the arrow next to the General item to expand it, choose File System from the list, and then click the Next button.** The Import from File system dialog box opens.

3. **Click the Browse button next to the From directory text field.** The Import from directory dialog box opens.

4. **Navigate to the `lib` directory below your extracted `BlazeDS` directory, select it, and then click OK.** The directory appears in the left pane of the Import from directory dialog box. Clicking the `lib` directory displays its contents in the right pane of the dialog box.

5. **Click the `lib` folder in the left pane and then click the check box next to each JAR file in the right pane.**

6. **Click Finish.** The `BlazeDS` library JAR files you just added appear beneath the `web/WEB-INF/lib` folder.

Next, you want to add these JAR files to the build path of your Eclipse project. To add the BlazeDS JAR files to the build path, follow these steps:

1. **Right-click the `jfib-ch15-p01` project in the Project Explorer view and then choose Build Path ⇨ Configure Build Path from the popup menu.** The Java Build Properties dialog box opens with the Libraries tab selected.

2. **Click the Add JARs button.** The JAR Selection dialog box opens.

3. **Click the arrow next to the `jfib-ch15-p01` project to expand it.**

4. **Click the arrow next to `web` to expand it.**

5. **Click the arrow next to `WEB-INF` to expand it and then click the arrow next to `lib` to expand it.**

6. **Click all the JARs in the list and then click OK.** The JAR Selection dialog box closes, and the JAR files are added to the list in the Library tab.

7. **Click OK.** The Java Build Properties dialog box closes.

Now all the libraries you need are in place. Next, you need to import some Flex classes into the `ArtWeatherService` class. Open the `ArtWeatherService` class in the editor by double-clicking it in the Project Explorer view. Add these `import` statements below the rest of the `import` statements at the top of the file:

```
import flex.messaging.messages.AsyncMessage;
import flex.messaging.messages.Message;
import flex.messaging.services.MessageService;
import flex.messaging.services.ServiceAdapter;
```

Next, change the class declaration statement (the statement that begins with `public class ArtWeatherService`) so that the `ArtWeatherService` extends the BlazeDS `ServiceAdapter` class. When you have done so, the class declaration should look like this:

```
public class ArtWeatherService extends ServiceAdapter implements
    Controller
```

Once you've made this change, Eclipse adds a squiggly red line beneath `ArtWeatherService`. If you mouse over `ArtWeatherService`, you see that `ServiceAdapter` is an abstract class with an abstract method called `invoke()` that you must implement when extending it. Add the `invoke()` method below the existing `handleRequest()` method. Here's the code listing for the `invoke()` method:

```
    /* (non-Javadoc)
     * @see flex.messaging.services.ServiceAdapter#invoke(flex.
    messaging.messages.Message)
     */
    @Override
public Object invoke(Message arg0) {
    AsyncMessage zipMsg = (AsyncMessage)arg0;
    String zip = (String)zipMsg.getBody();
    try {
        Map<String,String> model =
            buildModelForZipCode(zip);
        zipMsg.setBody(model);
        MessageService messageService =
            (MessageService)getDestination().getService();
        messageService.pushMessageToClients(zipMsg, false);
    }
    catch(Exception e) {
        e.printStackTrace();
    }
    return null;
}
```

The `invoke()` method in this class is much like the one in the chat application's `ChatService` class. In this application, however, instead of just returning a simple string value, `invoke()` returns a `Map` object that contains name-value pairs. Much like in the JSP view, the Flex application extracts the values from this object and then uses them to populate the UI components of the application.

That finishes the changes required on the Java side. Now you can move on to the changes required for the Web configuration. The first thing that's needed is the Flex `services-config.xml` file. Remember that this file defines the BlazeDS channels and services available to the Flex client for communicating with the code on the Java side. To create this file, follow these steps:

1. **Right-click the `web/WEB-INF` folder in the Project Explorer view and then choose New ⇨ Other from the popup menu.** The Select a wizard dialog box opens.

2. **Click the arrow next to General to expand it, click File, and then click Next.** The New File dialog box opens.

3. **Type services-config.xml in the File name text field and then click Finish.** The New File dialog box closes, and the new BlazeDS configuration file appears in the Project Explorer view.

Here's the code listing for the `services-config.xml` file:

```
<?xml version="1.0" encoding="UTF-8"?>
<services-config>
    <services>
        <default-channels>
            <channel ref="my-http"/>
        </default-channels>
      <service id="message-service"
          class="flex.messaging.services.MessageService">
          <adapters>
            <adapter-definition id="Ch15AWAdapter"
              class="com.wiley.jfib.ch15.mashup.service.ArtWeatherService"/>
          </adapters>
          <destination id="ArtWeatherAdapter">
            <adapter ref="Ch15AWAdapter"/>
          </destination>
      </service>
    </services>
    <channels>
      <!-- Simple HTTP -->
      <channel-definition id="my-http"
          class="mx.messaging.channels.HTTPChannel">
          <endpoint
            uri="http://localhost:8080/artweather/messagebroker/http"
            class="flex.messaging.endpoints.HTTPEndpoint"/>
      </channel-definition>
    </channels>
  </services-config>
```

This is a standard BlazeDS configuration file. The thing to note here is the destination ID: `ArtWeatherAdapter`. You use this destination later when you create the MXML file for the application. The messages sent to this destination use the HTTP channel created here, which directs them to the endpoint in the Java code by using the `MessageBrokerServlet`.

CROSS-REF For more on the structure of the `services-config.xml` file, see Chapter 14.

The `MessageBrokerServlet` definition, as well as some other Flex configuration details, must now be added to the `web.xml` configuration file for the Web application. Double-click `web.xml` to open it in the Eclipse editor. There are two blocks of XML that need to be added. First, add this block of XML to the file between the opening `<web-app>` tag and the `<servlet>` tag for the `SpringDispatcherServlet`:

```
<!-- Http Flex Session attribute and binding listener support -->
<listener>
```

```
            <listener-class>
               flex.messaging.HttpFlexSession
            </listener-class>
         </listener>

         <!-- MessageBroker Servlet -->
         <servlet>
            <servlet-name>MessageBrokerServlet</servlet-name>
            <servlet-class>
               flex.messaging.MessageBrokerServlet
            </servlet-class>
            <init-param>
                  <param-name>services.configuration.file</param-name>
                  <param-value>/WEB-INF/services-config.xml</param-value>
            </init-param>
             <load-on-startup>1</load-on-startup>
         </servlet>
```

Next, add this block of XML just above the existing `<servlet-mapping>` tag:

```
      <servlet-mapping>
            <servlet-name>MessageBrokerServlet</servlet-name>
            <url-pattern>/messagebroker/*</url-pattern>
      </servlet-mapping>
```

The Flex `MessageBrokerServlet` is now set up to receive channel requests from subscribers. The `MessageBrokerServlet` reads in the configuration from `services-config.xml` and uses that information to set up the destination endpoints and channels needed by the Flex client.

Everything is configured now, so create the Flex application MXML file by following these steps:

1. **Right-click the** Web **folder in the Project Explorer view and then choose New ⇨ Other from the popup menu.** The Select a wizard dialog box opens.

2. **Click the arrow next to General to expand it, click File, and then click Next.** The New File dialog box opens.

3. **Type** ArtWeather.mxml **in the File name text field and then click Finish.** The New File dialog box closes, and the `ArtWeather.mxml` file appears in the Project Explorer view.

Edit the `ArtWeather.mxml` file so that it matches this code listing:

```
      <?xml version="1.0" encoding="utf-8"?>
      <mx:Application
         xmlns:mx="http://www.adobe.com/2006/mxml"
         creationComplete="subscribeToWeather();"
         verticalGap="15">
         <mx:Script>
                  <![CDATA[
```

```
import mx.controls.Alert;
import mx.messaging.events.MessageAckEvent;
import mx.messaging.messages.AsyncMessage;
import mx.messaging.events.MessageEvent;
import mx.messaging.events.MessageFaultEvent;
import mx.managers.CursorManager;

private function subscribeToWeather():void
{
        consumer.subscribe();
}

public function getWeather():void
{
        if(zip.text.length != 5 || isNaN(zip.text as Number))
        {
                Alert.show("Please enter a 5 digit zip code");
                return;
        }
        var msg:AsyncMessage = new AsyncMessage();
        msg.body = zip.text;
        producer.send(msg);
        zip.text = "";
        CursorManager.setBusyCursor();
}

public function resultHandler(re:MessageEvent):void
{
        var model:Object = re.message.body;
        cityStateLabel.text = "Forecast for" +
                model["cityState"];
        todayPhoto.source = model["todayPhotoUrl"];
        tomorrowPhoto.source = model["tomorrowPhotoUrl"];
        todayForecast.text = "Today: " +
                model["todayCondition"];
        todayHigh.text = "High: " + model["todayHigh"];
        todayLow.text = "Low: " + model["todayLow"];
        tomorrowForecast.text = "Tomorrow: " +
                model["tomorrowCondition"];
        tomorrowHigh.text = "High: " + model["tomorrowHigh"];
        tomorrowLow.text = "Low: " + model["tomorrowLow"];
        CursorManager.removeBusyCursor();
}
```

```
                  public function faultHandler(fe:MessageFaultEvent):void
                  {
                          Alert.show("FAULT: " + fe.faultString);
                          CursorManager.removeBusyCursor();
                  }

                  public function acknowledge(event:MessageAckEvent):void
                  {
                  }
          ]]>
</mx:Script>
<mx:Producer id="producer"
        destination="ArtWeatherAdapter"
        acknowledge="acknowledge(event);"
        fault="faultHandler(event);"
/>

<mx:Consumer id="consumer"
        destination="ArtWeatherAdapter"
        message="resultHandler(event);"
        acknowledge="acknowledge(event);"
        fault="faultHandler(event);"
/>
<mx:Label id="headerLabel" horizontalCenter="0"
        text="ArtWeather - More Than Just A Forecast"
        width="453" height="60"/>
<mx:Label id="cityStateLabel" horizontalCenter="0" text="" width="453"/>

<mx:HBox horizontalGap="50">
        <mx:Image left="10" id="todayPhoto"/>
        <mx:Image right="10" id="tomorrowPhoto"/>
</mx:HBox>
<mx:HBox horizontalGap="50">
        <mx:Label left="10" id="todayForecast" text=""/>
        <mx:Label right="10" id="tomorrowForecast" text=""/>
</mx:HBox>
<mx:HBox horizontalGap="50">
        <mx:Label left="10" id="todayHigh" text=""/>
        <mx:Label right="10" id="tomorrowHigh" text=""/>
</mx:HBox>
<mx:HBox horizontalGap="50">
        <mx:Label left="10" id="todayLow" text=""/>
        <mx:Label right="10" id="tomorrowLow" text=""/>
</mx:HBox>
<mx:TextInput id="zip" horizontalCenter="0"/>
```

```
<mx:Button id="submit" horizontalCenter="0" click="getWeather()"
label="Submit"/>
<mx:Label id="yahooCredit" text="Weather data provided by Yahoo! Weather."
horizontalCenter="0"/>
<mx:Label id="flickrCredit" text="Photos retrieved from Flickr. All photos
are the property of their owners. ArtWeather claims no ownership."
horizontalCenter="0"/>
</mx:Application>
```

CROSS-REF For more on the MXML tags in this example and the structure of a Flex application in general, see Chapter 4.

The <mx:Producer> and <mx:Consumer> tags are set up to send and receive data by using the ArtWeatherAdapter destination. In the getWeather() function, the ZIP code is taken from the text field and then sent to the Java server by using the producer. The result handler function defined in the producer tag is invoked when the data from the Java server is returned. The Map object from the Java side is returned as a plain object in Flex. The values are retrieved from the object by using the names used when they were put in the Map on the Java side. These values populate the UI elements.

Create another new file by using the same steps you used to create the ArtWeather.mxml file. Name the file ArtWeather.html. This is the HTML wrapper for the compiled SWF file. Edit the file so that it matches this code listing:

```
<html>
<head>
<title>ArtWeather - More Than Just A Forecast</title>
</head>
<body>
<object classid="clsid:D27CDB6E-AE6D-11cf-96B8-444553540000" codebase="http://
   download.macromedia.com/pub/shockwave/cabs/flash/swflash.
   cab#version=9,0,124,0" width="100%" height="100%"
id="ArtWeather.swf">
  <param name="flashvars" value="versionChecked=true">
  <param name="src" value="ArtWeather.swf">
  <embed pluginspage="http://www.macromedia.com/go/getflashplayer" width="100%"
   height="100%"
    flashvars="versionChecked=true"
    src="ArtWeather.swf"
    name="Art Weather"
  />
</object>
</body>
</html>
```

Finally, to build this application and deploy it to the JBoss server, you need to add a couple of things to the `artweather-build.properties` file and the `build.xml` build script file. First, add these lines to the end of the `artweather-build.properties` file:

```
APP_ROOT=web
FLEX_HOME=c:/flex/sdk
```

Next, add a couple of items to the `build.xml` file. First, add this XML code between the end `</path>` tag and the `<target name="usage">` tag:

```
<taskdef resource="flexTasks.tasks"
    classpath="${FLEX_HOME}/ant/lib/flexTasks.jar"/>
```

Finally, add the following `<mxmlc>` task tag after the ending `</javac>` tag inside the `<target name="build">` tag:

```
<mxmlc file="${APP_ROOT}/ArtWeather.mxml"
   keep-generated-actionscript="false">
   <load-config filename="${FLEX_HOME}/frameworks/flex-config.xml"/>
   <source-path path-element="${FLEX_HOME}/frameworks"/>
   <services>web/WEB-INF/services-config.xml</services>
</mxmlc>
```

Make sure that all your files have been saved and then click the Ant view tab to switch to the Ant view. Double-click the `build-and-deploy` target. The Java code and MXML code compile, and then the application is packaged up into a WAR file and deployed to the JBoss server.

Follow these steps to test the `ArtWeather` application:

1. **Click the Servers tab to switch to the Servers view.**
2. **Click the green Start button to start up JBoss.**
3. **Once JBoss has started, open your Web browser, type** http://localhost:8080/ artweather/ArtWeather.html **in the address bar, and then press Enter.** The application opens and displays the text entry field for the ZIP code.
4. **Type your ZIP code and then click the Submit button.** After a short time, the application displays your two-day forecast and a photo for each day. See Figure 15.18 for an example.

Skinning the Flex mashup UI

This application currently uses the default Flex styles for all the UI elements. You skin the fonts and colors of the application by using CSS and then replace the default Flex button with one of your own. You need three buttons: `bn-down.png`, `bn-up.png`, and `bn-over.png`. They should be approximately 125 × 25. Place them in the Web directory along with your MXML and HTML files.

FIGURE 15.18

The Flex version of the `ArtWeather` application. This application uses the default Flex properties for all the UI elements.

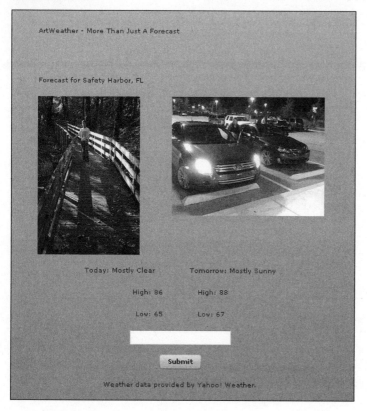

Create the CSS file for your application in Eclipse by following these steps:

1. **Right-click the `Web` folder in the Project Explorer view and then choose New ⇨ Other from the popup menu.** The Select a wizard dialog box opens.

2. **Click the arrow next to General to expand it, click File, and then click Next.** The New File dialog box opens.

3. **Type ArtWeather.css in the File name text field and then click Finish.** The New File dialog box closes, and the `ArtWeather.css` file appears in the Project Explorer view.

Edit the `ArtWeather.css` file so that it matches this code listing:

```
Application {
    backgroundColor: #000000;
```

```
}
Button {
    upSkin: Embed("bn-up.png");
    downSkin: Embed("bn-down.png");
    overSkin: Embed("bn-over.png");
}
.headerLabel {
    fontFamily: Verdana;
    fontSize: 18pt;
    fontWeight: bold;
    color: #FFFFFF;
}
.cityStateLabel {
    fontFamily: Verdana;
    fontSize: 12pt;
    fontWeight: bold;
    color: #FFFFFF;
}
.dataLabel {
    fontFamily: Verdana;
    fontSize: 10pt;
    color: #FFFFFF;
}
```

In this CSS file, a single style is being applied to the `Application` and `Button` types. The `Button` CSS style is a good example of CSS skinning. In this case, the actual graphics used to display the buttons are being swapped out; this happens instead of new colors and fonts being applied to the application. Remember that `Embed` means that the graphics files are compiled into the final SWF file and don't need to be referenced from or even exist in the Web application. The resulting SWF file is larger and thus takes longer to load initially, but the images load more quickly. While this may not make a big difference for an application with one button, it's important to know that the option exists.

The three remaining styles are named with a leading dot. They're not applied to any UI component type globally. Instead, individual components apply them by using the `styleName` attribute.

To import this style sheet into the MXML file, add this `<mx:Style>` tag directly after the `<mx:Application>` tag:

```
<mx:Style source="ArtWeather.css"/>
```

Finally, add `styleName` attributes to each of the `<mx:Label>` tags. The `headerLabel` and `cityStateLabel` styles should be used in the labels with those IDs. The `dataLabel` style should be used for the rest of the labels.

Save the files. Go to the Servers view and then stop JBoss. Switch back to the Ant view and then run the `build-and-deploy` target once again. When the build has finished, restart JBoss and then load the application in your browser again. The look and feel of the application have changed, and the button graphic has been swapped out with your `bn-up.png` file. Fill in your ZIP code and then click the button, noticing the mouse over and mouse down states of the button changing as you do. The final application should look something like Figure 15.19.

FIGURE 15.19

Skinning the Flex application by using CSS has completely changed the look and feel of the interface.

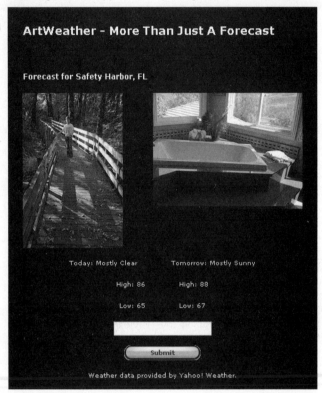

Summary

In this chapter, you learned about Web application mashups, which retrieve data from multiple data sources and combine that data into new services. You learned about third-party libraries, such as flickrj, a Java implementation of the Flickr API. You created a mashup by using data from a Yahoo! Weather RSS feed and Flickr, as well as using the Apache `commons-httpclient` library, XPath, and the Flickr API. Finally, you learned how to enhance the default look and feel of a Flex application by using skinning with both CSS and ActionScript code.

Chapter 16

Advanced Development

I n the previous chapters, I discussed a number of topics and concepts that you can use to create Web applications by using Java and Flex. These were all stand-alone applications with a singular purpose, such as a storefront for Internet shopping.

Another domain of applications involves those that serve the needs of a business or organization. These applications often serve multiple types of users with different needs, and data often needs to be shared among these applications. In this chapter, I discuss some of the more advanced needs of these applications and a number of libraries that can help you implement these solutions by using Java and Flex.

IN THIS CHAPTER

Advanced Java concepts

Advanced Flex concepts

Advanced Java Concepts

Writing the types of applications mentioned above is typically a large undertaking. In addition to the main business logic of these applications, the development team must address global concerns that encompass the set of applications as a whole, such as authentication, security, and reporting. Fortunately, Java libraries exist to help with all these concerns. Let's take a closer look at enterprise application development in Java and some of the libraries available to help you in developing these types of applications.

Enterprise-level Java development

Enterprise can mean many things in terms of software. Some consider enterprise software to be applications used in the management and internal processes of businesses. This definition encompasses things such as customer relationship management (CRM), sales force automation, and workflow. Others refer to any large-scale software application as an enterprise application. Whatever the definition, there are a few things that most enterprise applications need to concern themselves with:

- **Security.** An enterprise application typically involves some type of networked functionality, be it HTTPS requests in Web applications or pure socket connections in intranet applications. It's important to allow access to an application to only those users who are meant to have access. Furthermore, users may be assigned one or more user roles, each of which may grant some level of access to the user.

- **Interoperability.** Enterprise applications rarely live in a vacuum. Often, an organization deploys multiple related applications, such as a sales application for end users and an inventory application for internal users. The inventory application should be able to inform the sales application when inventory levels are low. Communication and interoperability between Web applications are vital to ensuring that systems such as these run smoothly.

- **Scalability.** As the number of users of an application grows and the amount of data handled by the application grows with it, it's critical to ensure that the application can handle the increased load. Careful upfront planning about the expected application load and data amounts is vital in making sure that your application can scale as needed to meet demand.

Although dedicated hardware and load-balancing solutions are typically used to handle scalability issues, Java libraries are available that help address each of the other two concerns. Let's look at each one in more detail.

Enterprise application security with Spring Security

Security in an enterprise application focuses on two basic questions: "Who are you?" and "What are you allowed to do?" In each of these cases, the "you" in question is known as the *principal*. The principal doesn't necessarily need to be a user sitting at a computer terminal. It could just as easily be another application calling into a Web service or some hardware device that receives data from the Web application.

The "Who are you?" question is answered through authentication. *Authentication* is the process of providing a set of credentials to the application to establish identity within that application. The combination of username and password is a typical means of user authentication for an application. Supplying such credentials may be required for any access to the application or may be required only for user-specific areas of the application, such as profile information or payment method details. Spring Security supports many of the most widely used authentication mechanisms, such as basic HTTP authentication, LDAP (Lightweight Directory Access Protocol, a directory querying protocol used by many organizations for resource access across a network), and others.

Once a user is authenticated (that is, the application knows who the principal is), the question of what the user is allowed to do comes into play. When a user attempts to access some piece of an application, the application determines whether the user has *authorization* to do what he or she is trying to do. If so, the application allows the user to access that functionality. If not, the user is presented with an error page or message stating that he or she isn't authorized to access that functionality. Authorization can also be used to completely hide areas of an application from a user. For example, a view can be presented with one or more links omitted based on the currently authenticated user's authorization.

The Spring Framework provides its own security framework called Spring Security. Spring Security was formerly known as Acegi Security but was rebranded to better identify its ties with the core Spring Framework.

Spring Security's chief advantage is that it allows you to keep your main application code and business logic separate from any security code needed to perform the authentication and authorization necessary for your application. Spring Security handles authentication and authorization through a series of interceptors and filters. An *interceptor* matches requests to an application that match a provided URL pattern and hands the request off to a filter chain to deal with the authentication and authorization requirements of the application.

Adding Spring Security to your application can be as simple as adding some configuration details to your `web.xml` configuration file and the Spring application context configuration XML file. As a simple example, let's look at the configuration for an application that contains one Spring controller that can be accessed by anyone and one that requires a user to be authenticated as an administrator user.

> **CROSS-REF** For more on the configuration found in `web.xml` and Spring application context configuration files, see Chapter 6.

The configuration in `web.xml` involves adding a servlet filter that sends requests through a Spring `FilterToBeanProxy` filter class:

```
<filter>
    <filter-name>springSecurityFilterChain</filter-name>
    <filter-class>
            org.springframework.web.filter.DelegatingFilterProxy
    </filter-class>
</filter>
<filter-mapping>
    <filter-name>springSecurityFilterChain</filter-name>
    <url-pattern>/*</url-pattern>
</filter-mapping>
```

The `DelegatingFilterProxy` class is the entry point into the Spring Security filter chain. The `DelegatingFilterProxy` is defined with the Spring application context. The configuration looks like this:

```
<?xml version="1.0" encoding="UTF-8"?>
<beans:beans xmlns="http://www.springframework.org/schema/security"
    xmlns:beans="http://www.springframework.org/schema/beans"
    xmlns:xsi="http://www.w3.org/2001/XMLSchema-instance"
    xsi:schemaLocation="http://www.springframework.org/schema/beans
```

```
http://www.springframework.org/schema/beans/spring-beans-2.0.xsd
http://www.springframework.org/schema/security
http://www.springframework.org/schema/security/spring-security-2.0.1.xsd">
    <http auto-config="true">
        <intercept-url pattern="/generalResource.html"
            access="ROLE_USER" />
        <intercept-url pattern="/adminResource.html"
            access="ROLE_ADMIN" />
        <intercept-url pattern="/**"
            access="IS_AUTHENTICATED_ANONYMOUSLY" />
    </http>
    <authentication-provider>
        <password-encoder hash="md5"/>
        <user-service>
        <user name="appadmin"
            password="2740231e18bd5c7bebb98628ab83c79f"
            authorities="ROLE_ADMIN,ROLE_USER" />
        <user name="chuck"
            password="9bd97baef2b853ec00cc3cffd269f679"
            authorities="ROLE_USER" />
        <user name="matt"
            password="b312ba4ffd5245fa2a1ab819ec0d0347"
            authorities="ROLE_USER" />
        </user-service>
    </authentication-provider>
</beans:beans>
```

This configuration file defines a few URL interceptors that will intercept requests for those URLs and then pass them through the Spring Security filter chain. The `/generalResource.html` URL is authorized to be accessed by principals granted the `ROLE_USER` authority. The `/admin Resource.html` URL is authorized to be accessed by principals granted the `ROLE_ADMIN` authority. The last interceptor uses the pattern `/**`, which matches any URL. It's marked as `IS_ AUTHENTICATED_ANONYMOUSLY`, meaning that no authentication or authorization is needed to access this resource. It's important to note that the interceptors will match more specific entries first, so the two specific URLs will match and check for the proper authority before the wildcard URL pattern is checked. This prevents those specific URLs from inadvertently matching the wildcard URL pattern and being authenticated anonymously.

The authentication provider at the end of the configuration file provides the means of authenticating the credentials passed into the application when a login is attempted. In this case, the usernames and passwords are contained in the configuration file, but authentication providers can be configured that check the credentials against a database table, an LDAP database, or even a plain text property file. The passwords in this file are MD5-hashed for added security, as noted by the `<password-encoder>` tag. It's possible to use plain text passwords here — this configuration file is located in the `WEB-INF` directory of the Web application, so the user can't access it through a browser. However, using plain text passwords in general isn't a good security practice.

When a user successfully logs into this application, an `Authentication` object is created that contains a `UserDetails` object with the user's credentials and granted authorities. When the `appadmin` user logs in, he or she has both the `ROLE_ADMIN` and `ROLE_USER` authorities, so he or she can access both of the secured pages. The `chuck` and `matt` users have only the `ROLE_USER` authority, so they can access the `/generalResource.html` page but not the `/adminResource.html` page. If a user without the proper authority tries to access `/adminResource.html`, he or she is presented with an access denied page.

Spring Security allows you to quickly set up basic authentication and authorization services for your application. It's also flexible enough to meet far more complex needs, such as integration with an LDAP server, making it a great choice for any Spring-based Web application.

Enterprise application interoperability with JMS

Applications within an enterprise often need to communicate with one another. For example, an inventory control system might keep track of what supplies an enterprise has in stock. When any supplies fall below a certain level, the inventory control system sends a message to the ordering system to let it know that supplies need to be ordered.

The Java Messaging System (JMS) API is the Java standard for allowing different applications or components of the same application to send and receive messages to and from one another. JMS provides a simple but highly configurable set of interfaces to facilitate this communication. JMS can be used to send messages directly to a single known location with high reliability or to send messages to multiple unknown subscribers.

JMS can be used in either of two messaging domains. A *messaging domain* is a specific set of rules defined by the JMS specification for each of the two messaging types. These two types are:

- **Point-to-point.** In point-to-point messaging, messages sent by a message producer are received by a single consumer. Messages sent by each producer are held in a message queue until the message consumer is ready to receive them. Thus, the message consumer doesn't need to be running at the time a message is sent by the producer in order to receive it. Messages are held in the message queue until they're received by the consumer or until they expire. When a consumer does receive a message, it must acknowledge successful receipt of the message to the producer. This messaging domain is most useful when high-reliability messaging between two specific components is necessary.

- **Publish/subscribe.** In the publish/subscribe messaging model, the producer sends each of its messages to a messaging topic. A *topic* is somewhat akin to a chat room in a chat application. Consumers in this model subscribe to one or more topics, and each message sent to a topic is received by all of the consumers subscribed to that topic. Typically, each of the consumers registers a message listener, which constantly listens for new messages and passes them along to the consumer as they arrive. The publish/subscribe messaging domain is useful when unknown types and numbers of components or applications might be listening for a certain message.

The publish/subscribe messaging domain should look familiar to you from the chat application in Chapter 14. That application uses Blaze DS to configure messaging channels and destinations, and includes producers and consumers in the Flex code. The Blaze DS messaging channels and destinations are roughly equivalent to topics in the JMS publish/subscribe messaging domain. The Flex <mx:Producer> and <mx:Consumer> components are analogous to the producers and consumers in the JMS API.

CROSS-REF   For more on Blaze DS and the Flex chat application, see Chapter 14.

Let's take a look at some JMS code. The following two code listings show a message producer and consumer class, respectively. These classes use the point-to-point JMS domain, meaning that the producer places messages in a message queue and the consumer retrieves messages from the message queue. This example doesn't go into detail about how to set up the JMS queue. Setting up JMS queues and topics varies from server to server. The documentation for the application server you're using explains how to configure JMS. These examples use a JMS queue named `"queue/test Queue"` — JBoss comes preconfigured with a JMS queue using this name, so no extra configuration is required to use this queue.

Here's the code listing for the JMS message producer:

```
import javax.jms.*;
import javax.naming.InitialContext;
import javax.naming.NamingException;

public class JMSPointToPointProducer
{
    QueueConnection queueConnection;
    QueueSession queueSession;
    Queue queue;

    public void sendTextMessageToQueue(String message) throws
JMSException, NamingException
    {
        InitialContext context = new InitialContext();
        Object resource = context.lookup("ConnectionFactory");
        QueueConnectionFactory queueConnectionFactory =
(QueueConnectionFactory) resource;
        queueConnection = queueConnectionFactory.
createQueueConnection();
        queueSession = queueConnection.createQueueSession(false,
QueueSession.AUTO_ACKNOWLEDGE);
        queueConnection.start();

        queue = (Queue) context.lookup("queue/testQueue");
        QueueSender queueSender = queueSession.createSender(queue);
```

```
            TextMessage textMessage = queueSession.
    createTextMessage(message);
            queueSender.send(textMessage);
            queueSender.close();
        }

        public void cleanup() throws JMSException
        {
            queueConnection.stop();
            queueSession.close();
            queueConnection.close();
        }

        public static void main(String args[])
            throws Exception
        {
            System.out.println("Starting message producer . . . ");
            JMSPointToPointProducer producer =
                    new JMSPointToPointProducer();
            producer.sendTextMessageToQueue("Hello, Consumer!");
            producer.cleanup();
            System.out.println("Ending message producer . . . ");
            System.exit(0);
        }
    }
```

The interesting method in this class is the sendTextMessageToQueue() method. The first couple of lines get the InitialContext, which is used in enterprise Java applications as a starting point for retrieving named resources configured in the application server by using the Java Naming and Directory Interface (JNDI). JNDI provides a standard Java API for looking up objects by name in a directory-like structure. The first thing that gets retrieved is a JMS QueueConnection Factory object. JBoss places both the point-to-point and publish/subscribe connection factories under the same JNDI name, "ConnectionFactory", so it's necessary to cast the object received from the InitialContext to the proper type — QueueConnection Factory, in this case.

The QueueConnectionFactory is used to create a QueueConnection, which in turn is used to create a QueueSession. The QueueSession is used to manage the queue that this producer deals with. Next, the start() method of the QueueConnection is called, which starts up the connection's message delivery operations. The specific queue that messages are sent to is also retrieved from JNDI by using the name "queue/testQueue". A QueueSender object is retrieved from the QueueSession by using this queue. The session is also used to create a TextMessage object. TextMessage is a subinterface of the JMS message interface, which all messages sent using JMS must implement. Finally, the QueueSender sends the text message, which is placed in the queue, waiting to be retrieved.

Here's the code listing for the JMS message consumer:

```java
import javax.jms.*;
import javax.naming.InitialContext;
import javax.naming.NamingException;

public class JMSPointToPointConsumer
{
    QueueConnection queueConnection;
    QueueSession queueSession;
    Queue queue;

    public static class MessageListenerImpl implements
    MessageListener
    {
        public boolean messageReceived = false;

        public void onMessage(Message msg)
        {
            TextMessage textMessage = (TextMessage) msg;
            try
            {
                System.out.println("Got A Message:    "
                        + textMessage.getText());
                messageReceived = true;
            }

            catch(Exception ex)
            {
                ex.printStackTrace();
            }
        }
    }

    public void listenToQueue() throws JMSException, NamingException
    {
        InitialContext context = new InitialContext();
        Object resource = context.lookup("ConnectionFactory");
        QueueConnectionFactory queueConnectionFactory =
                (QueueConnectionFactory) resource;
        queueConnection = queueConnectionFactory
                .createQueueConnection();
        queue = (Queue) context.lookup("queue/testQueue");
        queueSession = queueConnection.createQueueSession(false,
                QueueSession.AUTO_ACKNOWLEDGE);
        queueConnection.start();
        QueueReceiver queueReceiver = queueSession
                .createReceiver(queue);
```

```
        MessageListenerImpl listener = new MessageListenerImpl();
        queueReceiver.setMessageListener(listener);
    }

    public static void main(String args[])
        throws Exception
    {
        System.out.println("Starting message consumer . . . ");
        JMSPointToPointConsumer consumer =
            new JMSPointToPointConsumer();
        consumer.listenToQueue();
    }
}
```

The consumer class contains an internal class called `MessageListenerImpl`, which implements the JMS `MessageListener` interface. This interface contains a single method, `onMessage()`, which is executed upon receipt of a message from a queue. The message receiver is set up in the `listenToQueue()` method. A great deal of the setup in this method is the same as the setup in the `sendTextMessageToQueue()` method in the JMS producer example — the JMS `QueueConnectionFactory` and other queue objects are created in exactly the same way. Rather than creating a `QueueSender` object, the `QueueSession` is used to create a `QueueReceiver`. The `MessageListenerImpl` class is registered with the `QueueReceiver`, and at this point, it's ready for messages to come into the queue.

In these examples, simple text messages are being sent and received, but JMS allows more complex messages to be sent using serializable objects, collections of objects, or maps of name-value pairs. In this way, JMS provides great flexibility to share important data between modules and applications.

More library components

Many of the Java libraries and frameworks that I discuss in this book are general-purpose libraries that you will find yourself using in many or all of your Java Web applications. In addition to these libraries, there are a number of libraries for just about any specific piece of functionality that you might need in a Java Web application. In this section, I highlight a few that have proved especially useful in meeting some specific needs.

Jasper Reports and iText

Many applications have some sort of reporting requirements. Administrator applications for online stores might need reports for inventory, product sales, customer purchasing trends, and other data that helps an organization's decision-makers know how the business is performing. For applications written in Java, reporting can be added through the use of the Jasper Reports framework. Jasper Reports is an open-source Java reporting engine that adds reporting functionality to enterprise Java applications. Jasper Reports can output reports in many formats that can be viewed onscreen or printed, including PDF, HTML, and CSV (comma-separated values). You can find more information and a download link for Jasper Reports at `http://jasperforge.org/plugins/project/project_home.php?group_id=102`.

The design of a Jasper Report is defined in a JRXML file. JRXML is a dialect of XML specific to Jasper Reports, defining the report structure, data source, and layout. These JRXML files are compiled, either at runtime or during the application build process, into binary files with a .jasper extension. The .jasper file is populated with data from a specified data source. The data can be retrieved by using a query specified in the JRXML file and run against a java.sql.Connection object that wraps an active database connection, or it can come from a Java class that implements the Jasper Reports net.sf.jasperreports.engine.JRDataSource interface. This interface defines methods for retrieving the data for a given field and advancing to the next record in the data set used by the report.

The following two code listings show a very simple Jasper Report implementation. It doesn't use any dynamic data, but it does create two parameters to pass into the report structure definition.

First, here's the JRXML report definition:

```xml
<?xml version="1.0"?>
<!DOCTYPE jasperReport
  PUBLIC "-//JasperReports//DTD Report Design//EN"
  "http://jasperreports.sourceforge.net/dtds/jasperreport.dtd">

<jasperReport name="Simple Jasper Reports Example">
<parameter name="name" class="java.lang.String"/>
<parameter name="age" class="java.lang.String"/>
 <detail>
    <band height="40">
   <staticText>
   <reportElement x="100" y="0" width="200" height="20"/>
   <text><![CDATA[Hello. My name is ]]></text>
   </staticText>
   <textField evaluationTime="Report">
   <reportElement x="183" y="0" width="75" height="20"/>
   <textFieldExpression class="java.lang.String">
   <![CDATA[$P{name}]]>
   </textFieldExpression>
   </textField>
   <staticText>
   <reportElement x="211" y="0" width="200" height="20"/>
   <text><![CDATA[, and I am ]]></text>
   </staticText>
   <textField evaluationTime="Report">
   <reportElement x="257" y="0" width="75" height="20"/>
   <textFieldExpression class="java.lang.String">
   <![CDATA[$P{age}]]>
   </textFieldExpression>
   </textField>
   <staticText>
   <reportElement x="268" y="0" width="200" height="20"/>
   <text><![CDATA[ years old.]]></text>
   </staticText>
    </band>
  </detail>
</jasperReport>
```

In this JRXML file, two parameters called name and age are set up to be received by the report. There are a few static text elements that form a sentence. Because this is XML, the static text is enclosed in CDATA tags. The parameters are referenced by using the notation $P (such as $P{name}). Each of these elements is positioned by using x and y coordinates. It's possible to set up more complex layouts with Jasper Reports, including tables and even subreports.

Here's the Java class that populates this report:

```java
import net.sf.jasperreports.engine.*;
import java.util.*;

public class SimpleJasperReportsExample
{
    public static final String JRXML_FILE = "simpleJasperReport.
    jrxml";
    public static final String PDF_FILE = "simpleJasperReport.pdf";

    public static void main(String[] args)
    {
        JasperReport report;
        JasperPrint pdf;

        try
        {
            Map<String,String> hm =
                new HashMap<String,String>();
            hm.put("name","Chuck");
            hm.put("age","36");
            report = JasperCompileManager
                .compileReport(JRXML_FILE);
            pdf = JasperFillManager
                .fillReport(report, hm,
                    new JREmptyDataSource());
            JasperExportManager.exportReportToPdfFile(pdf,
                PDF_FILE);
        }
        catch (JRException jrex)
        {
            jrex.printStackTrace();
        }
    }
}
```

This Java application creates a HashMap and adds two String name-value pairs to it. These HashMap values correspond to the names of the parameters defined in the JRXML file. A Jasper Report instance is created by compiling the JRXML file. The report is then filled with data by using the JasperFillManager class. The JREmptyDataSource class implements the JRData Source interface and basically hands the report an empty data source. Any implementation of

JRDataSource could be passed in here. There are implementations provided with the Jasper Reports package that can retrieve data from JDBC result sets, Java collections, and more. The HashMap containing the two parameters to the report is also passed in here. Finally, the Jasper ExportManager class is used to write the report data out to a PDF file. The final PDF is shown in Figure 16.1.

FIGURE 16.1

This PDF was produced by the JasperExportManager using the report created by compiling the JRXML file and filling it with data.

Hello. My name is Chuck, and I am 36 years old.

Jasper Reports uses another library to export its reports to PDF. This library is called iText, and it's also available as a free, open-source library. iText is useful when you need to output PDFs from your application but don't need the full reporting framework provided by Jasper Reports. For example, if you'd like to create a printable view of a page in your application, iText can make that task much easier. The iText JAR file is included with Jasper Reports, which uses iText for PDF generation. iText can also be downloaded separately at www.lowagie.com/iText/.

Spring Framework has support for creating PDF views by using iText. Spring provides an Abstract PdfView class that does the work of setting up an iText document for you. Your application's PDF view class simply needs to extend AbstractPdfView, implement the buildPdfDocument() method to work with the iText document, and then add data to it as needed. This is very powerful because it means you can use the same Spring controller to retrieve the data needed by the client for both the HTML version and the PDF version simply by using different views in each case.

This code sample shows how to create a simple PDF using iText:

```
import java.io.FileOutputStream;
import java.io.IOException;

import com.lowagie.text.Document;
import com.lowagie.text.DocumentException;
import com.lowagie.text.Paragraph;
import com.lowagie.text.Font;
```

```java
import java.awt.Color;
import com.lowagie.text.PageSize;
import com.lowagie.text.pdf.PdfWriter;

public class SimpleITextExample
{
    public static void main(String[] args)
    {
        Document document = new Document(PageSize.LETTER);
        try
        {
            PdfWriter.getInstance(document,
              new FileOutputStream("simpleITextExample.pdf"));
            document.open();
            document.add(new Paragraph(
                "Hello. My name is Chuck, " +
                "and I am 36 years old!",
                new Font(Font.COURIER, 18,
                    Font.BOLD, new Color(0,0,0))));
        }

        catch (DocumentException dex)
        {
            dex.printStackTrace();
        }

        catch (IOException ioex)
        {
            ioex.printStackTrace();
        }

        finally
        {
            document.close();
        }
    }
}
```

iText was developed in Europe, so its default page size is A4, the European standard. iText documents can be constructed by using a number of convenient page size constants, such as `PageSize.LETTER` for standard U.S. letter-size pages. PDFs are built in iText by adding elements such as paragraphs to the PDF document. iText gives you a fair bit of control over font faces and styles in your paragraphs. The PDF is written out to a file by using a `FileOutputStream`. The PDF output from this application is shown in Figure 16.2.

FIGURE 16.2

The PDF output by the `SimpleITextExample` application. iText gives you a good deal of control over fonts and styling in your PDFs.

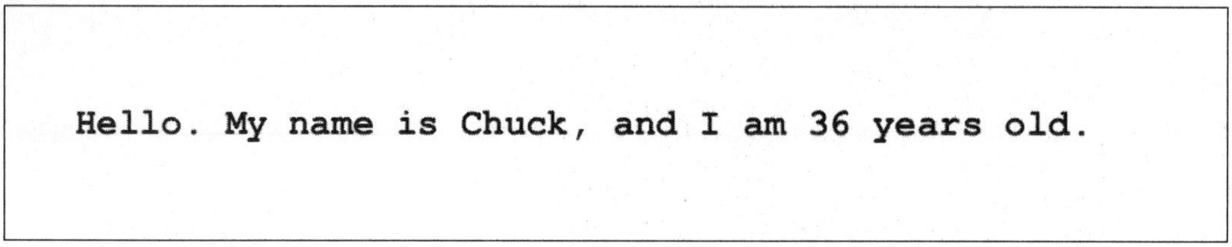

```
Hello. My name is Chuck, and I am 36 years old.
```

Quartz scheduler

Some applications may have requirements that call for a task to be performed at specific intervals or at set times each day or week. For example, an online store application might feed data into a data warehouse for reporting on a nightly basis. Rather than have someone log into an administration site and run this job manually, it would be beneficial to have the job run automatically on a set schedule. Quartz is an open-source Java job scheduling library that can be used to schedule jobs like these. Quartz can be downloaded at `www.opensymphony.com/quartz/`.

Quartz schedules tasks by using jobs and triggers. A *job* is a class that implements the Quartz scheduler's `org.quartz.Job` interface. The `Job` interface contains a single `execute()` method, which is run at a scheduled time. The scheduled time is determined by a trigger that's a subclass of the `org.quartz.Trigger` abstract class. The *trigger* contains the start time and end time for the job and the interval at which it fires. The job and the trigger are passed into an instance of the `org.quartz.Scheduler` interface that ties the job to the trigger.

Here's an example of a simple `Job` implementation class:

```
import java.util.Calendar;
import org.quartz.*;

public class CalendarOutputJob implements Job
{

    public CalendarOutputJob()
    {
    }

    public void execute(JobExecutionContext context)
      throws JobExecutionException
    {
        Calendar now = Calendar.getInstance();
        String currentDateAndTime = (now.get(Calendar.MONTH) + 1) +
                        "/" + now.get(Calendar.DAY_OF_MONTH) +
                        "/" + now.get(Calendar.YEAR) +
```

```
                                      " " + now.get(Calendar.HOUR_OF_DAY) +
                                      ":" + now.get(Calendar.MINUTE);
               System.out.println("Current Date/Time = "
                        + currentDateAndTime);
        }
    }
```

This `Job` class's `execute()` method simply gets the current date and time and then prints them out to the console. The `JobExecutionContext` object passed into the `execute()` method isn't used here, but it contains information about the trigger that has the schedule information for this `Job` and the `Scheduler` object that the job and trigger are registered with.

To see this job used on a schedule, look at this code sample:

```
    SchedulerFactory factory = new StdSchedulerFactory();
    Scheduler scheduler = factory.getScheduler();
    scheduler.start();
    JobDetail detail = new JobDetail("calendarOutputJob",null,
                                       CalendarOutputJob.class);

    Trigger trigger = TriggerUtils.makeHourlyTrigger(6);
    trigger.setStartTime(TriggerUtils.getDateOf(23,59,59));
    trigger.setName("calendarOutputTrigger");

    scheduler.scheduleJob(detail, trigger);
```

This code instantiates and starts a Quartz scheduler, which runs as long as the application is running and keeps track of the scheduled jobs for the application. The code then creates a new `JobDetail` object, which names the job and identifies the `Job` class that's executed. The trigger is instantiated next. This code creates a trigger that runs every six hours. There are also methods in the `TriggerUtils` class that can set up triggers to run at other intervals, such as certain days of the week, and optionally limit the execution to a specific number of times. The trigger's start time is set to one second until midnight (23:59:59 in 24-hour time notation) on the current date. Any other date in the future can also be specified if desired. Finally, the job detail and trigger are passed in to the scheduler, which associates the two and makes sure that the job represented by the job detail is executed.

Although this example is very simple, it demonstrates the power and flexibility of Quartz. Jobs can contain business logic of any level of complexity, make use of other classes in your application, and be tied to any number of schedules. Triggers can be created for practically any interval by using the `TriggerUtils` convenience class or using the concrete `CronTrigger` class by using standard UNIX cron job notation for those developers already familiar with cron, a UNIX command-line job scheduling utility. Spring also makes integrating Quartz into your Web applications easier. Spring provides a `JobDetailBean` class that can be configured by using standard Spring XML configuration. It has an `jobClass` property that can be set to a specific implementation of the `org.quartz.Job` interface in the configuration to enable that `Job` in your Web application. Anyone developing an application in need of scheduling functionality will find Quartz worth using.

Advanced Flex Concepts

Flex offers a wide array of components for display and interaction, and even some utility-based components. Another set of components that Flex offers is for reporting. These components are located under the Charts section of the Components panel. You can use the Flex data visualization components to build a more interactive experience with very little additional code required.

Requirements for charting components

The charting components are available in both versions of Flex Builder, either the stand-alone or the Eclipse plug-in. The standard versions of both the stand-alone and the Eclipse plug-in place a watermark over each component during runtime. This allows you to develop your application and get everything working; then, if you decide to use the components, you can purchase a professional license.

The professional version of Flex Builder needs to be purchased only once and offers the ability to use the charting components as well as the `AdvancedDataGrid` component.

 **NOTE** The professional version of Flex Builder isn't required for component use but is for distribution without the watermark.

Before developing the sample application, let's take a look at each of the charting component options. All of the charting components have similar syntax, which is covered later in this chapter. To start, here's the list of components:

- `AreaChart`
- `BarChart`
- `BubbleChart`
- `CandlestickChart`
- `ColumnChart`
- `HLOCChart`
- `Legend`
- `LineChart`
- `PieChart`
- `PlotChart`

All the components listed above, with the exception of `Legend`, are various shapes and formats for a charting application. A few of these components are shown in Figure 16.3. Let's look at how to configure one.

FIGURE 16.3

Displaying a couple charting components in a browser during runtime

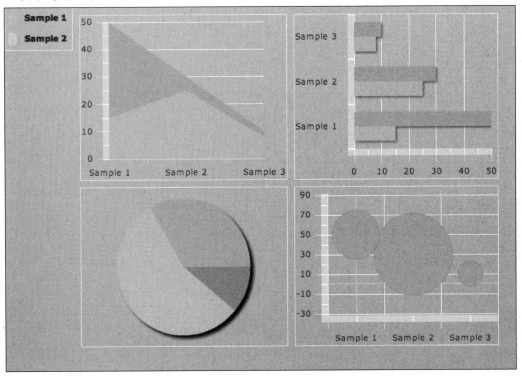

Configuring the charting component in Flex

To create a charting component, start by creating a new Flex project. Follow these steps:

1. **Right-click in the Flex Navigator and then choose New ⇨ Flex Project from the popup menu.** The Flex Project editor opens.

2. **In the Project Name text field, type** ChartingSample.

3. **Click Finish to build the project with all the default options set.**

Now that you have a project set up, the next step is to start writing the MXML code.

You should see the default code shown here:

```
<?xml version="1.0"?>
<mx:Application xmlns:mx="http://www.adobe.com/2006/mxml"
    layout="absolute">
```

```
        .
        .
        .
</mx:Application>
```

You can use any of the charting components in your applications. For this example, I use the BarChart to display sample sales data that are static in the Flex application.

Start by adding the <mx:Script> block, importing the ArrayCollection class, and defining a Bindable variable that will be attached to the BarChart component:

```
<mx:Script>
<![CDATA[

    import mx.collections.ArrayCollection;

    [Bindable]
    public var monthlySalesReport:ArrayCollection =
    new ArrayCollection([
            {Month:"Jan", Profit:2000, Expenses:1500},
            {Month:"Feb", Profit:1000, Expenses:200},
            {Month:"March", Profit:4000, Expenses:100}
        ]);

    ]]>
</mx:Script>
```

The monthlySalesReport is an ArrayCollection with objects placed inside. These individual objects are placed in the component dynamically and result in the view's being drawn.

The next step is to add the MXML that displays the charting component, as shown in Figure 16.4. This component has an id of barChart and a dataProvider of monthlySalesReport. The data provider is filled by the variable that you previously defined at runtime:

```
<mx:BarChart
    id="barChart"
    dataProvider="{monthlySalesReport}"
    showDataTips="true"
    x="10"
    y="10"
    width="546"
    height="220"
>
        .
        .
        .
</mx:BarChart>
```

494

The other specific parameter that's found within the charting component is `showDataTips`. This parameter tells the component to display information in a tooltip-style box when the user moves the mouse over the chart.

FIGURE 16.4

Showing the `BarChart` in the Design view of Flex Builder

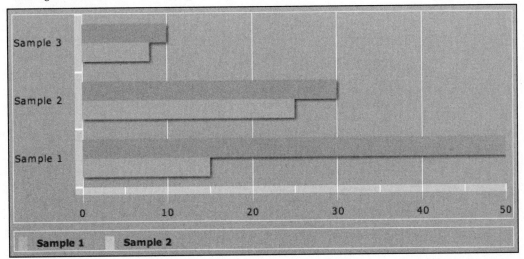

The chart is defined by MXML tags that are placed within the `BarChart` tag. The first portion defines the vertical placement and data viewing within the vertical axis:

```
<mx:verticalAxis>
    <mx:CategoryAxis
            categoryField="Month"
            dataProvider="{monthlySalesReport}"
    />
</mx:verticalAxis>
```

The following code, which is also placed within the main `BarChart` tags, contains the `BarSeries` sections. These tags define each of the individual bars in the `BarChart`:

```
<mx:series>
    <mx:BarSeries
            yField="Month"
            xField="Profit"
            displayName="Profit"
    />
    <mx:BarSeries
```

```
    yField="Month"
    xField="Expenses"
    displayName="Expenses"
/>
</mx:series>
```

The labels for the component are defined by the `xField` and `yField` parameters. The `display Name` is to tell the viewer which portion of the chart belongs to each value group, defined in the `Bindable` variable.

The last portion of the code is the `Legend`. This component displays each item's category in the chart. Usually, this component is placed below the chart; it doesn't need to be, but it's the optimal location within the MXML file.

```
<mx:Legend
    dataProvider="{barChart}"
    x="10"
    y="238"
    width="546"
    height="22"
/>
```

At this point, you've completed the sample `BarChart` application. You can now save and view the application in your browser, which should show the component with the data being displayed, as shown in Figure 16.5.

FIGURE 16.5

Displaying the completed `BarChart` application with data loaded and viewable

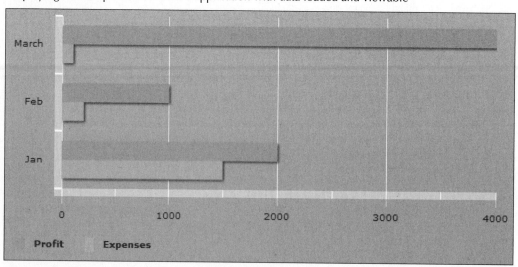

You may see a watermark on your version of the charting components if you don't
have a professional license for Flex Builder.

You have now completed the simple `BarChart` application; the following code block is the completed code for this application. You can expand your projects with this knowledge and begin adding Flex charting to your applications for a richer user experience:

```
<?xml version="1.0"?>
<mx:Application
    xmlns:mx="http://www.adobe.com/2006/mxml"
    layout="absolute"
>

<mx:Script>
<![CDATA[

    import mx.collections.ArrayCollection;
    [Bindable]
    public var monthlySalesReport:ArrayCollection =
        new ArrayCollection([
        {Month:"Jan", Profit:2000, Expenses:1500},
        {Month:"Feb", Profit:1000, Expenses:200},
            {Month:"March", Profit:4000, Expenses:100}
    ]);
  ]]>
</mx:Script>

 <mx:BarChart
   id="barChart"
   dataProvider="{monthlySalesReport}"
   showDataTips="true"
   x="10"
   y="10"
   width="546"
   height="220"
>
    <mx:verticalAxis>
        <mx:CategoryAxis
            categoryField="Month"
            dataProvider="{monthlySalesReport}"
        />
    </mx:verticalAxis>
    <mx:series>
        <mx:BarSeries
            yField="Month"
            xField="Profit"
            displayName="Profit"
        />
```

```
            <mx:BarSeries
                    yField="Month"
                    xField="Expenses"
                    displayName="Expenses"
            />
        </mx:series>
    </mx:BarChart>

    <mx:Legend
        dataProvider="{barChart}"
        x="10"
        y="238"
        width="546"
        height="22"
    />

    </mx:Application>
```

Summary

In this chapter, you learned more about enterprise development with Java and Flex. First, you learned about a few key concepts surrounding enterprise applications: security, interoperability, and scalability. You learned about the Spring Security framework for adding security to Web applications. Next, you learned how JMS allows different modules or applications to communicate with one another by using point-to-point or publish/subscribe domains. After that, you learned about other Java libraries that can be useful in many applications.

You also learned about Flex data visualization components. You first learned which components are available and then learned how to configure them for your own projects. Now that you know about these components and how to use them, you can include them in your own projects.

Appendix

Installing Adobe Flex and Adobe Flex Builder

B efore you can start using Flex, you need to install and configure it. There are three options for using Flex. First, you can use the stand-alone Flex Builder application, which is the IDE developed by Adobe, built on the Eclipse framework. Second, if you already use Eclipse, you can install the Flex plug-in, which gives you the same functionality in the editor that you already know. The third and final option is the Flex SDK (command line). The first two options require that you purchase a license from Adobe; the third option, SDK, is free. In fact, Flex (not the builder) is open source and allows the community to submit changes as well as publicly test the functionality. The general advantage of open source is a large support user base that's not restricted to Adobe professionals; the same is true for Flex.

Before installing the applications, let's take a look at some important points for each option.

Flex Builder:

- Is the self-contained IDE
- Was developed by Adobe specifically for Flex and ActionScript development
- Has the ability to load third-party Eclipse plug-ins, such as SVN and debugging tools

Flex (Eclipse plug-in):

- Leverages existing plug-ins and abilities within the stand-alone Eclipse IDE
- Is maintained by the Eclipse group
- Has the ability to integrate with Flex plug-ins and tools developed by Adobe

IN THIS APPENDIX

Downloading Flex and Flex Builder

Installing Flex Builder

Installing the Flex plug-in

Building a sample Flex application

Working with the Flex SDK

Flex SDK:

- Is open source, allowing outside developers to modify and update the code
- Offers a large user base of SDK developers to help you
- Doesn't require you to purchase a license unless you intend to use the Data Visualization components
- Offers command-line tools to help automate processes

Each option has its own benefits. The examples in this appendix use the Flex Builder option, developed and tested by Adobe, specifically with Flex and ActionScript as the focal points.

Now that you know about the three different options, let's look at how you go about installing and setting up each option. You start with the Flex Builder stand-alone application.

Downloading Flex and Flex Builder

Flex and Flex Builder can be purchased from a computer store, from Amazon.com, or directly from the Adobe site as a digital download. Now that most homes and businesses have faster Internet connections, downloading is a good option and much faster than shipping a product. The only difference is that you don't get the box to put on your shelf.

To download Flex directly from Adobe, start by opening your browser and navigating to the Flex product page on the Adobe site: `www.adobe.com/products/flex/`.

You see a link on the right side of the screen to purchase Flex. Click this link and then proceed with the on-screen options. Once you've purchased a license, a download link appears, which allows you to download a copy of Flex and Flex Builder. Save the file to a location you can remember.

The license normally is e-mailed to you after you purchase Flex. However, if you log in to the Adobe site, the license also appears in your recent purchases within your account.

Installing Flex Builder

Once you've downloaded the file, it's time to install Flex Builder. Follow these steps:

1. **Navigate to the location on your computer where you saved the installation file and then double-click the `FB3 Win` file to start the installation process.** The installation screen, as shown in Figure A.1, opens.

2. **Click OK to continue to the License Agreement screen, as shown in Figure A.2.**

3. **Read the license agreement, click the I accept the terms of the License Agreement radio button, and then click Next.**

FIGURE A.1

You can select a language on the first screen of the Flex installer.

FIGURE A.2

Accept the terms of the license agreement.

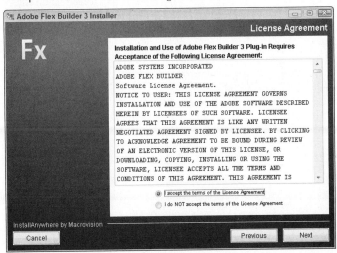

4. **On the next screen, as shown in Figure A.3, choose the location where you want to install Flex Builder.** Normally, you would use the default location. But you can also click Choose to open the Browse For Folder dialog box, as shown in Figure A.4, to pick a custom location. Click OK after choosing a new location.

5. **Click Next to install Flex Builder.**

Once the installation process completes, you're prompted to install Flash Player, which is used to debug your applications in Flex Builder. If you have Flash (IDE) installed, you probably already have Flash Player and can skip this step.

At this point, you have installed Flex. You can read on to learn how to install the plug-in version or jump to the end of this appendix to build a quick Flex application to make sure that everything is set up properly.

FIGURE A.3

Choose the install location for Flex Builder.

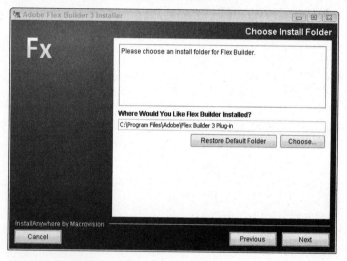

FIGURE A.4

You can choose a custom location to install Flex Builder.

Installing the Flex Plug-in

The Flex plug-in, which can be downloaded from Adobe or found on your Flex installation disc, requires that the third-party Eclipse application already be installed on your computer.

Downloading Eclipse

You may already have Eclipse installed from a previous project, so make sure that you check on that before attempting to install Eclipse. If you need to download Eclipse, navigate your Web browser to the Eclipse Foundation Web site at `www.eclipse.org/downloads/`, where you can get the latest stable version of Eclipse from the Eclipse downloads page, as shown in Figure A.5.

CROSS-REF For more on installing and configuring Eclipse, see Chapter 1.

FIGURE A.5

The Eclipse downloads page on the Eclipse Foundation Web site

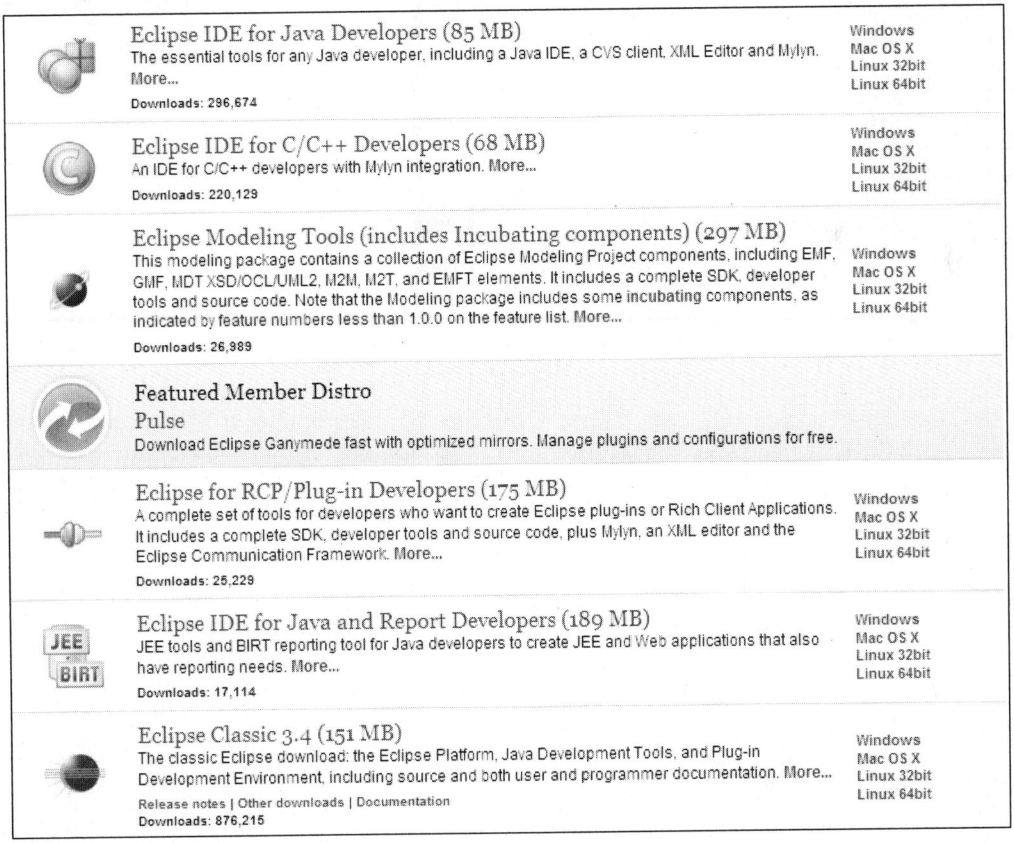

Installing Eclipse

Once Eclipse has been installed, it's time to install the Flex plug-in. Start by running the setup file located on the DVD from the boxed version or the directory you created from the digital download. The setup file is named FB3_Plugin_Win.exe.

The only screen that's different in the Flex plug-in version is the one where you choose the existing copy of Eclipse (previously installed) on the machine, as shown in Figure A.6.

FIGURE A.6

Choose the location where you want Eclipse to be installed on your machine.

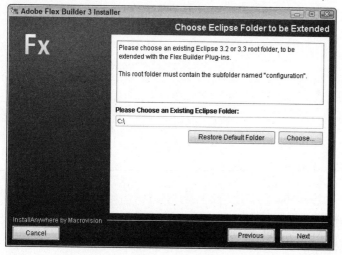

Follow the remaining screens to complete the install process. Once the plug-in is loaded, you're asked to install Flash Player, which is required to debug and test your applications.

Once Flash Player is installed, you're done. You can start Eclipse and then create a new Flex project by choosing New ⇨ Flex Project. You should see Design and Code tabs located in the editor; if you do, the Flex plug-in is running properly.

Building a Sample Flex Application

Now that you've installed Flex, whether it's the stand-alone version or the plug-in, you need to test the installation by creating a sample application.

Creating the application

This application involves simple `Label` and `Button` components that change a label when a user clicks a button. Start by creating a new Flex project by choosing File ⇨ Flex Project. Type a project name (**Sample**, for example) in the Project Name text field and accept all the other default options. Finally, click Finish to build the project.

The new project opens in the code editor, and you can start creating the code for the application. You should see the code from a default application in the editor, such as the following:

```
<?xml version="1.0" encoding="utf-8"?>
<mx:Application xmlns:mx="http://www.adobe.com/2006/mxml"
    layout="absolute">
</mx:Application>
```

All the code you add must be inserted between the `<mx:Application>` tags shown above.

Adding the MXML code

Start by adding the code for the `Label` component. This code adds a new label to the *stage* (where all your design components are placed in Flex) with some default text, which is replaced once the code is run:

```
<mx:Label width="300" id="lbl" text="A message will be here;
click the button" x="10" y="10"/>
```

Now add a `Button` to which you can attach an event handler to capture the event:

```
<mx:Button label="Update" click="changeLabel()" x="10" y="36"/>
```

The last portion of the code is the ActionScript that changes the label whenever a user clicks the Button component:

```
<mx:Script>

    <![CDATA[

        private function changeLabel():void
        {
                lbl.text = "Hello from Flex 3!";
        }

    ]]>

</mx:Script>
```

Testing the application

The application is complete. If you switch over to the Design view, you see the Label and Button components, as shown in Figure A.7. You can now test the application in a browser by choosing Run ⇨ Debug Sample or by pressing F11 on your keyboard. The application opens in your browser, and if you click the button, the Label component should update.

You've created your first Flex application. It's not the most useful of applications, but it allows you to see the most basic of applications built by using Flex.

FIGURE A.7

The Label and Button components on the stage in Flex

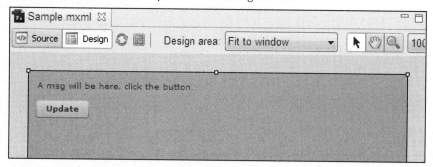

Working with the Flex SDK

The third option for using Flex is the open-source SDK. The SDK is provided by Adobe for free and allows a developer to run the entire process from the command line. This section describes how to obtain and install the SDK, as well as learn the basic process of creating a Flex application.

NOTE You need to use your own text editor to build applications by using the Flex SDK.

Before you can start developing Flex applications, you need to download the SDK. You can download the SDK from the open-source Adobe Web site: http://opensource.adobe.com/wiki/display/flexsdk/Downloads.

On the downloads page, you see the latest Flex 3 releases as well as beta versions, which are less stable but offer more functionality. For this process, you should use a stable release, such as version 3.1. There are two options when downloading the SDK:

- **Free Adobe Flex SDK.** This is the official product from Adobe, which comes with everything you need to build and deploy Flex applications.

■ **Open Source Flex SDK.** This package contains only the source code and doesn't include elements such as AIR or Flash Player, which aren't open source.

For the average developer who isn't looking to modify the core functionality of Flex, the Free Adobe Flex SDK version is the better choice. Click the link for this version to go to the Adobe downloads page, as shown in Figure A.8.

Click the link for the most stable version of the Flex SDK, read the license agreement, and then accept the terms by clicking the check box, which enables the download link.

When the download is complete, you can extract the SDK and then try out the samples located in the `samples/` directory. If you navigate to the explorer application located in `samples/ explorer`, you see a `build.bat` file. Double-click this file to open a command prompt and compile the SWF. Now when you look in the `explorer/` directory, you see the newly created SWF.

Run the `HTML` file by double-clicking the `Sample.html` file. Your default browser opens, displaying the sample explorer application.

FIGURE A.8

The Flex SDK downloads page on the Adobe Web site

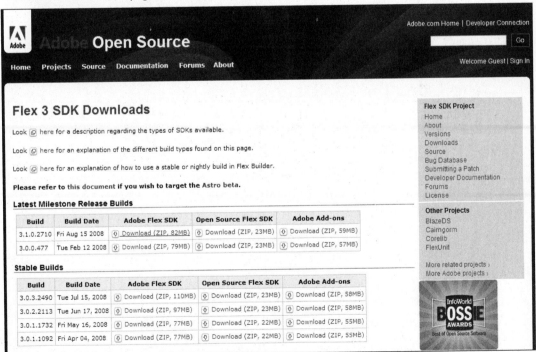

507

Building your sample application

Now that you've tested the samples that came with the SDK, you can compile your own sample file to understand how to work with the SDK. Start by creating a new MXML file with this code:

```
<?xml version="1.0" encoding="utf-8"?>
<mx:Application xmlns:mx="http://www.adobe.com/2006/mxml"
    layout="absolute">

    <mx:Script>
        <![CDATA[

                private function changeLabel():void
                {
                        lbl.text = "Hello from Flex 3!";
                }

        ]]>
    </mx:Script>

    <mx:Label width="300" id="lbl" text="A message will be here;
    click the button" x="10" y="10"/>
    <mx:Button label="Update" click="changeLabel()" x="10" y="36"/>

</mx:Application>
```

Save this new file as `Sample.mxml` to your desktop.

Compiling the application

Now open a command prompt and then navigate to the desktop. Once you're on the desktop, you can run the `dir` or `ls` command to make sure that your `mxml` file is located there. Next, type the path to the `mxmlc` file located in the `bin/directory` of the Flex SDK you previously installed.

The `mxmlc` command accepts an argument that's the name of the `mxml` file you want to compile into a completed application:

```
flex_sdk_3\bin\mxmlc Sample.mxml
```

After you run this command, you should see a `sample.swf` file appear on the desktop. This file is the compiled application. You can double-click this file, and it opens the application in a stand-alone Flash Player.

You've now created a Flex application by using the command-line tools and the open-source Flex SDK.

Glossary

ActionScript 3 The latest edition of the scripting language based on a draft proposal of ECMAScript 4 that Flex and Flash use to develop Web and desktop applications. See also *ECMAScript*.

Apache Ant A build and deployment utility written in Java that uses XML build scripts to divide build-and-deploy operations into separate targets made of one or more tasks.

Application programming interface (API) A set of functions in an application that's made publicly available to be used by other applications for the purposes of data interchange.

Array A data structure consisting of a group of elements that can be accessed by indexing or key names.

Bindable A data object that can be attached to (via an event handler) and send a notification when the value is modified. See also *data*.

BlazeDS An open-source Java Web application messaging technology, primarily used to send and receive data from applications written by using Adobe Flex or Adobe AIR.

Cascading Style Sheets (CSS) A standard style sheet language used to describe the presentation aspects — such as fonts, colors, layout instructions, and images — of the visual elements in a Web application.

Class An object-oriented construct found in Java, ActionScript, and other languages that includes properties and methods for manipulating those properties. Classes can be instantiated.

Command line A way to interact with a computer by typing commands after a prompt to perform certain tasks.

Compiler A program that translates source code and creates object code.

Constructor A special method used to create a new instance of a Java or ActionScript class by using the new keyword.

Data A collection of numbers, characters, and images or other outputs to be processed by the overall application.

Eclipse A popular open-source IDE for many programming languages. This is also the framework that Flex Builder is built on.

ECMAScript A scripting language that has been standardized by Ecma International in the ECMA-262 specification.

Flash Player A cross-platform application and multimedia player originally known as FutureSplash and created by FutureWare Software. It was acquired by Macromedia and renamed Flash. Since the merger of Adobe and Macromedia, it has been released under the Adobe name.

Flex An application development framework used to develop and deploy cross-platform rich Internet applications that run in the Adobe Flash Player or Adobe AIR runtime.

Flex Builder An IDE for Flex development built on the Eclipse IDE.

Flex data services An extension of the Flex eco-system that allows developers to create more advanced applications alongside Java or similar server technologies.

Flex SDK The freely distributed software development kit consisting of the Flex Framework and command-line development tools, such as compilers and debuggers. This kit doesn't require a purchased license and can create the same output as Flex Builder.

Function A portion of code within a larger program that performs a certain task while staying relatively independent of the other code. A function in Java development is known as a method.

Hibernate A Java object-relational mapping framework used to translate between Java objects and tables in a relational database.

HTTP Hypertext Transfer Protocol, a communication protocol used to transfer information across the Internet. This protocol is used in Flex to communicate with server-side scripting.

Inheritance A way to form new classes by extending classes that have been previously defined. The new class inherits properties and methods from the class it extends.

Interface An object-oriented construct that defines method definitions and constant values but provides no implementations of those methods. Classes can implement interfaces and must provide implementations for all methods in any interfaces that they implement.

iText A Java library for quickly creating PDF documents from within Java applications.

Jasper reports A Java reporting engine for building highly customized reports for Java applications.

Java An object-oriented programming language developed by Sun Microsystems, Inc., that uses structures and syntax similar to C++ but is compiled into platform-independent bytecode that runs in its own virtual machine.

Java Archive (JAR) An archive containing the classes and files that are part of a Java library or application. The JAR file format is based on the ZIP file format.

Java bean A Java class that conforms to a particular structural convention. A Java bean class contains one or more private properties, a public no-argument constructor, and public getter and setter methods for each of the properties that follow a known naming convention.

Java Database Connectivity (JDBC) A standard Java API that contains interfaces and classes used for writing applications that access or update data in a relational database.

Java Development Kit (JDK) A product of Sun Microsystems, Inc., containing a set of libraries and command-line tools used for Java application development, debugging, and execution.

Java Message Service (JMS) A Java enterprise API used for sending synchronous or asynchronous messages between modules or applications in a Java application server. Messages can be sent by using either a point-to-point or a publish/subscribe domain.

Java Runtime Environment (JRE) A product of Sun Microsystems, Inc., containing a set of libraries and command-line tools used for Java application execution.

JBoss An open-source Java application server used to run Java Web applications and enterprise applications.

JUnit An open-source Java unit testing framework.

Mashup An application that compiles data from multiple other applications and then combines it into a new service.

Method A portion of code associated with a class or object that's used to perform a certain task.

Model-View-Controller (MVC) An application design pattern that divides application code into a model layer representing the data, domain objects, and business logic of the application; a view layer representing the user interface elements of the application; and a controller layer that handles requests from the view layer, retrieves data from the model, and passes that data back to the view.

MySQL An open-source relational database management system.

Object A pragmatic container to store data and allow binding to other elements. This can also be a reference to a class instance when working with classes.

Object-oriented programming A programming process that uses objects and their interactions to develop applications and various computer programs. See also *object*.

Object-relational mapping A programming methodology by which the fields in Java objects are translated into fields in database tables through an intermediary XML mapping file.

Package A method used to group related classes and interfaces in an application. Classes in the same package have access to one another's protected properties and methods. In ActionScript, a package may also contain functions.

PureMVC A Model-View-Controller framework implementation written in ActionScript for use in Flex applications.

Quartz An open-source Java job scheduling system that allows Java applications to perform tasks at regular intervals or specific times.

Relational database A database that stores data in tables composed of columns that describe the data and data type being held and rows that contain data for a single instance of the data represented by the columns.

RESTful Representational state transfer, a type of architecture for Web services. This isn't a complete specification but is more of a best practice setup.

Spring Framework An open-source Java application framework consisting of a number of modules for developing Web applications.

Spring Security A Spring Framework subproject that provides security features for Spring-based Web applications. Spring Security can integrate with popular authentication and authorization mechanisms, such as LDAP.

Structured Query Language (SQL) The language used to create, retrieve, update, and delete data in a relational database.

Uniform Resource Identifier (URI) A string used to identify the name or location of some resource on the Internet. A URL used to identify the location of a Web page is one example of a URI.

Unit test A piece of code whose purpose is to test the functionality of another piece of code and determine whether it's functioning properly. A unit test typically tests the smallest possible testable piece of code (for example, a method in a Java class).

Variable A reference with a property that can be accessed once the variable has been defined.

Web Application Archive (WAR) An archive file that contains all the Java class files, static resources such as images and HTML files, and configuration necessary to deploy and run a Web application within an application server.

XML A language specification used to create customized and extensible markup languages. XML is frequently used in Web application configuration files as well as in Ant build scripts and as a data exchange format between Java and Flex.

XPath A language for retrieving specific nodes from an XML document by using a structure reminiscent of a directory listing.

Index

Symbols

/ (forward slash), 266
_ (underscore) character, 47
* (wildcard) character, 207

A

abstract method, 355
access modifier, 66
accessor method, 252
acknowledgeRec() function, 419
acknowledgeSend() function, 419
ActionScript file
    description of, 38
    ECMAScript, 62
    messaging example, 297
    MXML code and, 91–92
    sending data, 114
    trace message, 55
    version, 62
Add Foreign Key dialog box, 226
Add Library wizard, 176
addChild() method, 94
addEventListener() method, 94
addItem() method, 107
AddProductToCartService.java object
        listing, 358–359
Adobe sign-in screen, 76
Advanced tab (System Properties dialog box), 12
annotation, 179–180
Ant tool. See Apache Ant tool
AOP Developer Resources (Spring IDE plug-in), 32
AOP Extension (Spring IDE plug-in), 32

Apache Ant tool
    application development deployment, 367–368
    basic description of, 17
    build file, 17, 156–157
    configuration, 18–20
    console output, 162
    downloading, 18
    installation, 18
    target, 17, 82
    task, 82
API key, Flickr, 437–439
application context module (Spring Framework),
        125
application development
    best practices, 307–309
    build.xml file, 365–366
    code modularity, 308
    DAO (data access object), 310
    data access layer, 348–349
    data, adding to database, 318–319
    deployment, 367–368
    foreign key, 315–316
    Hibernate JAR file import, 325
    Hibernate mapping file, 343–346
    Java build path configuration, 327–328
    library import, 325–326
    model layer, 329–330
    multiapplication integration, 83–84
    MySQL Connector/J driver import, 325
    MySQL database creation, 310–312, 314–317
    new project setup, 319–322
    product table, 317–318
    separation of interface and implementation,
        308–309

application development (*continued*)
service layer, 355–358
testing, 367–368
user table, 314–315
AreaChart component, 492
array, 239
ArrayCollection class, 494
ArrayList collection, 294
artweather.jsp file, 456–457
ArtWeather.mxml file listing, 469–472
ArtWeatherService class listing, 452–455
assertion methods, 192
asynchronous communication, 69, 113
asynchronous event, 381
asynchronous messaging, 407
AsyncMessage class, 407
AsyncMessage object, 288
authentication, 478, 480–481
authorization, 478–479
auto-incrementing function, 257
automatic memory management, 5

B

BarChart component, 492, 494, 496–497
bin directory, 127
bin folder, 47
binary Java class file, 7
bindable data provider, 268
bindable variable, 297–299
bin-debug folder, 44
BlazeDS
downloading, 286
features, 285
installation, 286
messaging-config.xml file, 291–292
ServiceAdapter class, 292
turnkey development, 286
Web application folder, 294
Web path to, 296
blocking process, 381
bn-down.png file, 473

bn-over.png file, 473
bn-up.png file, 473, 476
boolean data type, 6
break point, 56
Breakpoints view (Flex Builder), 57–58
Browse for Folder dialog box, 27, 29
BubbleChart component, 492
build file (Apache Ant tool), 17
build properties file, 156–157
build-and-deploy target, 430, 462
Buildfile Selection dialog box, 161, 429
buildPdfDocument() method, 488
build.xml file, 158–159, 365–366, 425–427, 460–461
built-in library, 4
button click event, 93
button event, 384–385
bytecode, 62

C

C++ programming language, 62
callServer() method, 275, 379
camel case, 463
CandlestickChart component, 492
Cart.hbm.xml mapping file listing, 344–345
CartItem.hbm.xml mapping file listing, 345
CartItem.java object listing, 338–340
Cart.java object listing, 340–342
cascading style sheet (CSS), 463–465
charting
AreaChart component, 492
BarChart component, 492, 494, 496–497
BubbleChart component, 492
CandlestickChart component, 492
ColumnChart component, 492
configuration, 493
field, 496
HLOCChart component, 492
Legend component, 492, 496
LineChart component, 492
PieChart component, 492

`PlotChart` component, 492

`showDataTips` property, 495

vertical axis, 495

`xField` parameter, 496

`yField` parameter, 496

chat application

  `acknowledgeRec()` function, 419

  `acknowledgeSend()` function, 419

  basic description, 399

  `build-and-deploy` target, 430

  `build.xml` file, 425–427

  chat server, 403–407

  chat server connection, 430–431

  `ChatAdapter` value, 419

  `chat-build.properties` file, 426

  `chat.html` file, 419

  `Chat.mxml` file listing, 415–418

  Eclipse project setup, 400–402

  Flex code, 408–412

  `handleFault()` function, 418

  `randomName()` function, 418

  `receiveChatMessages()` function, 418

  `sendChatMessage()` function, 418

  `services-config.xml` file, 421–422

  `setUserName()` function, 418

  `subscribeToChat()` function, 418

  testing, 431–432

  `web.xml` file, 420–421

`ChatAdapter` class, 422

`ChatServer` class, 406–407, 422

check constraint, 206

class

  adding property to, 87

  `ArrayCollection`, 494

  `AsyncMessage`, 407

  attribute of, 87

  basic example, 86

  binary Java class file, 7

  building custom, 273–274

  `ChatAdapter`, 422

  `ChatServer`, 406–407, 422

  controller, 142–143

  `CronTrigger`, 491

  custom event, 380–381

  `DelegatingFilterProxy`, 479–480

  description of, 4

  `DriverManager`, 237, 243

  extending, 90–91, 147

  `Facade`, 69

  factory, 259

  `FilterToBeanProxy`, 479

  inheritance, 4, 90–91

  `InputStream`, 456

  instance of, 4

  `ItemRenderer`, 268, 272, 382

  `JavaFlexStoreAdmin`, 266–268

  `JavaFlexStoreEvent`, 266, 277–278

  `JavaServiceHandler`, 266, 276–277, 379–380

  `JREmptyDataSource`, 487

  listing, 6–7

  `ManageRenderer`, 266, 272–273

  `Mediator`, 69

  `MessageBrokerServlet`, 421, 468–469

  `MessageService`, 408

  method, 86

  `MouseEvent`, 93

  multiple classes in same file, 89–90

  object-oriented programming, 4

  `PopUpManager`, 279

  `ProductEditor`, 266, 270–271

  `Proxy`, 69

  `Restrictions`, 264

  `ServiceAdapter`, 292, 403, 467

  `SessionFactory`, 259

  `SimpleCommand`, 70

  skin, 464–465, 475

  `StoreBaseService`, 355–357

  subclass, 4

  superclass, 4, 351

  `Transaction`, 263

  `TriggerUtils`, 491

  `URLLoader`, 275

  `XPath`, 449

class declaration, 6, 147

Class Folder Selection dialog box, 260–261

`<class>` tag, 257

`click()` function, 93

`close()` method, 243

code. *See* listing

code modularity, 308

code structure

    Java and Flex similarity, 62–67

    tag, 62

collapsing file section, 145

`ColumnChart` component, 492

column, table, 203–204

comma-delimited list, 207

command-line tools, MySQL database server, 215

comma-separated value (CSV), 485

`commons-httpclient.jar` file, 448

compilation error, 164

Components view (Flex Builder), 52

`config` object, 263

configuration

    Apache Ant tool, 18–20

    charting component, 493

    Eclipse IDE, 22–24, 26–27

    FlexUnit framework, 189–190

    JBoss application server, 14–16

    JDK, 11–13

    MySQL database server, 213–216

configuration file

    Hibernate framework, 258–260

    messaging, 291–292

Confirm Table Edit dialog box, 223, 225, 228, 314

`conn` variable, 242

`Connection` interface, 233, 242

Console view (Flex Builder), 58

constraint

    check, 206

    not-null, 206, 221

    unique, 206

constructor, 6

`Consumer` component, 288–289

controller class, 142–143

`Controller` interface, 68–69, 357

controller layer (MVC pattern), 67, 70, 124, 141

Create a Java Project wizard, 169, 236

`creationComplete` event, 297

CRM (customer relationship management), 477–478

`CronTrigger` class, 491

CSS (cascading style sheet), 463–465

CSV (comma-separated value), 485

custom event class, 380–381

customer relationship management (CRM), 477–478

D

DAO (data access object), 310

data access layer, application development, 348–349

data definition language (DDL), 218

data dictionary, 219

`data` property, 100

data provider, 94–95

data type

    boolean, 6

    date field, 204

    integer, 221–222

    number field, 204

    variable character field, 204

database application. *See also* JDBC; relational database

    adding methods for, 279–281

    class imports and variable definition, 278

    connection, 278–284

    defining the project, 265–266

    designing the, 266–268

    file outline, 266

    listing, 281–284

    main application code, 278

    product editor popup, 269–271

    product grid, 272–273

database communication

    adding class method, 275

    custom data class, 273–274

    response from server, 276–277

database metadata, 219
dataField property, 299
DataGrid component, 268, 272–273
dataProvider property, 298, 494
date field, 204
DDL (data definition language), 218
Debug mode, Flex Builder, 55
declaration
    class, 6, 147
    package, 6, 65, 86
DELETE method, 115
delete statement, 208
DelegatingFilterProxy class, 479–480
dependency injection, 124
deployment
    application development, 367–368
    mashup, 462
Design view (Flex Builder), 52
destination property, 288, 298
destination service
    subscribing to, 289–290
    unsubscribing to, 290
development tool, Java and Flex similarity, 73–75,
    77, 80, 82
dialog box
    Add Foreign Key, 226
    Browse for Folder, 27, 29
    Buildfile Selection, 161, 429
    Class Folder Selection, 260–261
    Confirm Table Edit, 223, 225, 228, 314
    Download File, 440
    Extended Interfaces Selection, 331
    Flex Project, 116
    Implemented Interfaces Selection, 144, 249,
        332–333, 450
    Import, 132–133
    Import File system, 444–445
    Import from directory, 134, 323, 412
    Import from File system, 320
    Import Select, 322, 444
    JAR Selection, 138–140, 246–247, 447
    Java Build Path, 328

    Java Settings, 238
    MySQL Table Editor, 221–224, 227, 312–313
    New ActionScript Class, 377
    New File, 256, 344, 415
    New Flex Project, 267, 295, 374
    New Folder, 131, 148, 255, 321–322, 443
    New Java Class, 145, 171, 240, 250, 332, 406,
        449–450
    New Java Package, 142–143, 169–170, 239
    New MXML Component, 269
    New Project, 168, 442
    New Server, 41–42
    New Spring Project, 128–130, 442
    New User Variable, 12–13
    Open JAR, 425
    Open Perspective, 38–39
    Preferences, 423
    Run On Server, 50–51
    Runtime, 424
    Select a wizard, 168, 178, 235
    Show View, 160, 367, 428
    Software Updates and Add-ons, 31
    Superclass Selection, 351
    System Properties, 11–12
    Workspace Launcher, 22
directive
    JSP, 149–150
    tag library, 150
directory
    bin, 127
    creating, using Eclipse IDE, 128–132
    src, 127
    web, 127
dispatchEvent() method, 373
dist directory, 324
distribution, Spring Framework, 125
Download button (JDK), 8
Download File dialog box, 440
downloading
    Apache Ant tool, 18
    BlazeDS, 286
    Eclipse IDE, 503

downloading (*continued*)
Flex Builder, 74, 500
Flex SDK, 506–507
FlexUnit framework, 189
Flickr, 439–440
Hibernate framework, 245
JBoss application server, 14
MySQL Connector/J driver, 234
MySQL database server, 209–210
SLF4, 246
Spring Framework, 125
driver, JDBC, 234
DriverManager class, 237, 243

E

EAR (enterprise application archive), 17
Eclipse IDE
basic description of, 20, 499
configuration, 22–24, 26–27
creating new project in, 128–130
directory structure creation, 128–132
downloading, 503
editing XML file in, 256
folding feature, 145
install directory, 80
installation, 21–22, 504
Java Build Path setting, 136, 138
license agreement, 35
mashup application, 441–445
new project creation, 319–322
project configuration, 130–131, 133, 135–136
Spring IDE plug-in for, 30–34
welcome page, 22–23
workspace in, 22
ECMAScript, 62
enterprise application
basic description, 477–478
interoperability, 478, 481–483
scalability, 478
security, 478–480

enterprise application archive (EAR), 17
environment variable, 12–13
error
compilation, 164
forcing in test, 200
incorrect URL, 164
evalSelector value, 408
event
button click, 93
event listener, 194–195
MouseEvent class, 93
execute() method, 70, 243, 490
expanding file section, 145
Expressions view (Flex Builder), 57
Extended Interfaces Selection dialog box, 331

F

Facade class, 69
factory class, 259
fail() method, 180
failed unit testing, 181
field, charting, 496
file listing page (Spring Framework), 126
file outline, database application, 266
file, collapsing/expanding, 145
FileOutputStream object, 489
filter, 48
FilterToBeanProxy class, 479
finally block, 243
Flex Builder
Adobe sign-in screen, 76
basic description, 499
break point, 56
Breakpoints view, 57–58
Components view, 52
Console view, 58
debug message, 54–58
Debug mode, 55
Design view, 52
download page, 75–76

downloading, 74, 500
Eclipse install directory, 80
Expressions view, 57
Flex Navigator view, 39, 81
Flex Properties view, 52–53
installation, 74–75, 77, 80, 500
installation location screen, 78
license agreement, 77, 500
logging framework, 59–60
Pre-Installation Summary screen, 79
project screen creation, 45
project types, 37–38
red X indicator, 48
redeploying application, 52
sample Flex application, 104–110
Source view, 52
States view, 52
trace() function, 54
trace message in, 54–56
Variables view, 57–58
Web browser, 50–51
Flex Library project
creation, 46–47
description of, 38
Flex Project dialog box, 116
Flex project type. *See also* Java and Flex similarity
creation, 38–43
description of, 37
Flex Development perspective, 38
folder structure, 44–45
testing configuration of, 48–53
Flex Properties panel, 117
Flex SDK
downloading, 506–507
sample application, 508
FlexDataGrid control, 292
flex_libs folder, 44
flex_src folder, 44
flexTasks.jar file, 425
FlexUnit framework
adding to Flex project, 189–190
assertion methods, 192

basic description of, 188
configuration, 189–190
downloading, 189
low-level testing, 189
test class development, 193–194
test suite, 194–197
unit test development, 190–191
FlexUnit Runner application
filtering results, 197–198
forcing errors in test, 200
results of previous test, 199
specific information, gathering more, 198
Flickr service
API key, 437–439
downloading, 439–440
project page, 440
flood control, messaging, 287
folder
bin, 47
bin-debug, 44
flex_libs, 44
flex_src, 44
html-template, 45
lib, 320, 413
src, 45, 47
folder structure, Flex project type, 44–45
folding feature, 145
foreign key, 205, 315–316
forward slash (/), 266
function. *See also* method
acknowledgeRec(), 419
acknowledgeSend(), 419
auto-incrementing, 257
getter, 66–67, 88, 252
getXML(), 271
handleFault(), 418
logEvent(), 59
randomName(), 418
receiveChatMessages(), 418
sendChatMessages(), 418
setMessage(), 56–57
setter, 66–67, 88, 252

function (*continued*)
   setUserName(), 418
   subscribeToChat(), 418
   trace(), 54, 59

G

garbage collector, 5
GET method, 115
getProperty() method, 252
getRequestedData() method, 70
getter function, 66–67, 88, 252
getXML() function, 271
getXMLFromOperation() method, 357, 362
global configuration file, 245
GUI tools, MySQL database server, 216–217

H

handleFault() function, 418
handleRequest() method, 141, 164–165, 456
handleResponse() method, 276–277, 379
HashMap object, 487
heap size, 15
Hibernate framework
   basic description of, 244–245
   configuration file, 258–260
   downloading, 245
   global configuration file, 245
   Hibernate Core package, 245–246
   main application class, 261–264
   mapping file creation, 253–254, 257–258,
      343–346
   MySQL database server with, 246–250
   session, 245, 258
   transaction, 245
Hibernate Web site, 245
hibernate.cfg.xml configuration file,
      347–348, 364
HLOCChart component, 492
HTML wrapper, 472
html-template folder, 45

HttpClient object, 456
HTTPService tag
   handling response of, 115
   sending data using, 114–115

I

ICommand interface, 70
id property, 100
<id> tag, 257
IMediator interface, 69
Implemented Interfaces Selection dialog box, 144,
      249, 332–333, 450
Import dialog box, 132–133
Import File system dialog box, 444–445
Import from directory dialog box, 134, 323, 412
Import from File system dialog box, 320
Import Select dialog box, 322, 444
import statement, 146
Import wizard, 411
importing JUnit unit testing library, 168
index.html file, 48
information_schema data (MySQL database), 219
inheritance, 4, 90–91
init() method, 94, 197, 288, 388
inner join, 230–231
InputStream class, 456
insert statement, 207–208, 222
installation
   Apache Ant tool, 18
   BlazeDS, 286
   Eclipse IDE, 21–22, 504
   Flex Builder, 74–75, 77, 80, 500
   JBoss application server, 14
   JDK, 8–11
   JRE, 10
   MySQL database server, 210–212
   Spring IDE plug-in, 31–34
instantiation, 6, 250
integer data type, 221–222
integration, Java and Flex similarity, 83–84
interceptor, 479–480

interface
    Connection, 233, 242
    Controller, 68–69, 357
    ICommand, 70
    IMediator, 69
    IProxy, 69
    IStoreDao, 349–350
    IXmlSerializable, 329–331
    Job, 490
    JRDataSource, 487–488
    MessageListener, 485
    NamespaceContext, 449–450
    PreparedStatement, 234
    ResultSet, 234, 242
    separation of implementation, 308–309
    Serializable, 251–252, 330
    Statement, 234, 242
interoperability, 478, 481–483
invoke() method, 292, 294, 403, 467
IProxy interface, 69
isProperty() method, 252
IStoreDao interface, 349–350
item renderer
    defined, 96
    MXML component file creation, 98–100
    overriding a value, 100–104
    setting up, 96–98
ItemRenderer class, 268, 272, 382
iText library, 488–489
IXmlSerializable interface, 329–331

J
JAR Selection dialog box, 138–140, 246–247, 447
Jasper Reports, 485–488
Java and Flex similarity
    code structure, 62–67
    development tool, 73–75, 77, 80, 82
    integration and, 83–84
    library, 62–67
    MVC implementation, 67–71
    unit testing, 71–73

Java bean, 66, 252
Java build path configuration, application
        development, 327–328
Java Build Path dialog box, 328
Java Build Path setting, 136, 138
Java Database Connectivity. *See* JDBC
Java download Web site, 9–10
Java Messaging System (JMS), 481–485
Java Naming and Directory Interface (JNDI), 483
Java programming language. *See also* Java and Flex
        similarity
    automatic memory management, 5
    class declaration, 6
    constructor, 6
    garbage collector, 5
    heap size, 15
    instantiation, 6
    library, 4
    method, 6
    as most popular choice of Web development, 3
    object-oriented programming, 4
    package, 6
    portability, 3
    support, 3
    syntax, 5
    write once, run anywhere concept, 4
Java Runtime Environment. *See* JRE
Java SE Development Kit. *See* JDK
Java Server Pages Standard Tag Library
        (JSTL), 150
Java Service Handler, 376–380
Java servlet, 48
Java Settings dialog box, 238
Java Virtual Machine (JVM), 242
JavaFlexStoreAdmin class, 266–268
JavaFlexStoreEvent class, 266, 277–278
JavaFlexStoreEvent.as object listing, 381
JavaFlexStore.mxml object listing, 391–395
JavaScript Object Notation (JSON), 436
JavaServiceHandler class, 266, 276–277,
        379–380
java.sql.Connection object, 486

JBoss application server
   configuration, 14–16
   downloading, 14
   installation, 14
   run.bat startup batch file, 14–15
   Servers view, 163
   welcome page, 16–17
JBoss Web site, 14
JDBC (Java Database Connectivity)
   Connection interface, 233
   driver, 234
   MySQL Connector/J driver, 234
   overview, 233
   PreparedStatement interface, 234
   ResultSet interface, 234
   Statement interface, 234
   using with MySQL database server, 235–239
JDK (Java SE Development Kit)
   binary Java class file, 7
   configuration, 11–13
   current version, 8
   Download button, 8
   DriverManager class, 237
   environment variable, 11–12
   installation, 8–11
   license agreement, 8, 10
   New User Variable dialog box, 13
   user variable, 13
JMS (Java Messaging System), 481–485
JNDI (Java Naming and Directory Interface), 483
Job interface, 490
jobClass property, 491
JobExecutionContext object, 491
join, 230–231
JRDataSource interface, 487–488
JRE (Java Runtime Environment)
   Add JRD wizard screen, 25
   installation, 10
   System Library, 139
JREmptyDataSource class, 487
JRXML report definition, 486
JSON (JavaScript Object Notation), 436

JSP directive, 149–150
JSTL (Java Server Pages Standard Tag Library), 150
JUnit unit testing library
   adding to project build path, 175
   basic description of, 167
   importing, 168
   Library screen, 176
   test case, 178, 185
   test suite, 177, 187–188
JVM (Java Virtual Machine), 242

K

key, table, 205–206
keyword
   private, 6, 66
   public, 6, 66
   void, 6

L

Label component, 271
labelFunction property, 299–301
language parameter, 166
LDAP (Lightweight Directory Access Protocol), 478
Legend chart component, 492, 496
lib folder, 320, 413
library
   built-in, 4
   Java and Flex similarity, 62–67
   JRE System Library, 139
   mashup, 436
Library screen (JUnit unit testing library), 176
license agreement
   Eclipse IDE, 35
   Flex Builder, 77, 500
   JDK installation, 8, 10
   Spring IDE plug-in, 34
Lightweight Directory Access Protocol (LDAP), 478
line number, 144
LineChart component, 492

List control, 408

<listener> tag, 421

listenToQueue() method, 485

listing

    AddProductToCartService.java object, 358–359

    Apache Ant target, 82

    artweather.jsp file, 456–457

    ArtWeather.mxml file, 469–472

    ArtWeatherService class, 452–455

    build.xml file, 158–159, 365–366, 426–427, 460–461

    button click event, 93

    callServer() method, 275

    Cart.hbm.xml mapping file, 344–345

    CartItem.hbm.xml mapping file, 345

    CartItem.java object, 338–340

    Cart.java object, 340–342

    chat.html file, 419

    Chat.mxml file, 415–418

    ChatServer class, 406–407

    class example, 6–7

    Controller interface, 68–69

    database application, 281–284

    Flex and JavaScript code structure similarity, 62–65

    Flex application example, 109–110

    getter function, 88

    getXML() function, 271

    handleResponse(), 276–277

    hibernate.cfg.xml configuration file, 347–348

    IStoreDao interface, 349–350

    IXmlSerializable interface, 331

    Java Service Handler, 377–378

    Java syntax, 5

    JavaFlexStoreAdmin class, 267–268

    JavaFlexStoreEvent class, 277–278

    JavaFlexStoreEvent.as object, 381

    JavaFlexStore.mxml object, 391–395

    JavaServiceHandler class, 276–277, 379–380

    JMS message producer, 482–485

    log4j.properties file, 346–347

    LogInService.java object, 359

    main method, 241–242

    ManageRenderer class, 272–273

    messaging, 301–303

    ProductDetailsPopup object, 385–386

    ProductDetailsService.java object, 360

    ProductEditor class, 270–271

    Product.hbm.xml mapping file, 345

    ProductItem.mxml object, 383–384

    Product.java object, 335–338

    ProductListService.java object, 360–361

    RetrieveCartService.java object, 361

    services-config.xml file, 422, 468

    setter function, 88

    ShoppingCartListItem.mxml object, 384–385

    SimpleCommand class, 70

    spring-dispatcher-servlet.xml file, 363–364, 458

    StoreBaseService class, 356–357

    StoreDao class, 351–354

    test case, 185–186

    unit testing, 71–73

    User.hbm.xml mapping file, 346

    User.java object, 333–335

    web.xml file, 49, 154, 420–421, 459

    xmp.jsp file, 362

    YWeatherNamespaceContext class, 451–452

load() method, 263, 275

log4j.properties file listing, 346–347

logEvent() function, 59

logging framework (Flex Builder), 59–60

LogInService.java object listing, 359

loosely coupled code, 124

low-level testing, 189

M

main method, 239, 241–242

main.html file, 49

ManageRenderer class, 266, 272–273
mapping file, 245, 253–254, 257–258
mashup
    advanced example, 436
    builder tools, 436
    build.xml file, 460–461
    defined, 435
    deployment, 462
    Eclipse project creation, 441–445
    libraries for, 436
    user interface, 465–466, 473–475
    writing the, 448–449
Mediator class, 69
memory
    automatic memory management, 5
    heap size, 15
memory leak, 5
MessageBrokerServlet class, 421, 468–469
MessageListener interface, 485
MessageService class, 408
messaging. *See also* chat application
    configuration file, 291–292
    Consumer component, 288–289
    destination service, 289–290
    displaying to client, 287
    flood control, 287
    Java back end portion, 291–293
    JMS (Java Messaging System), 481–485
    listing, 301–303
    point-to-point, 481
    Producer component, 287–288
    publish/subscribe, 481–482
    sending a message, 288
    server-side destination, 286–287
    services-config.xml file, 286
    user interface, 296
messaging domain, 481
messaging-config.xml file, 291–292
metadata, 219
method. *See also* function
    abstract, 355
    accessor, 252

addChild(), 94
addEventListener(), 94
addItem(), 107
assertion, 192
buildPdfDocument(), 488
callServer(), 275, 379
class, 86
close(), 243
DELETE, 115
dispatchEvent(), 373
execute, 70, 243, 490
fail(), 180
GET, 115
getProperty(), 252
getRequestedData(), 70
getXMLFromOperation(), 357, 362
handleRequest(), 141, 164–165, 456
handleResponse(), 276–277, 379
init(), 94, 197, 288, 388
invoke(), 292, 294, 403, 467
isProperty(), 252
Java programming language, 6
listenToQueue(), 485
load(), 263, 275
next(), 243
onMessage(), 485
POST, 115
PUT, 115
send(), 288
setUp(), 180, 182
start(), 483
subscribe(), 289–290
tearDown(), 180
toXML(), 329, 342
unsubscribe(), 290
updateDisplayList(), 465
model layer (MVC pattern), 67, 69, 124, 141
model popup window, 279
modularity, 308
MouseEvent class, 93
MVC (Model-View-Controller) pattern
    controller layer, 67, 70, 124, 141
    interface code separation, 67

model layer, 67, 69, 124, 141
    PureMVC module, 69–70
    Spring Framework, 125
    Spring Web module, 68, 125
    view layer, 67, 69, 124, 141, 147
    Web application writing, 123–124
<mx:Label> tag, 475
MXML code
    ActionScript file and, 91–92
    MCML component code creation, 98–100
<mxmlc> tag, 428
<mx:Script> tag, 297
mx.skins package, 464
MySQL Connector/J driver, 234
MySQL database server
    application development, 310–312, 314–317
    command-line tools, 215
    configuration, 213–216
    database creation example, 220–224
    downloading, 209–210
    GUI tools, 216–217
    Hibernate framework with, 246–250
    information_schema database, 219
    installation, 210–212
    Instance Configuration wizard, 214
    JDBC with, 235–239
    mysql database, 220
    Query Browser, 218–220, 310
    registration process, 210–211
    root account configuration, 213
    schema, 218
    Select a Mirror screen, 211
    Setup screen, 212–213
    test database, 220
MySQL Table Editor dialog box, 221–224, 227,
    312–313

N

namespace, 91, 449
NamespaceContext interface, 449–450

New ActionScript Class dialog box, 377
New File dialog box, 256, 344, 415
New Flex Project dialog box, 267, 295, 374
New Flex Project wizard, 40
New Folder dialog box, 131, 148, 255, 321–322,
    443
New Java Class dialog box, 145, 171, 240, 250,
    332, 406, 449–450
New Java Package dialog box, 142–143, 169–170,
    239
New JavaServer Page wizard, 148–149
New JUnit Test Case wizard, 178–179
New MXML Component dialog box, 269
New Project dialog box, 168, 442
New Server dialog box, 41–42
New Server Runtime Environment wizard, 28
New Spring Project dialog box, 128–130, 442
New User Variable dialog box, 12–13
New XML File wizard, 152–153
next() method, 243
nonmodel popup window, 279
not-null constraint, 206, 221
number field, 204

O

object
    AsyncMessage, 288
    CartItem.java object listing, 338–340
    Cart.java object listing, 340–342
    config, 263
    DAO (data access object), 310
    FileOutputStream, 489
    HashMap, 487
    HttpClient, 456
    instantiation, 250
    JavaFlexStoreEvent.as object listing, 381
    JavaFlexStore.mxml object listing,
        391–395
    java.sql.Connection, 486
    JobExecutionContext, 491
    JSON (JavaScript Object Notation), 436

object *(continued)*
    `LoginService.java` object listing, 359
    `ProductDetailsPopup` object listing, 385–386
    `ProductDetailsService.java` object listing, 360
    `ProductItem.mxml` object listing, 383–384
    `Product.java` object listing, 335–338
    `ProductListService.java` object listing, 360–361
    `QueueSender`, 483, 485
    `RetrieveCartService.java` object listing, 361
    `ShoppingCartListItem.mxml` object listing, 384–385
    `TextMessage`, 483
    `User.java` object listing, 333–335
object-oriented programming, 4
object-relational mapping (ORM), 244
offline installation, JDK, 9
`onMessage()` method, 485
Open JAR dialog box, 425
Open Perspective dialog box, 38–39
ORM (object-relational mapping), 244
`<out>` tag, 151
overriding a value, 100–104

P

package
    path, 86
    using in reverse domain format, 85–86
    Web application, 142
package declaration, 6, 65, 86
page directive, 149
`parentApplication` property, 271, 273, 384
password parameter, 242
`<password-encoder>` tag, 480
`PATH` environment variable, 13
`<path>` tag, 159
payment solution, storefront application example, 395–396

PDF file, 488–489
`PieChart` component, 492
`PlotChart` component, 492
point-to-point messaging, 481
polymorphism, 4
popup, 269–271
popup window, 279
`PopupManager` class, 279
portability, Java programming language, 3
`POST` method, 115
post-colon syntax, 88
Preferences dialog box, 423
Pre-Installation Summary screen (Flex Builder), 79
`PreparedStatement` interface, 234
primary key, 205
`private` keyword, 6, 66
`Producer` component, 287–288
product editor popup, 269–271
product grid, 272–273
`ProductDetailsPopup` object listing, 385–386
`ProductDetailsService.java` object listing, 360
`ProductEditor` class, 266, 270–271
`Product.hbm.xml` mapping file listing, 345
`ProductItem.mxml` object listing, 383–384
`Product.java` object listing, 335–338
`ProductListService.java` object listing, 360–361
project directory structure, Web application, 126–127
property
    adding to class, 87
    defining as public, 87
    internal, 87
`<property>` tag, 159, 257, 346
Proxy class, 69
`public` keyword, 6, 66
publish/subscribe messaging, 481–482
PureMVC module, 69–70
`PUT` method, 115

Q

Quartz scheduler, 490–491
Query Browser (MySQL database), 218–220, 310
query, SQL
    basic description of, 206
    delete statement, 208
    insert statement, 207–208
    select statement, 207
    update statement, 208
QueueSender object, 483, 485
QueueSession object, 483

R

randomName() function, 418
real-time messaging system. *See* chat application
receiveChatMessages() function, 418
red X indicator, 48
registration, MySQL database server, 210–211
relational database
    basic description of, 203
    SQL queries, 206–209
    stored procedure, 209
    tables in, 203–206
Restrictions class, 264
<result> tag, 355
Results tab (MySQL Query Browser), 218
ResultSet interface, 234, 242
RetrieveCartService.java object listing,
    361
root account configuration, MySQL database server,
    213
Root folder path, 295–296
row, table, 203–204, 229
rs variable, 242
Run On Server dialog box, 50–51
run.bat startup batch file, 14–15
Runtime dialog box, 424

S

scalability, 478
schema, 218
Schema tab (MySQL Query Browser), 218
security
    authentication, 478, 480–481
    authorization, 478–479
    enterprise application, 478–480
    interceptor, 479–480
Security Extension (Spring IDE plug-in), 32
Select a Mirror screen (MySQL), 211
Select a wizard dialog box, 168, 178, 235
select statement, 207
send() method, 288
sendChatMessage() function, 418
sending data from Flex
    ActionScript approach, 114
    asynchronous communication, 113
    sample test, 116–120
    using HTTPService tag, 114–115
Serializable interface, 251, 253, 330
service layer, application development, 355–358
ServiceAdapter class, 292, 403, 467
service.configuration.file parameter,
    421
<services> tag, 428
services-config.xml file, 286, 421–422, 468
serviceURL property, 275
<servlet> tag, 155, 421
<servlet-mapping> tag, 421
SessionFactory class, 259
session, Hibernate framework, 245, 258
<set> tag, 346
setMessage() function, 56–57
setter function, 66–67, 88
setUp() method, 180, 182
setUserName() function, 418
ShoppingCartListItem.mxml object listing,
    384–385

Show View dialog box, 160, 367, 428
Simple Logging Facade for Java (SLF4), 246
`SimpleCommand` class, 70
site. *See* Web site
skin class, 464–465, 475
SLF4 (Simple Logging Facade for Java), 246
Software Updates and Add-ons dialog box, 31
Source view (Flex Builder), 52
Spring Framework
    application context module, 125
    container, 124
    dependency injection, 124
    distribution, 125
    downloading, 125
    file listing page, 126
    MVC pattern, 125
Spring IDE plug-in
    AOP Developer Resources, 32
    AOP Extension, 32
    basic description of, 30
    installation, 31–34
    license agreement, 34
    Security Extension, 32
    update, 31–33
Spring Web MVC module, 68, 125
`spring-dispatcher-servlet.xml` file,
    362–364, 458
`spring.jar` library, 135, 137
`spring-webmvc.jar` library, 135
SQL query
    basic description of, 206
    `delete` statement, 208
    `insert` statement, 207–208
    `select` statement, 207
    `update` statement, 208
`SQLException` value, 243
src directory, 127
src folder, 45, 47
`start()` method, 483
statement
    delete, 208
    insert, 207–208, 222

    select, 207
    update, 208
`Statement` interface, 234, 242
States view (Flex Builder), 52
stmt variable, 242
`StoreBaseService` class, 355–357
stored procedure, 209
`StoreDao` class listing, 351–354
storefront server application example
    application URLs, 373
    custom events, 380–381
    Flex project setup, 373–375
    Java Service Handler, 376–380
    main application, 387–391
    multiple server calls, 372–373
    payment solution development, 395–396
    product description popup creation, 385–386
    product viewer development, 382–385
    testing, 395
string
    array, 239
    defined, 6
`styleName` attribute, 463, 475
subclass, 4
`subscribe()` method, 289–290
`subscribeToChat()` function, 418
superclass, 4, 351
Superclass Selection dialog box, 351
support, Java programming language, 3
synchronous communication, 113
synchronous event, 381
synchronous messaging, 407
syntax
    Java programming language, 5
    post-colon, 88
Syntax tab (MySQL Query Browser), 218
System Properties dialog box
    accessing, 11
    Advanced tab, 12
    Environment Variables button, 12

T

table
  column, 203–204
  constraints, 206
  data type, 204
  key, 205–206
  row, 203–204, 229
tag
  `<class>`, 257
  code structure and, 62
  HTTPService, 114–115
  `<id>`, 257
  `<listener>`, 421
  `<mx:Label>`, 475
  `<mxmlc>`, 428
  `<mx:Script>`, 297
  `<out>`, 151
  `<password-encoder>`, 480
  `<path>`, 159
  `<property>`, 159, 257, 346
  `<result>`, 355
  `<services>`, 428
  `<servlet>`, 155, 421
  `<servlet-mapping>`, 421
  `<set>`, 346
  `<target>`, 159
  `<taskdef>`, 428
  `<web-app>`, 468
tag library directive, 150
target, 17, 82
`<target>` tag, 159
task, 82
`<taskdef>` tag, 428
teambuilding, 83
`tearDown()` method, 180
test case, 71, 73, 178, 185–186
test database, 220
test runner, 71
test suite, 71, 177, 187–188, 194–197
testing. *See also* unit testing
  Apache Ant installation, 19–20
  chat application, 431–432
  Flex Builder project configuration, 48–53
  forcing error in, 200
  JBoss installation, 16
  low-level, 189
`TextInput` component, 271, 408–409
`TextMessage` object, 483
thread, 259
`throws Exception` clause, 184
`toXML()` method, 329, 342
`trace()` function, 54, 59
trace message, 54–56
`Transaction` class, 263
transaction, Hibernate framework, 245
trigger, 490
`TriggerUtils` class, 491
`try` block, 183
try/catch block, 242–243
turnkey development, 286

U

underscore (_) character, 47
uniform resource identifier, 449
unique constraint, 206
unit testing. *See also* FlexUnit framework; JUnit
    unit testing library
  failed, 181
  Java and Flex similarity, 71–73
  listing, 71–73
  test case, 71, 73
  test runner, 71
  test suite, 71
`unsubscribe()` method, 290
update, Spring IDE plug-in, 31–33
update statement, 208
`updateDisplayList()` method, 465
URL error, 164
`URLLoader` class, 275
user interface, 296
user table, application development, 314–315
user variable, 13
`User.hbm.xml` mapping file listing, 346
`User.java` object listing, 333–335
`username` parameter, 242

V

value attribute, 151
value, overriding, 100–104
varchar field, 204
variable
    bindable, 297–299
    conn, 242
    environment, 11–13
    PATH, 13
    rs, 242
    stmt, 242
    user, 13
    xmlString, 362
variable character field, 204
Variables view (Flex Builder), 57–58
vertical axis, charting component, 495
view layer (MVC pattern), 67, 69, 124, 141, 147
void keyword, 6

W

WAR (Web application archive), 17
Web application writing
    build properties file, 156–157
    controller class, 142–143
    MVC pattern, 123–124
    package, 142
    page directive, 149
    project directory structure, 126–127
    web.xml configuration file, 151–152
Web browser (Flex Builder), 50–51
web directory, 127
Web site
    Hibernate, 245
    Java download, 9–10
    JBoss, 14

<web-app> tag, 468
WebContent folder, 45
WEB-INF folder, 320, 443
web.xml file, 48–49, 151–152, 362, 420–421, 459
welcome page
    Eclipse IDE, 22–23
    JBoss application server, 16–17
WHERE clause, 207–208
wildcard (*) character, 207
wizard
    Create a Java Project, 169, 236
    Import, 411
    New Flex Project, 40
    New JavaServer Page, 148–149
    New JUnit Test Case, 178–179
    New Server Runtime Environment, 28
    New XML File, 152–153
Workspace Launcher dialog box, 22
write once, run anywhere concept, 4

X

xField parameter, 496
XML file, 256
xmlString variable, 362
xmp.jsp file, 362
XPath class, 449

Y

yField parameter, 496
YWeatherNamespaceContext class listing, 451–452